THE FRENCH LANGUAGE

THE GREAT LANGUAGES

GENERAL EDITOR:
L. R. Palmer, M.A., D.Phil., Ph.D.
Professor of Comparative Philology in the University of Oxford

PUBLISHED

THE FRENCH LANGUAGE
By *A. Ewert, M.A., Litt.D.*

THE GERMAN LANGUAGE
By *R. Priebsch, Ph.D.* and *W. E. Collinson, M.A., Ph.D.*

THE SPANISH LANGUAGE, TOGETHER WITH PORTUGUESE
CATALAN, BASQUE
By *William J. Entwistle, M.A., Litt.D., LL.D.*

THE CHINESE LANGUAGE
By *R. A. D. Forrest, M.A.*

RUSSIAN AND THE SLAVONIC LANGUAGES
By *William J. Entwistle, M.A., Litt.D., LL.D.* and *W. A. Morison, B.A., Ph.D.*

THE LATIN LANGUAGE
By *L. R. Palmer, M.A., D.Phil., Ph.D.*

THE SANSKRIT LANGUAGE
By *T. Burrow, M.A.*

THE ROMANCE LANGUAGES
By *W. D. Elcock, M.A., L. ès L., D. de L'U. Toulouse*

THE ITALIAN LANGUAGE
By *Bruno Migliorini, Dott. in Lettere*
(abridged and re-cast by *T. G. Griffith, M.A., B.Litt.*)

IN PREPARATION

THE ENGLISH LANGUAGE
By *N. Davis, M.A.*

THE GAELIC LANGUAGES
By *Kenneth Jackson, M.A.*

THE SCANDINAVIAN LANGUAGE
By *Einar Haugon, M.A., Ph.D.*

INDO-EUROPEAN LANGUAGES
By *G. Bonfante, LL.D.*

THE HEBREW LANGUAGE
By *G. R. Driver, M.A.*

THE ANATOLIAN LANGUAGES
By *R. A. Crossland, M.A.*

THE GREEK LANGUAGE
By *L. R. Palmer, M.A., D.Phil., Ph.D.*

THE
FRENCH LANGUAGE

by

ALFRED EWERT, M.A., LITT.D.

LONDON
FABER & FABER LIMITED
24 RUSSELL SQUARE

FIRST PUBLISHED IN MAY 1933
BY FABER AND FABER LIMITED
24 RUSSELL SQUARE LONDON W.C.1
SECOND EDITION MARCH 1943
REPRINTED 1947, 1949, 1953, 1956, 1961,
1964, 1967 AND 1969
PRINTED IN GREAT BRITAIN
AT THE UNIVERSITY PRESS CAMBRIDGE

SBN 571 07019 1 (CLOTH)
SBN 571 05758 1 (FPCE)

Contents

CONTENTS

CONTENTS

[1] Pending a more extensive revision, the author has confined himself, on the occasion of the 1956 reprinting, and again of the present one, to the correction of a few minor errors and the addition of further bibliographical indications. The latter will be found on pages 407-11 and consist of particulars of the latest editions of works already mentioned and a strictly limited selection from relevant publications of recent years.

Foreword

This volume is not addressed to the specialist, who may well question the need of yet another general book on the French language. It represents an attempt to combine a history of the language with an historical grammar in the proportions required by the general reader and by those students who, while not specializing in philology, desire more detailed information than that supplied by existing books in English.[1] The older periods of the language have been considered not so much for their own sake as for their bearing on Modern French.[2] In spite of our endeavour to include whatever is essential, we cannot hope to have met fully the requirements of the readers we have in mind. A select bibliography has therefore been appended as a guide to further study.

It is our hope that in the upper forms of schools also this book may be of use, not merely for the concise account we have endeavoured to give of irregular verbs, formation of the plural, and the like, but as a modest attempt to place in their proper perspective a few syntactic problems, such as the use of the subjunctive. It should be one of the functions of historical grammar to inculcate the right attitude towards linguistic problems, and to lift the study of language above the plane of dogmatic assertion and pure empiricism. If it could begin to perform this function in our schools, less time would be wasted in misapplied logical reasoning and arid classification of morphological and syntactic exceptions.

As the language of a great nation and of a great literature,

[1] A. T. Baker, *Outlines of French Historical Grammar*, London, 1899; E. Weekley, *A Primer of French Historical Grammar*, London, 3rd ed. 1917; M. S. Brittain, *Historical Primer of French Phonetics*, Oxford, 1900; F. B. Luquiens, *Introduction to Old French Phonology and Morphology*, New Haven, revised ed. 1919.

[2] We had all the more reason for this procedure as a comprehensive account of the phonology and morphology of Old and Middle French by Miss M. K. Pope is shortly to appear. [Since published under the title: *From Latin to Modern French*, Manchester, 1934.]

French was bound to find a place of honour in a series devoted to the Great Languages. But its intrinsic claims are no less cogent. The historical study of the French language is an indispensable element in the special discipline provided by French studies. The student of French literature and French culture who neglects it will have but an imperfect knowledge of the most important literary movements in France, and his judgment on particular works and passages will often be falsified. One of the most brilliant facets of the genius of the race will be but a dull surface to him, for of no nation can it be more truly said than of the French that its language has been consciously and unconsciously fashioned in the image of the race.

Our debt to the many scholars who have written upon the French language or some aspect of it is very heavy. We have tried to acknowledge any special indebtedness in the body of the work or in the footnotes. Here we should like to say how much we owe to the monumental works of F. Brunot, W. Meyer-Lübke, and Kr. Nyrop; also to the books of A. Darmesteter, A. Dauzat, P. Fouché, E. Herzog, Th. Rosset, E. Schwan–D. Behrens, and K. Sneyders de Vogel. They have been constantly at our side, and it would be impossible for us to acknowledge in full detail what has passed directly or indirectly from them into this book.

It is a pleasant duty to record our deep obligation to Dr C. T. Onions, who has read the whole of the proofs and has placed his time and learning ungrudgingly at our disposal; to Mr H. E. Berthon, who has likewise read the proofs and has made many valuable suggestions; to Professor J. R. R. Tolkien for indispensable guidance in connection with Germanic loan-words; to Mr F. Whitehead, who kindly undertook the heavy task of preparing an index; and to the General Editor, the Publishers, and the officials of the Cambridge Press, who have combined to make our task as easy and pleasant as possible.

A. E.

Abbreviations and Symbols

C.L.   Classical Latin.
V.L.   Vulgar Latin.
L.L.   Low Latin.[1]
O.F.   Old French.
Mid.F.   Middle French.
Mod.F.   Modern French.
> 'becomes'.
< 'comes from'.
≠ 'by analogy with'.
orth.   'orthography'.
der.   'derivative' or 'derived'.

A hook, placed beneath a vowel, is used to indicate open quality, a dot to indicate close quality: thus *pö̦:r* (= *peur*), *pö̇* (= *peu*). A dot is placed beneath a consonant to denote the corresponding fricative: thus *ṭ*, *ḍ*, *ḅ* denote the initial sound of English *thin*, *then*, Spanish (*la*) *verdad*, respectively.

An acute accent placed after a consonant denotes palatalization: thus *vin'* (= *vigne*). When placed over a vowel it indicates tonic stress.

A tilde indicates nasalization: thus *ã* (= *an*). A colon indicates that the preceding vowel is long.

ə denotes the reduced *e* sound (*le*); cf. § 64.

j, *w*, *ẅ* denote the semi-consonants (*pied*, *Louis*, *lui*), and *i̯*, *u̯*, *ü̯*, the semi-vowels, corresponding to the vowels *i*, *u*, *ü* (*pie*, *loup*, *lu*) respectively.[2]

---

[1] We use the term Low Latin to denote all those species of written Latin (Late Latin, Church Latin, Law Latin) which reflect the decline of the Classical tradition and the influence of the vernacular (cf. § 3).

[2] The difference between a semi-consonant and the corresponding semi-vowel is very slight: in the former the consonantal (fricative) quality is more pronounced at the beginning of the breath-emission (*pied*), in the latter at the end (*bataille*). The difference is difficult to sasess in practice, and we have not attempted to maintain a rigid distinction between *j*, *w*, *ẅ* on the one hand, and *i̯*, *u̯*, *ü̯* on the other.

s, z denote the voiceless and voiced s sounds respectively (si, rose).

$š$, $ž$ denote the voiceless and voiced sh sounds respectively (cha*nte*, j*our*).

$ł$ denotes velar l; cf. § 43.

For k, k^i, k^a, g, g^i, g^a, see § 85.

For velar $ɑ$ and palatal a, see § 55.

We have used the term Vulgar Latin consistently to denote the spoken language only (cf. § 3). Consequently, Vulgar Latin forms are explicitly designated as such or are distinguished by an asterisk, except when they represent a phonetic transcription or regular development; e.g. *SUBITANUM > SOB'DANU > *soudain* (§ 96). Strict consistency would have demanded that, in the chapter on Phonology, both Latin and French forms be given in phonetic transcription; but we have not considered it necessary to do this in every case. The reader will therefore interpret FĪDEM > *foi* as meaning that Vulgar Latin FẸDE (orth. FIDEM) becomes Modern French *fwa* (orth. *foi*); cf. §§ 21–6, 84–5. For Latin nouns and adjectives the form given is, as a rule, the accusative, this being the case which has normally survived in Modern French (cf. §§ 173, 182). The quantity of Latin vowels is indicated only when special attention is to be called to it.

Occasionally letters are enclosed in parentheses to indicate that they have a purely orthographic value or that the corresponding sounds have disappeared: (H)ABERE, DOM(I)NUM. Alternatively the syncope of a vowel is indicated by an apostrophe: CAM'RA.

References to the Selections (Appendix A) take the form of a Roman numeral (indicating the number of the extract) followed by an Arabic numeral (indicating the line). For Old French syntax we have taken our examples, as far as possible, either from the Selections or from the *Chanson de Roland* (= *Rol.*) as edited by T. Atkinson Jenkins (Heath, 1924).

Chapter I

GENERAL AND EXTERNAL HISTORY

1. French is one of the group of languages which, derived as they are in all essentials from Latin, go by the name of Romance or Neo-Latin languages. They comprise: Sardinian, Italian, Roumanian, Rhaeto-romance, Spanish, Portuguese, Catalan, Provençal, French. Each of these languages represents the final term in the development of Latin as spoken in the respective parts of the Roman Empire. In each case the point of departure is the spoken tongue (Vulgar Latin) of the Roman soldiers, colonists, merchants, administrators, as opposed to the literary language (Classical Latin) of the Classical writers of Rome. The history of the French language is therefore concerned with the various changes through which Latin as spoken in Paris and its environs passed, with the elevation of this local language to the dignity of a national tongue, and with its adoption and development as the literary medium of French and French-speaking people throughout the world.

2. While the development of the French language is on the whole a gradual evolution in pronunciation, forms, vocabulary, and construction, with all the adaptations and adjustments to changing needs and conditions which that term implies, it is natural that the movement should have experienced its moments of relaxation and of accelerated progress, the latter generally coinciding with radical changes in social or political conditions. One can therefore establish several more or less distinct phases in the history of the French language. During the first centuries after the introduction of Latin into Gaul the language developed on practically the same lines as in the rest of the Empire. This period closed with the break-up of the Empire and is generally described as the Vulgar Latin period (to *ca.* 500). The second period is marked by a gradual

differentiation of the Latin of Gaul from that of the other parts of the Empire. It may be called the Gallo-Roman period and may be said to close with the establishing of a line of cleavage between the dialects of the North (Langue d'oïl) and of the South (Langue d'oc). The Old French period may be said to begin with the first French linguistic monument, the *Strasburg Oaths* (842), and to embrace that period of most striking literary activity—the twelfth and thirteenth centuries. The fourteenth and fifteenth centuries may at first glance appear to show more affinity with Old French than with Modern French, but compared with standard usage of the twelfth century they offer a contrast hardly less pronounced. One may accept 1328, the date of the accession of the Valois, as indicating roughly a time when a number of tendencies apparent in the preceding century come to a head and bring about a change in usage. The Middle French period is characterized by the decay of the classical usage of the twelfth century and general hesitation in pronunciation, flexions, and syntax. In spite of the efforts of grammarians and the formation of a literary school, this hesitation persists throughout the sixteenth century, and we may therefore conveniently take the Middle French period as embracing the fourteenth, fifteenth and sixteenth centuries, and the Modern French period as dating from the seventeenth century. The justification for making the divisions indicated lies largely in their practical convenience, and in some respects it would be more correct to describe the sixteenth and seventeenth centuries as constituting together the formative period of Modern French, the former representing the period of hesitation, experiment and tentative reform, the latter the stage of rational analysis, standardization and codification.

3. As indicated above, French is merely the modern form of the spoken Latin introduced into Gaul. Contrary to expectations there is very little evidence pointing to dialectal variations in the Latin spoken by the Romans who were the medium through which the language was transmitted to the various Roman provinces. Such differences as date

from its introduction are chronological rather than dialectal. Yet the existence of such dialectal variations is vouched for from the earliest times. It must therefore be assumed that, whatever their native dialect may have been, the Romans employed for general purposes a standard form of spoken Latin which developed, at most, regional variations of the type shown by the regional French of the present day. It is to this standard form of spoken Latin that we apply the term Vulgar Latin. Among the influences which helped to maintain the uniformity and homogeneity of spoken Latin in its early stages perhaps the most important was that of the literary language, to which it stands in a relatively constant relation. Vulgar Latin thus itself became a stable idiom, capable of maintaining its integrity even after the decline of culture had undermined the literary tradition, and disintegrating only when the complete destruction of that culture, the isolation of the various groups, and the changed political and social conditions made the maintenance of a conventional standard usage unnecessary and impossible. Vulgar Latin offers from the beginning a striking contrast with Classical Latin (§§ 21–5, 84–5 and Chap. v *passim*). But the changes which supervened in the Vulgar Latin period, while they are of capital importance for the future development of the Romance languages, are in themselves comparatively slight and bear witness to the extraordinary stability and still more the uniformity of Latin as spoken throughout the Empire. Even after the decline of the Classical tradition there remained various factors making for such uniformity: the close-knit fabric of the Roman Empire, the constant inter-communication, the founding of schools, the recognition of Latin alone as the official language and its use for public purposes throughout the length and breadth of the Empire. With the recognition of Christianity as the state religion, the Church became a powerful conserving factor from the linguistic point of view. Latin continued to be written but became honeycombed with Vulgar Latin features and rapidly deteriorated until the Carolingian reforms brought about a partial return to the

Classical tradition. Even in its debased form (Low Latin) the written language never ceased to influence the spoken language and to retard its evolution. In so far as it continued to maintain the tradition it has to be reckoned with as a factor making for uniformity. The hypothesis of a standard spoken Latin does not preclude the development of local dialectal features (particularly in pronunciation), but they would not find expression in monuments nor would they attract the notice of grammarians except in so far as they became regional. We cannot, it is true, find any evidence of such purely local features until the ninth century, yet it is inconceivable that they should not have existed. The extraordinarily rapid transformation of Vulgar Latin into a new language, such as we have it in the *Strasburg Oaths* and the *Eulalia*, presupposes a period in which the permeation of the vulgar tongue with dialectal features gradually reaches a saturation-point, and political and social disturbances provide the shock which crystallizes the language in a series of dialects. Thus it comes about that certain features must be described as old which do not come to the surface until relatively late.[1] A complete history of pre-literary French would present a much more kaleidoscopic appearance than the outline which we are constrained to give. It would have to reckon with a twofold development: a more or less standard and official Vulgar Latin presenting regional variations on the one hand, and highly differentiated local varieties of spoken Latin on the other.

4. The romanization of Gaul, which may be taken to begin with the formation of the Provincia Narbonensis (120 B.C.) and the conquest of the rest of Gaul (55 B.C.), brought with it the substitution of Latin for the native idiom of the Gauls. The latter was a Celtic tongue which it is impossible to characterize in detail, as only a few inscriptions of doubtful interpretation have come down to us. The examination of

---

[1] Cf. H. F. Muller, 'A Chronology of Vulgar Latin' (Beiheft 78 zur *Zeitschrift für rom. Phil.*), 1929. For another view, see F. G. Mohl, *Introduction à la Chronologie du latin vulgaire*, 1899.

Celtic elements in various languages and the historical study of Celtic languages and extant Celtic monuments have not yielded results which place beyond doubt the contention that certain developments in the Latin of Gaul are to be ascribed to the persistence of linguistic habits of the Celtic population (§§ 21, 35 a, 220). We do know that the language of the Gauls presented affinities with Latin, and this fact accounts in part for the readiness with which they seem to have abandoned their native idiom. Among other induce-ments to do so one may cite the advantages of Roman citizen-ship, the hope of advancement and material benefits generally, all of which were contingent upon the adoption of the official tongue. To these must be added the fact that with the spread of Christianity the diffusion of Latin was furthered by the Church, which employed Latin solely, at first in the form of Vulgar Latin and subsequently in the form of Low Latin. Before these combined forces the native idiom, inadequate for the new conditions of life and identified henceforth with an inferior culture, yielded ground rapidly, although it lingered on in the country districts as late as the third or fourth century. It has left its mark upon the vocabulary of the French lan-guage (§§ 503–4) and in particular upon place-names.[1] A dis-tinction must, however, be drawn between these primitive Celtic elements and later Celtic borrowings from the Bretons who emigrated from Britain to Armorica between the fifth and seventh centuries (§ 504).

5. The irruption of Germanic tribes in the fifth century, which resulted in the dismembering of the Empire and the establishing of various Germanic kingdoms, was responsible for the introduction of considerable Germanic elements into the Romance languages of the West and particularly into French. Northern Gaul was occupied by the Salian Franks, who adapted themselves readily to their new surroundings, showing a striking respect for Gallo-Roman property and maintaining more or less intact the Roman administrative system. Their conversion to Christianity and their cultural

[1] Cf. A. Longnon, *Les noms de lieu de la France*, Paris, 1920, pp. 27–71.

inferiority to the Gallo-Romans were a further inducement to give up their native language. But they introduced a large number of words (§§ 505–6), and their habits of speech were not without influence on the pronunciation of the Romance tongue (§§ 84, 103). In addition to Celtic and Germanic elements a certain number of Greek words found their way into Vulgar Latin during this period. As distinct from the earlier borrowings from Greek into the written or the spoken language, these later additions to the vocabulary are almost entirely connected with the Church and its services (§ 502).

6. The forces which tended to maintain a uniformity of language in the Vulgar Latin period gradually lose their strength in the Gallo-Roman period. The ties uniting Gaul, Spain and Italy remain for a time, but in an attenuated form; they are less important linguistically because they are maintained largely by the Church, which is now definitely in the Low Latin tradition. The old administrative cadre inherited from the Romans makes way for the feudal system which, with its self-contained and largely independent domains, fosters the development of local peculiarities of speech. The gulf between the spoken and the written language (Low Latin) grows ever wider in spite of the readiness with which the latter absorbs popular elements. By the Carolingian reform of the written language the opposition between the two is accentuated and the popular speech is free to evolve without the restraint imposed by a written tradition and in fact without a tradition of any sort. The varieties of speech under such conditions are well-nigh infinite, but communities which are united by bonds involving frequent intercourse will tend to follow a common evolution up to a point. It is in this sense that one can speak of dialects and groups of dialects. They are cultural rather than geographical divisions, and the forces which tend to produce uniformity often overleap physical, political, and administrative boundaries, and they do not remain constant. The play of these forces, rather than ethnological factors, would seem to have determined the forma-

tion of dialects and groups of dialects in the Gallo-Roman period. While this period offers no direct evidence of such sub-divisions, they are in their main lines fully constituted at the beginning of the Old French period and must therefore date from the period under consideration. The dialects developed fall into two main groups, a Northern (Langue d'oïl) and a Southern (Langue d'oc), the latter characterized particularly by the tendency to maintain Latin vowels intact, to maintain intervocal consonants, and to drop final consonants. The geographical boundary between the two is very roughly a line drawn from Bordeaux via Lussac and Montluçon to the southern boundary of the department of the Isère. The Langue d'oc developed its own literary language and its own tradition, but we are not concerned with its subsequent history except in so far as it influenced the Langue d'oïl. We may characterize the Gallo-Roman period as one in which the language of Gaul at first followed a line of development sometimes parallel with, but almost entirely independent of, that of Spain and Italy. But before the end of the period the line has frayed into a vast number of threads forming a network thrown over the map of France in such a way that one can draw no clear-cut boundaries without cutting across one or more threads, and that one can at most establish general areas of convergence, notably a Southern and a Northern. Similarly, within the Langue d'oïl, at the beginning of the Old French period, the dialects form a uniform network spread across the North of France in the sense that no dialect stands out more boldly than any other. To the North-East there is a close affinity between the dialects spoken in Picardy and the adjoining Walloon country; they may be taken to constitute the Picard-Walloon group. Similarly to the North-West Norman, to the West Poitevin, Saintongeais, Angevin, to the East Lorrain and Champenois, to the South-East Burgundian and Franc-Comtois, and finally in the Centre, favoured alike by its geographical and political situation, the dialect of the Île de France, called Francien or Central French, and destined to become the national tongue.

2-2

7. In accordance with this state of affairs the earliest documents in the vernacular are dialectal, particularly as there is as yet no strong national feeling and as no court or capital claims cultural pre-eminence. They are moreover utilitarian, clerical, or inspired by some Latin original—in any case not of national interest. First in point of time come the *Strasburg Oaths* (842), composed in a dialect which it is impossible to localize. They are followed by the sequence of *Eulalia*, composed about 880 at Saint-Amand-les-Eaux, in a Picard-Walloon dialect. The Clermont *Passion* and the *St Leger* date from the end of the tenth century and both present a mixture of Northern and Southern forms, probably due to the intervention of a Provençal scribe who substituted Langue d'oc for Langue d'oïl forms and in part re-wrote the Northern original. Except for the *Jonas*-fragment dating from the beginning of the tenth century and a number of glossaries, nothing further is preserved until we come to the *Vie de Saint Alexis*, composed about the middle of the eleventh century and preserved in three Anglo-Norman manuscripts, two dating from the twelfth and one from the thirteenth century. The language of the original is Continental and probably differed but little from Île de France dialect (Francien); what appear to be Norman traits may well be features of a slightly more archaic stage of Francien than that found in twelfth-century monuments. The twelfth century brought with it conditions favourable to the development of a standard literary language. On the one hand the chief princely houses developed an active and sometimes a brilliant court life. They were moreover drawn together by intermarriages and by a growing sense of nationality born of the Crusades. On the other hand the composers of epics were no longer sedentary but moved about from court to court. It was therefore natural that they should strive to express themselves in a medium devoid of the more pronounced dialectal features. The question of priority, which inevitably arose, seems to have been settled very quickly in favour of the Île de France dialect, largely because it was the language of the capital and of the

most influential of the various courts. The royal power had grown more sure of itself and Paris was already becoming in a real sense the capital city of the country. Our direct know ledge of the dialect of the Île de France in its pure state is very slight throughout this early period. It is, however, safe to assume that even in the twelfth century, as in the seventeenth, the literary language did not represent the pure dialect but a slightly artificial form, in which certain purely local traits were abandoned in favour of others that were more general or for other reasons more acceptable. With this qualification one may say that the literary medium was henceforth Francien, which those who wished to gain the ear of a wider public strove to write. It was only natural that they should succeed to a varying degree in shedding their native speech and that some should even continue to write in their local dialect, content to adapt it more or less to the recognized standard. The supremacy of Francien is never seriously challenged except for a brief period (towards the end of the twelfth century) by the Picard dialect. While the literary language countered this challenge, it nevertheless admitted a considerable number of Picardisms, which continue throughout the Middle Ages to figure in the works of writers who had no direct contact with Picardy.[1] A number of literary works not intended for the wider courtly circles continue to be written in more or less pure dialect, but this form of literature expires in the fifteenth century. From the thirteenth century onwards the standard language (more or less coloured by dialectal traits) takes the place of the local dialect in notarial acts and private contracts, but does not succeed in displacing Latin in royal charters and documents.

From the humble condition of a vulgar tongue in the Gallo-Roman period the French language thus emerges, and in the form of Francien becomes the medium for a rich literary output; it encroaches more and more upon the domain hitherto usurped by Latin, whether in works of a didactic

---

[1] Gertrud Wacker, *Über das Verhältnis von Dialekt und Schriftsprache im Altfranzösischen*, 1916.

and scientific nature or in public acts of municipalities and in annals. During this period it is characterized by a homogeneity, a sonority, and a vigour which it will never again attain. It possesses a great variety of sounds, rich and full vowels and diphthongs, a varied but harmonious system of verb forms, a simplified case system which allows of great freedom in word-order, and a homogeneous vocabulary in which the popular elements are supplemented in moderation by borrowings from Latin.

8. The development of the French language in the fourteenth and fifteenth centuries closely reflects the new political and social conditions. The decay of the feudal system leads to unrest and disorganization bordering upon anarchy, aggravated and prolonged by the Hundred Years' War. The balance of power as between classes, which had hardly been an issue before, now bulks large. With the rise of the bourgeoisie, horizontal divisions triumph over the old feudal vertical divisions. The dividing line between nobility and bourgeoisie becomes less distinct, while the cleavage between upper and lower bourgeoisie is accentuated. A utilitarian spirit pervades society and is reflected in literature. Great store is set by learning, and observation crowds out imagination. Hence prose is the natural medium. Poetic forms continue to be employed, but poetic fancy gives place to an intellectual exercise of the writer's powers of abstraction and elaboration. Never were pedantry and allegory more prevalent than in the literature of this period. Interest in the ancients, which is apparent in the fourteenth century and grows in the fifteenth, is largely inspired by the same spirit. There is little room for individualism in such an age and exceptions like Villon merely prove the rule. But out of the turmoil of the age there began to evolve a new conception of national unity, at first symbolized by, and later identified with, an absolute monarchy, which in spite of temporary setbacks slowly consolidated its position.

In conformity with the conditions indicated, the language does not show a unified forward movement but a multiplicity of changes, often conflicting. Many of the tendencies (reduction of the two-case system and elimination of the subject case, levelling influence of analogy in conjugations, etc.) that had begun to assert themselves in the Old French period now develop unchecked. The absence of a strong literary tradition favours the rapid change from a language still largely synthetic to one which, deprived of the forms and flexions essential to a synthetic structure, is groping towards the analytic structure characteristic of Modern French. The consequent hesitation, formlessness, and clumsiness in construction have their counterpart in pronunciation, which as late as the sixteenth century is characterized by fluctuation in usage and conflict of dialectal pronunciations. The adoption of Latin words, fostered by the revival of the study of the ancients and the activity of translators, and demanded by a literature predominantly didactic, utilitarian, and abstract, gradually transforms the vocabulary; for hitherto the Learned elements had been largely assimilated to the Popular. The breach between literary and popular usage is already widening. Externally the position of the vernacular undergoes a complete change. Francien, as the recognized literary medium, drives the dialects out of literature and reduces them to the status of mere patois. It is even extended to the domain of the Langue d'oc, which begins to furnish outstanding writers in the Northern idiom. Hand in hand with this extension in the field of literature goes the triumph of French over Latin in the chancelleries and in the royal administration generally. But it is not until the famous Ordonnances de Villers-Cotterêts (1539) that French is officially recognized and imposed as the language to be used in courts of law as well as in public and private contracts.

9. With all these gains French was still at the beginning of the sixteenth century considered an inferior tongue as compared with Latin, and its future seemed for the moment jeopardized by the New Learning. But the cultivation of Latin by scholars writing it in the best Ciceronian style was not calculated to make Latin a more living tongue. In fact,

the cultivation of a more 'classical' Latin prepared the way for the triumph of French. In scientific literature there was an obvious advantage in an international medium such as Latin provided, and French secured only a precarious foothold in this field. In theological literature, on the other hand, the polemical advantage of employing the vernacular was early recognized: Calvin's *Institution chrétienne* (1541) follows quickly upon the first version in Latin (1536). Furthermore, the demand of those who possessed no Latin to be allowed to share in the blessings of the New Learning was not to be denied. The dissemination of knowledge in the vulgar tongue was encouraged by successive monarchs and was regarded as a duty by many scholars. In this task the newly discovered art of printing was not only an aid but an incentive, it being to the commercial advantage of the printer to cater for as large a public as possible. But patriotic motives and the spirit of emulation, which animated writers and grammarians alike, were perhaps the decisive factors. The example had already been given by Italy, and it is from Italian writers that Du Bellay draws the bulk of his arguments for his *Defence et Illustration de la langue françoise* (1549). French is now to be, not merely the medium for the writer of tales, romances, farces, and chronicles; it is itself to be cultivated, improved and rendered illustrious. While the means to this end, suggested and in part applied by the Pléiade, sometimes ran counter to the genius of the French language, the earnest, conscious pre-occupation with the language as a medium marks a turning-point in its history. Henceforth the gulf between the language of poetry and everyday language will never be completely bridged, and arbitrary intervention will have to be reckoned with in the former, and eventually also in the latter. The scholar-poets of the Pléiade were aided and in part anticipated by a number of scholars who, inspired likewise by the New Learning, sought to introduce into French some of the fixity, regularity, and simplicity that had hitherto been the chief claims of Latin to priority. If their attempts at regularizing the spelling, whether on

phonetic[1] or on etymological[2] principles, at settling doubtful points of pronunciation and formulating rules of syntax,
proved abortive, the explanation lies partly in the fact that,
less fortunate than Malherbe and the grammarians of the
seventeenth century, they could not rely upon the sanction
of a fashionable 'bel usage' or the support of an official body
such as the Academy. The lack of a spirit of discipline among
writers and in society as a whole, the unequal level of culture
even at the court, and finally the social and political upheaval
of the Wars of Religion, rendered their efforts comparatively
fruitless. But many of their ideas were to be taken up by later
grammarians and they did help to create that vague notion of
a 'bel usage' which was to take definite shape in the following
century.

Throughout the sixteenth century the language is in travail.
The conflict of dialectal pronunciations continues. To the
hesitation between old and new there is added the struggle
between the spoken and the written word, for there is now
an ever-growing reading public, prone to model pronunciation upon the written symbol. Scholars and those acces-
sible to the admonitions of grammarians are influenced by
the reformed pronunciation of Latin, which they seek to
carry over into Learned words and even into such Popular
words as present a visible affinity with their Latin prototypes.
But already a 'correct' or standard usage is being elaborated,
and the condemnation of dialectal and popular Parisian
features has begun. In morphology the confusion is less
marked, but archaic and dialectal forms are still freely
used, although in many cases they have little more than an
orthographic value. In syntax and vocabulary the struggle
between old and new is more seriously complicated by the
Latinizing tendency of many writers. The cult of Latin
authors leads to the introduction of Latin words, the remodel-
ling of native words, and the attribution to them of Latin
meanings. In imitation of Latin many features which had

---

[1] Meigret, Pelletier, Ramus, Rambaud.
[2] Des Autelz, Dubois, R. Estienne.

been foreign to French syntax are introduced and the artificial revival of certain Old French features (e.g. omission of
article and of pronoun subject) is favoured. The imitation
of Latin periodic structure is carried to ridiculous lengths by
a few writers. In the latter half of the century the crisis is
past, so far as Latin influence is concerned. Montaigne's
syntax is still Latin in many respects, but his is a special
case, and it is significant that the vocabulary of the *Essais*
shows him to be anything but a 'latiniseur'. The Italian
influence emanating from the court of Catherine de Médicis
did not create more than a passing craze for speaking an
Italianized form of French, against which Henri Estienne
inveighed with such vehemence in his *Deux Dialogues du
nouveau langage françois italianizé* (1578). More important and
permanent are the numerous Italian words introduced in the
sixteenth century in all those fields where the French were
the pupils of the Italians (§ 516).

10. The general movement towards order and discipline,
which characterizes the seventeenth century, embraces literature and language no less than the political and social
organization. A rationalism that is tempered by a spirit
of discipline and has not yet hardened into the doctrinaire
philosophy of the eighteenth century contributes to this end.
The constitution of a polite society, whose life centres in the
salon and which eventually takes in the Court and a growing
portion of the town, brings with it a new attitude to language.
The theory of 'le bon usage' is elaborated and becomes
'le bel usage'. Its supremacy is assured by a unique collaboration of Précieuses, men of letters, and the newly
founded Academy. "L'usage", says Vaugelas, "c'est la façon
de parler de la plus saine partie de la Cour, conformément
à la façon d'escrire de la plus saine partie des Autheurs du
temps. Quand je dis la Cour, j'y comprens les femmes comme
les hommes, et plusieurs personnes de la ville où le Prince
reside, qui par la communication qu'elles ont avec les gens
de la Cour participent à sa politesse." It should be added
that to the moulding of this usage grammarians contributed,

although their chief rôle consisted in codifying and defending
it. The great writers not only reflect the mood of this society,
they are of it and use its language. Racine himself is not
ashamed to submit his work to the censorship of le père
Bouhours as the guardian and interpreter of 'le bon usage',
and we know from a letter of his with what diligence he
read, re-read and annotated the *Remarques* of Vaugelas. The
seventeenth century thus brought to fruition the ideas and
strivings of the age of the Pléiade. The process was a slow
one, but by the middle of the century we already find
Corneille moved to eliminate from his earlier works features
which had come to be regarded as reprehensible archaisms or
solecisms. By 1660 the work of purification and standardization is well on the way to completion, and the opposition
between the courtly aristocratic usage of society and of literature on the one hand, and popular usage on the other, is
clear-cut. The concessions which were made to certain genres,
such as comedy, do not modify the general picture. Every
aspect of the language was brought under review. Questions
of pronunciation were generally settled in accordance with
the prevailing practice in the salon, the voice of women
being in this matter supreme; but the tendency to model
pronunciation upon spelling persists. The elimination of
archaic forms is practically completed. In syntax usage
hardens, but still permits of many constructions since condemned in the name of logic. It is in vocabulary that the
new spirit is most clearly reflected. Malherbe heads the
reaction against the excesses and confusion of the sixteenth
century. Archaisms, dialectal forms, diminutives, neologisms,
and borrowed words are condemned. Clarity and precision
are insisted upon. Rationalism and the striving for refine-
ment combine to make each word a symbol for an abstract
idea. Connotation is eliminated in favour of denotation, and
consequently the abstract or periphrastic is preferred to the
concrete term; colour is sacrificed to line. The result is a
literary language which is an admirable instrument for the
psychological and dramatic literature of the seventeenth

century, but unsuited for lyric poetry or for colourful descriptive writing, and fated to lose contact with all save the restricted life of the salon. Thus it happened that towards the end of the century, when society itself became less exclusive and new ideas demanded expression in literature, the limitations of the medium became apparent. The opposition to neologisms was then relaxed, but the aristocratic and abstract character of the language persisted.

11. At first glance the eighteenth century appears merely to have continued the seventeenth, making an artificial medium of what had been a living form embodying the tastes and aspirations of its age. It is true that the opposition between a fashionable 'bel usage' and popular speech persists and hardens, that writers and public manifest a slavish respect for the language of the seventeenth-century classics; but dogmatic rationalism and the progress of science have left their mark in language as in literature. Simplicity, regularity, and clearness are now to be cultivated in the name of reason and logic. Grammarians are no longer to be heeded merely as the interpreters of 'le bon usage' but as the protagonists of Reason in matters linguistic. Devoid of historical sense, they elaborate the idea of a philosophical grammar based upon logic. Hence the great rôle played by the *Grammaire générale et raisonnée de Port-Royal* of Arnauld and Lancelot (1660). The ideal of a perfect language plays a part analogous to that of the ideal state. It is in this spirit that Voltaire judges the language of Corneille. The application of logic results in regularity and stiffness in construction, word-order being made almost inflexible and the language losing much of its variety and suppleness. The demands which are made upon it are substantially the same as in the seventeenth century, except that the popularizing of scientific knowledge introduces into general use a growing number of technical terms. A first influx of neologisms at the beginning of the century is arrested and Voltaire can still say: "L'essentiel est de savoir se servir des mots qui sont en usage". But in the latter half of the century a rising tide of neologisms (mostly

taken from the technical vocabularies of the sciences) invades the literary language. Changing fashions favour the introduction of many foreign words. But the distinction between noble and common words is rigidly maintained so far as poetry and sustained discourse are concerned. The ancien régime, in literature as in politics, presents to the end a Versailles façade, but the edifice is ready to crumble before a determined onslaught. In such writers as Rousseau and Beaumarchais can be seen the beginnings of a revolt against the artificiality and the cramping restrictions imposed and maintained in the name of 'le bon goût'.

12. The indirect linguistic effects of the Revolution are very great, but it was not accompanied by an immediate revolution in the literary language. A number of neologisms connected with politics and administration were naturally introduced, but in language the movement in the direction of logic and reason encountered no obstacle. It was the language itself that proved an obstacle to the revolution in literature. It was only when the latter was well under weigh that the frontal attack on the restrictions, the revolt against the artificiality and insufficiency of the language, began. In prose Chateaubriand had prepared the way, but it is the *Préface de Cromwell* (1827) that sounds the charge. The programme of the revolutionary movement is vividly presented in Victor Hugo's *Réponse à un acte d'accusation* (dated 1834, but actually composed in 1854). The forces of reaction—the Academy, the grammarians, university professors, the survivors of the salons—succumb to the Romantics, whose watchword is Liberty and whose aim is to break down the restrictions imposed on the literary language from the time of Malherbe, to restore to literature the whole of the spoken language. Content is now to determine form and the 'mot propre' comes into its own. Neologisms and even archaisms are to be made available for the artist's ends. The subsequent changes represent practically a liquidation of the Romantic programme. With the Realists the democratization of the language is carried rapidly forward; the language of the

lowest classes, slang, provincialisms are utilized. Later schools exploit the increased resources of the language in directions avoided by the seventeenth and eighteenth centuries: all the subsidiary and suggestive connotations are employed to achieve colour, relief, violent contrast, the vague, the hazy outline; both plastic and musical values are exploited. It is not surprising that with all these experiments the claims of clearness and order should at times have been ignored and that a condition bordering upon disintegration should at the present day be threatening the French language. The spoken language reflects more closely the changed social and political conditions resulting from the Revolution. With the elimination of the nobility and the salon, the language of the educated middle class as a whole comes to be recognized as standard usage. Certain popular features of pronunciation (*wa* for *wę*, *j* for *l'*) become universal. The technical languages of industry, commerce, science, politics, furnish an ever-growing number of neologisms; borrowings from foreign languages (particularly English) abound and Learned formations threaten to distort the vocabulary. Later political changes in the nineteenth century have had no effect, but other factors, such as the spread of education, accentuate certain lines of cleavage. The opposition between polite usage and popular usage gives place to a distinction between cultivated speech and colloquial speech, the former clinging closely to the written language, the latter influenced by popular speech and slang. Popular speech in its turn tends on the whole to become more refined but presents many varieties according to trade or occupation.

13. Externally, the progress of French has been steady. It is true that in some fields the struggle between French and Latin continued down to the Revolution. Latin was still used in the seventeenth century for occasional verse and formal discourses, but the victory of French in literature proper is consecrated in the masterpieces of the Classical School. In the sciences Latin lingered on into the eighteenth century, but French shared with Latin the rôle of an inter-

national scientific language. In education the French language played a very insignificant part under the ancien régime; although in country districts the local patois was often employed, instruction in the secondary and higher institutions of learning was generally given in Latin. The movement in favour of French received the support of the Revolutionary governments, which were hostile to Latin. The secularization of educational institutions was accompanied by decrees making French the medium in all schools and imposing the teaching of French, which had hitherto received scant attention. But while French had thus triumphed successively in administration, literature, and education, it was far from being universally employed in daily intercourse. Administrative centralization and the preponderance of Paris helped to foster its use in the provincial towns, but the local patois continued to be used even there. In the country districts and throughout the South generally French was still a foreign idiom in the seventeenth and a great part of the eighteenth century. Even the revolutionary project for the destruction of all patois (1791) did not get beyond a pious wish. French came to be recognized, in theory at any rate, as the principal language, but it was left to various powerful agencies of the nineteenth century (compulsory education, military service, the press) to reduce the local idioms more and more to a subsidiary rôle and to prepare their gradual elimination.

14. Geographically, the domain of the French language (including dialects) in Europe is much as it was in the Middle Ages. Within the political boundaries of France there are computed to be still nearly two million persons whose mother tongue is not French (Alsatians, Bretons, Provençaux, etc.), against whom are to be set some four million French-speaking citizens of adjacent countries (Belgium and Switzerland). Beyond the seas its domain embraces, not only the present colonies, but French-Canada. Nearly all the two and a half million French-Canadians are descended from the six thousand colonists of the seventeenth and eighteenth centuries,

who came from various provinces, but particularly from the North-West (Normandy and Perche). The language of the peasant (*habitant*) is a mixed, archaic form of French, an imperfect elaboration of a standard spoken language on the basis of the dialects of the original settlers, in which Norman traits are common, but which shows the influence of other dialects, notably Saintongeais. The speech of the urban population approximates much more closely to standard French but is characterized by lax articulation of consonants and is permeated with Anglicisms, against which a vigorous campaign has for some time been waged.

15. The extension of the French language to England is the most important incident in the external history of Old French. The infiltration of French had begun under Edward the Confessor, but the mass movement follows the Conquest and the rapid subjugation of the English. Not only did French become the language of the Court, of parliamentary procedure and of the courts of law; it produced a large and varied body of literature in the twelfth and thirteenth centuries, and before the middle of the thirteenth century it had become the chief language of daily intercourse in all save the lowest classes. Not least among the debts we owe to the Anglo-Normans is the transcription of many Old French works, often in unique or superior manuscripts. The decline of the French language follows upon the national movement under Henry III, and English quickly recovered its place in ordinary use (latter half of the thirteenth century), more slowly in official life. French remained the Court language as late as the fifteenth century and was not displaced by English in records of lawsuits until the eighteenth. It has left its mark upon legal vocabulary and in such parliamentary formulae as *le Roi le veult* and *le Roi s'advisera*, not to mention the vast number of French elements which have become completely naturalized in the general vocabulary of English. The French language was brought over in the main by Normans, who were in the majority, not only in the ranks of William's soldiers, but among the many French monks and ecclesiastics settled

in England during his reign. But other influences are to be traced in the French of England, notably from the South-West (Angevin) and from the North (Walloon and Picard). By the middle of the twelfth century it had begun to develop features of its own, and its evolution anticipates in many respects subsequent developments in Continental French (cf. §§ 62 note, 184). With the interruption of regular communication with the Continent in the thirteenth century and the rise of English, Anglo-Norman deteriorated rapidly, the literary language showing a curious mixture of archaisms and innovations. Before the end of the thirteenth century French is clearly for many writers no longer a completely natural medium but a language to be cultivated. This becomes more and more marked in the course of the fourteenth century, and it is significant that the fifteenth has, apart from legal and public documents, nothing to show save grammatical treatises and manuals.

For the cultivation of French as a second language, its utilization for literary purposes in Italy (Franco-Italian epics and romances, Marco Polo, Rusticiano of Pisa) and elsewhere, its rise and decline as the language of diplomacy, its cultivation as the *lingua franca* of polite society (notably in the eighteenth century), see Brunot, I, pp. 358–99 and v, pp. 135–431; Petit de Julleville (Brunot), VI, pp. 866–92 and VIII, pp. 861–3; Dauzat, *Histoire*, pp. 573–8 and § 701 (Bibliography).

Chapter II

PRELIMINARY CONSIDERATIONS

16. We may define a language as a system of words (groups of articulated sounds) used by a group of human beings to exchange their thoughts. In studying a language we may therefore proceed from the psychological to the physical and examine the means adopted by the language for the rendering of thoughts (whether simple notions or complex processes), or taking as our point of departure the physical symbols, we may examine their nature, their evolution and their utilization for the exchange of thoughts. The former might be called the natural method of approach, for speech-activity consists in the analysis of a concept (more or less complex) and the communication of the concept in analytic form. Thus the concept of 'John writing a letter to Peter' may take the following analytic form: *John—is writing—a letter—to Peter*, which the organs of speech are charged to reproduce in audible form. In the mind of a Frenchman the same concept would take the form *Jean écrit une lettre à Pierre* or *Jean est en train d'écrire une lettre à Pierre*, etc. In such a sentence one can distinguish two kinds of elements: (*a*) those which are recognized as units in virtue of the meaning they convey (*Jean, lettre, Pierre*) and (*b*) those which enable the reader to reconstruct the concept. The latter include not only such particles as *une, à,* but also flexions, word-order, and intonation. Our study would therefore resolve itself into an examination of the means employed by the language to denote certain objects, qualities, or actions, and to render such notions as tense, person, mood, number, gender, or such relations as we describe by the terms 'direct object', 'indirect object'.

The second method begins with the physical and examines the sounds of which speech is composed (Phonology), the groups of sounds which are recognized as units in virtue of the meaning they convey, their form and utilization (Vocabulary). Finally it examines those devices (flexions, prepositions, word-order, etc.) which serve to present in an analytic form a given concept. These may be studied from the purely formal point of view (Morphology) or from the point of view of use (Syntax). Such a treatment runs the risk of giving a false picture of speech-activity, but it presents definite practical advantages. Similarly the division of the field as indicated is artificial and presents obvious disadvantages, such as the separate treatment of form and function or meaning. Practical convenience must be our excuse for adhering to the time-honoured practice.

17. We have defined a language as a system of words, and upon analysis we find that from a physical point of view each word consists of one or more sounds. A change in the form of a word may therefore come about in one of two ways: (a) the quality of one or more of the constituent elements may be changed by a modified articulation, (b) there may be suppression, addition, substitution, or re-grouping of the constituent elements (vowels and consonants) independently of such modification. The former is called sound-change.

Sound-changes are a natural concomitant of speech-activity. We have seen that the latter implies the translation into audible sounds of a sound-picture existing in the mind of the speaker. This sound-picture might be described as a synthetic photograph (for which the analogy of a sound-film is appropriate up to a point) of a series of impressions received through the ear. A change in pronunciation may result from a distortion of the picture, such as might be produced by faulty perception or prolonged contact with persons possessing an abnormal articulation. But it also results from the failure of the individual to render the sound-picture accurately, from his failure to check slight deviations from the norm represented by the picture. In other words, the movement of the organs of speech is capable of variations so slight that they escape notice. Where such deviations are shared by a sufficiently large percentage of the population (community, tribe or nation) the synthetic photograph recorded through the ear is insensibly distorted. A new norm henceforth exists and we may say that a sound-change has been accomplished. Sound-change is therefore a gradual process, mechanical, regular, and involuntary. Thus FIDEM has by a series of slight changes ($f\varrho de > f\varrho\varrho de > fei\underline{t} > fei > foi > fo\varrho > fw\varrho > fwa$) become *foi*. Such changes may therefore be summed up in the form of sound-laws stating that at a given time, in a given place, under given phonetic conditions, a certain change in pronunciation took place. It is obvious that the term 'law' is here used in a special sense. It is in no sense an enactment, nor has it the universal application of a physical law. It is in fact a statistical law deriving its validity from the accuracy and completeness of the statistics. But as it records a mechanical and involuntary change it should, if accurately framed, admit of no exceptions. As already indicated, three conditions must be observed. (*a*) Chronology. A sound-law merely states what happened at a given time. Therefore only the words existing in the language at that date will be affected. Words entering it later will not undergo the change in question; they may appear to do so, but that is due to an analogical adaptation, the sounds of the borrowed word being rendered by what are felt to be their normal equivalents in the language (§§ 499–501). A distinction must therefore be drawn between native words and borrowed words. Borrowing has taken place at all periods in the history of Latin, but from the point of view of French, those words are described as Borrowed which came into the language after the date of the earliest change which differentiated French from the other Romance idioms. Among the Borrowed words a further distinction is made between Learned words (borrowed from Latin or through Latin, whether Classical or Low) and Foreign words borrowed from other languages. French words of Latin origin therefore fall into two classes, Popular and Learned, the former undergoing all the phonetic changes which have transformed Latin into French, the latter showing only some of these changes.

Compare Popular *poivre* (< PĬPER), *fièvre* (< FĔBREM), *gré* (< GRĀTUM), *suer* (< SŪDĀRE) with Learned *livre* (< LĬBRUM), *célèbre* (< CĔLĔBREM), *avocat* (< ADVOCĀTUM), *stupide* (< STŬPĬDUM). Etymological doublets consisting of a Popular and a Learned form of the same word are common: *maire* and *major* (MAJOR), *parole* and *parabole* (PARABOLA), *voyage* and *viatique* (VIATICUM), etc. (*b*) Geography. A sound-law merely states what happened in a given place, more precisely a given speech-community. Forms showing hard *c* (= k) for the normal *ch* (= š), e.g. *cage*, *cabaret*, etc., although they may be Popular 'langue d'oïl' forms, are borrowed and constitute nothing more than apparent exceptions to sound-laws applicable to the Île de France dialect. That is to say, each dialect has its own sound-laws; some of these are peculiar to itself, some it shares with other dialects. It is beyond the scope of this book to indicate how far each sound-law of the Île de France dialect applies to other dialects, but a few general indications are given in the Appendix (A). (*c*) Phonetic conditions. Isolative changes, i.e. changes which take place independently of varying phonetic conditions, are rare. An example is the change *u* (< ū) to *ü* (§ 32). Generally sound-changes are Combinative, i.e. governed by position within a word or phrase. Account must be taken, not merely of such phonetic conditions as are indicated in conventional orthography, but of conditions such as accent and syllabification. Compare the development of *ę* (< Ē) in TĒLA > *toile*, MERCĒDEM > *merci*, FRĒNUM > *frein*, RACĒMUM > *raisin*, VĒNĪ > *vin*(*s*), VINDĒMIA > *vendange*, DĒ > *de*. Cf. §§ 45–7.

18. A change in the articulation of the component elements thus brings about a change in the form of the word, just as in an orchestra a change in the quality of the component notes alters the character of the chord. But the word has an identity such as is denied to the component sounds. It is recognized as a unit in virtue of the meaning it conveys or the function it fulfils. It has both content and form. The latter is a conventional grouping of sounds, which serves as the audible symbol of the former. This implies that the word

may undergo a modification quite independent of sound-change. The modification affects that phase of speech-activity which is purely psychological and precedes the mechanical reproduction of the sound-picture in the form of audible sounds. The change of form thus brought about is generally involuntary, but it is not mechanical. It is dependent upon the psychological processes of speech-activity and subject to the associations which characterize all thought. When a word is called forth by an impulse of the brain, it may be accompanied by others which present some sort of affinity with it. If they obtrude sufficiently, the image to be translated into sound is no longer clear-cut; it is coloured, or its outlines are cut into, by other images. The result is often a new word preserving to greater or less degree the physiognomy of the old. Thus O.F. *il trueve* has given place to *il trouve* under the influence of those forms which are accented upon the ending and therefore regularly show *ou* (*trouvons*, *trouvez*, etc.); cf. §§ 309, 312. Such changes are sometimes described as sound-substitution, but the term is misleading in that it refers merely to the result. What has happened is not that *ou* has been substituted for *ue*, but that a new form *il trouve* has been created on the analogy of *nous trouvons*, etc. While it is easy to see how such changes of form take place in the speech of the individual, it is more difficult to account for their generalization; but it will be observed that they are particularly frequent in periods which lack a strong literary tradition (e.g. the Vulgar Latin and the Middle French periods). Weight of numbers and frequency of use generally decide the issue, but often the scales are so evenly weighted between the tendency to conserve the form and the associative influences that there is a prolonged period of hesitation, and the ultimate result may appear accidental. It is precisely in this field that some of the most interesting linguistic problems are encountered; and, while it is impossible to formulate laws governing such phenomena, it is possible to classify them and to distinguish tendencies. They reveal what is sometimes vaguely called the instinct of the language, the inherited tendencies and predispositions which, while remaining constant over prolonged periods, may insensibly decline or grow in strength, or change.

19. The changes which result from associative processes may be classified as follows:

(*a*) Changes resulting from similarity of sound, function or meaning. Levelling out of anomalies in conjugations and declensions (Chap. IV *passim*), or levelling out as between cognate forms such as the simple word and its derivative (§ 531). Substitution of prefix or suffix (§ 523). Folk Etymology, a term loosely used to denote the modification of a little-known word under the influence of a well-known word with which it is fancied to have some etymological connection (§ 587). Contamination, the modification which results when two words for the same notion present themselves to the mind at the same time and fuse (ALTUM + Germ. hōh > *halt, haut*, or O.F. *tempeste* + *orage* > O.F. *oreste*); cf. § 520.

(*b*) Back-formation or analogical regressions. As an example we may take the word *avoine*. Under the influence of the movement to restore *wę* for *ę* (< *oi*) (§§ 72–3), we find in certain words an analogical (false) regression from *ẽ* (< *ẽi*) to *wẽ*, which after being denasalized developed to *wa*; e.g. *avoine* for *aveine* (< AVĒNA).

(*c*) Changes which may be in part the result of conscious effort. Changes in pronunciation under the influence of the written language, particularly in borrowed words (§§ 54, 110–11). Terms of endearment (*Margot* for *Marguerite*). Thieves' slang. Differentiation and reaction: hesitation between two pronunciations is utilized to distinguish meanings (*frais* and *froid*, *raide* and *roide*, cf. § 72), or a sound-change is not allowed to proceed to its logical conclusion if the result would be a homonym or a duplication (§§ 60, 127).

Apart from the cases cited under (*b*) and (*c*), where its rôle is difficult to assess, conscious intervention is comparatively rare. One must take into account the activity of the

schoolmaster in imposing 'correct' pronunciation, the intervention of grammarians in the sixteenth and seventeenth
centuries, the conscious deformation of words with a burlesque
or euphemistic intention.

20. A special place must be assigned to certain tendencies
which assert themselves sporadically and which sometimes
result in a change of usage, viz. Assimilation, Dissimilation,
Metathesis. They represent a form of sound-substitution, but
result from the momentary escape of the organs of speech
from the control of the mind. Assimilation is the substitution
of a sound which has just been articulated, or is about to be
articulated, for the normal sound. Thus *écarquiller* has arisen
from older *écartiller*, and in O.F. *cerchier > chercher* initial
ch (= š) was by anticipation substituted for *c* (= s < ts). This
form of assimilation, which might be called harmonic or
dittological, is to be distinguished from the kind found in
sound-change (§§ 86–95). Dissimilation results from a tendency to avoid the repetition of a particular sound at too
short an interval. This may result in the suppression of a
sound or the substitution of another for it: *cinq* <CINQUE for
QUINQUE, *voisin* < *VĘCINUM for VĪCĪNUM, *pèlerin* <PELEGRINUM
for PEREGRINUM, and popular *colidor* for *corridor*. Metathesis is
the accidental transposition of a sound within a word: *fromage*
for *formage* < (CASEUM) *FORMATICUM. Sometimes two sounds
exchange places: *moustique* for Spanish mosquito, *étincelle*
< *STINCILLA for SCINTILLA.

In the following chapter attention will be given primarily
to sound-changes, and no attempt will be made to deal
at length with the apparent exceptions indicated in § 19.
Similarly the more detailed discussion of Learned words will
be reserved for Chapter VI.

Chapter III

PHONOLOGY

A. *VOWELS*

1. VULGAR LATIN DEVELOPMENTS

(a) ACCENTUATION

21. NATURE OF THE ACCENT. It would appear that in Classical Latin the accent combined pitch and stress, i.e. the voice was raised on certain syllables, which were at the same time stressed. In Vulgar Latin the musical element seems to have largely disappeared, leaving practically a pure stress (expiratory) accent. This expiratory accent was particularly strong in Gaul, a feature which has sometimes been ascribed to Celtic influence.

There were three degrees of stress: a full stress ('), a secondary stress (`), and a weak stress (relatively an absence of stress), whence a classification of tonic, countertonic, and atonic vowels or syllables respectively. Thus in CÈREBÉLLUM the first E is countertonic, the third tonic, the counterfinal E and the final U are atonic. The degree of stress is not absolute but relative. The relative stress as between the syllables of a single word is generally constant. Within a phrase or sentence the relative stress as between words is largely determined by their syntactic function, with the result that certain words, generally monosyllables (pronouns, NON, ES, ERAT, ERIT, BENE, MALE), may be articulated with full, secondary, or weak stress according to their function (cf. § 145). Thus MĒ when it is fully stressed develops into *moi*, but when it is joined proclitically to the following or enclitically to the preceding word it is weakened to *me* (mə) and may subsequently lose its vowel (O.F. *nem* for *ne me*). Certain monosyllabic words are uniformly unaccented (DE, AD, IN, PER, PRO, ET, NEC, AUT, SI); also SINE, IBI, UBI, QUOMODO.

22. PLACE OF THE ACCENT. In Classical Latin the tonic accent falls, (*a*) in words of two syllables, on the first (CÁNEM), (*b*) in words of three or more syllables, on the penultimate syllable if that syllable is long (i.e. if it contains a long vowel, a diphthong, or alternatively a short vowel followed by a consonant belonging to the same syllable) (AMÁRE, CEREBĔLLUM), otherwise on the antepenultimate (TÉPĬDUM, ÍNTĔGRUM). The initial syllable bears a secondary stress if there are one or more pre-tonic syllables (CÈREBĔLLUM).

In Vulgar Latin the accent remained on the same syllable, with the following exceptions:

(*a*) Proparoxytons whose penultimate vowel is followed by explosive + *r* are paroxyton in V.L. Thus INTĔGRUM, TONĬTRUM and the like are accented upon the second syllable in V.L.

(*b*) When accented *i* and *e* are in hiatus with a following vowel, the accent passes to the latter, with the result that *i* and *e* become semi-consonantal and have the common value *j*. Thus MULIEREM and PARIETEM are pronounced *mǫljẹre* and *par(j)ẹte* respectively in V.L.

(*c*) In numerals denoting tens the accent was thrown back upon the distinctive element (VÍGINTI, TRÍGINTA).

(*d*) Many changes of stress are due to analogy or result from morphological changes (§ 285). Thus in MERCURI DIES (> *mercredi*) the accent shifted to the first syllable by analogy with LÚNAE DIES, etc.; CADÉRE appears for CÁDĔRE by assimilation to verbs of the Second Conjugation (§ 284). In the written language tradition was generally strong enough to resist these tendencies. Compound verbs, if they were still felt to be such, were re-composed in V.L., often with a corresponding shifting of the accent (CON-VÉNIT, RE-TÉNET for C.L. CÓNVENIT, RÉTINET). It should be noted that re-composition does not always involve a change of accent (*ATTÁNGIT for ATTÍNGIT, etc.).

---

¹ According to C.L. rules of syllabification single consonants, or groups consisting of explosive + *l* or *r*, go with the following syllable. In the case of other groups the first consonant closes the preceding syllable.

For the accentuation of borrowed words, cf. §§ 499–501, 518–20.

The stress accent is of capital importance for the development of the Romance languages,[1] resulting as it does in a threefold development of vowels according as they were tonic, countertonic or atonic (see below). Hardly less fundamental was the change whereby C.L. distinctions of quantity gave place in V.L. to distinctions of quality.

(b) Quality

23. As a result of the tendency to give to long vowels a close, and to short vowels an open quality, the distinction of quantity led to a new distinction of quality in V.L. It is not clear at what date the process began, but by the end of the third century it is completed. It may be tabulated thus:

$$\text{C.L.} \quad \breve{A} \ \bar{A} \ \breve{E} \ \bar{E} \ \breve{I} \ \bar{I} \quad \breve{O} \ \bar{O} \ \breve{U} \ \bar{U}$$
$$\qquad\quad\ \ \vee \ \ | \ \vee \ | \ | \ \vee \ |$$
$$\text{V.L.} \quad a \quad \ e̜ \ \ e̜ \ \ i \quad o̜ \ \ o̜ \ \ u$$

It will be seen that V.L. does not perpetuate the distinction between Ă and Ā. In the greater part of the Empire Ĭ and Ŭ became so open, and Ē and Ō became so close, that they fell together as e̜ and o̜ respectively. Hence the confusion between E and I, O and U observable in Late Latin inscriptions and documents (SEMPETERNIS MUNIRIBUS DEPOTATA, C.I.L. v, 8958) Accordingly the I in FĬDEM and the E in CRĒDO give the same result in French (*foi* and *crois*); similarly PLŌRAT > *ploure* > *pleure* and GŬLA > *goule* > *gueule*.

The C.L. diphthongs AE, OE are reduced in V.L. to e̜ and e̜ respectively (CAELUM = V.L. K'E̜LU > *ciel*; POENA = V.L. PE̜NA > *peine*). In a few words it would appear from later developments that AE had been reduced to e̜ (PRAEDA = V.L. PRE̜DA, perhaps under the influence of PRE̜SA (< PREHENSA), whence *proie*; SAEPEM = V.L. SE̜PE > O.F. *soif* 'hedge').

The only other diphthong that had persisted in C.L. was

[1] Cf. G. Paris, *Étude sur le rôle de l'accent latin dans la langue française*, Paris and Leipzig, 1862.

AU, but it had in certain words been reduced in Classical times to o (CODA for CAUDA). This was probably a dialectal development: the literary language generally maintained AU and it persisted in V.L. except in words which begin with AU and have U in the following syllable: AUGUSTUM = V.L. AGOSTU > *aost* > *août*, AUGURIUM = V.L. AGURJU > *eür* > *(h)eur*, cf. *bonheur*, *malheur*. The *u* element of the diphthong here disappeared by dissimilation (§ 20). Beside the AU which was inherited from C.L. there existed in V.L. a secondary *au* which developed from *av'*cons. or *ab'*cons. (§§ 42, 84).

(c) QUANTITY

24. Thus the C.L. distinction of quantity had been obliterated, but towards the end of the Empire there developed a new distinction of quantity. This bore no relation to the C.L. but was determined by position. If the vowel was free (followed by a single consonant or by explosive + *r*) it became long. If it was blocked (followed by two or more consonants, except the combination explosive + *r*) it became short. This is explained by the fact that in the former case the syllable ended in a vowel (hence called an open syllable); but in the latter case it ended in a consonant, thus leaving correspondingly less time for the articulation of the vowel; e.g. FẸ-DE (FĬDEM), PẸ-TRA (PĔTRA), but VĔR-GA (VĬRGA), PǑR-TA (PǑRTA). The new distinction of quantity has important consequences in the later development of tonic vowels (§§ 32–3). The distinction was less marked in the case of countertonic vowels, while atonic vowels do not appear to have been affected.

It often happens that a vowel which was free in C.L. becomes blocked at some later stage through the loss of a vowel. Thus VĬRĬDEM early became VẸRDE, whence *vert*, while in a word like HABĒTIS (>*avoiz*) the unaccented vowel was not lost until after the change ẹ > *ei* (later *oi*) (§ 33). Conversely the early loss of N in the group NS left the preceding vowel free (MENSEM > MẸSE > *mois*) (§ 84).

The V.L. groups BJ, KJ, LJ, MJ, NJ, PJ, VJ block the preceding vowel, but accented ę and ǫ before such groups develop as though free, under the breaking influence of *j* (§ 36).

(d) VOWELS IN HIATUS

25. Two contiguous vowels are said to be in hiatus if they belong to separate syllables. The first vowel is therefore in an open syllable, but it does not always show the regular development of a free vowel because of the special phonetic condition created by the hiatus (see § 44). Moreover, in V.L. the hiatus was generally reduced in the following ways:

(a) Two identical vowels fused: CO(H)ORTEM > CǪRTE > *cour*, PRE(H)ENDERE > *prendre*.

(b) Atonic I, E in hiatus with a following vowel became semi-consonantal *j* (FOLJA, VINJA) (§ 22 b). Atonic U in hiatus similarly became semi-consonantal *w* (ANNUALEM > O.F. *anvel*); cf. § 103.

26. In the following section we shall consider the evolution of the V.L. vowel system down to 1300. It will be seen that some of the changes there discussed begin in the V.L. period and are therefore shared by other Romance languages. Others begin in the Gallo-Roman period and are shared by Provençal. We have for convenience grouped together cognate phenomena of various dates but indicate their relative chronology wherever possible.

2. THE OLD FRENCH VOWEL SYSTEM

The development of V.L. vowels in Old French is conditioned above all by the degree of stress with which they are articulated. We shall therefore consider in turn atonic, tonic and countertonic vowels.

(a) ATONIC VOWELS

27. Atonic vowels are naturally articulated with less tension than tonic or countertonic vowels and fine distinctions

of quality are obliterated, with the result that *ẹ* and *ę*, *ọ* and *ǫ* fall together. Further, the V.L. quantitative distinction (if it ever existed in atonic vowels, cf. § 24) was not maintained. Gallo-Roman therefore inherited from V.L. the atonic vowels *a, e, i, o, u,* which were presumably short and were already tending to weaken and disappear.

(i) THE UNACCENTED PENULT OF PROPAROXYTONS

28. The atonic vowel in this position offered least resistance and C.L. already shows traces of its effacement: CAL(I)DUM, etc. In the later stages of V.L. it disappeared in an ever-increasing number of words: COM(I)TEM, CAM(E)RA, PLAT(A)-NUM, whence *comte, chambre, plane.* The tendency to syncope was particularly pronounced in the V.L. of Gaul with its strong expiratory stress (§ 21). The result is that Old French possesses no proparoxytons except a few Learned words introduced after the reduction to paroxytons had taken place (*ángele, imágene, húmele, vírgene,* etc.). But these were likewise reduced before the end of the Old French period (*ange, image, humble, vierge*).

(ii) FINAL AND COUNTERFINAL VOWELS

29. These persist in V.L. in a weakened form with a tendency to confuse *e* and *i, o* and *u.* In Old French, *a* remains in a weakened form as so-called feminine *e* (= ə) (cf. § 64): BONA > *bonne,* AMAS > *aimes.* This change dates from about the end of the eighth century. *e, i, o, u* generally disappear (about the seventh century), but they persist in the form of the weakened supporting vowel *ə* in the following cases: (*a*) before a group of consonants (AMENT > *aiment*); (*b*) after a group of consonants requiring a supporting vowel, notably cons. + *l, r, m, n,* excepting *kl, gr, gn, rm, rn* (DUPLUM > *double,* PATREM > *peḍre* > *père,* *HELMU (Germ. h e l m) > *helme* > *heaume,* ALNUM > *alne* > *aune*). The group may be primary, i.e. inherited as such from Latin, or secondary, i.e. developed subsequently through the loss of a vowel (MASCULUM > MASC'LU > *masle* > *mâle*). In the absence of any supporting vowel an

ə is developed (INSIMUL > ENSEM'L > *ensemble*, MINOR > MEN'R > *mendre* later *moindre* ≠ *moins*). It will be seen that ə persists even after the reduction of the group which originally required the supporting vowel (*père, heaume, aune, mâle*). For the apparent exceptions presented by borrowed words, cf. § 500.

30. Where three syllables precede the tonic, the vowel of each of the first two normally bears a secondary stress, but analogical influences have interfered with the normal development (ÌNGÈNERÁRE > *engendrer*, RÈCÙPERÁRE > *recouvrer*, ÀMÀRITÚDINEM > *amertume*, but LÌBERÀTIÓNEM > *livraison*, *ÀRBORÌSCÉLLUM > *arbreissel*, Mod.F. *arbrisseau*).

For the development of final and counterfinal vowels in hiatus, cf. § 44.

(b) TONIC AND COUNTERTONIC VOWELS

31. The V.L. quantitative distinction was fully maintained in the case of tonic vowels and is responsible for a twofold development according as the vowel was long or short by position (§ 24). The strong expiratory stress with which they were articulated further caused them to absorb or attract neighbouring sounds, thus modifying their own point of articulation or forming diphthongs. The same factors have to be taken into account in the case of countertonic vowels; but the stress being weaker, they are less potent. We shall in the first place consider the development of tonic and countertonic vowels independently of such modifying influences and then consider the effect of the latter.[1]

(i) TONIC BLOCKED VOWELS

32. Tonic vowels when blocked, i.e. short, remained unchanged, except that the point of articulation of ǫ changed slightly and it became ṵ, which in the course of the Old French period probably became still more close (> ṵ). The point of articulation of *u* (< ū) shifted forward and upward,

---

[1] Cf. the tables given in §§ 45-7, where examples will be found.

giving *ü*; but this change affects every *u* (< ŭ) regardless of stress or position. *au*, whether primary or secondary (§ 23), became *ǫ*, that is, a monophthong intermediate in position between the two constituent elements of the diphthong.

(ii) TONIC FREE VOWELS

33. Tonic vowels when free, i.e. long, tend to diphthongize. The first stage in this process was a doubling of the vowel. In virtue of its being in an open syllable, the vowel was lengthened, and coming as it did under a strong expiratory stress, we may assume that doubling resulted from the concentration of stress on the beginning and end of the vowel, the middle portion being slurred. Taking *ẹ* as an example, the first stage would be *ẹeẹ* leading up to *ẹẹ*. Then followed a differentiation of the two elements, facilitated perhaps by unequal distribution of stress. Thus *ẹẹ > ẹe > iẹ > ié*. Similarly *ę > ęę > ęi > ọi, ǫ > ǫǫ > ǫǫ > úǫ > úe > uẹ > uǒ, ọ > ọọ > ọu > ǒu*. The vowels *i* and *u* did not diphthongize, the reason being that, as they are the extreme front and back vowels respectively, their point of articulation is more stable and no differentiation takes place. As for tonic free *a*, it appears in French as the monophthong *e*, but indirect evidence points to *aa > aę* as the intermediate stages. *au* regularly became *o* (§ 23).

(iii) COUNTERTONIC VOWELS

34. The articulation of countertonic vowels was less tense than that of tonic vowels and therefore the V.L. qualitative and quantitative distinctions were less fully maintained. The result was on the one hand confusion of *ẹ* and *ę*, and to some extent of *ǫ* and *ọ*, and on the other a tendency to shorten all vowels. Countertonic vowels therefore do not diphthongize and they tend to weaken. Their weak articulation renders them particularly liable to various sporadic changes (cf. § 20).

Dissimilation. *i* is dissimilated to *e* before following tonic *i* in DĪVĪNUM > *devin*, VĪCĪNUM (V.L. vęk'ınu) > *veisin* > *voisin*, FĪNĪRE > O.F. *fenir*.

Assimilation. *e* is assimilated to a following tonic *a* in sĭlvaticum > *salvage* > *sauvage*, *bĭlancia > *balance*.

e > *a* under the opening influence of a following *l* or *r* in *zelosum > *jalos, jaloux*, mercatum > *marchié* > *marché*, per > *par* (preposition and prefix). This is perhaps a dialectal pronunciation which the literary language adopted only in certain words such as the above; cf. belare > *beler*, permittere > *permettre*.

For the special form which the influence of labials, nasals, and palatals took in the case of countertonic vowels, see below.

The development of countertonic *o* and *u* (< ū) presents many irregularities, owing partly to the loose articulation of countertonic vowels (frūmentum > *froment*, pŏrcellum > *pourceau*, tŏrmentum > *tourment*), partly to the analogical influence of cognate forms (§ 531) and of orthography (§§ 65–7, 155). Many apparent exceptions to the regular change *o* > *u* are due to the fact that the words in question are later borrowings (*novembre, opinion, volume*) or have been remodelled under the influence of Latin (*colombe, colonne* for earlier *coulombe, coulonne*).

The countertonic vowel disappeared early between initial consonant and *r* in directum > *dreit* > *droit*, *directiare > *drecier* > *dresser*, *veracum > *vrai*, *corrotulare > *croller* > *crouler*.

(c) Modifying influences

(i) PALATALS

35. The influence of palatals on vowels is progressive or regressive and shows itself in the following ways:

(*a*) Palatalization of the vowel. This we may define as a shifting of the point of articulation upward and forward towards the front of the hard palate. Thus the passage from *u* (< ū) to *ü* may be described as a palatalization of *u*; the fact that it takes place independently suggests that the tendency to palatalization was naturally strong in Gaul, and this would in its turn account for the readiness with which

Old French vowels attracted a palatal element. Palatalization of vowels is generally progressive, e.g. countertonic free *a*
is raised to *e* by a preceding palatal (CABALLUM > *cheval*).

(*b*) The shifting of the point of articulation may take place
while the vowel is actually being articulated, i.e. the shape
of the oral cavity may be modified during the emission of
breath which produces the vowel, the tongue being arched
towards the hard palate at the beginning or at the end of the
emission. The result is, not a uniform palatalization of the
whole vowel, but a palatalization of the initial or of the final
stage, in other words a diphthong consisting of *i* + vowel or
vowel + *i* (CANEM > *chien*, *PECTORINA > *peitrine* > *poitrine*). This
is the process which is sometimes referred to as the disengaging
or giving off of a yod (= *j*) by the palatal, the yod combining
as semi-vocalic *i̯* with the vowel. *i̯* is simply absorbed by a
contiguous *i*, whether the latter be a monophthong or an
element of a diphthong (DĪCERE > *dire*, RĒGEM > *rei*). Its adjunction may result in the creation of a triphthong beginning
and ending in *i*, in which case the triphthong is reduced to *i*
(CĒRA > *cieire > *cire*, similarly NĔGAT > *nie*, MĔDIUM > *mi*, MER-
CĒDEM > *merci*). In like manner tonic free *a* between palatals
gives *i* through *iei (JACET > *gist*).

36. The palatal may affect the vowel directly or indirectly:

(i) The palatal may itself combine in the form of *i* (cf.
§ 92) with the preceding vowel to form a diphthong (PLAGA
> *plaie*, MAJOR > MAJ'R > *maire*, HŎDIE > (H)QJE > (*h*)*ui*).

(ii) The palatal may persist (intact or modified) and at
the same time disengage an *i* sound which combines with the
vowel (CARUM > *chier* through K'AR > *k'ier* > *t'ier* > *tš̌ier*; *CAR-
RICARE > *chargier*).

(iii) The palatal may first of all palatalize a neighbouring
consonant which is later depalatalized, the palatal element
combining in the form of *i* with the vowel (CEREVISIA > *cervoise*
through the stages K'ERVẸS'A > *t'erveise* > *tserveise*, CŎRIUM
> *cuir*, VŌCEM > *voiz*, GLŌRIA > *gloire*, DORMITŌRIUM > *dortoir*).

l' is not depalatalized if it remains medial or final, and it

therefore does not give off an *i* sound. The *i* which appears
in spelling is merely part of the compound graphy *ill* or *il*
for palatalized *l'* (*l* mouillé). The preceding vowel does not
show diphthongization except in the case of tonic *ę* and *ǫ*
(§ 91) (VĚTULUM > vęklu > *vieil*, FŎLIA > *feuille*, but VALEAM
> *vaille*, AURICULA > *oreille*, FILIA > *fille*, *GENUCULUM > *genouil*).
If by the loss of a vowel medial *l'* is subsequently brought
into contact with a following consonant, it is depalatalized
but does not give off an *i* sound, whence *travauz* (< *traval's*),
vieuz, genouz, etc. For the influence of *n'*, cf. § 40.

(iv) The groups *bj, kj, mj, vj, pj* preserved the syllabification
b-j, k-j, m-j, v-j, p-j. The preceding vowel was thus blocked
and remained unchanged, with the exception of tonic *ę* and *ǫ*
(*LĚVIUM > *liège*, but CAVEA > *cage*); *k* alone was later palatalized (*GLACIA > *glace*); in the remaining cases *j* developed
as though initial (§§ 91, 93).

37. Special mention must be made of the phenomenon
known as mutation (= the German *Umlaut*), which may be
described as the palatalization of a tonic vowel by a long
final *i*. The vowels *ę* and *ẹ* are raised to *i* (FĒCĪ > *fis*, TĚNUĪ
> *tin(s)*) and *ǫ* to *ü* (FŬĪ > *füi* later replaced by analogical *fus*).
Other vowels remain unaffected.

(ii) NASALS

38. Nasalization is the assimilation of a vowel to the following nasal consonant (*m, n, n'*), i.e. the uvula, which closes
the nasal passage for all oral (non-nasal) sounds, is allowed
to open in anticipation of the following nasal consonant, thus
giving a nasal quality to the vowel. Open vowels nasalize
more readily and more markedly than close vowels. Consequently *i* and *ü* were the last vowels to be nasalized and the
nasalization was never very pronounced. In Old French,
tonic vowels were nasalized, whether they were free or blocked.
Countertonic vowels were nasalized when blocked; but when
free, only *o* was nasalized (SŎNARE > *sonner*, DŌNARE > *donner*). The date at which the various vowels were nasalized
cannot be determined precisely, but *a* and *e* were probably

nasalized before the ninth century, the remainder between the ninth and twelfth centuries.

39. The diversion of the current of air (nasalization) is but one aspect of the influence of nasals. They also change the point of articulation of the preceding vowel and make it more close, the vowels affected being $ę$ ($<$ blocked $Ĕ$) and $ǫ$ ($<$ blocked $ŏ$), which become $ẹ$ and $ọ$ respectively and are then nasalized. This same influence has prevented the diphthongization of $ǫ$ when followed by a nasal. Old French thus originally possessed the nasal vowels $ã, ẽ̜, ĩ, õ̜, ũ$, but before the end of the Old French period the natural tendency for nasalized vowels to become open had already asserted itself. In the case of $ẽ̜$ this led to a lowering through $ẽ$ to $ã$ as early as the twelfth century, except before n'. The diphthongization of tonic free $ẹ, ę, ǫ$ was not arrested, the result being the nasalized diphthongs $iẽ, ẽ̜i, uõ$ (later $uẽ$). Free tonic a before a nasal gave $ãi$ (later $ẽi$), which lends support to the suggestion that ae (ai) was the intermediate stage in the normal development $a > e$ (§ 33).

40. n' nasalized a preceding vowel in the same way as m, n. When it became blocked or final, n' was depalatalized and gave off an i, which combined with the preceding vowel (§ 89). When it remained medial it was not depalatalized and did not give off an i, but the palatal nature of the consonant prevented the lowering of $ẽ$ to $ã$: CASTANEA $> chastaigne$ ($=$ tšastãn'ə), DIGNAT $> deigne$ ($=$ dẽn'ə), LINEA $> ligne$, CICONIA $> ceogne$, Mod.F. $cigogne$.

(iii) LABIALS

41. The influence of labial consonants is progressive or regressive. It is weaker than that of palatals and nasals, and its effect is to round the front vowels e, i (particularly in the countertonic position), the normal result being $ö$ and $ü$ respectively (*BĪBERATICUM $> bevrage > beuvrage > breuvage$, *AFFĪBULARE $> afibler > affubler$), but there are many exceptions (*FEMARIUM $> femier > fumier$, GEMELLUM $> gemel > jumel$ later $jumeau$).

42. *ƀ* (< v or b; §§ 23, 84), if brought into contact with a following consonant, is vocalized and combines as *u* with the preceding vowel (AVICELLUM > AUK′ELLU > *oisel*, PARA-BOLA > PARAULA > *parole*).

For the influence of the semi-consonantal *w*, which resulted from atonic *u* in hiatus, see §§ 345(3), 348, 350.

(iv) VOCALIZATION OF L

43. Before a consonant, *l* had a velar pronunciation (*ł*) in Vulgar Latin, that is to say, the tongue was arched towards the velum. It therefore approximated to the normal tongue-position for *u*, and in the course of the eleventh and twelfth centuries *ł* lost its liquid (consonantal) quality, persisting in the form of vocalic *u* (§ 45, col. *e*).

If by the loss of a vowel Latin intervocalic *l* was subsequently brought into contact with a following consonant, it likewise took a velar pronunciation and was vocalized, combining as *u* with the preceding vowel. But in this case the preceding vowel had begun to evolve as a free vowel, whence PALOS > *pels* > *pieus*, *CAELOS > *ciels* > *cieus*, SŌLOS > *sous*, *seus* (later *seuls*), SŎLET > *sueut > *sieut* (cf. § 44 *a*).

(v) VOWELS IN HIATUS

44. Latin cases of hiatus (primary) have been dealt with in §§ 22 *b*, 25. The loss of intervocalic consonants in Gallo-Roman (§ 98) created further such cases (secondary hiatus), which were reduced as they arose:

(*a*) Tonic vowel + *u* was early reduced: *a* + *u* > *ou* (CLAVUM > *clou*); *ę* + *u* > *iéu* (GRAECUM > *Grieu*); *ǫ* + *u* gave a triphthong *ueu*, the first element of which became *i* by dissimilation (LŎCUM > *lueu > *lieu*, JŎCUM > *jueu > *jieu*), or was absorbed by a preceding labial or velar (FŎCUM > *fueu > *feu*, similarly SARCŎPHĂGUM > *sarkeu*, CŎQ(U)UM > *keu*); *ǫ* + *u* > *ǫ́u* > *óu* (DUOS > *dous* > *deus*, LUPUM > *lou* > *leu*). The diphthong *eu* of Celtic and Germanic loan-words was treated as though the two vowels were in hiatus (Celtic leuca > *lieue*, Germ. speut > *espieut* (later *épieu*), Germ. streup > *estrieu*).

(*b*) Tonic vowel + *i* was early reduced: *a* + *i* > *ái* (AMA(V)I > *amai*).

(*c*) Countertonic *a* + tonic vowel. This secondary hiatus persisted in Old French, but *a* was weakened to *ə* (MATURUM > *meür*, A(U)GURIUM > *eür*, *SAPUTUM > *seü*). In S.E. and S.W. dialects and sporadically in other dialects *a* is found for *e* (*fahu* for *feü* < *FATUTUM formed on FATUM).

With the progressive weakening and disappearance of intervocalic consonants, many further cases of hiatus were created in the Old French period (§ 60).

[For §§ 45–7, see pp. 43–5.]

48. The accompanying tables summarize the development of tonic and countertonic vowels down to about the middle of the twelfth century. To complete the information there given the following should be added:

Tonic vowel + secondary *ł* (< *l* or *l'*), §§ 43, 36 (iii).

Tonic vowel + *l'*, § 36 (iii).

Tonic vowel + *n'* (medial), § 40.

Tonic free A between palatals, § 35 (*b*).

Countertonic A in hiatus, § 44 (*c*).

Countertonic free A preceded by palatal, § 35 (*a*).

Countertonic free O before nasal, § 38.

Sporadic developments affecting countertonic vowels, § 34.

49. The quality of *e* (< tonic free A). The original quality of this *e* is uncertain, but down to the middle of the twelfth century it never rimes with *ę* and rimes with *ę* only in a few words (*ert, Deu*, etc.). If we bear in mind such rimes and if we accept the view that the intermediate stage in the change A > *e* was *aę* (§ 33), we may conclude that *e* (< A) was still more open than *ę* and approached in quality the vowel of English *can*. There may also have been a quantitative distinction, *e* (< A) being longer than *ę* or *ę*. From about 1150 this threefold distinction begins to give place to a twofold distinction; *e*, whatever its provenance, being pronounced *ę* in

45. TONIC VOWELS—BLOCKED

	(a)	(b)	(c)	(d)	(e)
V.L.	Independent	+ i̯	Before *m, n*	Before *n′* + cons. or *n′* final	+ *l*
a	a PARTEM > *part*	ái > ę́i > ę FACTUM > *fait*	ã ANNUM > *an*	ã́i > ę́i PLANGIT > *plaint*	áu SALVUM > *sauf*
ę	ę TĔSTA > *teste*	i LĔCTUM > *lit*	ẽ > ã VĔNTUM > *vent*	ĩ INGĔNIUM > *enging*	éau > eáu BĔLL(O)S > *bęls* > *beaus*
ẹ	ẹ MĬTTERE > *metre*	ę́i > ǫ́i TĒCTUM > *toit*	ẽ > ã FĬNDERE > *fendre*	ę́i FĬNGĔRE > *feindre*	ę́u > ǫ́u CAPĬLL(O)S > *chevęls* > *cheveus*
i	i VĪLLA > *ville*	i DĪC(I)T > *dit*	ĩ QUĪNTUM > *quint*	ĩ SCRĪNIUM > *escring*	i *FĪL(O)S > *fis*
ǫ	ǫ PŎRTA > *porte*	ų́i > üí NŎCTEM > *nuit*	õ PŎNTEM > *pont*	ǫ́i LŎNGE > *loing*	óu FŎLL(E)S > *fous*
ọ	u RŬPTA > *route*	ǫ́i ANGŬSTIA > *angoisse*	õ ŬNDA > *onde*	ǫ́i PŬNCTUM > *point*	óu AUSCŬLTAT > *escoute*
u	ü NŪLLUM > *nul*	úi > üí FRŪCTUM > *fruit*	ũ̈ *ALLŪM(I)NAT > *allume*	ų́i > üí JŪNIUM > *juin*	ü NŪLL(O)S > *nus*
au	—	—	—	—	—

46. TONIC VOWELS—FREE

C.L.	V.L.	(a) Independent	(b) After a palatal	(c) + i̯	(d) Before m, n
ă ā	a	e MARE > mer	ié ié before m, n CARUM > chier CANEM > chien	ái > ę́i > ę PLAGA > plaie	ái > ę́i MANUM > main
ĕ ae	ę	ié PĔDEM > pied	ié CAELUM > ciel	i LĔGO > li(s)	ié BĔNE > bien
ē ĭ oe	ẹ	ẹ́i > ọ́i HABĒRE > aveir > avoir	i ī before m, n CĒRA > cire RACĒMUM > raisin	ẹ́i > ọ́i RĒGEM > rei > roi	ę́i VĒNA > veine
ī	i	i VĪVUM > vif	—	i AMĪCA > amie	ī VĪNUM > vin
ŏ	ǫ	úo > úe > uę́ > uǫ́ BŎVEM > buef	—	ų́i > üí HŎDIE > hui	uǫ́ > uę́ CŎMES > cuens
ō ŭ	ọ	ọ́u > ọ́u NEPŌTEM > neveu	—	ọ́i VŌCEM > voiz	õ DŌNUM > don
ū	u	ü MŪRUM > mur	—	ų́i > üí LŪCENT > luisent	ũ ŪNA > une
au	au	ǫ AURUM > or	—	ọ́i GAUDIA > joie	—

47. COUNTERTONIC VOWELS

	(a) Independent	(b) + i̯	(c) Before m, n + cons.	(d) Before n′ + cons.	(e) + l
V.L.					
a	a BARONEM > baron ARGENTUM > argent	ái > ę́i > ę RATIONEM > raison	ã MANTELLUM > mantel	ą́i > ę́i *PLANCTIVUM > plaintif	áu FALCONEM > faucon
ẹ) ę) e	e LĔVARE > lever VĬRTUTEM > vertu	éi > ói *PECTORINA > poitrine	ẽ > ã ĬNVOLARE > embler	ę́i CĬNCTURA > ceinture	óu *FĪL(I)CARIA > fougiere
i	i VĪLLANUM > vilain	i TĪTIONEM > tison	ĩ LĬNTEOLUM > linceul	—	i *FĪL(I)CELLA > ficelle
ǫ	free > ǫ > u blocked > ǫ PRŎBARE > prouver MŎRTALEM > mortel	ói *FŎCARIUM > foüer	õ CŎMPUTARE > conter	ǫ́i *ACŎGNITARE > acointier	óu SŎL(I)DARE > souder
ọ	u PLŌRARE > plourer	ói PŌTIONEM > poison	õ NŌM(I)NARE > nommer	ọ́i PŬNGERE + HA- BET > poindra	óu CŬLTELLUM > coutel
u	ü *ŪSARE > user	úi > üí LŪCENTEM > luisant	ũ̈ LŪNAE DIEM > lundi	—	—
au	ǫ PAUSARE > poser	ói *GAUDIOSUM > joieus AV(I)CELLUM > oisel	—	—	—

a closed syllable (i.e. before a consonant which continued to be sounded), e whenever by the loss of the following consonant it had come to be in an open syllable.

The distinction between oi ($< ei$ or $< au + i$ or $< a + ui$) and oi ($< o + i$) disappeared in the course of the twelfth century; cf. the subsequent identical development of oi in *avoir*, *roi*, *toit*, *joie*, and *voiz*, *angoisse*.

50. Towards the end of the twelfth century the French language thus possessed the oral vowels $a, e, e, i, o, u, ü, ə$; the oral diphthongs $au, ie, oi, ou, ou, üi, uo$; the triphthongs eau, ieu; the nasal vowels $ã, ẽ, ĩ, õ, ũ$; the nasal diphthongs ei, ie, $oi, ue, üi$. Further changes, some of which had already begun before 1200, transformed this system in the course of the thirteenth century. Of these the principal are:

Tonic o ($<$ AU) $> o$, except when preceded or followed by r (cf. §§ 53, 65).

The first element of the ascending diphthongs $ie, üi, ie, üi$ becomes semi-consonantal, whence $je, üi, je, üi$. Similarly $ieu > jö$.

The reduction of ou to u, ou and uo to $ö$ is practically completed by the end of the century.

oi, whatever its provenance, came to be pronounced oe before a consonant in the thirteenth century, and the first element tended to become semi-consonantal (we). In other positions oi was maintained down to the sixteenth century. Similarly $oi > we$.

ue existed in only a few words (*buen*, *cuens*, etc.) and may have been a dialectal development. Such forms have given place to forms with undiphthongized $õ$ (*bon*).

51. Towards the end of the thirteenth century we have therefore the oral vowels $a, e, e, i, o, o, u, ü, ö, ə$; the oral diphthongs au, oi; the triphthong eau; the nasal vowels $ã, ẽ, ĩ, õ, ũ$; the nasal diphthongs ei, oi; and the following combinations of semi-consonant and vowel: $je, jö, we, üi, je$ $we, üi$.

The fourteenth and fifteenth centuries present no clear-cut evolution of this system, but rather a conflict of old habits

fo pronunciation and new tendencies, complicated by dialectal features. As this conflict continues into the sixteenth
century and is reflected in modern pronunciation, we shall
for convenience reserve the discussion of such new tendencies
(elimination of *ə*, reduction of *wę* to *ę*, *je* to *e*, denasalization,
etc.) for the following section No new vowel sounds (if we
except variations in the quality of certain vowels) developed
in the course of the fourteenth and fifteenth centuries, and
we shall therefore take as our point of departure the vowel
system as constituted at the end of the thirteenth century and
examine its development in Modern French.

3. MIDDLE AND MODERN FRENCH DEVELOPMENTS[1]

52. We have seen that the development of the Old French
vowel system was conditioned by two factors, accent and
position (closed or open syllable). In so far as its evolution
continued to be natural (mechanical), the same factors remain decisive. But a fundamental difference between Modern
French and Old French lies in the progressive elimination
of the tonic accent (the stress falling on a particular syllable
of a word) in favour of the group-accent (§§ 145–9). The fact
that the group-accent falls almost invariably upon the tonic
syllable of the last word in the speech-group is largely
responsible for the comparative stability of tonic vowels. The
tendency to stress the initial syllable (particularly the initial
syllable of a group; cf. § 147) produces still further fluctuation
in the articulation of countertonic vowels. Consequently the
quality and quantity of the vowels of a particular word may
vary according to the place which the word occupies in the
speech-group. It is therefore inexact to attach to a particular
symbol (*a*, *e*, etc.) in a given word one definite quality, and
more correct to describe it as denoting a zone within which
the quality of the vowel gravitates according to its place in
connected speech. But various factors have combined to

[1] For this section we have utilized extensively the works of Rosset and
Herzog. Cf. also the many interesting observations in Dauzat, *Histoire*,
pp. 126–51.

restrict these fluctuations. The consciousness of the word as a unit, which obviously grows stronger with the increasing influence of the written language in modern times, is the most important of these and fosters the generalization of *one* pronunciation for each word. For words which constantly recur in the same position or which uniformly bear a sense-accent (e.g. numerals) the selection is made naturally. For other words orthography, the intervention of grammarians, fashion, and various analogical influences narrow the zone of variation. But in spite of levelling influences the number of words presenting such slight fluctuations is very large. Certain vowels (*a* and *e*) are more affected than others. It is mainly to the variation in stress and, to a lesser degree, in syllabification that such fluctuations as Modern French presents must be attributed. It is no contradiction of this to say, for example, that certain groups or individuals favour one particular variety of *a* (§ 55); what is implied is that in their speech the fluctuations are regularly confined within the narrower limits of palatal or velar *a*. We may say that in the articulation of vowels Modern French presents us with varieties of speech which develop within a zone so small that they are covered by a common orthographic symbol and do not constitute a striking departure from standard usage.

The weakening of the tonic stress renders the vowel less subject to the modifying influence of neighbouring consonants, and Modern French offers in this respect a striking contrast with Old French.

53. The new law of position which begins to operate as early as the twelfth century (§ 49) results in a new differentiation of quality which cuts across etymological distinctions. The tendency is to pronounce with a close quality vowels in an open syllable, and with an open quality vowels in a closed syllable (i.e. followed by a consonant belonging to the same syllable). The first vowel to be affected was *e* (twelfth century), followed by *o* (thirteenth century), and somewhat later by *ö*. The tendency reaches its climax in the sixteenth century. The position of the vowel may change in the course

of time through the elimination of a consonant (e.g. *s* before consonant) or the reduction of hiatus (*e-age* > *âge*) accompanied by lengthening of the vowel, or through the creation of a new group of consonants by the loss of a vowel (§§ 60–1). The loss of final *ə* (§ 62) has caused the preceding vowel to become blocked (*père* now pronounced *pɛ:r*, but as late as the seventeenth century *pɛ-rə*). The resulting conflict between the old and the new is reflected in a hesitation between the open and close qualities, which often extends over prolonged periods. A further cause of hesitation is the tendency to carry the final consonant over into the next syllable whenever a word beginning with a vowel follows (§ 137).

54. The natural evolution of the French language is therefore a continuous process, the same in kind from beginning to end, and showing at most a change of direction, which was initiated towards the end of the thirteenth century. As in the Old French period, the mechanical (phonetic) evolution is constantly interrupted by various analogical changes. These are particularly common in the Middle French period and are to be observed above all in the conjugation of the verb. But what distinguishes the later development of the language is the intervention of various external factors which arrest, reverse, retard or modify the natural evolution. They represent the application of the selective procedure which is implied in the formation and conscious elaboration of a standard spoken language. The conception of a standard spoken language is an ideal which appears to have been but dimly envisaged before the sixteenth century, imperfectly conceived by the grammarians of that age, defined and in a large measure realized in the seventeenth century. Its neutral position between the learned and popular tendencies exposed it to influences from both directions. Of the two the learned influence is the more clearly discernible; it dates from the introduction of numerous Learned words in the later Middle French period. Such words are pronounced in the first place as written, and give the initial impetus to the tendency to model pronunciation upon spelling. With the

great increase in the numbers of those who read, this tendency is strengthened and extended. The habit of investing Popular words with a written form approximating as nearly as possible to Latin (§ 163) invited further deviations from traditional pronunciation on the part of those who made any pretension to learning and culture. There thus developed two pronunciations, a learned and a popular. The segmentation of the latter, with the resulting opposition between a standard usage and popular usage in the narrow sense (the usage of the 'petit peuple'), takes place somewhat later, and there is no direct evidence of it until the sixteenth century. From that time onwards the history of French pronunciation is the story of the gradual extension of the standard usage to an ever-widening circle, of the efforts to regularize and codify it, of the give-and-take which characterizes its relation to the learned pronunciation on the one hand and the popular on the other. In tracing the evolution of modern standard usage we have therefore to consider the influence of orthography and of Latin, the intervention of the schoolmaster, the dictates of fashion, the adoption or rejection of popular tendencies. We may distinguish three stages in this evolution: a period of hesitation and uncertainty which extends from the fourteenth to the sixteenth century, a period of sifting, stabilizing and codifying which embraces the greater part of the sixteenth and the whole of the seventeenth century, and a period of liquidation, in which the bulk of the decisions taken in the seventeenth century are ratified and accepted by all, if and when they speak 'correct' French. The consolidation of the work accomplished in the seventeenth century has been rendered easier by the many factors which make for standardization, such as the spread of education, the development of the press, military service, administrative centralization. The attempt of the many to conform to 'correct' usage is accompanied by the adoption of certain popular features (*oi* = wa, *ill* = j) and a growing tendency to model pronunciation upon the written word. Apart from such phenomena the sounds of the language have remained stable since the seventeenth century. At most they have developed slight differentiations of quality in the already existing range of vowels.

A

55. There is no evidence to indicate that the modern distinction between the front or palatal a and the back or velar ɑ obtained in Old French. The tendency to confuse e and a which is noticeable in Old French (cf. § 56) supports the view that O.F. a was normally a front vowel, its point of articulation approaching that of ẹ.[1] The velar pronunciation (ɑ) seems to have developed gradually in the Middle French period and is connected with the lengthening of a which resulted from the absorption of a hiatus vowel (e-age > âge) or the loss of a consonant (haste > hâte). In such cases a has generally been supplied with a circumflex accent. The modern tendency to favour the palatal pronunciation when the letter a has no such accent may be taken to mark the persistence of an old habit. Velar ɑ is found in the sixteenth century before pre-consonantal or final s (paste, bas) which had become mute (§§ 123, 125) and before intervocal s or z (fasse, base). Modern French maintains velar ɑ in such cases but presents many exceptions (cf. Nyrop, Manuel, §§ 104 and 173). In the seventeenth century long a is always velar, but owing to changes in syllabification and to the influence of neighbouring consonants, both palatal a and velar ɑ can now be either long or short (patte = pat, part = paːr; froid = frwɑ, pâte = pɑːt), though generally tonic ɑ is long. The palatal and velar qualities are clearly recognizable, but the distribution of the two sounds varies very greatly, some Parisians preferring ɑ and some Frenchmen from the provinces a. As a general rule a is favoured whenever the vowel bears no circumflex accent or is unstressed, and it predominates in rapid speech. After a labial, velar ɑ is usual and one would accordingly expect wɑ (orth. oi), but wa is preferred (§ 73). Before n', a has sometimes become e under

[1] Cf. M. K. Pope, a, ã, ɑ, ãn, in French and Anglo-Norman (in Kastner Miscellany, 1932, pp. 396–402).

the influence of spelling, *aign* being interpreted as *ai* (= *e*) + *gn* (= *n'*), *araignée*, *saigner*, etc.

ER : AR

56. If our assumption that O.F. *a* was normally palatal (i.e. front) be correct, any factor which tended to make *ẹ* still more open would lead to a hesitation between *ẹ* and *a*. Such an influence was exerted by a following *r* (cf. English *clerk*, *Derby*, etc.), particularly in an initial syllable.[1] While there is ample evidence of the resulting confusion between *er* and *ar* in Old French and Middle French, it is not until the sixteenth century that it becomes general. It appears to have been common in the dialects of the Centre and particularly in popular Parisian speech. With the gradual development of a refined usage and the growing influence of grammarians, the distinction between a popular or dialectal pronunciation (*ar*) and a cultured pronunciation (*er*) hardened, the claims of the latter being strengthened by orthography, which generally preserved etymological *er*. It soon became an affectation to pronounce *er* for *ar* in words where the latter was etymological. To some extent the fluctuation between *er* and *ar* was eliminated in the sixteenth century, but in the majority of cases the modern pronunciation was definitely established in the seventeenth. In most words the traditional form triumphed (*charrette*, *chariot*, *charme*, *carquois*, *jargon*, *sarment*; *apercevoir*, *herse*, *serge*, *tertre*, etc.). In some *er* triumphed over etymological *ar* (*asperge*, *cercueil*, *guérir*, *serpe*), in others *ar* replaced etymological *er* (*dartre*, *harceler*, *marquer*). In a few words the hesitation persisted down to the eighteenth century (*catarrhe*, *épervier*); *cercelle* was still in use beside *sarcelle* in the nineteenth century. The triumph of *er* or *ar* respectively depended upon a variety of factors, the authority of grammarians, changing fashion, orthography, and frequency of use. Thus the aping of the cultivated pronunciation (*er*) by the lower classes led to a reaction in favour of *ar*, and this may

---

[1] Cf. also the passage from *e* to *a* when nasalized (§ 39) and the development of a glide *a* between *ẹ* and *u* (< *l*; §§ 45 *e*, 71).

account for the triumph of *ar* in *boulevard*.[1] Words of a
technical or popular character, being spurned by the polite
society of the seventeenth century, naturally preserve the
popular pronunciation (*dartre, hargneux, parpaing*). The popular
tendency to open *e* to *a* is also found in other positions, but
orthography proved a sufficient deterrent except in the case
of *wẹ* (< *oi*); cf. § 73.

E

57. We have seen that the Old French distinction between
ẹ, *ę* and *e* (< A) had been obliterated and that from the
thirteenth century *e*, whatever its provenance, tended to be
pronounced *ę* before a consonant, and *ẹ* when final. The
tendency of *e* to become *ę* was more marked before some
consonants than before others, with the result that in many
cases there was hesitation. The varying dates at which final
consonants became mute and their partial restoration (§§ 125–
30), the lengthening of vowels consequent upon the loss of
a consonant (§ 53), and the conflict of dialectal pronunciations contributed to the uncertainty. The result was that
while in the majority of cases *e* became definitely either *ẹ* or
ę, in many words usage fluctuated and gravitated round a
point midway between *ẹ* and *ę*. We have thus a threefold
distinction: close *ẹ*, open *ę*, intermediate *e*. The latter is a
very unstable type and is first recognized as a separate variety
in the seventeenth century. Its instability is increased by the
fact that no diacritic sign is available to distinguish it from *ẹ*
and *ę*, which in principle are denoted by *é* and *è* respectively.
Intermediate *e* may therefore appear in writing as *é* or *è* or *e*
according to the shade of quality it assumes. But it should be
noted that the use of accents is often determined by the habits
and predilections of printers rather than by pronunciation
(cf. Extr. XVII and notes). The modern distribution of these
three *e* sounds dates in the main from the latter part of the
seventeenth century, when pronunciation was fixed in doubtful cases and certain arbitrary distinctions were made. Under

[1] But possibly a mere substitution of suffix (cf. §§ 520, 523).

the group-accent the quality is more clearly defined, ǫ alone
being found in a closed syllable and ẹ predominating in an
open syllable. But the tendency to confuse intermediate *e* and
open ǫ persists to the present day. The following cases call
for special comment.

58. The normal development whereby final *e* becomes
close was interfered with by seventeenth-century grammarians who, basing themselves upon orthography, interpreted *ai* as ǫ in certain cases (*balai, paix, souhait*, etc.). While
ẹ was accepted for *j'ai, je sais*, the 1st pers. fut. -*ai*, the 1st
pers. past definite -*ai*, open ǫ was imposed in the imperfect
indic. -*ais*, etc. and the conditional -*ais*, etc. The distinction
thus set up between *chantai, chanterai* and *chantais, chanterais*
is gradually breaking down as the result, on the one hand,
of the inherited tendency to close final vowels, on the other,
of the tendency to pronounce *ai* as ǫ and the popular exaggeration of the distinctive pronunciation ǫ. Normally in
present-day French, final *e* is close in *chantai, chanterai* and
intermediate in *chantais, chanterais*, but often in popular speech
the former is open and the latter close. Similarly -*êt*, -*et* in
words like *forêt, sujet*, which were pronounced ǫ at the end
of the seventeenth century, are now normally intermediate,
in popular speech often ǫ. The same remark applies to *accès,
après, procès, succès*.

59. Countertonic *e*, when it did not become ə (§§ 44 *c*,
60), was always less clearly articulated than tonic *e*. It was
probably intermediate *e* with a tendency to become close
when free, and open when blocked. The close quality is
clearly defined whenever the syllable bears a sense-stress.
Various disturbing factors must be reckoned with, such as
the influence of orthography and analogy (*cesser, bêtise* show
ǫ by analogy with *cesse, bête*), uncertainty in syllabification,
and above all the influence of Learned words which, as the
result of the Erasmian reforms, propagated the pronunciation ẹ in the initial syllable (*périr*, etc.). Here too the spelling
ai helps to maintain ǫ (*aigu, prairie*). In hiatus, *e* is close
(*géographie*)

ə

60. Countertonic *ə*, which had resulted from free *e* and to some extent from other vowels (§§ 34, 44 *c*), began to disappear in the fourteenth century if it had in the meantime been brought into contact with the following vowel (SECŪRUM > *se-ur* > *sûr*, VIDĒRE > *ve-oir* > *voir*, ROTUNDA > *re-onde* > *ronde*). Between consonants countertonic *ə* remained (*chemin*) but tended to become mute in the sixteenth century, in the first instance between labial and *l* (*p'lotte, b'listre*). Here again the grammarians, supported by orthography, intervened to rescue the threatened syllable. Their task was made easier by the substitution of *ę* for *ə* in many words. This substitution resulted from a variety of causes. The most potent was perhaps the new pronunciation of Latin, which generalized the pronunciation of countertonic *e* as *ę* in Learned words. These in their turn influenced Popular words (*séjour*), particularly if the latter were readily associated with their Latin prototypes (*trésor*). A similar influence is exerted by foreign words (*régate, ténor, bédouin, revolver*). Confusion of prefix accounts for the substitution of *dé-, ré-, tré-* for *de-, re-, tre-* (*défendre, réduire, trépied*). The analogical influence of stem-accented forms accounts for *chérir, lévrier, péter,* and the like. Other cases may be attributed to the hesitation resulting from a conflict of dialectal pronunciations, *ę* for countertonic *ə* being a well-known dialectal trait in the seventeenth century.

61. Counterfinal *ə* in hiatus with the tonic vowel disappeared sporadically in the thirteenth century, more frequently in the fourteenth and fifteenth. In the sixteenth century it survives only in spelling (cf. § 68). In hiatus with the preceding countertonic vowel it was more tenacious (*prierai*), but did not persist in the sixteenth century although still sometimes counted as a syllable in poetry (*vraiement*). Between consonants counterfinal *ə* had begun to disappear in Old French, particularly before or after *r*. The efforts of grammarians and purists to preserve the syllable were unsuccessful. From the seventeenth century, *e* in this position has

a purely graphic value, except in the following cases:
(a) When a supporting vowel is required to avoid a group of
three consonants (*âprement, tremblement*; cf. § 142). If two *ə*'s
are separated by a consonant, one is kept (generally the first)
in order to avoid such a group (*échevelé*=ešəvlẹ). (b) When
it separates two identical consonants (*honnêteté*). Analogy has
sometimes been responsible for the substitution of *ẹ* or *ę* for *ə*
(*achèvement* ≠ *achève, caresser* ≠ *caresse*, etc.).

62. Final *ə*, when it followed immediately upon the tonic
vowel, had begun to become mute in the fourteenth century,
and in the fifteenth century it gradually disappeared, the
preceding vowel being lengthened. After consonants, final *ə*
continued to be sounded in Middle French[1] but disappeared
in popular speech in the sixteenth century, often carrying
with it the last consonant of a difficult group (*notre, autre*,
pronounced *not', ot'*). But its preservation in the written
language and the fact that it served as the sign of the feminine
caused the grammarians of the sixteenth and seventeenth
centuries to stand out for its retention. For a time their
efforts were partly successful, *ə* persisting well into the seventeenth century after *j* (*paie*=pẹjə), before a pause, and
generally in sustained discourse. An important consequence
was the preservation of final voiced consonants (*vide, raide*,
etc.) and their persistence even after the elimination of *ə*.
From about 1660, *ə* ceased to have syllabic value except after
a group consisting of consonant + *l* or *r*, where it continues
to be sounded (but cf. popular *fenet', vot', not'*, etc.).

63. The *ə* of those monosyllabic words which by reason
of their syntactic function receive no stress, shows considerable hesitation. In the seventeenth century *les, ces, des,
mes, tes, ses* were normally pronounced *lẹ*,... before a consonant, *ləz*,... before a vowel, and this continued to be the
rule in ordinary conversation as late as the end of the
eighteenth century. At that time *lẹ, lẹz*, which had hitherto
been confined to sustained discourse, became general. The

[1] In Anglo-Norman it began to disappear from about the middle
of the twelfth century.

alternative pronunciation *lę, lęz* dates from the eighteenth century. Of the three pronunciations which *cet* (*cette*) had in the sixteenth century, *sət* has survived in popular speech, *sęt* (supported by orthography) has been adopted in 'correct' speech, and *sẹt* has been abandoned.

Another instance of the substitution of *ę* for *ə* is furnished by the interrogative form of the 1st sing. pres. indic. of verbs in -*er* (*chanté-je*, etc.), where *ə* having become tonic was at the same time brought under the influence of the following *j*. Normally *ə* remains intact when it receives the group-stress (*faites-le, rendez-le*, etc.).

64. The quality of *ə* was in Old French that of a weakened *e*. Wherever it continues to be sounded, *ə* tends from the seventeenth century onwards to be pronounced with slight lip-rounding, and when accented (*faites-le, premier*) approximates to *ö*. Its instability is reflected not only in the tendency to disappear, which we have noted, but also in the great variations it presents according to position, stress, and the nature of neighbouring sounds. Thus, after labial consonants it tends to become *ö* or *ü* (*breuvage* for earlier *beuvrage, buvons*). Loss or weakening of *ə* is characteristic of rapid speech; retention and strengthening (tendency towards *ö*) are common in sustained discourse and when a special effort is made to speak distinctly. Cf. §§ 134, 142–3.

ọ ǫ u

65. One of the most striking features of sixteenth-century pronunciation is the hesitation between *o* and *u* in a large number of words. The battle between those who favoured *u* (ouïstes) and those who favoured *o* (non-ouïstes) went on throughout the century, and it was not until the early part of the seventeenth century that the pronunciation of all but a few words was settled. This hesitation seems to have existed to some extent from the beginning (cf. § 34), and it makes the history of *o* one of the most difficult and involved problems in the history of the French language. In many cases usage evidently fluctuated for long periods between a very close *o*

and a very open *u*. This uncertainty is reflected in orthography
(§ 155). As a general rule we find persisting in Modern
French the *u* which resulted from *o* in the cases specified in
§§ 45 (*a*), 47 (*a*), from *ou* (< *o* + *l*; § 50), and somewhat later
from *o* (< *au*) when final or followed by a vowel (CAULEM
> *chou*, LAUDARE > *loer* > *louer*). But in other positions the
tendency to close *o* to *u*, which continued throughout Middle
French, encountered the resistance of those whose pronunciation was consciously or unconsciously modelled upon the
written language, for the latter generally preserved or re-
introduced *o*, whether from mere conservatism or under the
influence of Latin. Thus it came about that tonic and countertonic *o* (< blocked *ǫ*) remained *o* (PǑRTA > *porte*, DǑRMIRE
> *dormir*), as did also tonic *o* (< *au*) when not final or followed
by a vowel (CAUSA > *chose*, AURUM > *or*).

66. But exceptions to these general rules are numerous
and reflect the uncertainty which prevailed throughout the
sixteenth century. The intervention of grammarians (who are
generally to be found upon the side of the written language
and who base many of their decisions upon orthography) and
the prejudice of polite society at the beginning of the seventeenth century against *u* as a popular and dialectal feature,
account for the triumph of *o* in many cases, but the reasons
which prompted a decision often remain obscure. In
literary and technical words *o* was generally favoured. For
the details of this involved question and the debates which
raged over individual words or series of words the reader
may be referred to Brunot, II, pp. 251–4, IV, pp. 177–8;
Rosset, pp. 67–83; Herzog, pp. 156–89. The following list
aims at being merely illustrative. *o* appears for countertonic
u (< blocked *ǫ*) in *ortie*, *formage* later *fromage*; for countertonic
u (< free *ǫ* and free *ę*) in Learned words (*moment*; *opinion*,
volume) and in Popular words which have been remodelled
under the influence of Latin (*soleil*, *oraison*; *colombe*, *colonne*;
for regular O.F. *souleil*, *ouraison*; *coulombe*, *coulonne*). *o* appears
for tonic *u* (< blocked *ǫ*) in *forme*, *morne*, *orme*, for regular
O.F. *fourme*, etc. *Adore*, *dévot*, *sobre* are Learned. *u* appears

for countertonic *ǫ* (< blocked *ǫ*) in *fourmi, pourceau, tourment*. Hesitation between *o* and *u* persisted through the greater part of the seventeenth century in *arroser, colombe, couleuvre, aujourd'hui, outarde, coussin, fourbu, fourmi* and many other words.

67. In many words, particularly verb forms, *u* appears for etymological *ö* by analogy (*ouvre, prouve, coule ≠ ouvrir, prouver, couler*, etc.; *époux, jaloux ≠ épouser, jalousie*, etc.). As regards the quality of *o* in cases where it survived, the modern distinction between *ǫ* and *ǫ* dates from the Middle French period, when the etymological distinction gave place to the distinction according to position (§ 53), *o* becoming close when free or followed by *z* (*tôt, gros, mot, chose*), and open when blocked or followed by *r* (*forme, ortie, or*). The distinction is clear-cut in the case of tonic *o*, particularly when it comes under the group-stress. Countertonic *o* tends to become open in Modern French (*roseau, potage*), but analogical influences are responsible for many exceptions (*rǫsier* beside *rǫse*) and the presence of a circumflex accent generally induces a close pronunciation (*ôter, clôture, côté, mômerie*, etc., but *o* is open in *hôpital, rôtir; hôtel* = ǫtęl or ǫtęl).

I Ü Ö

68. These vowels persisted unchanged. The hesitation between *ö* and *ü* in certain words, which made possible such rimes as *jeu* (< JŎCUM) : *jeu* (< *JACUTUM), e.g. Villon, *Testament*, l. 1736, in the fifteenth century and gave rise to many debates in the sixteenth, was cleared up in the seventeenth and leaves few traces in Modern French. It was due partly to a conflict of dialectal pronunciations: *ö* did not exist in Picard, where its nearest equivalent was *ü*. This feature together with other Picardisms had invaded Parisian speech. On the other hand the spelling *eu* had throughout the sixteenth century a twofold value. It represented not only *ö*, but also *ü* in words which had originally offered *ə* in hiatus with *ü*, *s(e)ur* (< SECŪRUM), *m(e)ur* (< MATŪRUM). Thus it came about that the grammarians, on the authority of spelling, some-

times condemned etymologically correct *ü* as a vulgar or
dialectal pronunciation; *heur* (*bonheur*, *malheur*) is an interesting
example of such a mistaken decision: the sixteenth- and
seventeenth-century popular pronunciation *ür* represents the
regular development of *e-ür* (< AUGURIUM), but Malherbe,
supported by Ménage and others, declared *ür* provincial and
imposed *ör*; a false association with *heure* (< HORA) facilitated
the triumph of *ö* and is responsible for the unetymological *h*.
Orthography is also responsible for the substitution of *ö*
for *ü* in *gageure*. Apart from such exceptions the traditional
pronunciation was restored in the seventeenth century, but
in *eucharistie*, *eunuque*, *Eugène*, *Europe*, *Eustache*, *ö* did not
triumph definitely until the beginning of the nineteenth
century.

69. The distinction between open and close *ö* is modern
and is determined by position. *ö* is close in an open syllable
or if followed by *ž*, *z*, *t*, *tr* (*peu*, *Maubeuge*, *menteuse*, *meute*,
feutre), and open in a closed syllable (*peur*, *peuple*). When
the vowel is not stressed the distinction is less clear-cut and
ǫ̈ tends to predominate (*feuillage*). In hiatus, *ö* is close
(*bleuâtre*).

AU

70. *au* (< *a* + *l*) seems to have persisted as a diphthong as
late as the sixteenth century, but it had clearly begun to be
reduced to *o*. The testimony of grammarians is conflicting
and probably reflects changing usage; *o* was generalized
before the end of the sixteenth century (*haut*, *animaux*).

EAU

71. According to the testimony of Erasmus and Meigret,
eau was still a triphthong at the beginning of the sixteenth
century, but before the middle of the century it had become
a diphthong *eo*, which was reduced to *o* before 1600 (*beau*,
eau(*e*), *beauté*). In popular Parisian speech *eau* appeared as
iau (> *jo*), which is probably of dialectal origin (but cf.
Dauzat, § 101) and persisted down to the nineteenth century.

WĘ (OI)

72. The Old French diphthong *oi* had by the end of the thirteenth century reached the stage *wę*, and the tendency to eliminate the labial element had already begun to assert itself. The earliest sporadic examples of *ę* for *wę* date from that century. In the fifteenth century *ę* for *wę* was perhaps already a feature of Parisian pronunciation (Brunot, I, 406). It is moreover characteristic of Norman, where it developed directly from older *ei*, and the large number of Normans who migrated to the Capital undoubtedly helped to generalize it. In the sixteenth century it was usual in the Capital and the Court. The grammarians inveighed against this 'careless' pronunciation, which they wrongly attributed to Italian influence and which they sought at the same time to brand as a vulgarism. Their campaign was continued by the grammarians of the seventeenth century, powerfully supported by the bar and the salon. The result was a partial restoration of *wę* in the language of polite society and later of the common people. But for a great part of the seventeenth century there was hesitation, a conflict between *wę*, which was consciously cultivated, and *ę*, which was the final term of a natural evolution. Hence such doublets as *harnais—harnois, raide—roide, raideur—roideur, Français—François*. In the more common words *ę* was too firmly established to be eradicated: *craie* (< CRĒTA), *dais* (< DĬSCUM), *faible* (< FLĒBILEM), *frais* (Germ. frisk), *marais* (Germ. marisk), *monnaie* (< MONĒTA), *paraître, connaître*; particularly in cases where spelling had been brought into line with the pronunciation *ę*: *tonnerre* < O.F. *tonoire* (< TONĬTRUM), *verre* < O.F. *voire* (< VĬTRUM). *Anglais, Français, Écossais, Hollandais* (beside *Danois, Suédois*, etc.) are explained by the fact that they were in frequent use at this time. Similarly *ę* was kept (and approved by Vaugelas) in the endings of the imperfect indicative and the conditional *-ais, -ait*, etc. (cf. § 58).[1] The spelling *oi*, which had been

---

[1] The labial semi-consonant remained intact in *wĕ, wi, wĭ* (*loin, fruit, juin*); cf. § 77.

phonetic in the twelfth century, continued to be used in spite of the suggestion made by Nicolas Berain (1675) to substitute *ai*. This orthography was adopted by Voltaire, but not recognized by the Academy until 1835.

73. By a strange irony the grammarians by their attempts to impose *wę* prepared the way for the triumph of a still more popular feature: *wa* for *wę*. The change *wę* > *wa* is akin to the change *er* > *ar* (§ 56) and is a specifically Parisian feature (cf. *alle* for *elle*, etc.). It became common in popular Parisian speech of the sixteenth century. Noted by Palsgrave (1530), condemned as vulgar by Henri Estienne (1582), Theodore de Bèze (1584) and others, it was eschewed by the polite society of the seventeenth century but adopted by the bourgeoisie towards the end of the century. It continued to gain ground in the eighteenth, and *wę* lost its last stronghold with the fall of the Monarchy and the dispersal of the Court. Wherever it had been restored it became *wa*.

74. We have it on the authority of grammarians (Erasmus, Henri Estienne) that *oi* when final or before a vowel persisted as a diphthong in the sixteenth century. Palsgrave (1530) declares that the *oy* of *roy*, *moy*, *moyen*, etc. had the same value as in English *boye*, *coye*, etc. But before the end of the century final *oi* had become *wę*. Before vowels there was still hesitation in the seventeenth century between *oj*, *węj*, *waj* (a hiatus-*j* having in the meantime developed) (*royal*, *moyen*).

JE JÖ JẼ

75. *je* had a twofold origin. It resulted (*a*) from tonic free *a* preceded by a palatal or palatalized consonant, (*b*) from tonic free *ę*. In the latter case it persisted. In the former it was almost invariably reduced to *e* at a later date. From the fourteenth century onwards, *j* was absorbed by a preceding *š*, *ž*, *n'*, *l'*, although the spelling *ie* persisted down to the sixteenth century. If preceded by other consonants, its reduction is due to analogy, which affected the numerous verbs in -*ier*, bringing them into line with verbs in -*er* (*laissier*, *laissiez*, *laissierent*, *laissié* are replaced by *laisser*, *laissez*, etc.). This

reduction of *je* to *e* becomes general in the fifteenth century and is completed in the sixteenth, but *je* remains intact in the suffix *-ier* (< -ARIUM), and in *pitié, moitié*. After explosive + *l* or *r*, *je* has become *ije* in Modern French (*encrier, tablier*).

The reduction does not affect *jö*, which persists intact (*cieux, curieux*), nor *jẽ* (cf. § 77).

NASAL VOWELS AND DIPHTHONGS

76. The natural tendency of nasal vowels to open (§ 39) gradually brought about a change in quality during the Middle French period and resulted in the changes $\tilde{\imath} > \tilde{e} > \tilde{\varepsilon}$, $\tilde{u} > \tilde{o} > \tilde{\rho}$, $\tilde{e} > \tilde{\varepsilon}$, $\tilde{o} > \tilde{\rho}$, which are practically completed in popular speech before the end of the sixteenth century. But $\tilde{\varepsilon}$, $\tilde{o}$, $\tilde{\rho}$ continued to be used to some extent in the seventeenth century. The tendency to confuse $\tilde{a}$ and $\tilde{o}$, of which there are traces in Old French, becomes more pronounced with the velarization of *a* (§ 55); it is common in popular speech of the sixteenth and seventeenth centuries and persists in certain parts of France to the present day.

77. The O.F. nasal diphthongs *iẽ*, *üĩ* had been reduced to *jẽ*, *wĩ* respectively before the sixteenth century (§ 50). *jẽ* showed a tendency to become *jã*, as rimes of the fifteenth century show (*an : paroissien*, Villon; *mendiants : liens*, G. Alexis). *jã* for *jẽ* was a feature of popular Parisian speech in the sixteenth century, but the grammarians had no difficulty in banning it from polite usage. The popular word *fiente* (*fienter*) represents the sole survival of this feature. In such words as *escient* and *orient*, *jã* is due to the fact that *ie* was originally disyllabic (O.F. *escïent, orïent*). Similarly in Learned words (*patience, science*) *ie* was disyllabic in the sixteenth century and *en* in Learned words was pronounced $\tilde{a}$, whence the modern *pasjã:s, sjã:s*. But Learned words which were in common use (*chrétien, quotidien*, etc.) or which were borrowed after 1600, when the pronunciation of Latin *en* as $\tilde{e}$ had been adopted, show *jẽ*. Another popular tendency of the seventeenth century, the reduction of *jẽ* to $\tilde{e}$, persists in present-day

popular speech (*bẽ* for *bjẽ*, etc.). The development *ẅĩ* > *wẽ* is parallel to *ĩ* > *ẽ* (§ 76).

ẽi and *õi* had been reduced to *ẽ* and *wẽ* respectively before the sixteenth century but persisted sporadically as diphthongs. The attempt of seventeenth-century grammarians to preserve a distinction between *ẽ* (< *ãi* and *ẽi*) and *ẽ* (< *ĩ*) must be regarded as artificial and dictated by the spelling. Similarly *õi*, where it had not already been reduced, gave place to *wẽ* before the end of the sixteenth century.

DENASALIZATION

78. In Old French, vowels were nasalized by a following nasal consonant, whether it was final, was followed by a consonant or was followed by a vowel. In the last case *m* and *n* were often written double after *a*, *o*, *e*, the first *m* or *n* denoting the nasalization of the preceding vowel, the second denoting the consonant which was pronounced (*bonne* = bõnǝ, *femme* = fãmǝ). No orthographical device denoted the nasalization of a vowel before *n'* (*montagne* or *montaigne* = mõtãn'ǝ), unless we interpret the alternative graphy *ngn* as such. Before a following consonant or when final, the nasal consonant was pronounced in Old French and partly assimilated in pronunciation, and sometimes in spelling, to the following consonant, *m* becoming *n* before a dental, *n* becoming *m* before a labial (COMPUTARE > *conter*, INVOLARE > *embler*). But before the end of the Middle French period it had by a process of progressive assimilation been absorbed by the preceding nasal vowel, *m* and *n* being thus reduced to a common and purely orthographic function (*conte*, *comte*, *compte* = kõ:tǝ).

79. The tendency to denasalize nasal vowels and diphthongs before intervocal *m*, *n*, *n'* probably began to manifest itself in the Middle French period, but we have no evidence of its effects before the sixteenth century, when they are apparent in the speech of the Capital. One of the first vowels affected was *ã*, followed quickly by *ẽi* and more slowly by

the rest. While the process was not completed in all cases before the end of the seventeenth century, the preservation of the nasal vowel before intervocal *m*, *n* was regarded as a provincialism from about 1650. Nasalization seems to have persisted rather longer in the case of countertonic vowels. Before a word beginning with a vowel, the final nasal consonant is pronounced (cf. § 135) and the preceding vowel is normally denasalized (*bon ami*), but the nasal quality is sometimes preserved by analogy (*bien aimable*).

80. The denasalized vowels naturally show the changes in quality which nasalization had brought about, but orthography (which had not always kept pace with these), the intervention of grammarians, and analogical influences are responsible for many exceptions.

ã > *a*. As *ã* in many words represents older *ẽ* (§ 39) and as *e* had been retained in spelling (§ 155), there is often discrepancy between spelling and pronunciation in Modern French, *e* being pronounced *a* in such words as *femme*, *rouennais*, *solennel*, and in adverbs in -*emment* (*prudemment*). *ã* continued to be sounded in Learned words to the end of the seventeenth century and even later in adverbs in -*emment*. In *emmancher*, *emmener*, *enamourer*, *enivrer*, *enorgueillir* it has been maintained to the present day under the influence of numerous words beginning with *en* + consonant, where *ã* regularly persisted (*enfermer*). In *ennui* the triumph of *ã* (analogical) over *a* was not secured until the nineteenth century. Under the influence of orthography *e* has displaced regular *a* in *ennemi*, *étrenne*; *e* for *a* is now also common in *solennel*, *indemnité*. Hence such doublets as *panne* (with change of spelling) beside *penne*, both going back to O.F. pãnə (< PENNA). The quality of *a* is velar (=ɑ), except in *femme*, *couenne*, *panne*.

81. *ẽ*. In the case of *ẽ* < *ĩ* (*voisin*, *voisine*) polite usage of the seventeenth century favoured denasalization to *i*. Its triumph over popular *e* is due to the support which it received in the spelling, and perhaps also to the fact that *i* was not so completely nasalized before intervocal *m*, *n*, *n'* as were the more open vowels, and had therefore not merged with *ẽ*.

These considerations do not of course apply to *ẽ* (< *e* before medial *n'*), which regularly became *ę*, whence *enseigne* (ãsęn'), *deigne* with change of spelling *daigne* (dęn'), beside *ligne*, *vigne*.

82. *õ* (orth. *un*) normally gives denasalized *ö* in popular speech of the seventeenth century, but polite usage adopted *ü* for the same reasons as it adopted *i* for *e* (< *ẽ* < *ĩ*) (§ 81), yet *ö* persisted in popular speech as late as the eighteenth century and in certain parts of France to the present day. Adjectives in -*un* and the indefinite article *un* when linked with a following word beginning with a vowel should accordingly have been pronounced *ön* (§§ 79, 135), but *õn* was often restored by analogy, and in popular speech *ün* (under the influence of the feminine). For example, *un autre* is pronounced *önǫ:trᵉ* beside the more generally accepted *õnǫ:trᵉ* and the popular *ünǫ:t(rᵉ)*. In the sixteenth century no distinction was apparently made between *un autre* and *une autre*, both being pronounced *õnotrə*, which partly explains the common confusions of gender in texts of that period (cf. § 194).

83. *õ* > *o*, which alternates with *u* in the seventeenth century (§§ 65–7). Before *n'* also, *õ* was regularly denasalized to *o* (*vergogne*, *cigogne*), but in a number of words *oi* (= wa) has displaced *o*. This is due partly to analogy, partly to a false interpretation of the common spelling *ign* (= n'), *oign* being wrongly read as *oi* + *n'* instead of *o* + *n'*. Thus it came about that *élogner*, *temogner* (the normal development of O.F. *esloignier*, *tesmoignier*) had to contend with *éloigner*, *témoigner*, which found support in *loin*, *témoin*. Ménage's decision in favour of the latter (*Observations*, p. 313) was accepted; *roignon*, which also found favour with him, was not adopted. Other examples are *soigner*, *poignet* (influenced by *soin*, *poing*).

B. *CONSONANTS*

1. VULGAR LATIN DEVELOPMENTS

84. The Classical Latin alphabet possessed the following consonants: B, C, D, F, G, H, I (J), K, L, M, N, P, Q, R, S, T, U (V), X.[1] These symbols do not accurately represent the sounds of the spoken language, still less the consonant system of Vulgar Latin of the Late Empire. The following are the more important V.L. developments; others are for convenience dealt with in connection with O.F. developments.

v (uncial u, cursive *uu*) is the symbol corresponding in Classical times to the semi-consonant *w*. This early became a bilabial fricative (ƀ) which in its turn became, perhaps as early as the fifth century, the labio-dental fricative (*v*) which survives in French. It remained *w* in the groups GU, QU, with a tendency to disappear even in V.L., except before *a* (COCUS for COQUUS). If preceded by a vowel and followed by *u* it disappeared (RIUS for RIUUS). A secondary *w* developed from unaccented *u* in hiatus (VIDUA > VẸDWA, whence *veuve*). The initial *w* of words borrowed from Germanic towards the end of the V.L. period was rendered by *gw* (Germ. warda > *GWARDA, whence O.F. *guarde*).

b between vowels became the bilabial fricative ƀ and its subsequent history is identical with that of ƀ < *w* (DEBERE > *devoir*, FABA > *fève*). If by the loss of a vowel ƀ was subsequently brought into contact with a following consonant, it became *u* (PARABOLA > PARAULA, whence *parole*).

m and *n* when final disappear completely in V.L., except in accented monosyllabic words (REM > *rien*, NON > *non* accented, *ne(n)* unaccented). The antiquity of this change as regards *m* is vouched for by its elision in Latin poetry and is reflected in the forms of early inscriptions.

---

[1] I was the regular symbol for both the vowel (*i*) and the semi-consonant (*j*). Y, Z, CH, PH, RH, TH occur only in Greek loan-words.

n before *s* became mute at an early date and the preceding vowel was lengthened (MENSEM > MĘSE > *mois*, MENSURA > MĘSURA > *mesure*).

r was often assimilated to a following *s* (SURSUM > SUSU > *sus*, DORSUM > DOSSU > *dos*).

h was regularly mute in current speech from the third century onwards, but Learned influence maintained it for a time. The aspirate *h* sound was re-introduced in Germanic loan-words: O.F. *halberc* (Germ. halsberg).

l had in V.L. a velar quality when followed by a consonant (§ 43).

tl, a group which resulted from the loss of an intervening vowel, became *kl* (VĔTULUM > VĘKLU > *vieil*).

Words beginning with *s* + consonant developed a prosthetic *e* (sometimes written I) in V.L. whenever the preceding word ended in a consonant (SPINA > ESPINA > O.F. *espine*, SPATHA > ESPATA > O.F. *espe(d)e*, SCOLA > ISCOLA > O.F. *escole*).

85. C, K, Q are symbols for the hard *k* sound. In V.L. the point of articulation of *k* varied according to the point of articulation of the following vowel. Before front vowels (*e, i*) the tongue was arched towards the middle of the hard palate, giving a medio-palatal explosive, for which we have adopted the symbol k^i. Before *a* the tongue was arched towards the back of the hard palate, giving a post-palatal explosive (k^a). Before back vowels (*o, u*) the tongue was arched towards the velum, giving a velar explosive (k); cf. §§ 93–4.

Similarly Vulgar Latin possessed three *g* sounds: g^i, g^a, *g*. g^i had before the end of the V.L. period become semiconsonantal *j* and therefore coalesced with *j* (= C.L. J) and *j* which resulted from unaccented *i* or *e* in hiatus (§ 25 *b*), from the reduction of *gj* and *dj* (§§ 93–4), and from Greek ζ (*jaloux* derived from ZELUS, Gr. ζῆλος).

2. THE OLD FRENCH CONSONANT SYSTEM

86. The development of Vulgar Latin consonants in French is conditioned by the place which they occupy in the word, by the nature of the preceding or following consonant, and to a lesser degree by the nature of the preceding or following vowel (LEVARE > *lever*, but PAVONEM > *paon*; PAGANUM > *paiien*, but RUGA > *rue*). The readiness with which they are assimilated to a following consonant and various other phenomena suggest that V.L. consonants were articulated with the crescendo effect which still characterizes French as opposed to English vowels and consonants. That is to say, the articulation of the consonant begins weak and reaches its maximum energy or tension near the end. For this reason assimilation is nearly always regressive; the articulation of the first consonant of a group has not reached its maximum before the articulation of the second begins. The former tends therefore to be pronounced weakly and at the same time to shift its point of articulation towards that of the latter, often to the point of disappearing. The same crescendo trend is responsible for the development of so-called glide-consonants (§ 100).

87. Assimilation of a different kind affects a single consonant between vowels. Here the consonant, caught between two sonorous elements, becomes voiced if it was originally voiceless, the vibration of the vocal cords being allowed to continue instead of being momentarily interrupted. At the same time the consonant tends to be articulated more laxly, the tongue tending to remain in the free position which it must assume for the articulation of the preceding and following vowels (VITA > *vida* > *viḍe* > *vie*).

88. Assimilation may also take the form of palatalization: under the influence of a neighbouring palatal sound the normal articulation of a consonant is modified by arching the tongue forward and upward in the direction of the hard palate (e.g. *n'* in Modern French). In principle all non-palatal consonants are susceptible to this influence and in

Vulgar Latin appear to have been so palatalized, but some of them preserve no trace of palatalization in Old French.

89. *l'*, *n'*, which result from palatal + *l*, *n*, or from *l*, *n* + *j*, developed in Gallo-Roman (FILJA > *fil'a* > *fille*, and similarly VIG(I)LAT > *veille*, INSIGNAT > *enseigne*, VINEA > *vigne*, VERE-CUNDIA > VER(E)GONJA > *vergogne*). But upon being brought into contact with a following consonant, *l'* had become *ł* before the O.F. period and therefore gave regularly *u*, the palatal element disappearing without trace, except that a following *s* was changed to *ts* (orth. *z*): TRIPALIUM > *traval'* (orth. *travail*), but *TRIPALIOS > *traval's* > *travałts* > *travauts* (orth. *travauz*, *travaux*). *n'* was also depalatalized when brought into contact with a following consonant, the palatal element persisting in the form of *i* (which combined with the preceding vowel) and a following *s* becoming *ts* (orth. *z*). In the twelfth century final *n'* was similarly depalatalized (PUGNUM > *poing*, PUGNOS > *poinz*). At the end of the twelfth century we therefore find *n'* persisting if it remained inter-vocal, *l'* persisting if it remained intervocal or final. For the subsequent history of these consonants cf. §§ 113, 129.

90. In some cases depalatalization had supervened before the O.F. period (even when the consonant remained inter-vocal) and the palatal element appears in the form of *i*, which combines with the preceding vowel: *rj* > *r'* > *ir*, *sj* > *s'* > *iz* (*is* when final) (PARIA > *paire*, MANSIONEM > *maison*, *PERTUSIUM > *pertuis*).

91. In the groups *bj*, *mj*, *pj*, *vj*, the semi-consonant was articulated with the following syllable and therefore shows the same development as initial *j* (> *dž*); the consonant closes the preceding syllable, is not palatalized, but is sub-sequently assimilated to *dž* (< *j*): *RABJA (C.L. RABIEM) > *ra(b)džə* (O.F. *rage*), LEVJARJU (*LEVIARIUM) > *le(v)džier* (*legier*), SIMJU (SIMIUM) > *sindžə* (*singe*), *REPROPJARE > *re-pro(p)tšier* (*reprochier*). The same syllabification appears sporadically with other consonants: LIN-JU (LINEUM) > *linge*, LAN-JU (LANEUM) > *lange*, ESTRAN-JU (EXTRANEUM) > *estrange*. Similarly *rg^i* > *r-j* > *rdž* (ARGENTUM > *argent*).

92. The palatal sound may persist while at the same time palatalizing the neighbouring consonant. Thus *k*, *g* before a consonant (except *l*, *n*, § 89) became the spirant χ (= Germ. *ch* in *dicht*) which palatalized the following consonant and later combined with the preceding vowel as *i*; the consonant was subsequently depalatalized, the palatal element combining in the form of *i* with a following *e* (< tonic free A) : FACTA > *faχt'a* > *faite*, *FRĬG(I)DUM > *freit*, LAXAT > *laisse*, NĬGRUM > *neir*, LAXARE > *laissier*.

93. Lastly, palatalization may cause at the same time a shifting of the point of articulation and the disengaging of the palatal element in the form of a sibilant (*s*, *š*, *ž*) :[1] *tj* > *t'* > *t's'* (*CAPTIARE > *chacier* with assimilation of *p*); *kⁱ* and *kj* > *k'* > *t'* > *t's'* (CENTUM > *cent*, *ARCIONEM > *arçon*); *kᵃ* > *k'* > *t'* > *t'š'* (CARUM > *chier*); *gᵃ* > *g'* > *d'* > *d'ž'* (GAUDIA > *joie*); initial *j* > *dj* > *d'* > *d'ž'* (JAM > *ja*, GENTEM > *gent*, DIURNUM > *journ*). When intervocal, *t's'* (< *tj* or *kⁱ*) > *d'z'* > *idz* > *iz* (VICINUM > *veisin*, RATIONEM > *raison*); in combination with a preceding *s* it gives *is* (ANGUSTIA > *angoisse*, CRESCENTEM > *creissant*) as does also *t's'* (< *kj*) (*PISCIONEM > *peisson*).

The palatalization of *kⁱ* caused the point of articulation to shift forward until it reached that of *t'*, whose subsequent development it shares. This fusion explains orthographical hesitations of the type AMICITIAM—AMICICIAM, INITIUM—INICIUM which are so frequent in Late Latin documents.

94. The palatalization of *kᵃ* and *gᵃ*, which is characteristic of certain Langue d'oïl dialects, including Central French, as opposed to other Northern dialects (Norman and Picard), to Provençal and the remaining Romance languages, took place about 800 and suggests that by that date *a* had passed from the velar (Latin) to the palatal or forward position (cf. § 55). As the point of articulation of *a* is not so far forward as that of *e* and *i*, the palatalization of *kᵃ* and *gᵃ* was less pronounced

---

[1] The resulting groups *t's'*, *t'š'*, *d'ž'* probably preserved their palatal quality throughout the O.F. period, but in the following pages we shall for convenience note them *ts*, *tš*, *dž* respectively; for their later reduction to *s*, *š*, *ž*, respectively, see § 108*a*.

than that of k^i, whence the difference in the development of t' ($<k^i$) and t' ($<k^a$), the latter being parallel to that of d' ($<g^a$). Intervocal k^a and g^a are not affected by this later palatalization, as k^a had in the meantime become g^a and with original g^a had become a spirant; cf. § 102, col. (b).

The development of the dental element before j is to be explained as a strengthening of the articulation of the initial consonant.

95. Assimilation of a consonant to a following vowel (apart from the palatalizing influence of e, i, a, and the voicing of intervocal consonants) is rare and presupposes a close affinity between vowel and consonant. Thus intervocal b ($<$ v, b) is absorbed by a following rounded vowel (§ 84). Cf. also the later absorption of a nasal consonant by a preceding nasal vowel (§ 78).

For the vocalization of l, see § 43.

96. The chief consonantal changes down to the end of the twelfth century are classified in the tables on pages 76–83, according to the position they occupy within the word: initial, medial, and final; singly or in groups of two or more.

The position of consonants is often altered by the loss of neighbouring vowels or consonants. Thus s of MENSEM is the last of a group in C.L., but intervocal in V.L. MẸSE, and final in French *meis*, *mois*; the g of FRIGIDUM ceased to be intervocal and became the first of the group gd through the loss of unaccented i. Groups which existed as such in Latin are called primary, those which developed in Gallo-Roman or French are called secondary. An apostrophe (indicating the loss of a vowel or consonant) is employed to distinguish the latter. In the case of a secondary group, account must be taken of the changes which a consonant may have undergone before being brought into contact with another. Thus the t of *SUBITANUM had become d before i disappeared, whence SOB'DANU ($>$*soudain*); whereas in DEBITA $>$ DEB'TA $>$ *dette*, t was brought into contact with b before it could become d. We have thus evidence for establishing the relative chronology of the two phenomena, loss of unaccented vowels and voicing of intervocal consonants, but it is evidence which must be carefully sifted. Thus in the change AMATIS > *amez*, *i* did not drop out before *t* became *d*, as might appear at first sight; if it had, *á* would not have developed as a free vowel. Here the secondary group *d's* developed first and then became *ts* by assimilation of the voiced *d* to voiceless *s*. Occasionally two developments are preserved, e.g. O.F. *coute* < COB'TU < CUBITUM, beside *coude* < COB'DU < CUBITUM. Similar chronological considerations apply in the case of final consonants (§ 101).

97. Initial consonants (§ 102, col. *a*), whether single or followed by another consonant, generally remain unchanged, except V.L. k^i, k^a, g^a, *j*. This also applies to the initial consonant of a syllable if the preceding syllable ends in a consonant (§ 102, col. *g*), except that *sk* became by metathesis *ks*, whence *is* (NASCO > *nais*, CRESCO > *creis*). For the group cons. +*j*, cf. §§ 88–94 and § 102, col. (*f*). The prosthetic *e* which had developed in V.L. before initial *s* + cons., whenever the preceding word ended in a consonant (§ 84), had become permanently attached to such a group before the twelfth century; note that in the *Eulalia* (II, 22) we still find *une spede* (O.F. *une espee*, Mod.F. *une épée*).

98. Less resistance is offered by consonants in other positions. Intervocal consonants tend to weaken and disappear (§ 87). Single consonants between vowel and *r* develop as though intervocal (§ 102, col. *b*).

99. The first consonant of a group (§ 102, cols. *c*, *d*, *f*) tends to be assimilated partially or completely (§§ 88, 90–2), but *r*, *f* persist unchanged, as do *b* before *l*, and *t* before *s*. For the development of *m*, *n* before consonant, cf. § 78. Primary *ns*, *rs*, *ds* had been reduced in V.L. to *s* (§ 84), which therefore becomes voiced. Double consonants became single in O.F., with the exception of double *r*, which persisted as such if it remained intervocal (TERRA > *terre*, but FERRUM > *fer*, CURRIT > *court*).

100. Groups of three consonants (§ 102, col. *e*) are reduced, generally by the elimination of the middle consonant,

except in the combinations consonant + labial or dental + *l* or *r*, consonant + dental + *s*, and *ng'l*, *nk'l*, *nk'r*, *rk'l* (UNGŬLA > *ongle*, AVUNCŬLUM > *oncle*, ANCŎRA > *ancre*, CIRCŬLUM > *cercle*). The resulting group of two consonants may be further reduced by assimilation of the first element, but in certain cases the elimination of the middle consonant results in the formation of a glide-consonant. The latter develops before the first consonant has been brought into such close contact with the last consonant as to be assimilated. The loss of the middle consonant causes the first to be correspondingly lengthened, and the characteristic rising tension (cf. § 88) is therefore exaggerated to the point of producing an explosive. This so-called glide develops simultaneously with the disappearance of the middle consonant and shows the influence of the latter in that it is voiced or voiceless according as the latter was voiced or voiceless: PULV(E)REM > POL'RE > *poldre*, similarly *FULGEREM > *foldre*, VINCERE > *veintre*, PLANGERE > *plaindre*, INVOLARE > *embler*, CARCEREM > *chartre*, SURGERE > *sourdre*, MARMOR > *marbre*, NASCERE > *naistre*.

A glide develops in the same way in the secondary groups *m'r*, *m'l*, *n'r*, *l'r*, *z'r*, *s'r*, which result from the loss of a vowel: CAMERA > *chambre*, *TREMULARE > *trembler*, TENERUM > *tendre*, MOLERE > *moldre*, CONSUERE > COSERE > *cousdre*, *ESSERE > *estre*.

101. Final consonants develop differently according as they are unsupported (preceded by a vowel) or supported (preceded by a consonant). A distinction must also be drawn between consonants which were final in Latin (primary) and those which by the loss of final vowels became so at a later stage (Romance or secondary).

Supported final consonants (§ 102, col. *i*) remain, secondary voiced finals becoming unvoiced (TARDUM > *tart*, LONGUM > *lonc*). The supporting consonant may disappear, but the final consonant persists in O.F. (VALET > *valt* > *vaut*).

Unsupported final consonants (§ 102, col. *h*) show considerable fluctuations. Before a pause they tend to weaken and disappear: *ḍ* (< intervocal *d*) > *ṭ*, which disappears in the eleventh century. But various influences have counteracted this tendency. For example, *s* fulfilled a morphological function (cf. § 182) and this fact undoubtedly prolonged its existence. The same remark applies to *t* in verb endings (CANTAT > *chantet* > *chante*̣*t*). The striking contrast which French presents with other Romance languages (including Provençal) in maintaining final consonants may be partly due to the very important rôle of the schoolmaster in Northern Gaul. If the consonant persists, it is in its unvoiced form (NOVEM > *neuf*). Within a speech-group (i.e. if the word is closely associated with a following word) the normal development of the final consonant would be that of an intervocal consonant if the following word begins with a vowel, that of the first consonant of a group if the following word begins with a consonant (cf. Mod.F. *neuf heures*, *neuf kilos*, but *il y en a neuf*). But against this has to be set the consciousness of the word as a separate entity. This recognition of the word as a unit was not equally potent at all periods of the language but appears to have been particularly strong in the O.F. period. There is therefore from the beginning a tendency to generalize the unvoiced final (*vif*, *mois*). The resulting conflict accounts for the many anomalies in the treatment of final consonants, not only in Old French, but in Modern French, where the powerful influence of the written language favours the preservation of the word as a separate phonetic entity (cf. §§ 125–31).

[For § 102, see pp. 76–83.]

103. *w*, which had resulted from an unaccented *u* in hiatus with a following vowel, had early disappeared when preceded by two consonants and in the group *kw* before *u* (§ 84). Elsewhere it had persisted and its development in Old French may be summarized as follows:

Initial *gw* (< Germanic *w*) and *kw*, whether initial of the word or of the syllable, were reduced during the O.F. period to *g* and *k* respectively, although spelling may remain unchanged: Germ. warda > *guarde* > *garde*, Germ. werra > *guerre*; QUARE > *car*, QUINDECIM > *quinze*; LINGUA > *langue*.

	(a)	(b)	(c)	(d)	(e)
	Initial	Medial			
		Between vowels or vowel and *r*	Before *l*	Before other consonants	Middle of group[1]
p	p	> b > ḅ > v	b	(−)	(−) But cons. p + l, r remains
	PONTEM > *pont* PROBARE > *prouver*	CREPARE > *crever* CAPRA > *chievre*	DUPLUM > *double*	RUPTA > *route*	COMP(U)TARE > *conter* RUMP(E)RE > *rompre*
b	b	> ḅ > v (−) before o, u	b	(−)	(−) But cons. + b + l, r remains
	BONUM > *bon* BREVEM > *brief*	DEBERE > *devoir* LABRA > *levre* TABONEM > *taon*	MOB(I)LEM > *mueble*	SUBTILEM > *soutil*	GALB(I)NUM > *jalne, jaun* MEMBRUM > *membre*
w	> ḅ > v	> ḅ > v (−) before o, u	—	(−)	(−)
	VIVERE > *vivre*	LEVARE > *lever* PAVONEM > *paon*		*JOV(E)NEM > *juene*	SOLV(E)RE > *soldre* Cf. § 100
f	f	—	f	—	(−) But cons. + f + l, r remains
	FIDEM > *foi* FRENUM > *frein*		*GAROF(U)LUM > *girofle*		FORF(I)CES > *forces* INFLARE > *enfle*
t	t	> d > ḍ > (−)	t'l > kl > l'	(−) But t's > ts	(−) But cons. + t + r, s remains
	TALEM > *tel* TRABEM > *tref*	VITA > *vie*	VET(U)LUM > *vieil*	PLAT(A)NUM > *plane* AMAT(I)S > *amez*	AEST(I)MARE > *esmer* FENESTRA > *fenestre* FORT(I)S > *for.*

NOTE. (−) denotes the loss of the sound in question.
— indicates that the case does not arise.
[1] For the development of glide-consonants, see § 100.

CONSONANTS TO 1200

(*f*)	(*g*)		(*h*)	(*i*)
			Final	
+*j*	Last of group		Unsupported	Supported
tš	p	Lat.	—	·—
APPROPIARE > *approchier*	SERPENTEM > *serpent*	Rom.	f *CAPUM > *chief*	p CAMPUM > *champ*
dž	b	Lat.	—	—
TIBIA > *tige*	CARBONEM > *charbon*	Rom.	f TRABEM > *tref*	p *CORBUM > *corp*
dž	v	Lat.	—	—
ABBREVIARE > *abregier*	SERVIRE > *servir*	Rom.	f VIVUM > *vif*	f CERVUM > *cerf*
—	f	Lat.	—	—
	INFANTEM > *enfant*	Rom.	—	—
After vowel > iz After cons. > ts but stj > is POTIONEM > *poison* INFANTIA > *enᶠance* ANGUSTIA > *angoisse*	t FONTANA > *fontaine*	Lat.	> ṭ > (—) AMAT > *aime*(ṭ)	t AMANT > *aiment*
		Rom.	> ṭ > (—) GRATUM > *gre*(ṭ)	t PARTEM > *part*

The development of final consonants here tabulated is that
normally found before a pause (cf. § 101).

For Initial *h*, see §§ 84, 109, 115.

	(a)	(b)	(c)	(d)	(e)
	Initial	**Medial**			
		Between vowels	Before *l*	Before other consonants	Middle of gro
d	d	$>$ ḍ $>$ (−)	d'l$>$ll$>$l	(−) But d's$>$ts	(−) But cons. $+$d$+$r remai d's$>$ts
	DURUM $>$ *dur* DRAPPUM $>$ *drap*	VIDERE $>$ *v(e)oir*	MOD(U)LUM $>$ *moule*	*ADMIRARE $>$ *amirer* AUD(I)S $>$ *oz*	ORD(I)NEM $>$ *orne* PERD(E)RE $>$ *perdre* SURD(O)S $>$ *so*
s	s	z	(−)	(−) But sp, st remain, st's$>$ts; sk$>$is	s
	SERVIRE $>$ *servir* SPINA $>$ *espine* Cf. § 97	PAUSARE $>$ *poser*	I(N)S(U)LA $>$ *i(s)le*	AS(I)NUM $>$ *a(s)ne* ASPERUM $>$ *aspre* HOSTEM $>$ *ost* HOST(E)S $>$ *oz* CRESCUNT $>$ *croissent*	*DEXTRARIUM $>$ *destrier*
r	r	r	r	r	—
	REM $>$ *rien*	FARINA $>$ *farine*	MER(U)LA $>$ *merle*	CARBONEM $>$ *charbon*	
l	l	l	(−)	$>$ ł $>$ u	—
	LUNA $>$ *lune*	TELA $>$ *toile*	NULLA $>$ *nule*	PALMA $>$ *paume* CAL(I)DUM $>$ *chaut*	
m	m	m	m'l$>$mbl	m But $>$ n before dental	(−) But rm'n$>$r
	MURUM $>$ *mur*	AMARUM $>$ *amer*	*TREM(U)LARE $>$ *trembler*	GAMBA $>$ *jambe* SEM(I)TA $>$ *sente* TEM(PU)S $>$ *tens*	DORM(I)TORIU $>$ *dortoir* GERM(I)NARE $>$ *germer*

CONSONANTS TO 1200—*continued*

(f)	(g)		(h)	(i)
			Final	
+*j*	Last of group		Unsupported	Supported
>j in V.L.	d	Lat.	>ṭ>(—) AD>a(ṭ)	—
	TARDARE >*tarder*	Rom.	>ṭ>(—) FIDEM>*foi*(ṭ)	t TARDUM>*tart*
iz But ssj>is	s But after l′, n′, nn, >ts	Lat.	s BONAS>*bones*	—
MA(N)SIONEM >*maison* MESSIONEM >*moisson*	VERSARE >*verser* PUGN(O)S >*poinz* *GENUC(U)L(O)S >*genolz* ANN(O)S>*anz*	Rom.	s NASUM>*nes*	s URSUM>*ours*
ir	r	Lat.	r COR>*cuer*	—
VARIUM>*vair*	LABRA>*levre*	Rom.	r CARUM>*chier*	r FERRUM>*fer*
l′ FILIA>*fille*	l Palatal +l>l′ MOB(I)LEM >*mueble* AURIC(U)LA >*oreille*	Lat.	l FEL.>*fiel*	—
		Rom.	l TALEM>*tel*	l BELLUM>*bel*
ndž SIMIUM>*singe*	m ARMA>*arme*	Lat.	(—) BONAM>*bone*	—
		Rom.	n RACEMUM >*raisin*	m VERMEM>*verm*

	(a)	(b)	(c)	(d)	(e)
	Initial	Medial			
		Between vowels	Before *l*	Before other consonants	Middle of gro
n	n	n	—	n But > m before labial; n'm > m	(−)
	NASUM > *nes*	PLANARE > *planer*		PLANTA > *plante* INFA(N)S > *emfes* AN(I)MA > *ame*	DIURN(O)S > *jours*
k	k	(−)	k + l > l'	i But ks + cons. > s + cons. ktj > ts	(−) But remains nk'l, nk'r, rk'l sk + cons. > is + cons nkt > int
	COLLUM > *col* CREPARE > *crever*	SECURUM > *s(e)ur*	AURIC(U)LA > *oreille*	FACTUM > *fait* *DEXTRARIUM > *destrier* *DIRECTIARE > *drecier*	MISC(U)LARE > *mesler* AVUNC(U)LUM > *oncle* ANC(O)RA > *ancre* CIRC(U)LUM > *cercle* CRESC(I)T > *croist* PUNCTUM > *point*
g	g	(−)	g + l > l'	i But gn > n'	(−) But remains ng'l
	GUTTA > *goute* GRANDEM > *grant*	AUGUSTUM > *a-oust*	REG(U)LA > *reille*	FRAGRARE > *flairer* DIGNAT > *deigne*	*MARG(U)LA > *marle* UNG(U)LA > *ongle*

CONSONANTS TO 1200—*continued*

(*f*)	(*g*)		(*h*)	(*i*)
			Final	
+*j*	Last of group		Unsupported	Supported
n′	n But pal. + n > n′ mn > m rm'n > rm	Lat.	n NON > *non* Cf. § 84	—
LINEA > *ligne*	ALNUM > *alne* DIGNAT > *deigne* *DAMNATICUM > *damage* GERM(I)NARE > *germer*	Rom.	n BONUM > *bon*	n > (—) CORNU > *cor(n)*
—	k But sk > is	Lat.	k or i or (—) AB HOC > *avuec* FAC > *fai* ILLAC > *la*	—
	FALCONEM > *falcon* CRESCUNT > *croissent*	Rom.	i *VERACUM > *vrai*	k PORCUM > *porc*
—	g	Lat.	—	—
	BURGUNDIA > *Bourgogne*	Rom.	—	k LONGUM > *lonc*

	(a)	(b)	(c)	(d)	(e)
			Medial		
	Initial	Between vowels	Before l	Before other consonants	Middle of gr
k^1	ts CENTUM > cent	iz PLACENT > plaisent	—	—	—
k^a	tš CANTAT > chante	> g^a > ij after $a, e,$ $(-)$ after i, o, u PACARE > paiier AMICA > amie JOCARE > jouer	—	—	—
g^a	dž GAMBA > jambe	> ij after a, e $(-)$ after i, o, u PAGANUM > paiien RUGA > rue	—	—	—
j g^1 }j dj	dž *JOVENEM > juene GENTEM > gent DIURNUM > journ	Post-tonic > ij ; Pre-tonic > ij before $a, e, o,$ $(-)$ before i, u CORRIGIA > courroie *APPODIARE > apoiier JEJUNUM > je-un	—	—	—

CONSONANTS TO 1200—*continued*

(f)	(g)		(h)	(i)
			Final	
+*j*	Last of group		Unsupported	Supported
ts But skj > is *GLACIA > *glace* *PISCIONEM > *poisson*	ts But sk¹ > is ANCILLA > *ancelle* VASCELLUM > *vaissel*	Lat.	—	—
		Rom.	its CRUCEM > *croiz*	ts SAL(I)CEM > *salz*
—	tš	Lat.	—	—
	*BLANCA > *blanche*	Rom.	—	—
—	dž	Lat.	—	—
	VIRGA > *verge*	Rom.	—	—
—	See preceding column	Lat.	—	—
		Rom.	i RADIUM > *rai*	—

In medial groups consisting of explosive + *w*, the explosive was assimilated to *w*, which became *u* if subsequently brought into contact with a following consonant (DEBU(I)T > *dut*, HABU(I)T > *out*), and became *v* or *u* if it remained intervocal (VIDUA > *veuve*, AQUA > *ewe* > *eaue* and *eve*). *nw* > *nv* (JANUARIUM > *janvier*). Cf. §§ 345, 348, 350.

104. The conditions under which consonants developed were so unstable, and disturbing influences so common and sporadic in their effect, that many apparent exceptions to the general rules set out above are to be noted. Some of these are accounted for by varying phonetic conditions, such as a change (or merely hesitation) in syllabification (cf. § 91) or, in the case of secondary groups, the date at which the constituent consonants were brought into contact (cf. § 96).

105. Sporadic tendencies, such as metathesis, harmonic assimilation and dissimilation, account for other irregularities (§ 20).

106. Many apparent exceptions to sound-laws are to be found in words which were borrowed subsequently to the change or changes in question. For the phonetic treatment of borrowed words, see §§ 499–501, 520. The following list may serve to illustrate such apparent exceptions. P: *epistre* (EPISTOLA), *propre* (PROPRIUS), *couple* (COPULA), *assomption* (ASSUMPTIO); B: *habile* (HABILIS), *libre* (LIBER); T: *nature* (NATURA), *titre* and *titele* (TITULUS); D: *prudent* (PRUDENS); K: *duc* (DUX), *difficile* (DIFFICILIS), *discipline* (DISCIPLINA), *cause* (CAUSA), *fecondité* (FECUNDITAS); G: *negoce* (NEGOTIUM), *regle* (REGULA), *fragile* (FRAGILIS).

107. Learned influence is responsible, not only for the introduction of words borrowed from C.L. and L.L., but for the retarding or reversing of popular developments (cf. § 500). Analogical influences account for many other apparent exceptions. Cf. the development of final consonants (§§ 101, 125–31).

108. The most striking developments dating from the thirteenth century are:

(*a*) The elimination of the dental element of the groups

ts, dz, tš, dž, which were reduced to *s, z, š, ž* respectively from about the middle of the thirteenth century and subsequently depalatalized (cf. § 93 note). Orthography does not record this change, except sporadically in the case of final *ts* (orth. *z*) > *s* (orth. *s*): *morz* (*morts*), *granz* (*grands*), *chacier* (*chasser*), *place, anz* (*ans*), *poinz* (*poings*), *compainz, genolz* (*genoux*), *cire, noiz* (*noix*); *onze*; *chanter, vache, manche, porche, sache*; *argent, gent, salvage* (*sauvage*), *joie, herberge, jugier* (*juger*), *tige.*

(b) The progressive reduction or elimination of final consonants, which however persist in spelling. Unsupported final *ţ* (§ 102 *h*) had ceased to be pronounced in the twelfth century. About the middle of the thirteenth century supported final *t*, which had hitherto been pronounced even after the loss of the supporting consonant (*plai(s)t, di(s)t*), began to disappear. Other unsupported final consonants (including *s: bones, chantes*), when preceded by *ə*, likewise began to become mute in the thirteenth century. Final *n'* > *n* and was absorbed by the preceding nasal vowel (*poing, tesmoing*) (cf. § 78).

(c) *s*, which had become mute before voiced explosives prior to the thirteenth century, now also ceased to be pronounced before voiceless explosives, although preserved in spelling (§ 169).

109. These changes are gradually generalized in the fourteenth century. In the fifteenth century, final *r*, which had hitherto resisted, began to disappear (§ 128); similarly *r* tended to disappear in the group *r* + cons. + *ə* (*rouges: courges, mesle: perle*, rime in Villon). Aspirate *h* also became mute for the most part before the sixteenth century (§ 115). The passage of intervocal *r* to *z* is attested, but does not become general until the sixteenth century (§ 116). These changes, together with others which began in the Middle French period, will be dealt with in the following section.

3. MIDDLE AND MODERN FRENCH DEVELOPMENT

110. The various factors which from the sixteenth century onwards have interfered with the normal phonetic development of vowels (§ 54) play an equally important and perhaps more striking part in the history of consonants. Here the Erasmian reforms in the pronunciation of Latin are of capital importance. The pronunciation that had made possible such puns as *requiescant in pace = Hé, qui est-ce?—Quentin—Passez!* gives place to a pronunciation in which each consonant is sounded. Whereas in the Middle Ages Latin was pronounced as though it were French, the scholars of the sixteenth and seventeenth centuries, having developed the habit of pronouncing Latin as written and sounding each consonant, may be said to have reversed the position: they endeavoured to 'correct' the pronunciation of the vernacular on similar lines. In the case of recent borrowings from Latin, which were essentially book-words, they had little difficulty in maintaining intact many consonants and groups of consonants which would in the normal course have been modified and brought into line with Popular words. Similarly, earlier borrowed words of limited currency were partially restored to their Latin pronunciation. In Learned words which had become more fully naturalized, and in many Popular words, the conservative and etymologizing tendency of orthography (§ 163) facilitated their efforts. But here they generally had to contend with habits of pronunciation which were too deeply ingrained to be modified. The tendency of grammarians to model pronunciation upon spelling proceeded, not from a mere worship of the written or printed word, but from a feeling that they were thereby restoring to the language some of the dignity which it, in common with Latin, had lost in the Dark Ages. Their contempt for the corruptions and abuses of popular speech are not to be interpreted as snobbery but as the grammarian's contribution to the 'Defence and Illustration' of the French language.

111. Thus we find from the sixteenth century onwards a

conflict between the popular and spontaneous evolution of French consonants, which made for simplification and reduction, and the learned, conscious attempt to arrest this evolution and to re-introduce consonants which had ceased to be pronounced. The polite society of the seventeenth century endeavoured to strike a balance between these tendencies. Modern refined speech shows remarkably few departures from seventeenth-century usage, and they are often to be attributed to the growing influence of the printed word in more recent times.

(a) Changes in the articulation of particular consonants

R

112. Latin *r* was evidently linguo-dental (i.e. produced by the vibration of the tip of the tongue against the upper gums) and persisted as such in the Romance languages. The modern French uvular R (produced by the vibration of the uvula) is a comparatively modern Parisian development, which has spread to the greater part of Northern France. In the South the medieval linguo-dental *r* predominates to this day, but even here uvular R is gradually spreading from the larger towns (Marseilles, etc.) to the countryside. While uvular R may have developed in isolated cases during the Middle Ages, such changes as *r* > *z* (voiced dental) in the sixteenth and seventeenth centuries show that it could not have been general before the eighteenth century, and the phonetic description given by Molière in *Le Bourgeois Gentilhomme* may be taken to represent standard usage of the time. Uvular R had become general in Parisian speech by the beginning of the nineteenth century. In the speech of the Parisian workman the point of articulation has shifted still further back, R becoming almost a guttural spirant with a slight vibration.

L' > J

113. The reduction of *l'* to *j* is also a popular Parisian feature, which is noted as such by the grammarians of the

sixteenth century and condemned as vulgar by those of the
seventeenth and eighteenth. But it became so general in
the eighteenth century, even beyond the Capital, that *j* was
accepted as the correct pronunciation from the beginning of
the nineteenth. *l'* lingers on only in the South, in Switzerland,
and in certain northern patois. The reduction is extended in
popular speech to the group *lj* (*escalier* pronounced *ęskaję*)
(cf. § 124).

114. The palatalization of consonants, which had been so
marked a feature in Vulgar Latin and Gallo-Roman, re-
appears in popular speech in the seventeenth century and
accounts for the confusion of *t'* (< *tj*) and *k'* (< *kj*), *d'* (< *dj*)
and *g'* (< *gj*) (*moiquié* for *moitié*, *Guieu* for *Dieu*, cited by Rosset,
p. 314). But the efforts of grammarians, supported by orthography, prevented this confusion from having permanent
results, and it disappears in the course of the eighteenth
century. The palatalization of *k* and *g* before *e, i, ü*, is attested
from the end of the seventeenth century and persists to the
present day in popular speech, as does also the palatalization
of *l* and *n* by a following *j* (§ 124).

H

115. Aspirate *h* had ceased to be sounded before the sixteenth century, but words in which it occurred continued to
be treated for purposes of elision and liaison as though they
began with a consonant. Even this habit had practically
disappeared in popular speech; but such as it was, it made
possible the arbitrary distinction between mute *h* and aspirate
h which the grammarians imposed. Furthermore, orthography continued to note aspirate *h*; and according to Scaliger,
in the course of the sixteenth century the French took to
pronouncing *h* in Latin. While the grammarians were unable
to restore the aspirate *h* sound (except in the narrow circle
of the learned), they imposed the arbitrary rule that words
which had formerly begun with aspirate *h* should be treated
as though they began with a consonant. This rule became
in the seventeenth century one of the many to be observed

by all who aspired to speak their language 'correctly'. They were compelled, then as now, to learn all the words which according to the dictates of grammarians and orthography begin with aspirate *h* and to distinguish them from words in which *h* has no significance whatever. The list as drawn up by Palsgrave has remained practically unchanged to the present day (cf. Rosset, p. 289). As for the slight aspirate sound which in Modern French sometimes accompanies the articulation of the initial vowel, it merely serves to mark more clearly the beginning of a word and bears no relation to etymology. It may be produced, for example, in *c'est une chose 'horrible* or *c'est une chose 'odieuse*, no less than in *c'est une chose 'honteuse*, and it usually accompanies emotional stress.

The decision between *'h* and *h* is sometimes taken on grounds which are not historical, e.g. *l'héroïsme* and *l'héroïne*, but *les héros* (= lę ęrǫ) to avoid confusion with *les zéros*, and thence in the singular *le héros*.

Certain words beginning with a vowel or mute *h* have for various reasons since the seventeenth century been treated as though they began with aspirate *h*: *le huit* (but cf. *dix-huit*), *le onze* by analogy with *le deux*, *le trois*, etc. The hesitation between *il dit que oui* and *il dit qu'oui*, *la ouate* and *l'ouate* dates from the seventeenth century, when *u* in hiatus became semi-consonantal *w*. Similarly *avant hier* (without liaison) beside *avant-hier*, which has evolved as a single word; *le huit* for *l'huit* may be in part due to the corresponding change *ü* to *ẅ*.

INTERVOCAL R > Z

116. The passage of intervocal *r* to *z* (cf. § 109), which is so common in popular speech of the sixteenth century, is an instance of the general tendency of intervocal consonants to weaken. The relaxed articulation of the linguo-dental vibrant *r* produces automatically the linguo-dental spirant *z*. In the sixteenth century this pronunciation (*z* for *r*) threatened to become universal, but the grammarians, aided by orthography (which maintained *r*), succeeded in banishing it from correct usage. In the seventeenth century it was confined to the lower classes, but it is significant that *leur* continued to be pronounced *löz* in liaison. *Chaire* and *chaise* represent the survival of the learned and etymological pronunciation beside the popular, the ιormer being reserved for the more specialized and technical meanings of CATHEDRA.

(*b*) GROUPS OF CONSONANTS

117. The popular tendency to assimilate adjacent consonants (regressively as a rule) persists to the present day in spite of the resistance offered by grammarians, purists, and orthography (*asbeste, obscur, absurde*). The more genuinely popular a word is or becomes, the more likely is this tendency to triumph. Recent borrowings, whether from dead or living languages, generally serve a period of probation in technical or special languages before they are fully naturalized, and therefore tend to be accepted in their learned form with consonant groups intact. The following brief indications[1] may serve to illustrate the many anomalies which result from the conflict.

118. Groups of three or more consonants, whether inherited from Latin or of secondary formation, had been reduced in Old French, with the exception of the group cons. + explosive + *l, r*; but with the learned restoration of consonants and the introduction of many borrowed words in the sixteenth and seventeenth centuries, they re-appeared: *b* was restored towards the end of the seventeenth century in the groups *bsk, bst* (*obscur, substituer*); *k* in *ksk, kst* and *t* in *std, stp* after the seventeenth century (*excursion, extraire, post-dater, postposer*). That such groups are contrary to French habits of pronunciation is clear from the popular tendency to break them up by articulating the constituent consonants in separate syllables and thus forming normal groups (*eks-tra*) or by introducing a feminine *e* (*bourg[e]mestre, arc[e]boutant*).

119. The loss of unaccented *ə* created new groups of consonants in many Popular words, but as *e* was maintained in

[1] Based for the most part upon Rosset and Herzog.

spelling and often re-appears in pronunciation (§§ 60–4), assimilation has rarely taken place except in regard to voice: *mętsẽ* (*médecin*), *saftję* (*savetier*), and with progressive assimilation, which is rare, *õ̃ʃfal* (*un cheval*), *aʃ́fę* (*achever*). As a rule the two consonants are articulated in separate syllables: *mad-mwazęl* (*mademoiselle*), *ǫr-vwa:r* (*au revoir*).

INITIAL GROUPS

120. *s* + cons. Initial groups consisting of *s* + cons. had in V.L. developed a prosthetic *e* (§ 84), and borrowed words introduced during the Old French and Middle French periods were normally treated in the same way in popular speech; this tendency persisted down to the beginning of the nineteenth century. But in the literary language certain borrowed words had persisted in their Latin form, although borrowed as early as the twelfth century (*splendeur, station, spirituel*). The grammarians had therefore little difficulty in maintaining intact the initial *s* + cons. of words which were newly borrowed or which had never been widely used, particularly as the group *s* + cons. was not unknown in popular speech, owing to the elimination of countertonic *ə* (§ 60). They could not hope to restore the group in Popular words, for here *s* had become entirely mute, although preserved in spelling (*estoile, espee*). Such a borrowed word as *estampe* represents a compromise between the popular development of a prosthetic *e* and the tendency to maintain *s* in Learned and foreign words.

ps had been reduced by the assimilation of *p* to *s* (*psaume, psautier, psalmiste, psalmodie*), but *p* was definitely restored in the eighteenth century.

MEDIAL GROUPS

121. *p* + cons. The etymologizing tendency of orthography had led to the restoration of *p* in many Popular words, but the attempt to restore it in pronunciation met with no success. In Learned words the tendency to suppress *p* continued, particularly after a nasal vowel. It was not restored until the end of the seventeenth century in *rédempteur* and *présomptueux*, and not until the nineteenth in *péremptoire* and *symptôme*. It persists as a mere graphy in many Learned words (*exempter, promptement, sculpter*) and in some Popular words (*corps, temps, sept, septième* beside *septante*). It serves to distinguish *compte* from its homonyms *comte* and *conte*.

b + cons. *b* having been restored in spelling in the prefixes *ab-, ob-, sub-*, came to be pronounced sporadically in the sixteenth century and regularly in the seventeenth. It is regularly unvoiced before a following voiceless consonant (*absolu, obtenir, subterfuge*).

d + cons. Etymological *ad-* had been restored in many Popular words, but as the *d* was not pronounced and as *a-* (< AD) was a very common prefix, the attempt to restore it was only half-hearted and resulted in many inconsistencies. *d* was restored in *adjectif, adverbe, adverse, adversité, admonition, admirer*, but not in *aversion, avocat*, etc. The spelling reform of 1740 merely perpetuated these inconsistencies by suppressing *d* wherever it was mute: *a(d)version*, but *adverse*. In this way arose the doublet *avenir—advenir*.

122. *k* + cons. This group existed only in Learned or semi-Learned words (*siècle*), and the efforts of grammarians to maintain it in later borrowings met with resistance throughout the seventeenth century, particularly for -*anc-*, -*onc-* (*k* was not sounded in *sanctifier*). In some words *c* continued to be written, although not pronounced (*practique, subjection*), as late as the seventeenth, or even the eighteenth century (*bienfaicteur*), but generally spelling was brought into line with pronunciation, which suppressed *c* (= k) in words which were commonly used, and preserved or restored it in others (*sanctifier, ponctuel, diction, antarctique, effectuer, affecter, affectation*). Owing to the restoration of *c* (= k) the group *cc*, when followed by *e, i*, came to be pronounced *ks* in Learned words in the seventeenth century (*accent, occident*). Similarly *xc*, which tended to be reduced to *s*, was maintained as *ks* (*excellent* for sixteenth century *e(x)cellent*). The seventeenth-century tendency to pronounce intervocal *x* as *gz* (as opposed

to sixteenth-century *z*) has been reversed in many words by learned influence (*vexer, maxime*), but initial *ex-* followed by a vowel continues to be pronounced *egz* (*examen, exemple, exercer*). Before a consonant, *x* had been reduced to *s*, but *k* was restored in the seventeenth century (*exclure, extrême*).

g + cons. In Popular words *gn* was merely a graphy for *n'*. In Learned words *gn* was pronounced *n* in the sixteenth century (*regne* = renə), but this pronunciation had to contend with the interpretation of the graphy *gn* as *n'*. The seventeenth-century attempt to restore *g* failed before these two established pronunciations. The hesitation between *n* and *n'* continued in the seventeenth century, but *n'* triumphed before 1700, except in a few words (*consigner, désigner, résigner, signe*), which adopted *n'* in the eighteenth, and in *signet* which still hesitates between *sinę* and *sin'ę*. Words borrowed since the seventeenth century preserve *g* (*diagnose, diagnostic, ignition, inexpugnable, pugnacité, stagnant*), although even here *gn* now tends to be pronounced *n'* (*incognito* = ẽkǫgnitǫ, but sometimes = ẽkǫn'itǫ). *gm* is maintained in Learned words (*énigme, dogme, flegme*) in spite of a popular tendency to assimilate *g*.

123. *s* + cons. By the end of the fifteenth century, *s* before consonant had ceased to be pronounced in Popular words and in those Learned words which did not remain confined to the written language. The grammarians attempted to restore *s* in the latter, just as they maintained *s* in pure book-words. The resulting hesitation persists throughout the sixteenth century and well into the seventeenth. Orthography helped to perpetuate the confusion by preserving *s*, whether pronounced or not, although lists were drawn up of words in which *s* was to be pronounced. The remaining words of doubtful pronunciation were settled in the eighteenth century, and the spelling reform of 1740, which suppressed *s* wherever it was mute, consecrated the decisions taken. Henceforth, wherever *s* appears in spelling before a consonant, it is pronounced. A survival of the old hesitation is to be seen in the double form *fenestré—fenêtré*.

The pronunciation of *s* in Learned words was the more

easily imposed as the group *s* + cons. existed in other Romance idioms from which words were borrowed (§§ 515–18) and had re-appeared during the sixteenth and seventeenth centuries in Popular words through the elimination of *ə* between *s* and a following consonant (§§ 60–1). The familiarity with spoken Italian may also have accustomed polite society to this grouping.

s was even restored in the seventeenth century in certain Popular words which had preserved it in spelling (*jusque, lorsque, presque, puisque*). *tandis que* still hesitates between *tādikə* and *tādiskə*.

124. Cons. +*j*. The natural tendency was for *j* to palatalize the preceding consonant, if both belonged to the same syllable. The popular confusion of *kj* and *tj, dj* and *gj* (§ 114) is still to be observed in patois. The palatalization of *l* led to a confusion of *lj* and the *l'* which had been inherited from Old French. Both are reduced to *j* in popular speech and continue to be so pronounced to the present day (*ęskaję* for *ęskalję*). Correct usage, as moulded by the grammarians, has restored the group *lj*. The parallel confusion between *n'* and *nj* has had a more lasting effect, and *nj* is commonly pronounced *n'* even in the everyday speech of the cultured classes of to-day (*ün'õ* for *ünjõ*).

(c) FINAL CONSONANTS

125. The threefold development of final consonants according to the position of the word (§ 101) is still preserved in *six, neuf, dix* (cf. *dix jours, il y en a dix, dix hommes*), but apart from such exceptions, it had largely broken down by the sixteenth century. Before a word beginning with a vowel the final consonant was to some extent maintained, but before a consonant or a pause it had generally ceased to be sounded in popular speech. The elaboration of a 'correct' usage brought with it a conflict between this popular tendency and a learned reaction; for the grammarians, inspired in part by the example of Latin (§ 110) and given to modelling

pronunciation upon spelling, strove to maintain or restore final consonants. Their efforts found support not only in orthography but in the natural reaction against the process of phonetic erosion which threatened monosyllabic words with extinction (*if, œuf*) and tended to create an excessive number of homonyms (*sens—sang, nef—nez*). They could moreover base themselves upon the analogy of cases where the final consonants continued to be sounded (*fer, ver*); cf. § 128. The number of such words was increased by recent borrowings, which were pronounced in the first place as written. The comparative ease with which final *k* and *f* were restored, as compared with *p, t, s,* is perhaps due to the prevalence of Learned words in *-c* (= k), *-f,* and the paucity of forms in *-p, -t, -s.* Further accessions resulted from the progressive elimination of *ə* (§§ 62–4). The rapid growth of a reading public favoured the restoration of final consonants, but still more the generalization of a single pronunciation for each word. Hence the modern system in which the final consonant is either preserved or dropped uniformly, whether the word comes before a pause or is followed by a word beginning with a consonant. A vestige of the old distinction is preserved in the modern rules of liaison (§ 135).

126. The conflict between popular and learned tendencies led to hesitation in the sixteenth and a great part of the seventeenth century, as can be seen from the remarks of grammarians and the vacillating orthography (*luc—luth, lilac—lilas, arsenac—arsenal*). Before the end of the seventeenth century this hesitation was eliminated in the majority of cases, but usage has reversed some of the decisions then taken and still shows hesitation in such words as *nerf, sens, mœurs, fait, mars, but, net, cerf, legs.* The final consonant of *combat, secret* was still sounded in the seventeenth century; of *drap, trop, galop,* in the eighteenth; of *mot, sot,* in the nineteenth. On the other hand, the final consonant of *net, os, cep* was not restored until the nineteenth century. Orthography continues to favour the restoration of the final consonant, particularly in the speech of the semi-lettered.

127. The final consonant is generally preserved in words of limited currency. The later the borrowing, the more likely is the consonant to remain (*accessit, déficit, hiatus, gratis, atlas, fat, albatros, vermouth, granit*). Similarly, archaic words preserve the final *s* (*hélas, jadis, sus, cens*). In common words the preservation of the final consonant is generally due to one or more of the factors indicated (§ 125). It serves above all to distinguish what would otherwise be homonyms: *sens* from *sang, donc* from *dont, soit* as an exclamation from *soi(t)* as a part of the verb, *tous* pronoun from *tou(s)* adjective, *os* from *eau, nef* from *nez*. This is particularly common in short or monosyllabic words, where there is often the further danger that the word may be reduced to a mere vowel (*if, œuf*). Analogy frequently exerts a decisive influence (*ours ≠ ourse, -if ≠ -ive, dot ≠ doter, heurt ≠ heurter*).

128. The treatment of final *r* illustrates most adequately the anomalies which have resulted. At the beginning of the sixteenth century this consonant persisted only in words where it had originally been followed by another consonant, *fer(r), enfer(n), hiver(n), ver(m)*, and perhaps also in infinitives in *-ir* and *-oir*, where the analogy of infinitives in *-re* may have operated. Supported by such survivals, the attempt to restore or preserve *r* met with considerable success (infinitives in *-ir, -oir*, words in *-our, -or, -ir, -ur, -ar(d)*, recent borrowings such as *cancer, steamer, revolver, ulster*); but it failed with the numerous infinitives in *-er* (the pronunciation *-ęr* being practically confined as early as the seventeenth century to sustained discourse and declamation), also in substantives and adjectives in *-ier* (except *fier*) and *-er* (except *amer, cher, cuiller, mer*, and the cases mentioned above, *fer*, etc.), in *monsieur, messieurs*. In the suffix *-eur* the final consonant had become mute by the sixteenth century. It was therefore confused with *-eux*, and an analogical feminine in *-euse* was sometimes created which survived after the restoration of *r* in the second half of the seventeenth century (*menteur—menteuse, liseur—liseuse*).

129. The case of final *l* is more complicated. In Popular words it was tending to disappear in the sixteenth century

(*chou*(*l*), *saou*(*l*), *cu*(*l*)), but was generally restored before the
end of the seventeenth under the influence of orthography
or of the feminine form (*nul—nulle, tel—telle*). Learned words
preserve final *l* (*calcul*) and favour its restoration in Popular
words. The resulting hesitation was utilized to distinguish
col from *cou*; *mol* and *fol* were reserved for liaison. After *i* the
treatment of *l* is complicated by the fact that the graphy *il*
could represent either *i+l* or *i+l'* and that *l'* was reduced
to *j* (which tends to disappear after *i*). Accordingly the final
consonant may be restored in the form of *l* (*avril, fil* (< FILUM),
cil (< CILIUM), *péril, vil*) or *j* (*grésil*). It is still mute in *chenil,
coutil, outil, fusil, gentil, sourcil* (but popular pron. *sursil ≠ cil*).
Some words still show hesitation (*nõbril : nõbri, gril : grij : gri,
bari : baril, furni : furnil*). *Fils* (< FILIUS), with restored *s*, replaced *fi*(*l*) (< FILIUM) which is still preserved in poetry in
rimes such as *crucifix : fils* (Lamartine, *Le Crucifix*). In familiar
speech *il, ils* are often reduced to *i* before a pause or a consonant (*s'il vous plaît, pleut-il?, qu'est-ce qu'ils disent?*).

130. The strength of popular habits of speech is shown by
the failure to preserve *s* as the sign of the plural, *s* and *t* in
verbal flexions and in many suffixes (*-et, -eux, -ot, -ard*), *r* in
-er infinitives. This has had far-reaching results in morphology and syntax. The flexional distinction between singular
and plural has to a large extent disappeared, and the article
is almost indispensable as an indication of number. In verbs
the personal pronoun is similarly called upon to make good
the loss of flexional distinctions (*je chante, tu chantes, il chante,
ils chantent*). The distinction between masculine and feminine, while in spelling still indicated by *e*, is in the spoken
language often indicated merely by the preservation of the
final consonant in the feminine, with or without a modification in the quality of the tonic vowel (*so—sot, ba—ba:s*); cf.
§ 191.

131. The tendency to unvoice final voiced consonants
(§ 101) persisted in the seventeenth century (*Jacop* for *Jacob*).
The campaign in defence of final *ə* (§§ 62–3) preserved the
preceding voiced consonant from this tendency (*vide, robe,*

digue). Although *e* is no longer sounded in such words, it may be said to have left a deposit in the *ə*-like resonance which accompanies the final voiced consonant. Supported by such cases, the voiced consonant has sometimes been restored under the influence of orthography: *nord, sud* were advocated in the seventeenth century for normal *nort, sut,* and *sud* was adopted. *g* for *k* dates from the eighteenth century in *joug, zigzag,* and from the nineteenth in *bourg* and *legs,* the graphy *legs* for O.F. *lais* having been adopted owing to false analogy with LEGATUM (cf. § 163). In words borrowed since the seventeenth century the final voiced consonant is generally preserved (*club, grog, whig*).

C. *SYNTACTIC PHENOMENA*

132. We have hitherto considered words as separate entities, but their form is also subject to modification according to their place or function in a speech-group. The latter may consist of a single word (*Venez!*) or of a series of words (*Faites-moi le plaisir de m'accompagner!*). Phonetically it consists of a succession of syllables articulated without a pause (*fɛtmwal(ə)plɛzi:rdəmakõpan'ɛ*) and is therefore sometimes called a breath-group. Semantically it represents a single concept (§ 16), but the constituent elements (words) have an individuality of their own which they tend to conserve The consciousness of the word as a unit may result in a modification of normal syllabification (§§ 137, 144) or in a closer phonetic union between those words within the group which are intimately connected syntactically (§ 135). The changes in form which result from such phonetic or semantic groupings have been loosely summed up under the heading Syntactic Phenomena. They affect (1) Syllabification (Elision, Liaison, etc.), (2) Accentuation (variation in stress and pitch).

1. SYLLABIFICATION
(Hiatus, Elision, Aphæresis, Liaison, Syncope)

133. If a word ending in a vowel is followed by a word beginning with a vowel, both vowels may persist in hiatus (*et après*). In rapid speech slurring sometimes takes place and a diphthong may result (*il y a une raison*), or the first vowel becomes a semi-consonant (*Qu'y a-t-il?* =kjati?, *Celui qui est la* =sęlwïkjęla). Before so-called aspirate *h* the hiatus has been artificially maintained (§ 115).

134. If the final vowel is *ə*, it is elided, although orthography does not record the elision except for *je, me, te, le, se, ce, de, ne, que*, most compounds of *que*, and the particle *entre*. Elision of *ə* has been the rule since the earliest texts, but exceptions are encountered at all periods of the language. The hiatus was often maintained before proper names (*au roi de Elenie*; cf. A. Tobler, *Vom französischen Versbau*, 5th ed. pp. 55–73). O.F. *se* (<sɪ) was regularly elided, whence Mod.F. *s'il, s'ils*; O.F. *s'on* (xɪɪɪ, 25), *s'elle* were replaced by *si on, si elle*, when *si* triumphed over *se* (§ 466). *a* is still elided in *la* (art. and pron.), but O.F. *m', t', s'* gave way to *mon, ton, son* in Mid.F. The elision of other vowels was optional and rare, as in O.F. *si* (< sɪc), *qui, li* (m. nom. s. of def. art.), *ço, jo, lo. Tu* sometimes appears as *t'* in Old French and in modern popular speech, but this may represent the elided form of analogical *te* (§ 237).

Modern French shows considerable hesitation in the elision of *e* and *a* (and in the articulation of a liaison-consonant) before initial *i, u, ü* in hiatus, according as the latter develop semi-consonantal or semi-vocalic value. Elision is usual in Popular words (*l'huile, l'oiseau*, cf. also *un oiseau, mon oiseau*), less common in Learned and foreign words (*l'yeuse, l'hiatus*; but *le wagon, la ouate, le yacht*). For non-elision before numerals and before aspirate *h*, cf. § 115.

The reduction of the hiatus by the elimination of the second vowel (aphæresis) is found in Old French only (*si est*> *si'st, lui en*> *lui'n, qui en*> *qui'n*).

135. Hiatus is in many cases avoided by the articulation of a liaison-consonant. Generally the consonant is etymologically justified and perpetuates the Old French practice of preserving the final consonant before a word beginning with a vowel (§ 101). But at the beginning of the sixteenth century this practice was breaking down before the popular tendency to suppress all final consonants (§ 125). The modern rules of liaison date in the main from the seventeenth century, when the hesitation in the pronunciation of final consonants was utilized to avoid hiatus between two consecutive words. The grammarians, anxious to maintain final consonants, strove to extend the use of liaison-consonants. Polite usage effected a compromise: for the liaison-consonant to be pronounced it was necessary, not only that both words should belong to the same speech-group, but that there should be a close syntactic connection between them (*vous avez, il vous aime, les enfants, nos amis, vient-il?, pas encore*) or that they should form fixed locutions (*un sang impur*). The rules of the grammarians were more faithfully observed in sustained discourse and in declamation. Popular speech continued to suppress final consonants. The same distinctions of usage obtain at the present day, but standard usage tends more and more to reflect the popular aversion to liaison and to condemn its excessive use as pedantic. It remains obligatory between article and substantive, adjective and substantive, pronoun and verb, auxiliary verb and participle or adjective, between a preposition, adverb or conjunction and the following word, interrogative verb and pronoun, verb and preposition; optional between verb and direct object, substantive and verb, substantive and adjective. There is also a marked tendency to articulate laxly those liaison-consonants which are preserved. Their number is not large: *z, t, n* are the most common, *p, k, v* less so, while *r* is confined to sustained discourse or declamation. Final *s* and *f* appear as *z* and *v* respectively (*pas encore, neuf heures*); *p, t, k* remain voiceless in spite of the spellings *d, g* (*trop aimable, un froid hiver, un sang impur*). The articulation of final *n* in liaison brought with it the denasalization of the preceding vowel (*bon ami*), but learned influence reacted against this popular tendency (§ 79).

136. Occasionally a liaison-consonant is introduced which is not etymological. This is a popular feature and is due to a misguided attempt to imitate the liaisons characteristic of refined speech, the consonants most frequently employed being *z* and *t*. Generally some analogical influence determines the choice of the consonant (*quatre[z]hommes*, *le bal des Quat'zArts*, *mille[z]amitiés*, *j'ai[z]été*, *Malbrough s'en va-t-en guerre*). Such false liaisons (called 'cuirs', 'velours', or 'pataquès') are attested in popular speech from the seventeenth century onwards (cf. Rosset, pp. 277 ff.), but do not as a rule find acceptance in standard usage. A striking exception is furnished by the interrogative form of the 3rd sing. pres. indic. of *-er* verbs (*donne-t-il?* *aime-t-il?*), where *t* is not to be interpreted as a survival of etymological *t* (DONAT, AMAT), which had long since disappeared, but as a false liaison-consonant introduced by analogy with *dit-il, fait-il,* etc. *Entre quatre[z]yeux* has, by a surprising dispensation, been sanctioned by the Academy.

137. The liaison-consonant is invariably carried over into the next syllable in accordance with the prevailing rules of syllabification (*lę-zǫm, vu-zavę*). Consequently such linked forms have occasionally been falsely interpreted in popular speech: (*lę)zyeux* (*les yeux*) has given a popular verb *zyeuter*. Cf. also *un nombril* for *un ombril*.

138. A word ending in a vowel generally remains intact, if followed by a word beginning with a consonant; but in popular speech the final vowel is often dropped, particularly if the preceding consonant is the same as the initial consonant of the following word. Such forms as *qu'a-vous?* (*qu'avez-vous?*), *sa-vous?* (*savez-vous?*) were even taken up into the literary language of the sixteenth century (cf. Brunot, II, p. 276). But in standard usage and in the literary language the vowel chiefly affected is *ə*.

139. The progressive weakening of monosyllabic words

used proclitically had often resulted in the reduction of the vowel to *ə* (*le*, *me*, *te*, etc.) (§ 21). When such words were, as the result of close syntactic connection, linked with the preceding word, the process was carried to the point of eliminating *ə* completely. This form of apocope is called Enclisis. Thus *à + le* (def. art.) > *al*, *de + le* > *del*, *en + le* > *enl*, reduced to *el* (*al conte*, *del tens*, *el mostier*), and with vocalization of *l* before a word beginning with a consonant, *au*, *du* (for *deu*), *eu* respectively. For *eu* the form *ou*[1] appears from the thirteenth century onwards (XI, 34; XII, 96) and continues in use down to the fifteenth century. The connection with *en* having been lost sight of, *ou* was confused syntactically and phonetically with *au* and was replaced by it (XVII, 33; cf. the legal formula *en mon nom et au sien*).[2] Similarly *à + les* > *als*, reduced to *as*, which was gradually replaced by *aux* (≠ *au*); *aux* appears as early as the thirteenth century; *de + les* > *dels*, early reduced to *des* (≠ *les*); *en + les* > *enls* > *els* > *es* (XIII, 10), still used in the sixteenth century, preserved as a literary archaism in the seventeenth, and surviving in *bachelier ès lettres*, *maître ès arts*, and the like.

140. The enclisis of the personal pronouns *me*, *te*, *se*, *le*, before a word beginning with a consonant, which still obtains in modern speech, with certain qualifications (see below), is no longer noted in writing as it was down to the fourteenth century (*sis = si se*, *nem = ne me*, *sim = si me*, *oul = où le*, *kis = ki se*). With the change *ləs > lẹs* (§ 63), the common Old French enclisis of the pronoun *les* (*kis = ki les*, *luis = lui les*) disappeared.

141. After the imperative, *le* is maintained if it bears the group-accent (*fais-le*). If it is not so accented and is followed by a word beginning with a vowel, it is elided in the Classical

---

[1] *ou* being the normal unaccented form corresponding to tonic *eu* (*mourir* : *meurt*).

[2] The definite article is no longer used after *en*, except in set expressions (*en l'espèce*, *en l'air*, *en l'an* 2000, *en la saison des pluies*). The instinctive avoidance of *en* + def. art. even goes to the length of substituting *dans* for *en* after such verbs as *consister* whenever the definite article follows (*Le bonheur consiste dans la vertu*).

poets (*Ou bien faites-le entrer*..., *Le Misanthrope*, ii, v); cf. also
viii, 29. The modern artificial rule against such an elision
must be attributed to the analogical influence of *faites-le* used
as an independent phrase and therefore with group-accent
on *le*.

142. In the case of polysyllabic words the treatment of
final *ə* is in Modern French governed by the so-called 'loi
des trois consonnes', which stipulates that when *ə* is preceded
by two consonants and followed by a third, it must be pronounced (*Charles douze, presque pas, reste-là, notre père*). The
same law applies when there is a succession of syllables con-
taining *ə*, the usual practice being to drop every other *ə*:
je le sais (žəlsẹ), *je ne le sais pas* (žənləsẹpɑ), *c'est ce que je te
disais* (sẹskəžtədizẹ), but *ce que je ne veux pas* (skəžənvǫpɑ)
(cf. Nyrop, *Gram. Hist.* i, § 294).

The initial consonant of a word, if followed by *ə*, is thus
often drawn into the preceding syllable: *le chemin* (ləš-mẽ),
au-delà (ọd-la), *la pelouse* (lap-lu:z); but cf. *chemin faisant*
(šəmẽfəzɑ̃), *une pelouse* (ünpəlu:z).

143. In familiar, rapid speech the elimination of *ə* often
takes place contrary to the 'loi des trois consonnes', the
preceding consonant being dropped at the same time:
maît(re) d'hôtel, à quat(re) pattes. The pronunciation of a word
like *quatre* may therefore vary considerably according to
position and circumstances. Before a vowel, it will normally
appear as *ka-tr*, *tr* being carried over into the next syllable
(*quatre hommes*); before a consonant, often *kat* (*à quatre sous*);
at the end of a speech-group, *katr* with a very faint *r* (*il faudra
se mettre en quatre*); in careful, slow speech, before a consonant
or before a pause, *ka-trə* (*Il y en a quatre, sans compter Jean*);
to which we might add *entre quatre[z] yeux* (cf. § 136).

No attempt can here be made to discuss the many anomalies,
fluctuations and contradictions which the treatment of *ə* presents. They result not only from the conflict of inherited
habits of speech with new tendencies, of the written word
with the spoken, of the word as a separate entity with its
rôle in the speech-group; they exist as between different

classes of the community, and they occur in the speech of one and the same cultured person. According as he dictates a message, recites poetry, delivers a set oration, converses at ease in his drawing-room or is constrained to come quickly to the point, he will tend more and more to eliminate the feminine *e* from his discourse. We have here but one of the many features which give to the French language its flexibility and its adaptability to the mood and temper of the speaker.

144. If a word ending in a consonant is followed by a word beginning with a consonant, the resulting group of two or more consonants is often modified in modern popular speech. As a corollary to the 'loi des trois consonnes' an *ə* is developed between the second and third of a group of three consonants (*le turc[ə]pur, l'ours[ə]blanc, Ernest[ə]Blanc*, examples cited by Nyrop, *Manuel*, § 88). As a general rule cultured speech, which is more conscious of and guided by the written word, accommodates itself to such groups by accentuating the syllabic division (*urs-blã*). Occasionally an accessory *ə* of this kind is intercalated in an endeavour to give prominence to the final consonant: *post[ə]quam, post[ə]scriptum, post[ə]tonique, à l'Est[ə]de la France*. Such forms are due in part to a reaction against another popular tendency, the assimilation of the first consonant to the second (*pos(t)scriptum*). Such assimilations find grudging acceptance in cultured speech (*cap vert* = kabvẹːr, *avec Jean* = avẹgžã, *tête dure* = tẹddüːr).

2. ACCENTUATION

(a) STRESS

145. One of the most striking developments in the history of the French language is the gradual elimination of word-stress in favour of group-stress. In Latin the rhythm of the group was determined by word-stress (i.e. the alternation of tonic and atonic syllables), modified at most by a slight increase of stress on words which logic or emotion singled out for special emphasis. Accordingly, short words of purely syntactic significance tended to be pronounced with less

stress and to play the same part in the group rhythm as
atonic syllables. They therefore grouped themselves round
the nearest tonic syllable, proclitically with the following or
enclitically with the preceding. If such words received a
logical stress equivalent to normal tonic stress, they show the
same development as tonic syllables (cf. the twofold development of mē > *me* and *moi*, § 21).

146. The tonic stress was perhaps the most important
single factor in the phonetic history of the Romance languages,
and it was particularly strong in Gallo-Roman and Old
French. It led to the loss or reduction to ǝ of the Latin
post-tonic vowels, and all Popular words were therefore
stressed on the last syllable unless that syllable contained
an ǝ. The first syllable continued to be articulated with
secondary stress, and counterfinal syllables, caught between
two stresses, were to a large extent eliminated. Proclitic
and enclitic words were still further reduced, and often little
remains of them except the characteristic consonant (§ 139).
Group-stress, as distinct from tonic stress, was apparently
still determined in Old French by logic and emotion, but
a tendency to stress the final syllable of a group can be traced.
It finds support in versification, which by means of assonance
or rime gives prominence to the final syllable. At the same
time the first syllable of a group received a marked stress
(perhaps already in Latin) and there is a tendency to place
in this position words which it is desired to emphasize.

147. It was undoubtedly in the Middle French period that
the group-stress began more and more to overshadow the
tonic stress and that the characteristic accentuation of Modern
French was developed. This change is clearly connected with
the gradual elimination of ǝ, a change which made all
Popular words oxytonic. Words which had been accented on
the first syllable in Latin thus became monosyllabic. Other
Popular words (except derivatives) generally preserve in addition to the tonic syllable only the initial (countertonic).
Consequently in Middle French, if we except Learned words,
a speech-group consisted largely of tonic syllables, often con-

secutive or separated only by countertonic syllables, and (apart from a dwindling number of feminine *e*'s) proclitic monosyllables. The constituent syllables of a group thus tended to be reduced to a common level, but the oxytonic rhythm of the language was maintained by strengthening the stress on the final syllable of the group. From the point of view of stress, the word is therefore replaced by a group with the strongest stress on the final syllable and a secondary stress on the initial. Word-stress being thus eliminated, the intervening syllables are stressed according to meaning, the more significant elements receiving a sense-stress. In polysyllabic words the sense-stress often falls on the initial syllable, for such words are to a large extent derivatives (*prémier, férmier, máladie, máisniée*) or verb forms. This tendency, coupled with the tendency to stress the initial syllable of a group, completes the elimination of the tonic stress, and a definite turning-point in the history of French pronunciation is thus reached. From the nature of the process it is impossible to assign a definite date to this turning-point, but indirect evidence suggests that in its main features the modern accentual system was constituted by the end of the sixteenth century. In Modern French the tonic stress is uniformly preserved only if the word is used by itself (i.e. constitutes a group in itself) or if it is the final word of a group. Nothing could illustrate more clearly the triumph of group-stress than the fact that even an unaccented enclitic pronoun receives a stress if it happens to stand in the final position (*faites-le*); cf. § 141.

148. Modern French has thus developed a rhythm which distinguishes it clearly from all other European languages. It is in principle an oxytonic rhythm (emphasised by a rising intonation), the final syllable receiving somewhat more stress than the preceding syllables. An interesting exception to this rule has been noted by Herzog (*op. cit.* p. 63), viz. that if the final syllable ends in *õ*, there is a tendency to transfer the stress to the penultimate syllable. Our impression is that this applies to disyllabic words only (*Vous avez raison*) and

is perhaps due to an instinctive desire to stress the significant element (i.e. the first syllable), *ŏ* being reduced to the rôle of a mere supporting vowel. Words of more than two syllables (*condition, floraison*) do not appear to be so affected. Normally there is also a stress on the initial syllable of the group, or if it be a proclitic (*je, ne*, etc.), the following syllable. The intervening syllables are unaccented, but in longer groups one can observe a slight rhythmical but irregular alternation of stressed and unstressed syllables. None of these rhythmical variations in stress are very pronounced, and they are at every moment overshadowed by the stress which is given to various syllables according to the emotion of the speaker (*Il veut absólument partir*) or the meaning (*Je loge au prémier étage*).[1] The rhythmical (group) stress, the emotional, and the logical may fall upon different syllables or combine to give a particular prominence to one and the same syllable. Emotional stress and logical stress are not peculiar to French, but it is in the prominence which the elimination of the tonic stress (word-stress) secures to them that the special virtue of the French tongue lies, its flexibility and suppleness, its claim to be considered the eloquent language *par excellence*. The rhythm of the language reflects directly the emotion of the man.

149. The etymological stress lives on in the form of a group-stress whenever a word comes at the end of a group, but as the word moves to other positions in the group the stress disappears. Consequently the word loses its consistency. The quality and quantity of vowels vary: *ã* is distinctly shorter in *Que penses-tu?* than in *Qu'est-ce que tu penses?*; *ö* is a tense vowel in *Il fait ce qu'il peut*, but tends towards *ə* in *Qu'est-ce que cela peut être?* (cf. §§ 52, 64). But nothing could be more erroneous than to interpret such variations as indecision or lax articulation. The dominant character of French pro-

---

[1] Sense-stress is not to be confused with the emphatic stress so common in English, e.g. I live on the *first* floor. To secure such emphasis French resorts to other devices, as for example, *C'est au premier (étage) que je loge* (cf. § 484).

nunciation remains the crisp, energetic, distinct articulation of both vowels and consonants.

(b) PITCH

150. Variations of pitch in connected speech constitute what is called Intonation. Nothing is known of the historical development of French intonation. It is probable that the tonic stress continued, as in Latin, to be accompanied by a slight pitch-accent, and the close connection between stress and pitch variations in Modern French lends some support to this hypothesis. In Modern French, variations of pitch, like variations in stress, are determined not by etymology but by the constitution of the speech-group. A slight raising of the pitch is natural with increase of stress, and as the rise in pitch generally extends over adjoining syllables, we find that within a normal speech-group a rising intonation is characteristic of Modern French speech. But syllables which bear a sense-stress or emotional stress are usually distinguished by a more pronounced change in pitch, generally a rise (*C'est épatant!*; *Vous avez mille fois raison!*; *Ça coûte horriblement cher!*) but sometimes a fall. Similarly the group-accent may be accompanied by a more pronounced raising of the pitch if attention is to be called to the fact that the speaker has not completed his thought (*Je vais vous dire*); a lowering indicates finality (*Je n'ai plus rien à vous dire*) or the end of the last of a series of groups. Variations of pitch, in so far as they express certain emotions, do not differ markedly from those of other languages, e.g. the rising intonation of direct questions. They are, in French, variations upon a fundamental theme—the characteristic rising melody of the normal speech-group.[1]

---

[1] We have omitted as not strictly relevant to our purpose the consideration of speech-groups in combination and of sub-groups. We would refer the reader to the works of Klinghardt and of Herzog mentioned in the Bibliography.

Chapter IV

ORTHOGRAPHY[1]

151. When the first documents in the vernacular were composed, the Latin alphabet was naturally employed. The spoken language had not yet evolved so far as to render the Latin orthographic symbols unsuitable, particularly as the pronunciation of Latin had by that time become contaminated by the vernacular. The earliest documents were written down by clerks who had hitherto written only Latin, and for them the phonetic equivalents of the Latin letters were no longer those of Classical but of Merovingian Latin. The Carolingian reforms affected orthography and syntax much more than pronunciation, and Latin continued to be pronounced more or less like French: thus the orthographic confusion between *i* and *e* might be to a large extent eliminated by these reforms, but *c* before *e* and *i* continued to be pronounced as *ts*. Consequently, we shall find that *e* and *i* are identified in Old French spelling with the corresponding vowel sounds, while *c* remains an ambiguous symbol.

152. The adaptation of the Latin alphabet presented more difficult problems in the case of the new sounds that had developed in the vernacular. The earliest monument (the *Strasburg Oaths*, Extr. No. 1) illustrates the difficulties with which a scribe accustomed to Latin was faced. The scribe of this document is sometimes content to employ the Latin word (*pro* 3, *quid* 7, *nunquam* 7, *in damno sit* 8), quite apart from Learned (*christian* 3) and semi-Learned (*sagrament* 11) forms, or to employ traditional (etymological) symbols for new sounds (*cist* 5 = *cest*, *int* 13 = *ent*), incorrect *i* for *e* (*prindrai* 7). He adopts an imperfect notation for diphthongs (*savir, podir* 4 for *saveir, podeir*) or keeps the traditional spelling

[1] In addition to the works mentioned in the Bibliography, cf. particularly Meyer-Lübke, *Hist. fr. Gram.* I, ch. 3.

(*poblo* 3, *meon* 8, *vol* 8); but cf. *dreit* 6, *plaid* 7, *pois* 13. He is obviously at a loss over the new sound *ə* (*nostro* 3, *salvarai* 5, *fradre* 5, *fradra* 6, *suo* 12), and makes a hesitating use of *dh* to indicate the fricative *ḍ*, a stage which the intervocal dental had by this time reached (*ajudha* 5, *cadhuna* 6, *Ludher* 7; cf. *podir* 4, *fradre* 5). The change *kj* > *ts* is recorded in *fazet* 7, *p* > *v* in *savir* 4. Consequently, the linguistic interpretation of this document, which shows in general an archaizing tendency, bristles with difficulties; e.g. the interpretation of *dunat* 5, *conservat* 11 as Presents, and of *jurat* 11 as a Preterite, depends largely on the evidence furnished by the corresponding German version of the Oaths.

153. The manuscript of the *Eulalia* (Extr. No. 11) shows marked progress, and already the admirable orthography of the twelfth century is foreshadowed. The scribe is still often content with the Latin spelling (*rex* 12 = *reis*, *inimi* 3 = *enemi*), but makes interesting attempts to spell phonetically (*manatce* 8, *czo* 21, *lazsier* 24), and adopts *ch* as a symbol for *k* before *e*, *i* (*chi* 6, 12, *chielt* 13 = dialectal *kielt*, *chieef* 22 = dial. *kief*). The diphthongs, allowing for dialectal variations, are remarkably well noted (*bellezour* 2, *veintre* 3, *ruovet* 24, etc.).

154. The orthography of the literary texts (particularly *chansons de geste*) of the twelfth and thirteenth centuries is well-nigh as perfect as is possible with the Latin alphabet, and, all things considered, remarkably uniform. This uniformity presupposes the elaboration of rules and the careful training of scribes. Such evidence as we have suggests that the latter were trained, and transcribed their manuscripts, in the jongleurs' schools. As the works they transcribed were intended to be sung or recited, and not read, their orthography aims at rendering the spoken word and suggests auditory as opposed to visual images. They continue and improve upon the orthography of such works as the *Eulalia*, i.e. they eliminate from the Latin spelling those Latin letters which had ceased to be pronounced and employ existing symbols or combinations of symbols to render as phonetically as possible the new sounds (particularly diphthongs) which developed. They succeeded in creating a system of spelling which, while not perfect, corresponds more closely with the spoken language than at any subsequent stage in the history of the French language. This applies particularly to the standard literary language of about the middle of the twelfth century. It will be seen at once that its chief defect lies in the utilization of one symbol for a rather wide range of related sounds, or even for widely differing sounds. But this was inevitable, unless new symbols had been evolved.

155. Thus ẹ, ẹ, e (< A), ə were all denoted by a common symbol e. The ẹ which resulted from the reduction of ai continued to be denoted by ai, but also with growing frequency by e. The modern distinction between i and j, u and v, was (as in Latin) not observed. ü (< ū) was denoted by the traditional graphy u (v), but the same symbol was also used in Norman and Anglo-Norman for ǫ or u (< ǫ). Elsewhere ǫ was denoted by o, with a consequent confusion with o for ọ. The notation of diphthongs and triphthongs (ie, üi, ei (oi), ou, eau, ieu) was at first phonetic, but tended to become traditional and thus to represent an obsolete pronunciation: uö was rendered by ue (sometimes oe), representing the older pronunciation ue; öu was rendered by ou, later by eu; ai and au (where they persisted as diphthongs) and ou (< o + ł) were spelt ai, au, ou respectively. The nasalization of vowels and diphthongs (ĩ, ũ, ẽi, iẽ, õi, uẽ, üĩ) was not noted in spelling, except by a hesitating use of the doubling of medial m, n, and perhaps by the graphy ngn (n'). The change ẽ > ã is reflected in an extensive use of the phonetic spelling an (regularly employed in the manuscripts of Chrétien de Troyes' works; cf. Extr. No. VI), but tradition and an etymologizing tendency proved too strong: the etymological spelling (en) was preserved or restored in the majority of cases. The graphy an is frequently used as late as the seventeenth century (cf. XVIII b, 26; also XVI passim) and has survived in a number of words (sans, langue, etc.). In the same way the later change ãi > ẽi was only sporadically noted in spelling.

156. *ts* ($< k^i$ or $< tj$ after a consonant) was denoted by *c* (and when it became final by *z*), which had already received this value in Church Latin. In words where *ts* occurred before *a, o, u* (*ço* $<$ ECCE HOC), the use of *c* created ambiguity, which was sometimes obviated by the substitution of *ce* (after *e* had become mute), less frequently of *cz* (cf. *czo* in the *Eulalia*, 21). *ts* ($< t + s$ or $<$ *sts* or $< s$ after *l′, n′, nn*) was denoted by *z* (*amez, oz* $<$ HOSTES, *vielz, poinz, anz*). *tš* ($< k^a$ or $< pj$) was denoted by *ch*, a graphy in which *h* originally rendered the aspirate quality of Greek χ and later served to indicate the fricative quality of palatalized *k*. The graphy *ch* has been preserved throughout all the subsequent changes $k′ > tš > š$. *dž* ($< g^a$ or $< bj, mj, vj$) was denoted by *g* before following *e, i*, by *j* (and sometimes by *g*) in other cases, in conformity with traditional spelling (GENTEM $>$ *gent*, JAM $>$ *ja*). *l′* was denoted by *ill* (*il* or *ill* when final), the *i* serving to indicate the palatal element. *n′* was denoted by *gn, ign, ngn*; *gn* being traditional in such words as *legne* $<$ LIGNA, *i* (of *ign*) rendering the palatal element, *n* (of *ngn*) probably indicating nasalization. The semi-consonant *j* is rendered by *i* (*j*), which, as we have seen, also renders *i* and *dž*. *v* is rendered by *u* (*v*), which also renders *ü* and *u*; to obviate this confusion *o* was sporadically employed for initial *u* (vowel) in such words as *oeil, oef*, and later an *h* was occasionally prefixed, as in *huis* (to distinguish *uis* from *vis*); *vu* is often denoted by *w*. *w* was rendered by *u* in the groups *qu* and *gu* ($<$ Germ. *w*), and when the labial element disappeared (cf. § 103) *qu* became a symbol for *k*, *gu* being preserved as a graphy for hard *g* before *e, i* (*guerre*).

157. *y* (as a graphy for *i*) was at first sparingly used and confined to Learned words. *x* (or a symbol interpreted as *x*) was frequently employed as an abbreviation for final *us* (*animax, Dex*), but as early as the twelfth century it came to be considered as a variant of final *s*, and *u* was re-introduced (*animaux, Dieux*). Subsequently *x* was extended to many plurals (§ 185). *h* had ceased to have any phonetic value in Latin, but continued to be used fitfully by scribes, sometimes contrary to traditional spelling (*hermite, hermine*).

It was also adopted as a graphy for the aspirate *h* of words borrowed from Germanic (*heaume, hameau*).

158. The etymologizing and Latinizing tendency of scribes is further seen in the fluctuating use of double consonants beside the more common (and phonetic) single consonant.[1] In the case of *s, r, m, n*, this doubling had however a phonetic significance. Intervocal *ss* served to distinguish voiceless *s* from voiced *s* (=z). In the earlier documents *rr* is generally kept in conformity with etymology and represents a survival of double *r* (i.e. a more prolonged vibration) in speech; but exceptions are numerous (cf. § 337). The common doubling of *m* and *n* probably serves to indicate nasalization (cf. § 78).

159. The imperfections of this system are due to economy in the use of symbols (the same symbol being used to denote a variety of sounds) and to traditionalism. Adherence to the traditional symbol means that when phonetic evolution has caused two originally distinct sounds to coalesce, orthography has at its disposal two symbols for the same sound (*en : an*, *g : i (j), ai : e*, etc.). By a discriminating use of such alternative spellings homonyms may be distinguished to the eye, but so long as works were written to be sung or recited such a distinction was of little consequence.

160. The system we have described represents on the whole an admirable adaptation of traditional symbols to the purposes of phonetic notation. But with the elaboration of a more or less standardized usage there came into being a new tradition, to which French orthography has practically adhered ever since. Subsequent changes in pronunciation are but rarely indicated, and even before the end of the Old French period orthography had ceased to be phonetic in many respects. The reduction of *öu* and *uö* to the monophthong *ö* is not indicated; and *eu*, less frequently *ue, oeu, ueu*, continued to be used as symbols for this sound. After the reduction of *ou* to *u* in such forms as *mout* (< *molt*), *escouter* (< *escolter*), a new graphy (*ou*) was available and was gradually

---

[1] This fluctuation is a characteristic feature of Anglo-Norman (cf. Extr. No. v); but cf. also No. XII, notes.

adopted in order to distinguish *u* from *ü*. The hesitation between the graphies *o* and *ou* reflects a corresponding hesitation in pronunciation (cf. §§ 65–6). The change *ei* > *oi* brought with it a corresponding orthographic change, but the subsequent evolution of *oi* was not indicated, except for an occasional use of *oe* or *oue* to render *we̜* (cf. §§ 72–4). The reduction of diphthongs to a combination of semi-consonant + vowel is likewise not indicated (*pied, lui*). The graphies *c, ch, z, g, i* (*j*) continued to be used after the elimination of the dental element (*t*)*s*, (*t*)*š*, (*d*)*z*, (*d*)*ž*. Pre-consonantal *s*, although mute, was retained in spelling. *ai* was generally restored wherever it was the etymological equivalent of *e̜* (*fait* is preferred to *fet*). Final unsupported *t* was retained long after it had ceased to be pronounced. Although *l* had been vocalized to *u* before a consonant, it continued to be used freely to denote the new sound, sometimes in addition to the new sound (*moult*), occasionally for *u* not resulting from *l* (*nevolz* for *nevouz* (< NEPOTES) in the *Roland*, 2420). The reduction of final *ts* to *s* is not regularly noted by *s* (for older *z*).

161. A number of archaic spellings were thus perpetuated, but the rapid deterioration of orthography from the fourteenth century onwards is due above all to the introduction of superfluous letters. These are of two kinds: (1) Letters introduced by analogy (*vifs* for *vis* ≠ *vif*, *perds* for *perz*, *pers* ≠ *perdent*, etc.). These were common in the Old French period but became more and more numerous in Middle French and led to such spellings as *animaulx*, in which *l* (or *u* < *l*) is represented by *u*, by *l*, and by *x* (= *us*). (2) Etymological letters introduced under the influence of the Latin etymon (real or supposed). Such letters are comparatively rare in Old French (e.g. *corps* in the *Eulalia*, 2). With the revival of interest in the Ancients and the translation of Latin works, such spellings rapidly increased. The passage from a literature intended to be sung or recited to one intended for reading is a decisive factor, for the aim of the scribe is no longer to suggest an auditory but a visual image, to invest the word with a form which shall individualize it. The norm is no longer provided by

the scribes of the *chansons de geste* but by those charged with
the engrossing of legal charters and documents, and with the
transcription of works of a more learned or didactic character.
It is a mistake to ascribe the introduction of etymological
letters to scholars and pedants.[1]

162. The development of French orthography from the
fourteenth century onwards is determined almost entirely
by the preponderant rôle of the legal fraternity and particularly of the lawyers' clerks. The development of the royal
courts and of numerous other jurisdictions (ecclesiastical,
baronial, etc.) and the introduction of written procedure
rapidly multiplied the number of documents of all kinds.
A modern brief is a mere bagatelle beside the mountains of
depositions, indictments, rebuttals, judgments, and reports
which an insignificant case involved in medieval procedure.
This incredible mass of documents, ranging from mere scrawls
to carefully engrossed documents, was the work of the vast
community of lawyers' clerks employed at Paris and elsewhere. The clerks were not only numerous, they formed a
powerful order, of which the most important community was
the Basoche of Paris with its king, its constitutional rules, and
a power analogous to that of a modern trade-union. It
was from among their number that the court-officers and
magistrates were recruited. The majority of the outstanding
writers (Jean de Meun and many others) were clerks or connected with the law, and in the sixteenth century such writers
as Calvin and Rabelais were brought up in a legal atmosphere
and naturally adopted the orthography of the clerks. In this
way it received an added weight of authority. It is probable
that the majority of scribes from 1300 onwards were clerks.

163. The considerations and principles which guided the
clerks (*praticiens*) were of a mixed kind. They wrote under
the general supervision of the magistrates. The latter were

---

[1] Reference to the Extracts (Appendix A) will show that etymological
spellings are already very common in the *Quinze Joyes de Mariage* (No.
XIII). They are most numerous in Rabelais (No. XIV), after which they
show a steady decline (Nos. XV–XVIII).

concerned to establish a more or less traditional usage and to bring orthography (and to some extent pronunciation) into line with Latin, which was still used for certain purposes and persisted as a barbarous *lingua franca* until standard French came to be generally used throughout France. As in earlier times, the influence of Latin orthography was all the more potent in that the Latin in use before the Renaissance was a sort of Latinized French, intelligible to the poorest scholar. The introduction of superfluous letters provided a means of distinguishing homonyms and was encouraged for this reason also. Thus we find the clerks applying more or less consciously the two principles which M. Beaulieux calls the principle of 'rapprochement' and the principle of 'differentiation'. The former aims at securing a similarity of form as between words which are etymologically related or associated by analogy of some kind or other: *mes* comes to be written *mets* under the influence of *mettre*; *les* or *lais* (verbal substantive of *laisser*) becomes *legs* under the influence of LEGATUM, to which it is only related semantically; similarly *pois* (< PENSUM, supine of PENDERE) becomes *poids* under the influence of PONDUS (a mistaken etymology). The principle of differentiation, which seeks to distinguish homonyms, may operate at the same time, as was undoubtedly the case in all three examples cited above: *legs* is distinguished by its spelling from *lai, lait, lais, laie*; *mets* from *mai, maie, mais*; *poids* from *pois, poix*. Practical considerations decide, and the principle of differentiation is normally applied only if the homonyms are likely to be confused owing to similarity of meaning or function.

164. The introduction of superfluous letters is also prompted by a desire to give more body to words which the process of phonetic erosion had reduced, in some cases almost to the vanishing-point. But in this direction the scribes were clearly actuated by a less worthy motive, the desire for gain. As they were paid by quantity they proceeded with characteristic lack of scruple to write an excessively large and sprawling hand. A check was placed upon this by specifying the

number of words per page, and the redundancy of many legal formulae is doubtless due in part at least to the efforts of scribes to counter this regulation. Then instructions were issued prescribing the number of lines per page and the number of letters per line, but the scribes were equal to the occasion: they fell back upon such spellings as *animaulx*, *genoulx*, etc. It is in such hands that fate left the elaboration of the orthography which was to remain authoritative throughout the fifteenth and sixteenth centuries and which Modern French perpetuates to a large extent. Behind it was the whole weight of the law, so imposing at that time. And this weight was concentrated at the Capital, in the Parlement, the Palais, and the Châtelet (to which were attached the Basoche and kindred corporations). It is through them that the orthography (and to some extent the pronunciation of the Capital) was extended to the provincial courts and to the provinces in general.

165. As might be expected, this orthography is uniform in its general aspect, the same in literary works as in legal documents throughout France, but in detail it is far from regular and uniform. There is little attempt to spell phonetically. Calligraphic considerations outweigh the orthographic: *x* continued to be treated as a variant for final *s*; *z* was often retained, although the group *ts* which it denoted had been reduced to *s*; it became an archaic variant of final *s* and was favoured as such. *y* as a variant of final *i* had an extraordinary vogue, being favoured because it served to indicate more clearly the division of words in the sprawling calligraphy of the scribes and stood out more clearly from neighbouring *m*, *n*, *u*; moreover it was more ornate and occupied more space. Changes in pronunciation since the twelfth century are ignored: the reduction of *ie* to *e* (*mangier* > *manger*) is one of the few changes which gradually find expression. The graphy *sc* for *ss*, which is found as early as the thirteenth century, is much favoured, particularly in the suffix *-esce* (for *-esse*) and initially, where association with Latin is sometimes partly responsible (*scavoir* for *savoir* (< *SAPÉRE) by association with SCIRE?). The influence of Latin is also to be seen in such spellings as *pauvre* for *povre*, *aile* ₁or *ele* (< ALA), *clair* for *cler* (< CLARUM). But the most striking feature is the use of superfluous letters which the introduction of many Learned words fostered and whose number was slightly increased by scholars and humanists of the sixteenth century (*dipner* for *di(s)ner* by association with δειπνεῖν).

166. The first attempts at reform date from the sixteenth century and are indirectly inspired by the revival of learning. The reform of Latin pronunciation, while not completely successful, resulted in the restoration of a great many sounds that had disappeared from pronunciation but not from spelling. The close correspondence between spelling and pronunciation which Latin now presented roused a number of scholars to emulation: they aimed at reforming French spelling so that it too might reflect accurately the sounds of the spoken language; but the force of tradition, the tendency to Latinism, and practical considerations proved too strong. The most influential of them, Robert Estienne, abandoned his early ideas of reform in favour of a thoroughly conservative attitude, and in the successive editions of his famous *Dictionaire françois-latin* (1539 ff.) he simply adopts the orthography of the *praticiens*. His authority was sufficient to defeat the advocates of phonetic systems of spelling (Meigret, etc.), whose cause was moreover weakened by their own lack of consistency and the multiplicity of their systems. More fortunate were the discreet attempts of Ronsard and his disciples to simplify spelling, to distinguish *i* and *j*, *u* and *v*. Their reforms were in part abandoned by their own authors but largely adopted by the Dutch printers (Plantin, the Elzevirs) who, in the seventeenth century, flooded the country with their books, and gradually accustomed the public to a more simplified system. The cause of reform found many protagonists in the seventeenth century. The Précieuses favoured a simpler and more phonetic orthography; the process of simplification went on but slowly, in spite of the insistent demands of various writers and grammarians and the bold reforms suggested by Richelet (1680), e.g. *acord, receu, mélancolie*. In the course of the century a large number of superfluous letters were eliminated; but spelling remained for the most part an academic question, and the practice of such cultured persons as Mme de Sévigné reveals an amazing irregularity, one may almost say a sovereign contempt for the minutiae of spelling. The printer was generally left free to adopt the orthography he thought fit.

167. The history of the diacritic signs shows the same hesitation. The cedilla, apostrophe, tréma, hyphen, circumflex and grave accents were unknown in the Middle Ages; the acute accent was occasionally used to indicate the tonic stress, more frequently to show that two contiguous vowels are to be pronounced separately, or to distinguish *i* from contiguous *m, n, u, v*; sometimes it was placed over monosyllabic *a* (HABET), *u* (AUT), etc. All of these signs began to be used by grammarians and printers in the sixteenth century. The acute accent was first used by Robert Estienne in his *Dictionarium* (1530) to distinguish final *ę* from *ɞ* The cedilla (originally a small *z*) was borrowed from the Spanish by Geoffrey Tory (1530), but its use did not become general until much later: *cz, ce* or *s* were commonly used in the sixteenth century (for modern *ç*). The grave accent was sparingly used (*à, là*), although theorists employed it for a variety of purposes (e.g. to denote *ɞ*). The apostrophe (to indicate elision) was introduced by Geoffrey Tory (1529), the tréma (to indicate diæresis) and the circumflex accent (to indicate contraction) by Sylvius (1532), the hyphen by Montflory (1538); the apostrophe was frequently employed where Modern French preserves *e* (*un' heure*, etc.; cf. Extr. No. XVI, 21, 25, 28). The general adoption of these diacritic signs (and the rejection of many others) was long delayed, and throughout the sixteenth century both theory and practice show hesitation. Thus Ronsard began by making a liberal use of accents and of the tréma, but later returned more or less to the practice of Robert Estienne. The Dutch printers were largely responsible for the more extensive and regular

use of diacritic signs. Pierre Corneille was the first to advocate
the use of the grave accent to indicate the open quality of
e (*è*), but his example was not followed. We print in Appendix A an extract from Molière and two Fables of La Fontaine
which will serve to illustrate the usage of seventeenth-century
printers. It will be seen that the acute accent continued to
be used sparingly in pre-tonic syllables, that the grave accent
is almost confined to the particles *à*, *où*, *là*, and that *-és* still
alternates with *-ez*. It is significant that *s* before a consonant
is generally preserved, but that a circumflex accent on the
preceding vowel takes its place wherever the space thus saved
will avoid running over into the next line. The stroke over
a vowel to mark the omission of a following *m* or *n* is also
used for the same purpose. The distinction between *i* and *j*,
u and *v* is not regularly observed by printers, although it had
been recognized as desirable and partly applied in the sixteenth century. The tréma is often used to distinguish vocalic *u* from consonantal *u* (= *v*).

168. When the first edition of its Dictionary appeared
(1694), the Academy had not yet become the court of appeal
in matters orthographical. Its spelling is decidedly archaic
and continues the tradition of Estienne, only grudgingly
admitting some of the reforms of Ronsard and the Dutch
printers, with some of the simplifications which had taken
place in general usage. It favours the retention of superfluous
letters which serve to distinguish homonyms, less consistently
those which have a purely etymological significance. Thus it
suppresses *l* in such words as *au(l)tre*, but keeps it in *aulne*,
aulx, *faulx*, *faulcher*, *pouls*, *poultre*; suppresses *c* in *poin(c)t*,
effe(c)t, *droi(c)t*, *frui(c)t*, but keeps it in *contract*, *oinct*, *prefect*;
keeps *t* before *s* (*enfants*, *innocents*) contrary to general usage;
efuses to sanction the suppression of *s* before a consonant
and the graphy *-és* for *-ez*, but adopts the circumflex accent
to denote contractions of the type *seur—sûr*, and the distinction between *i* and *j*, *u* and *v*.

169. The rationalistic grammarians and philosophers of
the eighteenth century naturally reacted against the illogicali-

ties and contradictions of traditional orthography. The private practice of even the most cultured persons still shows a contempt for regularity and consistency in spelling, but printed works show a gradual elimination of capricious and redundant graphies. The Academy, guided by the progressive abbé d'Olivet, sanctions a number of important reforms in the third edition of its Dictionary (1740). Many superfluous letters are dropped (*de(b)voir, a(d)vocat, v(u)ider*, etc.) and many double consonants, which had ceased to have a phonetic value, are simplified; *t* is suppressed between *n* and *s* (*enfans, innocens*), and *i* replaces *y*, except where the latter is equivalent to *ij* (*payer*) or is etymological. Pre-consonantal *s* is replaced by the circumflex accent on the preceding vowel (by the acute on pre-tonic *e*), and the grave accent is allowed to share with the device of doubling the following consonant (*appelle*) the rôle of indicating open *e* (*gèle*). The fourth edition (1762) replaces *-ez* by *-és* in the plurals of substantives and participles; archaic *z* thus remains in the 2nd pers. plural ending *-ez* and in a few words where it is etymologically unjustified: *nez* (< NASUM), *chez* < *ch(i)es(e)* (< CASA).

170. In the nineteenth century spelling became standardized and personal caprice was eliminated: not to spell in accord with established usage is interpreted as ignorance. The Academy became the recognized authority. It has maintained its conservative attitude, the most noteworthy decisions being those embodied in its sixth edition (1835). These include the restoration of *t* between *n* and *s* (*enfants, innocents*) except in *gens* (which no longer has a singular) and the adoption of *ai* for *oi* wherever it had become *ę*. The latter 'reform' had been advocated by Nicolas Berain in his *Nouvelles Remarques sur la langue françoise* (1675) and taken up by Voltaire, who carried it through in his *Siècle de Louis XIV*. The seventh edition (1878) brought a few minor changes of the type *rythme* for *rhythme*, the suppression of the hyphen between *très* and the following adjective or adverb, the substitution of *-ège* for *-ége* (*privilège*).

171. French orthography thus remains essentially tradi-

tional, very few graphies being strictly phonetic. The same sound or group of sounds may be rendered in a variety of ways: *ö* by *eu*, *œu*, *ue*; *pẽ* by *pain*, *peins*, *peint*, *pin*. One and the same symbol may serve to render a variety of sounds: *g* = *g* in *grand*, = *ž* in *gens*, = *k* in *sang impur*, and has no value in *doigt*, *poing*, *bourg*, etc., while *gn* = *n'* in Popular words (*vigne*) and = *gn* in Learned words (*stagnant*); *u* = *ü* in *une*, = *ẅ* in *lui*, = *w* in *aquarelle*, = *ǫ* in *album*, and has no value in *qui*, *gui*, etc. The feminine of *pǝti* is *pǝtit*, yet the latter is distinguished from the former by adding an *e* to the purely orthographic *t* of the masculine form. The majority of words show one or more letters which have no value: the seven letters of *agneaux* render three sounds *an'ǫ*. To sum up, Modern French orthography presents on the one hand symbols which correspond to the pronunciation of the twelfth century, and on the other a host of letters introduced by the *praticiens* of the Middle French period. The 'reforms' of the modern period have resulted in little more than a codifying and standardization of usage and the elimination of some of the more absurdly superfluous letters. The campaign in favour of a simpler and more rational system seemed on the point of yielding results at the beginning of the present century France, with its highly organized and centralized educational system and the Academy as the recognized authority, appeared to present particularly favourable conditions for such a reform. But the conservatism of the Academy and the forces of tradition and of those vested interests (printers and publishers) which oppose spelling reform in all countries, have hitherto proved too strong.

Chapter V

MORPHOLOGY AND SYNTAX

172. The present chapter deals with those linguistic devices (flexions, particles, word-order) which serve to present a concept in analytical form (cf. § 16). They may be considered from two points of view: (1) we may examine the means adopted by the language to render certain psychological categories, e.g. command, wish, possession, motion towards or from, place, present, past, future; (2) we may examine the meaning conveyed or function performed by the devices the language possesses, e.g. the various functions of the preposition *de*, or of the subjunctive. Syntax is therefore not concerned merely with the grouping together of words to form sentences. It is concerned with such expressions as *John's hat* no less than with *John strikes Peter*, with SCRIBO (as a rendering of the concept of 'the speaker in the act of writing') or with ITE (as a rendering of the command to go) no less than with CURRIT PUER or FILIA MATREM AMAT. The study of flexions thus comes within the scope of syntax, and the flexions are themselves based upon syntactic relations; e.g. the Latin accusative ending -M is a regularized mode of indicating the direct object.

The history of the French language consists largely in the abandonment of flexions in favour of particles and word-order, in the passage from a synthetic to an analytic language. This movement had begun in Vulgar Latin and is in part consequent upon phonetic changes, which progressively eliminated or reduced flexional distinctions. Thus, to repair the havoc created by phonetic erosion in the declensions, the language had recourse, not to the creation of new case-endings, but to the utilization of particles. Classical Latin had already made a liberal use of prepositions (DE, AB, AD) to denote relations which were not indicated clearly enough by case-endings, or to make finer distinctions than could be made by case-endings alone. Such uses were greatly extended by analogy, but the rapid acceleration of the movement must be attributed to new modes of thought, a demand for greater expressiveness and explicitness. Thus CANTABIT gave place to CANTARE HABET (§ 281), not merely because CANTABIT and CANTAVIT had in pronunciation coalesced, but because CANTARE HABET renders the future in a more explicit, expressive way (cf. Mod.F. *je vais chanter* for *je chanterai*). The ultimate result has been that in modern spoken French the place of the flexions has been largely taken by particles (pronouns and prepositions): sing. *lə garsõ*, pl. *lę garsõ*; 1st sing. *žə dǫn*, 2nd sing. *tü dǫn*; but the two devices are often used side by side: *lə žurnal, lę žurnọ; žə dǫn, nu dǫnõ*.

It is therefore obvious that the separate treatment of forms (Morphology) and use (Syntax) is artificial and that such a division is justified only by convenience. We have endeavoured to effect a partial compromise by combining both in one chapter.[1] For similar practical reasons we have included in the present chapter certain features (gender of substantives, formation of particles) which belong strictly speaking to Word-formation. The space at our disposal does not allow of more than the barest outline of syntactic developments. Certain syntactic devices (variations in stress, pitch, duration), which are so important in the spoken language, have had to be omitted almost entirely, and attention given primarily to literary usage, with only occasional references to popular speech. The latter continues the natural tendencies of the language and is less susceptible to the claims of logic, but in cases of conflict between mere tradition and logic it may prefer to follow the latter; in a word, it is a more natural form of speech-activity, one in which, now feeling, now logic, now tradition, determine the form of utterance.

[1] The Old French forms given in the paradigms are normally those of the early twelfth century.

A. *SUBSTANTIVES AND ADJECTIVES*

SUBSTANTIVES

173. The Classical Latin case system was early reduced in Vulgar Latin. On the one hand phonetic changes (the elimination of *-m*, the confusion of unaccented *u* and *o*, *i* and *e*) obliterated the formal distinctions, and on the other the general analytical trend of the language led to the more extensive use of prepositions to indicate syntactic relations. In Gaul the genitive, dative, ablative, and vocative disappeared in the Vulgar Latin period, leaving the nominative (which took over the functions of the vocative) and the accusative (which was sometimes used as a dative or genitive and was the case with which all prepositions were used). Old French presents a few survivals of the genitive plural (*gent paienor, tens ancienor* III, 1), but these forms had already become adjectival in function, if not in form. The genitive singular survived in *lundi* (LUNAE DIEM), *mardi* (MARTIS DIEM), *mercredi* (MERCURI DIEM), *jeudi* (JOVIS DIEM), *vendredi* (VENERIS DIEM), *samedi* (*SAMBATI DIEM); the ablative singular in the adverbial suffix *-ment* (MENTE) (cf. § 446).

174. The distribution of substantives as between the different declensions underwent a series of changes. Those of the Fourth Declension were assimilated to the more numerous substantives of the Second (CANTUS, FRUCTUS, PORTUS). Those of the Fifth were absorbed by the First (*GLACIA, *FACIA, *RABIA for GLACIES, FACIES, RABIES), with the exception of a few which passed to the Third (FIDES, RES). Neuter substantives in -U(M), whether of the Second or Fourth, generally became masculine substantives of the Second (*FERRUS, *AURUS, *CASTELLUS, *CORNUS; also *CAPUM (> *chief*) for CAPUT, whence *CAPUS (> *chiés*)); neuter substantives of the Third likewise became masculine (PIPER, COR, FEL, NOMEN). But the neuter plural in -A was often used in a collective sense and treated as a feminine substantive of the First Declension: FOLIA (> *feuille*), GAUDIA (> *joie*), LABRA (> *lèvre*) Occasionally the singular persists as a masculine substantive alongside of such forms: O.F. *feuil* beside *feuille*, *cervel* (*cerveau*) beside *cervelle*, *grain* beside *graine*. Neuter substantives in -s (TEMPUS) survive in Old French as indeclinable substantives (*tens*); other neuter substantives of the Third (FLUMEN, NOMEN) joined the *murs* Class in Old French.

175. Analogical influences were responsible for a further reduction before the end of the Vulgar Latin period. The feminine plural in -AS came to be used for the nominative (-AE) as well, perhaps by analogy with the singular, where the nominative and accusative were identical (PORTA : PORTA(M) : : *PORTAS : PORTAS). The nominative plural of masculine substantives of the Third Declension was remodelled on the analogy of the Second, whence *PATRI for PATRES ≠MURI. The nominative singular of those imparisyllabic substantives in which the accent remains on the same syllable throughout (MONS, MONTEM) was remodelled on the accusative, by analogy with parisyllabics (CANIS, CANEM), whence *MONTIS (> *monz*). Feminine substantives of the Third which have -s in the nominative singular tended to be assimilated to the more numerous substantives of the First, the nominative being re-modelled on the accusative (cf. §178).

OLD FRENCH DECLENSIONS

176. Old French maintains to a large extent the simplified flexional system of Vulgar Latin. This is due in the main to the preservation of final *s* (cf. § 101), which enabled the distinction between the nominative and accusative to be kept. It would probably have disappeared, had it not been for the development of a literary tradition and the important rôle played by the schools of Gaul (cf. § 182).

Old French substantives fall into the following classes:

177.   MASCULINES

CLASS I

	Sing.	Pl.
Nom.	murs	mur
Obl.	mur	murs

This class includes:

(a) Substantives in -US of the Second Declension (including V.L. accessions; § 174).

(b) Masculine parisyllabics with nom. sing. in -S (PANIS> *pains*), and re-modelled imparisyllabics, of the Third Declension (*MONTIS > *monz*; § 175).

(c) Neuter substantives in -U(M), -R (*chastels, cuers*).

CLASS II

	Sing.	Pl.
Nom.	*pedre*	*pedre*
Obl.	*pedre*	*pedres*

This class includes:

(a) Substantives in -ER of the Second Declension (MAGISTER > *maistre*).

(b) Masculine parisyllabics of the Third Declension which did not have -s in the nom. sing. (PATER > *pedre*).

178.   FEMININES

CLASS I

	Sing.	Pl.
Nom.	*porte*	*portes*
Obl.	*porte*	*portes*

This class comprises feminine substantives in -A of the First Declension (including V.L. accessions; § 174).

CLASS II

	Sing.	Pl.
Nom.	*flor(s)*	*flors*
Obl.	*flor*	*flors*

Here belong feminine substantives of the Third Declension (including those which passed from the Fifth to the Third in V.L.; § 174). This class differs from Feminine Class I in that the nom. sing. in -*s*, which is etymological in many substantives (LEX, FIDES, FINIS), is common in twelfth-century French (regular in Chrétien de Troyes). In the thirteenth

century such nominatives in -*s* are still found (x, 3), but they
disappear in the fourteenth. It is not clear whether -*s* here
represents a survival of the Latin ending or is due to the
influence of masculine substantives of the *murs—mur* type,
where *s* is the distinctive sign of the nom. sing. If the former
is the correct explanation, then the absence of the *s* in early
Old French may be attributed to the influence of the more
numerous feminine substantives of Class I, which make no
distinction between the nominative and the oblique case.

IMPARISYLLABICS

179. The phonetic development of substantives which
present a varying number of syllables in the nominative and
accusative, and which had not been re-modelled (cf. § 175),
created a distinction which affects the stem no less than the
ending. Those in which the accent remained on the same
syllable had mostly been re-modelled (**MONTIS* for MONS), but
in a few the original nominative persisted. Feminine imparisyllabics are, by the elimination of the nominative,
assimilated to Class II, with the exception of SOROR.

WITH FIXED ACCENT

	Sing.		Pl.	
Nom.	(*h*)*om*,	*cuens*	(*h*)*ome*,	*conte*
Obl.	(*h*)*ome*,	*conte*	(*h*)*omes*,	*contes*

WITH SHIFTING ACCENT

	Sing.	Pl.
Nom.	*emperedre*	*emperedor*
Obl.	*emperedor*	*emperedors*

Similarly: *abes—abét, abét—abez*; *ber—baron, baron—barons*;
compaing—compaignon, compaignon—compaignons; *enfes—enfant,
enfant—enfanz*; *fel—felon, felon—felons*; *niés—nevot, nevot—
nevoz*; *sendre—seignor, seignor—seignors*; *prestre—proveidre, proveidre—proveidres*; and one feminine: *suer—soror, sorors—sorors*.
A further series of masculine imparisyllabics in -O, -ONEM
and -US, -ONEM, arose in Vulgar Latin with the Latinization of

Germanic names: *Hüe* (HUGO)—*Hüon* (HUGONEM); *Otes*—
Oton; *Naimes*—*Naimon*. The analogous formation of Vulgar
Latin feminine substantives in -A, -ANEM may be due to the
influence of such forms: *none*—*nonain, nonains*; *Eve*—*Evain*.

INDECLINABLES

180. Parisyllabic substantives whose stem ends in *s* are
thereby precluded from preserving the distinction between
the nominative and accusative, and are in Old French indeclinable: *cors, meis, pais, piz* (< PECTUS), *tens, voiz*.

181. The distinctive feature of the Old French declension
of substantives is the preservation of -*s*, and this was accentuated by the change which its presence sometimes
brought about in the final consonant of the stem:

s combined with *d, t, st*, to give *ts* (graphy *z*): *piez*—*piéṭ*;
escuz—*escuṭ, oz* (HOSTES)—*ost* (HOSTEM).

s > *ts* (graphy *z*) under the influence of preceding *l', n'*
(which were depalatalized) or *n* (< MN, NN): *uelz* later *ieus*,
veux—*ueil* or *oeil*; *poinz*—*poing*; *danz* (DOMINUS)—*dan*; *anz*—*an*.
rns > *rz*: *jorz*—*jorn*.

Before *s* of the ending, *f, p, c* disappear: *bues*—*buef*; *cols,
cous*—*colp, coup*; *sas*—*sac*; while *ł* (< *l* or *l'*) is vocalized to *u*:
chevaus—*cheval*.

182. The flexional system outlined above began to dis-
integrate in the course of the twelfth century, and that it
should have done so at such an early date may be due to
the fact that it had been in some measure artificially maintained. The first sign of disintegration is the uncertainty in
the use of the flexional -*s* which distinguished the nom. sing.
of most masculine substantives and was fitfully maintained
in certain feminine substantives (cf. § 178). Masculine substantives of Class II tend to be assimilated to Class I, often
adding *s* in the nom. sing. (*peḍres, freres*, etc.); and the same
tendency may be observed in imparisyllabics (*compainz, bers,
empereres*, etc.). This uncertainty in the use of flexional -*s* was
one of a number of factors which led early to a con.usion

of the nominative and the oblique forms, and the elimination
of the two-case system. In fact, the Old French two-case system appears as a momentary stabilization of the process which
tended naturally to the complete elimination of flexions and
to the development of a purely analytic language. Syntactic
influences, therefore, combine with phonetic developments
(e.g. the tendency of final *s* to become mute before a word
beginning with a consonant) to make it increasingly difficult
to maintain the cases. The distinction of form gradually gives
place to a distinction which depends entirely on the place
of the words in the sentence and upon auxiliary devices, such
as prepositions. The impersonal *on* alone preserves the distinction of form, in that it can only be used as the subject
of a sentence, whereas *homme* (like other accusatives) has
become generalized. The confusion of the nominative and
the oblique case sometimes took the form of a substitution
of the former for the latter (*filz, fils* for *fil*), but as the oblique
form was far more frequently used and as flexional *s* tended
in any case to become mute, it is as a rule the oblique (accusative) case that has survived.

183. Old French nominative forms survive in a few words,
generally terms in frequent use as subjects or vocatives, or
preserved in fixed locutions: *ancêtre, chantre, copain* (for *com-
pain*, nom. of *compagnon*), *fils, gars* beside *garçon* (acc.), *on*
beside *homme* (acc.), *pâtre* beside Learned *pasteur, peintre,
prêtre, queux, sire* (< *SEIOR) beside *sieur* (< *SEIOREM); proper
names: *Louis, Charles, Jacques, Georges*. The nom. *suer, sœur*
(< SOROR), owing to its frequent use as a vocative, survived
at the expense of *soror* (< SOROREM) and gave rise to a new
plural *suers* (*sœurs*); *nonne* and *nonnain, pute* and *putain* have
survived as independent substantives.

184. While the two-case system was fairly well maintained in Central French throughout the twelfth century, it
had broken down more or less completely in Anglo-Norman
by 1200. In the course of the thirteenth century, Central
French too tends more and more to eliminate the nominative,
and by the end of the fourteenth the oblique form is general-

ized. Nominative forms continue to be used, but with little regard to the morphological value of flexional -*s*. This can be clearly seen from Villon's attempt to write a *Ballade en vieil françoys*.

185. By the beginning of the fifteenth century the case distinction had completely disappeared, and there remained only the distinction between singular and plural. This too disappeared when final *s* became mute, and survives only in those substantives which show a modification of the final consonant before -*s* (*animal—animaux*) or in liaison with a word beginning with a vowel (cf. § 135). In all other words the distinction of form is maintained only in spelling, and number can only be indicated in the spoken language by the form of the determinant (definite article, etc.), or by the context. The number of substantives which show a modification of the stem in the plural has been substantially reduced (*a*) by the re-modelling of the plural on the singular: *bals* for O.F. *baux*, pl. of *bal*; *conseils* for O.F. *conseus*, pl. of *conseil*; or, less frequently, the reverse: *genou* for O.F. *genoil*, pl. *genoux*; *chou* for O.F. *chol*, pl. *choux*. (*b*) by the preservation or restoration in spelling of letters which had ceased to be sounded; this led in many cases to their being pronounced (cf. § 110 ff.): *coqs* for O.F. *cos*; *sacs* for O.F. *sas*; *chefs* for O.F. *ches*, *chiés*. These two influences account for such double forms as *cieux—ciels*, *aïeux—aïeuls* (with distinction of meaning); they are still operative and are responsible for the tendency observable in present-day French to pronounce *bœufs* as *bœf*, *œufs* as *œf* For the use of *x* as the sign of the plural, see § 157.

ADJECTIVES

186. As in substantives, the nominative case and accusative case alone survived. The case distinction disappeared regularly in the singular of fem. -A forms and by analogy in the fem. sing. of other adjectives (cf. the nom. sing. *grant* (GRANDIS), *fort* (FORTIS), etc.) except imparisyllabics, and the fem. pl. of all adjectives. The masc. nom. pl. of adjectives of

the Third Declension was re-modelled on the analogy of the
BONUS type, whence *GRANDI for GRANDES. The nom. sing. of
imparisyllabics was re-modelled on the accusative (*VALENTIS
for VALENS, O.F. *vaillanz*). The neuter survived only in the
singular, being used exclusively as the attribute of an impersonal subject. It is in form indistinguishable from the
masc. acc. Adjectives whose stem ends in -*s* naturally show
no case distinction (*bas, corteis, franceis, gros*). Adjectives
which in Latin had a common form for the masc. and fem.
early showed a tendency to pass into the more numerous
BONUS -A -UM class, and such forms as TRISTA, ACRA are
attested from the Vulgar Latin period.

187. Old French adjectives fall into the following classes:

CLASS I *a*

	Sing.			Pl.	
	Masc.	Fem.	Neuter	Masc.	Fem.
Nom.	*bons*	*bone*	*bon*	*bon*	*bones*
Obl.	*bon*			*bons*	

To this class conform all Latin adjectives in -US -A -UM. Those
which developed a supporting *ə* (cf. § 29) naturally make no
distinction between the masc. acc. sing. and the fem. sing.,
between the masc. acc. pl. and the fem. pl., e.g. *rade* (= RAPI-
DUM or RAPIDA(M))—*rades* (= RAPIDOS or RAPIDAS).

CLASS I *b*

	Sing.			Pl.	
	Masc.	Fem.	Neuter	Masc.	Fem.
Nom.	*tendre*	*tendre*	*tendre*	*tendre*	*tendres*
Obl.	*tendre*			*tendres*	

To this class belong adjectives of three terminations in -ER
(TENER TENERA TENERUM). They differ from those of Class I *a*
only in presenting no -*s* in the masc. nom. sing.

CLASS II

	Sing.			Pl.	
	Masc.	Fem.	Neuter	Masc.	Fem.
Nom.	*granz*	*grant*	*grant*	*grant*	*granz*
Obl.	*grant*			*granz*	

To this class belong adjectives which in Latin had a common form for the masc. and fem. (FORTIS, GRAVIS, MORTALIS), including re-modelled imparisyllabics of the Third Declension (*vaillanz*). The feature of this class is the absence of *-e* in the feminine, no distinction being made between the masc. acc. sing. and the fem. sing., between the masc. acc. pl. and the fem. pl. As in fem. substantives of Class II, an occasional *-s* is found in the fem. nom. sing. (*granz, forz*); cf. *laquex* XI, 53.

IMPARISYLLABICS

	Sing.			Pl.	
	Masc.	Fem.	Neuter	Masc.	Fem.
Nom.	*mieldre*	*mieldre*	*mielz*	*meillor*	*meillors*
Obl.	*meillor*	*meillor*		*meillors*	*meillors*

This class consists exclusively of those synthetic Comparatives which had survived (cf. § 192).

188. What has been said in the foregoing paragraphs on the hesitation in the use of flexional *-s* and on the breakdown of the two-case system applies with equal force to adjectives. In the twelfth and thirteenth centuries adjectives of the *tendre* type (Class I *b*) frequently take *s* in the masc. nom. sing., as do also adjectives of the *grant* type (Class II) in the fem. nom. sing. The nominative disappears about the end of the fourteenth century and with it the distinction between the neuter and masculine. The distinction of number is also largely obliterated, as in substantives. Phonetic changes brought about by *-s*, while it was still sounded, maintain such distinctions as *royal—royaux*, but re-modelling of the plural on the singular (or vice versa) and the influence of orthography have often obliterated them: *sec—secs* (O.F. *ses*); *vif—vifs* (O.F. *vis*); *nouveau* (O.F. *nouvel*)—*nouveaux*; *beau* (O.F. *bel*)—*beaux*; *fou* (O.F. *fol*)—*fous*; *mou* (O.F. *mol*)—*moux*; *vieux* (O.F. *vieil*)—*vieux*; the forms *nouvel*, etc. being preserved in Modern French only if the following word begins with a vowel (cf. § 135). The plural of adjectives in *-al* appears regularly as *-aux*, but in recent borrowings it is often formed from the singular by merely adding s (*finals, fatals*); sometimes there is hesitation between -*als* and what is instinctively felt to be the normal plural (-*aux*): *finaux* is rare; *nasaux* seems to have triumphed; sometimes the plural is simply avoided (*glacial*).

189. The majority of Old French adjectives showed feminine forms in -*e*, and even those which originally lacked -*e* (Class II) were gradually re-modelled on the BONUS (*bons*) type. This process began in Vulgar Latin (cf. § 186) and is reflected in *doux—douce* (O.F. *dolce* < *DULCIA*), *fol—folle, mol— molle, corteis—corteise*. An increasing number of adjectives take -*e* in the Old French and Middle French periods: *grande* (attested eleventh century), *forte, verte, tele, quele, brieve, grieve* (all attested twelfth century); adjectives in -*al*, -*el*, -*il*, -*eur*, and present participles used adjectivally: *mortelle, generale, vile, gentille, vaillante, puissante*. But the etymological forms without -*e* continue to be used throughout the fifteenth and to some extent in the sixteenth century; they survive to the present day in certain fossilized expressions and proper names: *grand'mère, grand'rue* (where the apostrophe is wrongly introduced to indicate the supposed loss of -*e*), *Rochefort, Villefort,* and the adverbs *prudemment* (< PRUDENTE + MENTE), *constamment, diligemment, éloquemment, patiemment,* etc. (cf. § 446).

190. In a certain number of adjectives of the BONUS (*bons*) type, the masculine was re-modelled on the feminine, and they were thus brought into line with those adjectives (*rade*; § 187) which had from the beginning a supporting *ə* in the masc. and therefore did not distinguish masc. and fem. in the oblique case: *large* (O.F. *larc*)—*large, triste* (O.F. *triz*)—*triste, roide* (O.F. *roit*)—*roide, vide* (O.F. *vuit*)—*vide, chauve* (O.F. *chauf*)—*chauve*. A determining factor was undoubtedly the excessive divergence in form between masc. and fem.; but the feminine was adopted also because it was the more sonorous form and in some cases found more support in the Latin cognate forms (LARGUS, TRISTIS, etc.).

191. There was thus a whole series of adjectives which did not permit of a distinction of gender. With the disappearance of final *ə* this threatened to become true of all adjectives, but

the development of the final consonant had in the meantime created a further differentiation which allowed of a distinction of gender without the articulation of *ə*. (*a*) The consonant had become final in the masc., but remained intervocal in the fem. down to the time when *ə* became mute, whence a twofold development in *vif—vive, sauf—sauve, neuf—neuve, actif—active, blanc—blanche, sec—sèche*; also, before the re-modelling of the masc., *larc—large*, etc. (§ 190). O.F. *francesche* (FRANCISCA), *longe* (LONGA) were re-modelled on the masc. *franceis, lonc* (later *long*). (*b*) The disappearance from pronunciation of final consonants (§§ 125–31) coincided more or less with the disappearance of *ə*; the efforts made to maintain the latter, and its persistence in spelling, saved the preceding consonant from extinction and at the same time preserved the open quality of the tonic vowel. Feminine *-e* is in Modern French a mere graphic device indicating that the preceding consonant is pronounced and, in certain cases, that the preceding vowel is open. This function is shared to some extent by such devices as the doubling of the consonant and the use of accents: sǫ (*sot*)—sǫt (*sotte*), bõ (*bon*)—bǫn (*bonne*), bɑ (*bas*)—bɑːs (*basse*), ɛpɛ (*épais*)—ɛpɛːs (*épaisse*), ru (*roux*)—rus (*rousse*), žãti (*gentil*)—žãtiːj (*gentille*), lõ (*long*)—lõːg (*longue*), pəti (*petit*)—pətit (*petite*), grã (*grand*)—grãːd (*grande*), dɛrnjɛ (*dernier*)—dɛrnjɛːr (*dernière*), süžɛ (*sujet*)—süžɛt (*sujette*), kõplɛ (*complet*)—kõplɛt (*complète*). (*c*) If the stem ends in a vowel or in a final consonant which is pronounced, the distinction of gender disappears completely: *aigu—aiguë, cruel—cruelle, pareil—pareille, meilleur—meilleure.*

COMPARISON OF ADJECTIVES

192. The Comparative and the Superlative were normally expressed in Classical Latin by means of synthetic forms (MAJOR, MAXIMUS, etc.). In Vulgar Latin the analytic forms consisting of the adverbs MAGIS or PLUS + adjective, which were rare in Classical Latin, are gradually extended, and *plus* + adj. is the regular form in Old French. This development is in accord with the general analytic trend of the language.

A few synthetic forms of the Comparative have survived in Modern French: *maire* (< MAJOR)—*majeur* (< MAJOREM), *moindre* for O.F. *mendre* (< MINOR)—*mineur* for O.F. *meneur* (< MINOREM), O.F. *mieldre* (< MELIOR)—*meilleur* (< MELIOREM), *mieux* O.F. *mielz* (< MELIUS), *pire* (< PEJOR)—O.F. *pejor* (< PEJOREM), *plusieurs* O.F. *plusors*, *pluisors* (< L.L. PLURIORES influenced by PLUS). Others did not outlive the Middle Ages: *graindre*—*graignor*, *joindre*—*joignor*; *joindre* survives in the form *gindre*. For the declension of these forms, see § 187. Survivals of the synthetic Superlative are O.F. *pesmes* (< PESSIMUS) and *pruismes* (< PROXIMUS). The Old French forms in *-ismes* (-ISSIMUS) are Learned formations (*altismes*, *fortismes*, *grandismes*, *saintismes*), as are also the modern forms in *-issime*, which are partly due to Italian influence (*illustrissime*, *révérendissime*).

GENDER OF SUBSTANTIVES

193. The distribution of French substantives between the masculine and feminine gender is in the main inherited from Latin. For the fate of neuter substantives, cf. § 174. But the tendency to identify a certain ending with one or other gender continued in Vulgar Latin and French. We have already seen how neuter plurals in -A came to be treated as feminine substantives and how feminine substantives of other declensions tended to be assimilated to the -A declension (*GLACIA for GLACIES). Names of trees ending in -US passed from the fem. to the masc. under the influence of the ending: PINUS > *le pin* (It. Sp. pino), FRAXINUS > *le fresne* (It. frassino, Sp. fresno), and with them ARBOR > *arbre* (It. albero, Sp. árbol); FLOS, FLORIS joined the feminine substantives in -IS (but It. il fiore); SOREX and VERVEX (later BERBEX) were re-modelled on the analogy of RADIX RADĪCEM, etc. and became fem. *la souris, la brebis*.

194. Similarly French *ə* continues to be identified with the feminine gender. The tendency to treat as feminine the sub-

stantives ending in -*e*[1] is particularly strong if they begin
with a vowel, in which case the definite article, being elided,
does not help to maintain the distinction. In the sixteenth
century this also applied to the indefinite article (*un* and *une*
both being pronounced *ŏn* before a vowel); accordingly we
find considerable hesitation as to the gender of such words
in writers of that time. Thus *affaire* (< *à faire*; cf. x, 24;
xiv, 16), *limite* (LIMITEM m.) have, after a period of hesitation
in the sixteenth century, become fem.; *abîme, bronze, chanvre,
panache* have remained masc. in spite of similar hesitation.
This sometimes dates from the Middle Ages (*silence, navire,
ordre, mérite, doute*, xii, 40).

195. But more often other factors combine with the presence
of -*e* to induce hesitation and change. Thus *armoire* (ARMARIUM)
and *écritoire* (SCRIPTORIUM) have become fem. under the
influence of numerous fem. substantives in -*oire*. The etymologizing tendency of sixteenth-century scholars and grammarians is responsible for considerable hesitation and some
changes: *œuvre* (< OPERA), originally fem., was made masc.
to correspond with Latin neuter OPUS, but has survived as
such only in certain technical meanings (*l'œuvre de V. Hugo*
'his work considered as an artistic whole', *le gros-œuvre, le
sous-œuvre*); *délices* (DELICIAS), associated with DELICIUM, was
treated as masc. in the sixteenth century, and this gender
survives in the rarely used *le délice*.

196. Other changes result from formal or semantic associations: *alarme* (It. a l l' a r m e) becomes fem. in the seventeenth
century ≠ *arme*; *mensonge* (< *MENTITIONICA derived from
MENTITUS) becomes masc. ≠ *songe*; *rancœur* (for *ranqueur*) shows
change of both spelling and gender under the influence of
cœur. Semantic associations account for hesitation between
masc. and fem. in *après-midi* (usually masc.) ≠ older *après-
dinée, après-soupée*; *minuit* (O.F. *mie nuit*) was influenced by
midi and, after hesitation in the sixteenth and seventeenth

---

[1] The tendency is so strong that certain feminine substantives have
been provided with an unetymological *e* (*la cuillère*), and certain masculine substantives have been deprived of theirs (*pédant*).

centuries, became masc.; *gens*, regularly fem. in Old French (*gent* < GENTEM), has become masc. owing to its use in the plural as the equivalent of '*hommes*', the fem. surviving in set expressions (*vieilles gens, petites gens*) (cf. § 170); hesitation has led to the formulation of subtle rules at various periods, the latest finding being contained in the Ministerial Decree of 1901, according to which *gens* may be treated uniformly as a fem. substantive.

197. Change of gender sometimes results from change oi function: *rien* (< REM) as a fem. substantive did not survive the Old French period; as a negative particle it is logically neuter and is therefore treated as masc. (*Rien n'est arrivé*); *personne* used as an indefinite negative pronoun is similarly masc. (*Personne n'est arrivé*), though formerly sometimes feminine. Used as a substantive it is fem., but syllepsis is common in the plural (cf. *gens*) and was commended by Vaugelas (*Faire rire des personnes qui ne rient que quand ils veulent*, Mol. *Impr. de V*. sc. 1); *chose* is masc. when used with a neuter meaning in combination with *quelque* or *autre* (*Quelque chose est arrivé* but *Quelques choses sont arrivées*). Cf. the neuter use of *chose* in familiar language to denote a person (*Le Petit Chose*—title of a novel by A. Daudet).

198. As the above examples will show, a variety of factors may combine to induce hesitation or change. An interesting case is that of substantives in *-eur*. Abstract substantives in -OR became fem. in Vulgar Latin, probably under the influence of other abstract substantives, which are generally fem. Their number was increased by new formations in *-eur* (*froideur, laideur,* etc.). The scholars of the Renaissance attempted to restore the original gender, and their efforts found support in the confusion of *un* and *une* before a vowel (*un erreur*; cf. § 194) and in the existence of common masc. substantives in *-eur*: *heur* for *e-ür* (< AUGURIUM) and its compounds *bonheur, malheur* (cf. § 68); *pleur, labeur* (verbal substantives from *pleurer, labourer*). But after a period of hesitation the Old French gender prevailed, except in *humeur* (m.); *déshonneur* (m.) and *honneur* (sporadically treated as masc.

from the fourteenth century) were perhaps influenced by *bonheur*; (*bon*)*heur*, (*mal*)*heur*, *labeur* remain masc., although fluctuating in the Middle Ages.

199. Later borrowings from Latin show the same treatment of gender as Popular words, but hesitation was formerly very common, owing partly to the popular tendency to give them the gender corresponding with their ending or form (*cimeterre, épisode, exercice*), partly to the lack of a traditional gender in the case of derivatives (*automobile, armistice*). *Automobile* has been exposed to a variety of influences: it appears first as an adjective about 1875 (*une voiture automobile*); whence, by ellipsis, *une automobile*, which has to contend with *un automobile* (≠*domicile, ustensile*, etc.). Borrowings from foreign languages generally keep their original gender, but exceptions are common as the result of formal or semantic associations: *ombrelle* (It. ombrello), *romance* (Sp. romance) owe their fem. gender to association with substantives in *-elle -ance*; *populace* (It. populaccio) has become fem. after prolonged hesitation.

200. Some apparent changes of gender result from ellipsis: *un* (*chien de*) *Terre-neuve*, *le* (*vin de*) *Champagne*, *le* (*bateau à*) *vapeur*, *une* (*automobile de*) *trente chevaux*, *un* (*fiacre de*) *remise*, *une* (*horloge à*) *pendule* beside *le pendule* (PENDULUM) 'pendulum'. On the analogy of *la* (*fête de*) *Saint Jean*, etc., *la Noël* is found beside *le Noël* < (DIURNUM) NATALEM. A number of changes of gender are unexplained: *lierre* (m.), with agglutinated article, for *ierre* (< HEDERA); *été* (< AETATEM) ≠*hiver?*; *art* (< ARTEM) both masc. and fem. in O.F. as in Sp. and Prov.; *dent* (< DENTEM) both masc. and fem. in O.F.; *mer* (< MARE) ≠*terre?*; *paroi* (< PAR(I)ETEM).

201. Of the many hesitations that have not persisted one may further cite: (*a*) in Latin: DIES,[1] FRONS, PULVIS, PERDIX; (*b*) dating from the Middle Ages: *lange, mystère, office*; (*c*) frequent in the sixteenth century: *âge, cartilage, image, tige*; and as late as the seventeenth: *caprice, gage, mélange, orage, ouvrage, squelette*. The following still fluctuate: *après-midi, humour,*

[1] O.F. *di* (m.), i, 4; ii, 12. Survives in *midi, lundi*, etc.

automne, délice (masc. sing., fem. pl.). In other cases hesitation persists in an attenuated form with differentiation of meaning: *amour* (< AMOREM m.) is now masc., after prolonged hesitation dating from Middle French, but in the plural it is still sometimes fem. in poetic language; *espace* (< SPATIUM) now masc., but former hesitation has led to the preservation of *une espace* as a printing term; *foudre* (< FULGUR) has become fem. owing to final *e*, but *le foudre* is still permissible in the figurative sense *un foudre de guerre*; *période* (PERIODUS f.) masc. only in the sense of 'degree' or 'stage'; *voile* (< VELA) hesitated under the influence of VELUM, the hesitation being utilized to distinguish *la voile* 'sail' from *le voile* 'veil'.

202. In other cases the so-called double gender results from the phonetic and orthographic identity of two separate words. (*a*) Cognate words: *le crêpe* (< CRISPUM) 'crape'—*la crêpe* (verbal subst. from *crêper*) 'pancake'; *le critique* 'critic' —*la critique* 'criticism'; *le faune* 'faun'—*la faune* (der. from *faune* ≠ *flore*) 'fauna'; *le manche* (< *MANICUM from MANUS) 'handle'—*la manche* (< MANICA) 'sleeve'; *le mémoire* (*MEMORIUM) 'memoir'—*la mémoire* (MEMORIA) 'memory'; *le mode* (late borr. from MODUS) 'method' 'mood'—*la mode* (early borr. from MODUS) 'fashion'; *le poste* (It. posto) 'station' 'office'—*la poste* (< POSITA) 'mail'; *le garde, le guide, un aide, un enseigne, un manœuvre, un trompette* are derived from *la garde*, etc. with change of gender in accord with meaning 'he who guards', etc. (cf. § 548). (*b*) Words which have become homophonous through phonetic evolution and are not cognate: *le coche* (<?) 'passage-boat', *le coche* (Germ. kutsche) 'coach'—*la coche* (der. from *cochon*) 'sow', *la coche* (<?) 'notch'; *le faux* (< FALSUM)—*la faux* (< FALCEM); *le livre* (LIBER) 'book'—*la livre* (< LIBRA) 'pound'; *le mousse* (It. mozzo) 'cabin-boy'—*la mousse* (Germ. mos) 'moss'; *le page* (It.-Gr. paggio)—*la page* (PAGINA) 'page of book'; *le poêle* (PALLIUM) 'canopy'—*la poêle* (< PATELLA) 'frying-pan'; *le somme* (< SOMNUM) 'nap'—*la somme* (< SUMMA) 'sum', *la somme* (< SAGMA) 'burden'; *le tour* (verbal subst. from *tourner*) 'turn'—*la tour* (< TURREM) 'tower'; *le vague* (VAGUS)

'void'—*la vague* (Scand. vág-r) 'wave'; *le vase* (VAS) 'vase'—
la vase (Dutch wase) 'silt'.

DIFFERENTIATION OF FORM TO INDICATE SEX[1]

203. Substantives which denote persons or the higher
animals sometimes show a differentiation of form to indicate
sex. Those denoting persons are often adjectives used substantivally and therefore present a regular feminine form:
chrétien—chrétienne, jumeau (< GEMELLUM)—*jumelle* (< GEMELLA),
cousin—cousine, ami—amie, époux (< SPONSUM)—*épouse, paysan—
paysanne, voisin—voisine.* Many others follow the analogy of
adjectives: *baronne, lionne, chienne* (for older *lice* or *cagne*),
géante, formed on *baron,* etc., and even *vaurienne, fainéante.*
Sometimes it is the masc. that is analogical: *veuve* alone
existed in Old French; *veuf* is a modern creation on the
analogy of *neuf—neuve.*

204. Substantives in *-eur* present feminines of different
types. (*a*) *-eure* is rare in Modern French, e.g. *prieure,* an
analogical formation which has replaced older *prioresse,*
prieuresse, prieuse. (*b*) *-euse* (the result of a confusion of *-eur*
with *-eux,* cf. § 128) is common in forms derived from verbs:
liseur—liseuse, menteur—menteuse, blanchisseur—blanchisseuse. (*c*)
-eresse is found in *pécheresse* which is a re-modelling of O.F.
pecheriz (< PECCATRICEM), the unusual *-iz* being replaced by
-esse, and in *enchanteresse* = O.F. *enchantere* (< INCANTATOR)
+ *-esse.* (*d*) *-trice* was borrowed from Latin -TRIX, -TRICEM,
and is regularly used to form the fem. of Learned words in
-eur: *lecteur—lectrice, acteur—actrice.*

205. The ending *-esse* (also formerly written *-esce* and *-ece*)
is derived from L.L. -ISSA (borrowed from Greek -ισσα) which
was widely used: ABBATISSA > *abbesse,* DIACONISSA > *diacon-
nesse.* In French, *-esse* was used to form the feminine of many
substantives: *comte—comtesse, dieu—déesse*; later: *hôte—hôtesse,
docteur—doctoresse, âne—ânesse.* Many feminines in *-esse* did
not survive the sixteenth century (*clerc—clergesse*); *maîtresse*

[1] This section belongs strictly speaking to Chapter VI, but is introduced
here for convenience.

and *traîtresse* have triumphed, although formerly *maître* and *traître* served as both masc. and fem.

206. A derivative or cognate form is often used to supply a missing gender: *canard* is derived from the fem. *cane* under the influence of O.F. *malart*; *cochon* has given a derivative *coche*; *dindon* is a derivative of *dinde*; NEPOS, NEPOTEM and NEPTIS, NEPTEM could be used in Latin for either sex, but NEPOTEM (> *neveu*) was restricted in Vulgar Latin to the masc. and a fem. NEPTIA (> *nièce*) created on NEPTEM; *compagne* is the fem. corresponding to *compaing* (O.F. nom. of *compagnon*); *gouvernante*, *servante* (fem. of pres. part.) supply the fem. to *gouverneur*, *serviteur*; *mule* is the fem. of O.F. *mul* (< MULUM), since replaced by its derivative *mulet*. Borrowed feminine forms are: *empereur—impératrice*, *chanteur—cantatrice* (It. cantatrice) beside the popular *chanteuse*, *ambassadeur—ambassadrice* (It. ambasciadrice), *Hébreu—Hébraïque* (Lat.-Gr. HEBRAICUS). In other cases the distinction of sex is traditionally indicated by different words, which may or may not be cognate: *fils—fille*, *roi—reine*; but *frère—sœur*, *cheval—jument*.

207. Some substantives denoting persons possess no feminine (*écrivain*, *médecin*, *professeur*, *peintre*, *sculpteur*). This deficiency is made good, as required, by prefixing the word *femme* (*une femme auteur*, etc.) just as in Middle French the lack of a masc. of *veuve* was supplied by *un homme veuve*. But such devices are felt to be cumbrous, and various analogical feminines have been created, none of which has however been officially recognized (*autrice*, eighteenth century; *une auteur*, eighteenth century; and the monstrous Anglicism, *authoresse*, nineteenth century); *avocate* bids fair to receive this recognition. The same difficulty in the case of animals is overcome by adding *femelle*, the article remaining masc. (*un éléphant femelle*); the lack of a masc. being made good in a similar way (*une baleine mâle*). Some words vary in gender without varying in form (*élève*, *enfant*). Others show a contradiction between grammatical gender and sex (*la sentinelle*, *la vedette*, and metonymically used *connaissance*, *dupe*, *recrue*, *victime*, *bas-bleu*).

SYNTAX OF THE SUBSTANTIVE

208. The tendency to substitute a prepositional phrase for flexions persists through Vulgar Latin into French, but the oblique case continued in Old French to fulfil certain functions other than those of the direct object and the prepositional case. It was often used as an indirect object (I, 8, 11; II, 11; III, 27; IV, 49, 100) and also fulfilled the function of the Latin ablative in absolute constructions (I, 8; *Paien chevalchent, . . . halbers vestuz, Rol.* 710). With verbs of motion it is used to denote place, direction or manner (*Tant chevalchierent e veies e chemins, Rol.* 405; *Son petit pas s'en torne chancelant, Rol.* 2227); cf. Mod.F. *Je demeure place Saint Michel; aller son chemin; marcher grand train.* Time, duration, measure, price, continue to be denoted by the oblique case, but Modern French usage often requires a preposition where Old French dispensed with it: *Il est parti le lendemain; La représentation dure trois heures; Il a vendu cette maison cent mille francs;* but *Il n'a cessé de pleuvoir pendant trois jours.*

209. The oblique case of proper names or of substantives denoting persons or personified objects was often used to denote possession (II, 3; VI, 137; X, 70; XI, 64, 68). This construction gradually gives way to the construction with *de* in the fourteenth and fifteenth centuries, but it survives in fixed locutions (*le feu Saint Antoine, la Fête-Dieu, hôtel-Dieu*) and place names (*La Ferté-Milon, Pont-l'Évêque*) and in the conjunction of Christian name and family name (*Jean Latour*). An imitation of such survivals is to be observed in names of streets, institutions, firms (*place Gambetta, faubourg Montmartre, gare Saint-Lazare, l'affaire Dreyfus, style Louis XV*). This type of juxtaposition is much favoured in commercial language (*les pneus Michelin,* etc.) and has been extended to substantives other than those denoting persons (*timbre-poste*), the qualifying substantive being sometimes hardly distinguishable from a substantive used adjectivally (*un chapeau paille;* cf. *une robe marron*).

210. For cases of syllepsis in substantives which are singular in form but plural (or collective) in meaning, see § 380

A special point of interest is the number of the substantive in such expressions as *profils de femme*. In marked contrast with English, French shows a decided preference for the singular. In spoken French the question hardly arises, as the plural is generally indistinguishable from the singular. The rule is therefore a literary one and is consonant with the gradual rationalization of the French language: the qualifying substantive becomes generic, and therefore logic demands that it shall be singular (*peaux de bœuf*); when the substantive is itself qualified this naturally does not apply (*des peaux de bœufs d'Auvergne*); other exceptions are probably due to assimilation (*des articles de revues, des peaux d'animaux*). Assimilation also accounts for such constructions as *trente francs de perdus*; cf. the assimilation of gender in *une diable de maison, une drôle d'idée, une goutte de répandue*.

SYNTAX OF THE ADJECTIVE

211. Adjectives, whether used attributively or predicatively, agree in case, gender and number with the substantive they qualify. With O.F. *se clamer* 'to be called', *se faire* 'to become', *se tenir à* (*pour*) 'to consider oneself' the nominative is regular (IV, 1); but as the active meaning of these verbs had not been entirely obliterated, the accusative is sometimes found; cf. the Modern French hesitation between *elle a l'air bonne* and *elle a l'air bon*.

212. The survival of the neuter accounts for a number of apparent exceptions, for it was not only used predicatively with a neuter subject (*Ço est bel*) but adverbially in such expressions as *vendre chier*. Many of these have survived and others have been created by analogy (*parler bas, chanter faux, tenir bon, risquer gros, parler net, tomber juste, peser lourd, voir clair, marcher droit, tomber dru, tenir ferme, taper dur, sentir mauvais*). When such expressions are used passively and the adjective stands before the participle, there is in Old French a tendency to make it agree (*Con chiere achetee est vaillance*, Tobler, *Verm. Beitr.* I, p. 75 ff.); cf. also x, 96. A similar hesitation in the case of adjectives used adverbially with a following adjective existed in Old French, and the agreement is preserved in such expressions as *fenêtres grandes ouvertes, fleurs fraîches écloses*; *tout* regularly agreed with the adjective in O.F. (*set anz toz pleins, espees totes nues*); but in the seventeenth century Vaugelas and the Academy, interpreting *tout* as an adverb, succeeded after some resistance in imposing the invariability of *tout*, while admitting *toute, toutes* before a feminine adjective beginning with a consonant (*toute charmante, toutes charmantes*) on the ground of euphony Similarly Vaugelas' ruling (which now affects only spelling) has been accepted for *demi* and *nu* (*aller nu pieds, nu-tête*, but *pieds nus, tête nue*; *une demi-heure*, but *une heure et demie*. Cf. also *tenir haut la tête*, but *tenir la tête haute*; *avoir de l'argent plein ses poches*, but *avoir ses poches pleines d'argent*; *ci-joint la facture*, but *la facture ci-jointe*. The invariability of the adjective in such locutions as *Nous étions seul à seul*; *À quoi bon la guerre?* is likewise due to their adverbial force. The curious use of the feminine for a neuter idea in such expressions as *Vous en verrez de belles*; *en dire de bonnes* is probably due to ellipsis (of *choses* or *nouvelles?*). Various explanations have been given of *Il l'a échappé belle* (ellipsis of *balle?*); *belle* might here be explained as a mere spelling for the old neuter *bel* used adverbially.

213. The modern rule that an adjective qualifying several ubstantives stands in the plural, and in the masculine if they are of different genders, dates from Malherbe. Before him the same liberty obtained as in Latin, viz. to make the adjective agree with the nearest (XVI, 5) (§ 381); but exceptions to the modern rule are still numerous (*certificat de bonne vie et mœurs, des sentiments et des croyances religieuses*).

COMPARATIVE AND SUPERLATIVE

214. Of the synthetic forms, *meilleur, moindre, pire* (together with the adverbs *mieux, moins, pis*) alone survive as genuine comparatives in Mod.F., but *plus mauvais, plus petit, plus mal* have almost eliminated *pire, moindre, pis* from the spoken language, *moindre* being used only in the abstract sense. In popular speech *plus* is sometimes prefixed to such synthetic forms (*plus pire, plus mieux*).

215. The comparative was also used in O.F. and Mid.F. as a relative superlative (cf. Latin VALIDIOR MANUUM 'the stronger of the two hands'): *Tolent lor veies e les chemins plus granz, Rol.* 2464; *Et luy devions donner le nom du plaisir plus favorable, plus doux et naturel,* Mont. I, xx. This use has survived in Mod.F. only after a possessive pronoun or the partitive *de* (*C'est tout ce qu'il y a de plus beau*). Elsewhere the article is now compulsory, as is also its repetition if the adjective follows the substantive.

216. The absolute superlative, for which Classical Latin used the same form as for the relative superlative, is rendered in French by prefixing to the adjective an adverb of intensity (*bien, fort,* etc.); O.F. also used *par. moult, trop* (in the sense of *très: Trop nos est loinz Charles, Rol.* 1100). The choice of the adverb is often determined by passing fashion and a striving for effect, and the weakening through constant use leads to its replacement (*il est très riche—il est extrêmement riche—il est horriblement riche*).

217. If the second term of the comparison is a pronoun or substantive, O.F. generally introduces it by *de* (IV, 51; *Meillor vassal n'out en la cort de lui, Rol.* 775). This construction, which is a continuation of the Latin ablative construction, is preserved in Mod.F. only before a numeral (*plus de dix,* (*rancs*). In all other cases *que* (= Lat. QUAM) was used, and, as a negative is implied, an expletive *ne* was prefixed to the verb; but *ne* has never been compulsory and has practically disappeared from popular speech (cf. § 455). Old French often introduced *être* or *faire* as a 'verbum vicarium' before the second term of the comparison (*Plus est isnels que nen est uns falcons, Rol.* 1572), and this is still common in the seventeenth century. If the second term consists of two substantives, they were formerly linked by *ne* (seventeenth-century *nf* (*Plus est isnels qued esperviers n'aronde, Rol.* 1535); in Mod.F. by *et* or *ou*.

PLACE OF THE ATTRIBUTIVE ADJECTIVE

218. The position of the adjective was freer in O.F., and even in the sixteenth century (xv, 33; xvi, 86), than in Mod.F. This is most clearly illustrated by adjectives of colour (*la Ruge Mer, blanches mains*), which in Mod.F. always follow, unless used figuratively. Yet even in Mod.F. the place of the adjective is anything but fixed. One can at most say that the usual place is after the substantive, but that a number of common adjectives (often monosyllabic) generally precede (*bon, gros, jeune, long, haut, mauvais*, etc.). The place of the adjective is often determined by considerations of euphony and style: it is contrary to normal rhythm to place a long adjective before a short substantive. The differentiation of meaning according to position, which certain Mod.F. adjectives present, is likewise a gradual development and is due, partly to the tendency of adj. + subst. to become more or less fused and often to develop a special meaning (*sage femme, petit pain, un vrai conte* 'a pure fairy-tale'), partly to the tendency to place the adjective after the substantive if it preserves its full qualifying force (*une histoire vraie* as opposed to *fictive*, etc.). Consequently, if the adjective is used as a mere epithet or figuratively, it precedes; if used in its literal, full sense, it follows. This usage is most clearly exemplified in *ancien, brave, dernier, franc, grand, méchant, pauvre, petit, sage, triste, vrai*; for *certain, différent, même, propre, second, seul*, this differentiation did not yet exist in the seventeenth century.

NUMERALS

CARDINALS

219. The majority of the cardinal numerals are derived directly from Latin. Certain V.L. changes are to be noted: *cinq* < CINQUE for QUINQUE by dissimilation; *quatre* < QUATTOR for QUATTUOR with loss of *w* after two consonants; *dix-sept*, O.F. *dis et set* < DECEM ET SEPTEM for SEPTEMDECIM, and similarly *dix-huit* and *dix-neuf*; *vingt* < VẸNTI < VIGINTI (*i* for *ẹ*

under the influence of final *i*, cf. § 37); *trente* < TR(I)ENTA
< TRIGINTA; *quarante* < QUADRA(I)NTA < QUADRAGINTA; *cin-quante* < CINQUA(I)NTA < QUINQUAGINTA; *soixante* < SEXA(I)NTA
< SEXAGINTA. The distinction between MILLE sing. (> *mil*) and
MILIA pl. (> *mille* or *milie*) was lost sight of very early, and
down to the sixteenth century they were used indiscrimi-
nately; but in accordance with its etymology, *mille* as a numeral
never takes the sign of the plural in Mod.F., rarely in O.F.
The restriction of *mil* to dates is in force from the seventeenth
century. *Million* (for O.F. *mil milie* or *dis feis cent milie*) dates
from the fourteenth century and is modelled on It. milione.
AMBO survived in O.F. *ambes* (f.) and (in combination with
DUO) masc. *andui*—*an(s)dous*, fem. *ambesdous*; cf. Mod.F.
ambesas 'double ace'.

220. The vigesimal system (sometimes attributed to Celtic
influence, so far as French is concerned) was in common use
in the Middle Ages: *deus vins*, *trois vins*, etc. up to *dis huit
vins*; cf. English counting by scores. Of these forms only
quatre-vingts and *quatre-vingt-dix* have persisted (superseding
(*h*)*uitante*, *nonante*, which are now confined to patois).
Soixante-dix (for *trois vins et dis*) has similarly ousted *septante*.

221. *Un* was declined in O.F. like an adjective of Class I
(*bons*). *Deux* was also inflected in O.F.: Nom. *doi* (< *DUI)—
Obl. *dous*, *deus* (< DUOS); Fem. *does* (< DUAS). *Vingt* and *cent*
regularly take the sign of the plural when multiplied (*quatre
vingts*, *deux cents*), but sometimes remained uninflected in
O.F. The modern rule prescribing *vingt* and *cent* if another
number follows (*quatre-vingt-un*) is a recent artificial creation,
since annulled by Ministerial Decree (1901). The use of *et*
to link component elements (*dis et set*), which was general
in O.F., was finally abandoned in the sixteenth century (cf.
XVI, 58), except between *vingt*, *trente*, *quarante*, *cinquante* and a
following *un*, and in *soixante et onze*. After numerals ending
in *un* (*vingt et un*), the substantive normally stood in the
singular in O.F., but after a period of hesitation extending
into the seventeenth century the plural became the rule.

Ordinals

222. None of the Modern French ordinals are derived by uninterrupted tradition from Latin. Primum[1] was replaced by primarium > *premier*; secundum was displaced by alterum > *altre, autre* (XI, 49), which finally gives way to *second* (a twelfth-century borrowing) in the sixteenth century; tertius > *tierz, tiers* (uninflected in O.F.), tertia > *tierce* (XI, 49) survive in Mod.F. only in set expressions (*tiers état*) or technical language (*tierce majeure*, etc.); quartum > *quart* (XI, 49) and quintum > *quint* survive in the same way (*la fièvre quarte, Charles-Quint*); decimum > *dime* > *disme* ≠ *dis*, survives only as a substantive (*la dîme*). Such etymological forms as these were gradually replaced by new creations formed by adding to the cardinal numerals the suffix *-ième*, which appears in O.F. as *-i(s)me* (cf. XII, 79) and *-ie(s)me*. *Second* still maintains a precarious existence and can no longer be used in compounds (*vingt-deuxième*); *premier* similarly gives place to *unième* in compounds (*vingt et unième*). The suffix *-ain* (< -anum) was also used in O.F. to form ordinals (*premerain, quatorzain*, etc.). Some of these forms have survived as terms of prosody (*quatrain*) or in the feminine as collectives (*huitaine, dizaine, douzaine*, etc.).

223. The extensive use of cardinals for ordinals in Mod.F. (*le trois janvier, Louis Quatorze, chapitre six*) must be attributed to the habit of reading them as written (*III*, etc.): it is significant that the modern usage begins with the development of printing, although it does not become established until the end of the seventeenth century. *Premier*, owing to its frequent use, was not so affected (*le premier janvier*).

---

[1] O.F. *prin, prime* (< primum -a) has survived in a few set forms: *printemps* (primum tempus); the fem. sometimes appearing for the masc. (*de prime abord, primesautier* for earlier *prinsautier*).

B. *ARTICLES AND PRONOUNS*

THE DEFINITE ARTICLE

224. The definite article continues the Latin demonstrative pronoun ILLE. The O.F. forms are:

		Masc.	Fem.
Sing.	nom.	*li*	*la*
	obl.	*lo > le*	*la*
Pl.	nom.	*li*	*les*
	obl.	*les*	*les*

The development of the definite article consists in a progressive weakening and extension of ILLE. Used proclitically with substantives, it lost the first syllable (which was slurred over) and in the oblique cases shows the characteristic weakening of unaccented vowels. The feminine oblique *les* was carried into the nom.; the masc. nom. sing. *li* goes back to V.L. ILLĪ (cf. § 238). The oblique forms alone have persisted in Mod.F. For elision and enclisis of the definite article, see §§ 134, 139.

225. Even in C.L. the demonstrative force of ILLE is not always maintained, and in V.L. it rapidly weakens. Late Latin texts show a growing tendency to use ILLE (also IPSE) as an individualizing particle and reflect the general tendency of popular speech to achieve greater explicitness. In Mod.F. the demonstrative force survives only in set expressions like *de la sorte* (cf. XVII, 60), *du jour*; but in O.F. it was still clearly felt (III, 7) and the definite article still 'defined' or individualized sharply the substantive which it preceded. Hence the much more restricted use made of it in the earlier periods of the language and the possibility of fine distinctions such as Modern French cannot achieve. In general it can be said that O.F. uses the definite article whenever the substantive is to be singled out or individualized. Thus, abstract substantives, proper names, names of nationality in the plural (*Franceis, Sarrazins*), geographical names, substantives which denote a unique object (*ciel, terre*), seasons, points of time (*printemps, matin, dimanche*) did not take an article in O.F. With concrete substantives there was a certain amount of hesitation, the article being dispensed with if they were used in a generic sense, and reserved for the purpose of singling out a particular object or a definite number of objects. Accordingly, if the substantive is already individualized by some other means (dem. pron., etc.), the article is not used. For similar reasons the article was generally omitted (1) before the direct object if it more or less merged with the verb to form a compound (*dire verité, avoir faim*); Mod.F. presents many such cases (*tenir tête, livrer bataille, fermer boutique*, etc.); (2) if several substantives linked by *et* form a unit (*ciel et terre*); (3) after prepositions, if the substantive is not to be individualized (*aler a court, estre en maison*; cf. Mod.F. *à pied, à cheval, par terre, sans pitié*); such expressions tend to become purely adverbial and therefore to be preserved intact (cf. *amont, aval*, etc.); (4) in comparisons, where again the substantive is not individualized (*blanc comme neige*).

226. The extension of the definite article in the Mid.F. period was greatly favoured by the breakdown of the O.F. declension and the elimination of final *s*: this conferred upon the article the rôle hitherto played by the flexional endings (*l'homme—les hommes, le chant—les chants, la fleur—les fleurs*). Analogy also played its part, and gradually the article came to be little more than an adjunct of the substantive, losing entirely its demonstrative force and retaining in a limited degree its individualizing function. Generally in Mod.F. its omission implies that the substantive is no longer purely substantival and has combined with the verb to form what is practically a compound verb (*avoir raison* 'to be right'), or with a preposition to form what is in effect an adverbial expression (*avec courage* 'courageously', *à tort* 'wrongly', *par terre, sous bois*). This accounts for the hesitation in the case of substantives used predicatively or in apposition (compare *Il est français* with *C'est un Français*). Similar considerations account for the adoption of the article in *la France*, but its

omission in *en France*, and the hesitation (with a very slight differentiation) between *l'histoire de France* and *l'histoire de la France*. For the use of the article to form the superlative, see § 215.

THE INDEFINITE ARTICLE

227. The indefinite article developed from UNUS, which was occasionally used in C.L. in the sense of QUIDAM and is already used as an indefinite article in post-Classical writers. In French it appears as early as the *Sequence of Saint Eulalia* (II, 22) and is inflected like *bons*. Its extension is much slower than that of the definite article. It is rare in the twelfth and thirteenth centuries, and its function, that of singling out one unspecified object of a series, is not yet clearly defined. Like the definite article, it is dispensed with in O.F. unless the person or thing is to be singled out from others of the same class. Accordingly, it was not used in negative phrases, interrogative and conditional sentences, between verb and complement if closely linked (*donner réponse = répondre, rendre service = servir*), after prepositions, before substantives used predicatively, and in comparisons (XIII, 8).

228. The gradual extension of the indefinite article in Mid.F. is facilitated by the fact that it often corresponds to the plural of the partitive article (*un homme*, sing. of *des hommes*). Before *tel, autre, même, si*, and often before a qualifying adjective, it is omitted, even in the sixteenth and seventeenth centuries, where Mod.F. requires it (XIV, 9, 11, 34).

229. The plural *un—uns, unes* was used in O.F. and as late as the sixteenth century before substantives denoting pairs of objects or persons (*unes grandes narines; unes botes* XIII, 36; *uns esperons* XIII, 38). It was also used before plural substantives which have no singular or have a different meaning in the singular, or are used collectively (*uns grans dens;* cf. *Auc. et Nic.* sect. 24).

THE PARTITIVE ARTICLE

230. The early history of the partitive article is a much debated question (cf. Sneyders de Vogel, pp. 17–23, whose conclusions we have in the main adopted). To express the partitive idea (i.e. an unspecified portion of a whole) Latin employed the substantive alone, but in Late Latin three renderings are possible after a verb: (1) the accusative (EDERE PANEM), (2) the genitive (EDERE PANIS), (3) DE + the ablative (EDERE DE PANE). With the elimination of the genitive (§ 173), (2) naturally merged with (3), which was fairly common in L.L. but rare in C.L., and with (1), which was preferred. Accordingly, we find in O.F. occasionally *manger de pain* (only one example in the *Roland*) beside regular *manger pain* (XI, 42). To specify the whole from which the unspecified portion is taken, Latin could naturally employ such determinatives as pronominal adjectives (*Surge, sede et comede de venatura mea*, Gen. xxvii, 19). Similarly we find in O.F. from the earliest texts the type *manger de bon pain*, and also *manger du pain* meaning 'to eat an unspecified quantity, not of bread in general, but of *the* bread (specified by the definite article)' (*Por son seignor . . . deit hom perdre e del quir e del peil* = literally 'some of *the* skin and some of *the* hair (of one's own person)', *Rol.* 1012). But with the weakening of the definite article (§ 225) and its consequent use in a generic sense (*le pain* = bread in general), the phrase *manger du pain* came to denote, as it does in Mod.F., 'to eat an unspecified portion of bread' without any specification as to which bread; it therefore became equivalent to the common and traditional *manger pain*. The triumph of *manger du pain* over *manger pain* is due to the same causes as the extension of the definite article, but the struggle was more protracted. The partitive (*du, de la, des*) was still optional as late as the sixteenth century (XIV, 4, 48, 54), and it is sometimes omitted in the seventeenth century where modern usage would require it. The type *manger pain* survives in Mod.F. only in proverbs and set expressions (*avoir pitié, tirer profit*).

231. From what has been said we should expect the old construction *manger de bon pain* to persist, but with the extension of the definite article the alternative *manger du bon pain* developed. The latter was common in the sixteenth century (XVI, 72) and continues to find favour in popular speech and familiar conversation, in spite of the opposition of all the grammarians of the seventeenth century. The official rule that *de* is to be used if the adjective precedes, *du, de la, des* if the adjective follows, was formulated by Vaugelas, but it was not faithfully observed by seventeenth-century writers and is subject to certain restrictions in Mod.F. literary usage. In general one can say that *du, de la, des* are used if the adjective is more or less fused with the substantive, whether this is indicated by a hyphen (*des petites-filles*) or not (*des petites filles, du menu bois, de la bonne foi*).

232. The use of *de* after substantives or adverbs of quantity (*une foule, beaucoup, assez*) falls in a different category. Here we have merely the Romance equivalent of the Latin Genitive of the Whole (*magna pars hominum*), and therefore the partitive is not required (*assez de pain*, not *assez de du pain*). The analogy of such constructions (*assez de pain*) may have favoured the extension of the partitive article; according to L. Foulet (*op. cit.*) it was the point of departure of the partitive article. It is to be noted that throughout the Middle Ages adverbs of quantity hesitate between adverbial and adjectival functions (*assez pain* is common beside *assez de pain*). If the substantive denotes a specified object or series of objects, the definite article is introduced: *J'ai trouvé beaucoup des livres que vous m'aviez indiqués*; similarly *la plupart des hommes* (i.e. *hommes* conceived of as a calculable number of men), but *beaucoup d'hommes* (generic); *la foule des passants*, but *une foule de passants*. *Bien* is originally an adverb of intensity and continues to be followed by *du, de la, des*, although it has become purely quantitative (*bien des hommes*).

233. The negative particles *pas* and *point* were originally substantives denoting quantity (*pas d'hommes, point d'hommes*; cf. § 452), and therefore on all fours with such expressions of quantity as *assez d'hommes, une foule d'hommes*. Apparent exceptions, such as Voltaire's *Toujours du plaisir n'est pas du plaisir*, arise from the fact that the substantive does not depend on *pas*; in the sentence quoted, *du plaisir* is a genuine partitive, the predicate of a negative clause ...*n'est pas*....

234. Before a substantive used as subject or predicate the partitive article was rare in O.F. After a preposition it is found sporadically in Mid.F. and is far from universal in Mod.F. (*avec bonté*). It is usually dispensed with if the prepositional phrase is purely adverbial, e.g. *avec patience* 'patiently', but *avec de la patience* 'by means of or with the help of patience'.

235. From the point of view of meaning it is to be noted that the plural *des* generally denotes multiplicity and is the plural of the indefinite article (*des hommes*, pl. of *un homme*), but sometimes it denotes quantity (*des affaires*).

PRONOUNS

236. The C.L. flexional system was much more fully maintained in the case of pronouns, the dative being in part preserved (*cui, li, lui*) and the genitive with change of function (*lor*). The neuter survived to a large extent (*el, mien, iço*). As the degree of stress with which the pronoun is articulated (§ 145) varies with its syntactic function, it shows a twofold development and presents both tonic and atonic forms.

PERSONAL PRONOUNS
FIRST AND SECOND PERSON

237. EGO was reduced in V.L. to EO (I, 5), which became *jo* and was weakened to *je* when unaccented; the regular tonic form is *gié* (later *je*). Owing to their frequent use with a following verb, atonic NOS and VOS replaced tonic NOS and VOS, which would normally have given **nös* and **vös*.

O.F. DECLENSION

		Accented		Unaccented	
Sing.	nom.	*gié > je*	*tu*	*jo > je*	*tu*
	obl.	*mei > moi*	*tei > toi*	*me*	*te*
Pl.	nom.	*nos > nous*	*vos > vous*	*nos > nous*	*vos > vous*
	obl.	*nos > nous*	*vos > vous*	*nos > nous*	*vos > vous*

The unaccented forms persist in Mod.F.

The accented nominative forms *je*, *tu* give place to the accusative forms *moi*, *toi* (*c'est moi*, *c'est toi*) before the end of the O.F. period: *je*, *tu* are always unaccented in Mod.F.

THIRD PERSON

238. For the third person the demonstrative pronoun ILLE (which, used in another function, gave the definite article) was adopted. Used as a personal pronoun it presented in V.L. a number of deviations from the regular phonetic development. The first syllable of the oblique forms, which were in connected speech closely linked with the verb or a preceding preposition, was slurred and disappeared. The masc. nom. sing. ILLE and the dative ILLI became ILLĪ and ILLUI respectively under the influence of the interrogative forms QUĪ, CUI, whence *il* (cf. § 37) and *lui* respectively, the latter being also used as the tonic form of the accusative (cf. *cui*); the dative ILLĪ persisted when unaccented, giving *li* (m. and f.). The O.F. feminine accented form *li* (dial. *lei*, II, 13) presupposes a V.L. ILLAEI, which is explained as a contamination of ILLAE (dat.) +ILLUI; like *lui* it came to be also used as the tonic form of the accusative. The dative plural ILLIS (m. and f.) gave place to the genitive plural (ILLORUM > *lor*) (with change of function). The neuter ILLUD gave way to analogical ILLUM, whence accented nom. sing. *el* and unaccented acc. sing. *lo > le*. The fem. acc. pl. (ILLAS) was, as in substantives, used for both nominative and accusative. The O.F. atonic forms present a further series of irregularities, which result in part from their varying syntactic relations. The nominative forms are supplied by

the tonic *il, ele, el, il, eles,* which gradually become unaccented through proclitic use with the following verb; *lo, los, las* are weakened to *le, les,* but *la* persists.

O.F. DECLENSION

		Accented		Unaccented	
		Masc.	Fem.	Masc.	Fem.
Sing.	nom.	*il*	*ele*	*il*	*ele*
	dat.	*lui*	*li*	*li*	*li*
	acc.	*lui*	*li*	*lo > le*	*la*
Pl.	nom.	*il*	*eles*	*il*	*eles*
	dat.	*lor > leur*	*lor > leur*	*lor > lour*	*lor > lour*
	acc.	*els > eus*	*eles*	*les*	*les*

Neuter: Accented nom. sing. *el*—Unaccented acc. sing. *lo > le.*

Reflexive: the Latin SE persists as accented *sei > soi* and as unaccented *se.*

239. Of the accented forms only *lui, eus, ele, eles* survive, but with restricted functions (see below). The persistence of the nom. *ele* is due to the influence of the pl. *eles.* The accented datives *lui, leur* had from the end of the thirteenth century begun to supplant the unaccented datives *li, lour,* and eventually displace them. The masc. pl. *il* gave way in Mid.F. to analogical *ils,* which (owing to its proclitic use) tends to be reduced to *i* before a consonant, to *iz* before a vowel; this pronunciation was regular in the sixteenth century and still characterizes popular and familiar speech (*s'il vous plaît*). The neuter *el,* which appeared in O.F. as the subject of an impersonal verb, early gave place to *il*; but neuter *le* survives, though indistinguishable in form from the masc.

240. In C.L. the personal pronoun was used as subject of the verb only if required for emphasis, the verbal ending sufficing to indicate person. But in accord with the analytical tendency of V.L. the pronoun subject came to be used for greater clearness. The gradual breakdown of flexional distinctions makes its use necessary: it ceases to be used for emphasis and becomes an adjunct of the verb. O.F. occupies a position midway between the two extremes represented by C.L. and Mod.F., and the use of the pronoun subject is often governed by other considerations than clearness; e.g. it is used if the sentence would otherwise begin with an unaccented word. In Mid.F. the pronoun is more and more commonly expressed, but Latin influence reversed the movement for a time in the sixteenth century (XIV, 7, 13, 32, 34, 41, 53; XVI, 23). Since then its omission before a verb in the indicative or subjunctive is to be seen only in archaic expressions and fixed locutions (*Fais ce que dois*). The neuter pronoun subject *il* (for older *el*), the introduction of which before impersonal verbs is due to analogy, continued to be used sparingly even in the sixteenth century (XIV, 89) when it often has the value of modern *cela* (*Mais puis qu'il ne se peut,...apprenons à le soutenir de pied ferme*, Mont. I, 20). Such expressions as *tant y a que, peu s'en faut, mieux vaut* are relics of O.F. usage. In Mod.F., neuter *il* has given way in many cases to *ce*, particularly before the verb *être* (§ 258).

241. The pleonastic use of the personal pronoun subject (*Mais sávies hom* il *deit faire message*, Rol. 294; XII, 108) which was formerly common (*Un noble s'il vit chez lui dans sa province*, il *vit libre*, La Bruyère, Haase, 6, 1) is now confined to popular speech and to questions (cf. also *Moi, je crois*). In O.F. the personal pronoun could also be used with the imperative (*E! reis celestes, tu nos i fai venir!* Alexis, 335).

242. The use of the polite plural *vous* for *tu* dates from the V.L. period and may be due to the analogy of *nous* for *je*. In O.F. the modern usage is already foreshadowed, but there is much confusion (cf. XII, 59), particularly in Anglo-Norman, where such phrases as *Va t'en d'ici, tost levez!* and *tu faistes* are common. Under the influence of Latin, the sixteenth century tended to favour *tu*, but seventeenth-century texts show an exaggeration of the opposite tendency.

243. The use of tonic and atonic forms was in O.F. governed by the degree of emphasis which it was desired to give to the pronoun. The tonic form could be used as direct

or indirect object (VI, 87; VII *a*, 35); it was normal before the infinitive and the gerund (cf. *soi-disant*) and is found in this position as late as the sixteenth century. The elimination of the tonic stress in favour of group-stress (§ 145 ff.) caused the accented form to give way in such cases to the unaccented; it also favoured the adoption of the accented form after an imperative, where the pronoun is the last word of the group (*dites-moi, aidez-moi*); cf. § 147. In Mod.F. the tonic form is used after a preposition, after *c'est*, and in apposition with the pronoun subject if it is desired to emphasize the latter (*Moi, je pars*).

244. The use of *à* + tonic pronoun as an accented dative is in Mod.F. possible only if the atonic form precedes (*il me semble, à moi*); but with certain verbs the unaccented dative is regularly expressed by *à* + tonic pronoun, and not by the atonic form (*Il songe à moi*). The number of such verbs was much larger in the earlier periods of the language, and the prepositional construction was optional, e.g. O.F. could say *il me semble, il moi semble*, or *il semble à moi*; cf. VII *b*, 22; x, 46; XIV, 45. The indirect object is expressed by *à* + tonic pronoun if the direct object is a personal pronoun of the first or second person (*Je me fie à vous*; *Il m'a présenté à elle*); and in O.F. it could precede the verb (*Mieudre de moi a vos m'envoie*).

245. Neuter *le* was commonly used in O.F. to refer to a following clause (*Henris le sot que mult granz oz venoit sor lui*, Villehardouin, 322); this use was still common in the seventeenth century (*Il faut le dire que ce crime n'est que trop commun*, Bossuet, Haase, 6, 3). Where Mod.F. employs neuter *le* to refer to a preceding substantive without article or to a predicative adjective (*Êtes-vous mère de cet enfant? Je le suis*), the older practice, of which there are examples in the eighteenth century, was to make the pronoun agree (*Je la suis*).

246. The omission of the pronoun object if accompanied by another pronoun in the dative, which is general in the Middle Ages (XII, 71), was condemned by Vaugelas and other grammarians of the seventeenth century and is now met with only in popular speech.

247. The adverbs of place *en* (< INDE) and *y* (< IBI) gradually acquired a pronominal value and came to be used as the equivalents of *de* + pron. and *à* + pron. respectively. They also continue to be used as adverbs; *en* in particular is frequently used to establish a loose connection with what precedes or with some unexpressed thought in the mind of the speaker or listener (*J'en ai assez*; *Ne m'en veuillez pas!*). As a pronoun, *en* may be used as a possessive genitive (*J'ai vu ce pays*; *j'en connais les beautés*; cf. also XVI, 46); as a partitive genitive (*J'en ai vu des centaines*), often omitted even in the seventeenth century; as the object of a verb requiring *de* (*Je m'en souviens*), just as *y* is used with a verb requiring *à* (*Songez-y*). Whereas *en* and *y* were formerly used of persons or things, Mod.F. generally avoids their use when referring to persons, except *en* as a partitive (*J'en ai vu des centaines*). The latter use of *en* has been much extended in Mod.F., as has also the adverbial use of *en*.

248. Contrary to C.L. usage, the French reflexive pronoun can only refer to the subject of the clause in which it occurs, the unaccented form (*se*) being used with reflexive verbs, the accented (*soi*) being used after a preposition or predicatively. In O.F., *soi* was used in the same way as other tonic personal pronoun forms (XIII, 6, 97; cf. a survival in *soi-disant*), but from the twelfth century (IV, 16) it had to compete with *lui, eux, elle, elles*. The struggle between *soi* and *lui* continues to the disadvantage of *soi*, which is now used to refer to things (masc. sing.), but to a personal subject only if the latter is indefinite (*chacun pour soi*); in the seventeenth century it was still possible to say *Il porte de l'argent sur soi*; cf. XIV, 22, 100.

249. The pronoun object, whether tonic or atonic, could in O.F. precede or follow the verb, but the atonic form now always precedes. In the positive imperative it still follows, but has become accented (§ 147). If two pronoun objects precede, the direct object was formerly always placed first (*Je le vous donne*; cf. XII, 24, 70), partly because it was usually joined enclitically to the preceding word (*Jel vous donne*). This order is still preserved after the imperative (*Donnez-le-moi*), but elsewhere the modern usage, which places the indirect first unless it be *lui, leur,* was established about the end of the sixteenth century after a period of hesitation. The old practice of placing *en* before *y* (XII, 6; XIII, 78; *Conte de tes cognoissans combien il en est mort avant ton aage, plus qu'il n'en y a qui l'ayent atteint,* Mont. I, 20) disappeared in the seventeenth century. When the pronoun is the object of a verb + infinitive, it was formerly placed before the verb even when logically the object of the infinitive (IV, 90, 101; XII, 108; XVI, 78; XVIII *b*, 13; *Vous l'est-on venu dire?* Mol. *Mis.* 560). This is still the rule before *voir, entendre, envoyer, sentir, laisser,* or *faire,* + infinitive; elsewhere Mod.F. requires the pronoun before the infinitive if it is the object of the infinitive and not of the modal verb.

POSSESSIVE PRONOUNS

250. Analogy modified profoundly the development of the Latin possessive pronouns. The accented forms show a re-modelling of MEUS, TUUS, SUUS on the acc. sing. forms *mien* < MEUM, *tuen* < TUUM, *suen* < SUUM, and follow the adjectival declension Class I. The unaccented forms show no such re-modelling and can be explained by assuming that their proclitic use caused what stress there was to fall on the second element, the first vowel disappearing; **mos, *tos, *sos, *mas, *tas, *sas* were then further weakened to *mes, tes, ses* (cf. § 21).

		Accented		Unaccented	
		Masc.	Fem.	Masc.	Fem.
Sing.	nom.	*miens, tuens, suens*		*mes, tes, ses*	
			meie, toe, soe		*ma, ta, sa*
	obl.	*mien, tuen, suen*		*mon, ton, son*	
Pl.	nom.	*mien, tuen, suen*		*mi, ti, si*	
			meies, toes, soes		*mes, tes, se*
	obl.	*miens, tuens, suens*		*mes, tes, ses*	

251. From about the end of the thirteenth century, the strong forms of the second and third persons were re-modelled on the analogy of the first, whence *tien, sien.* Similarly, by analogy with *moie,* the forms *toie* and *soie* had developed beside *toe, soe;* but all the forms of the feminine gave way to new analogical forms *mienne, tienne, sienne,* before the end of the fourteenth century. Alongside of the masc. sing. *mes, tes, ses,* the forms *mis, tis, sis* also occur in O.F. and are due to the influence of the nom. pl. *mi, ti, si.* All the nom. forms disappear at the same time as the nominative of substantives and adjectives (*mes* has survived in *messire*).

The *a* of *ma, ta, sa* was regularly elided in O.F. before a word beginning with a vowel, but in the thirteenth century *mon, ton, son* begin to be used, whence Mod.F. *mon amie,* etc. Mod.F. *ma mie* results from a false interpretation of O.F. *m'amie.*

252. Under the influence of NOSTER, C.L. VESTER was replaced by VOSTER in V.L. The genitive plural ILLORUM came to serve as the corresponding possessive of the third person, whence O.F. accented *lor* (later *leur*), unaccented *lour.*

Accented

		Masc.	Fem.
Sing.	nom.	*nostre, vostre, lor*	
			nostre, vostre, lor
	obl.	*nostre, vostre, lor*	
Pl.	nom.	*nostre, vostre, lor*	
			nostres, vostres, lor
	obl.	*nostres, vostres, lor*	

Unaccented

		Masc.	Fem.
Sing.	nom.	*nostre, vostre, lour*	
			nostre, vostre, lour
	obl.	*nostre, vostre, lour*	
Pl.	nom.	*nostre, vostre, lour*	
			noz, voz, lour
	obl.	*noz, voz, lour*	

253. The contracted forms *noz, voz* are sometimes used in O.F. for accented *nostres, vostres,* and conversely *nostres, vostres* for *noz, voz* (Mod.F. *nos, vos*). Unaccented *nostre, vostre* give Mod.F. *nǫtre, vǫtre*. Unaccented *lour* was supplanted by *lor* (later *leur*), which in conformity with its etymology remained uninflected to the end of the thirteenth century, when it takes *s* in the plural; but its origin is still reflected in the fact that it shows no distinction of gender.

254. The unaccented forms of the possessive pronouns were generally used as adjectives only, but the accented forms, which are now almost exclusively substantival and accompanied by the definite article, could formerly be used attributively (I, 3; IV, 37; X, 76; II, 29; *Paien escrident: 'Aïde nos, Mahom, Li nostre deu, vengiez nos de Charlon',* Rol. 1906; cf. Mod.F. *un mien ami*) and predicatively (*'Dient il voir que la garde de l'abaie est moie?—Certes, sire, fis je, non est, ains est moie'*, Joinville, Sudre, p. 62). In the latter case Mod.F. generally employs *à* with a tonic personal pronoun (*Ce livre est à moi*). If it is desired to give emphasis to the possessive adjective, *à* + personal pronoun is in Mod.F. added after the substantive (*son livre à lui, à elle*). The use of *de* + personal pronoun to denote possession was formerly common, but is from the seventeenth century reserved for cases where clearness absolutely demands it.

DEMONSTRATIVE PRONOUNS

255. The weakening and partial loss of the C.L. demonstrative pronouns[1] led to the development in V.L. of forms in which the demonstrative was reinforced by prefixing the adverb ECCE. Old French preserves these agglutinated forms in the case of ILLE, ISTE, HOC.

---

[1] ILLE survives in the form of the definite article (§ 224) and the personal pronoun of the third person (§ 238). Hoc survives in *av(u)ec* (< AB HOC) and as an affirmative particle with the personal pronoun: *o je, o nos,* etc.; *oïl* (< HOC ILLE) > *ouï* > *oui* (= wi). Cf. also *ist* (< ISTUM) I, 4; *o* (< HOC) I, 6; II, 11, 18, 20.

		Masc.		Fem.		Neuter	
Sing.	nom.	*icil*	*icist*	*icele*	*iceste*	*icel*	*ices*
	obl.	*icelui*	*icestui*	*iceli*	*icesti*		
		icel	*icest*	*icele*	*iceste*	*icel*	*icest*
Pl.	nom.	*icil*	*icist*	*iceles*	*icestes > icez*		
	obl.	*icels > iceus*	*icez*	*iceles*	*icestes > icez*		

ECCE HOC > *iço*

256. Beside the forms *icil*, *icist*, etc. the abbreviated forms *cil*, *cist*, etc. appear from the beginning of the O.F. period and prevail. (*I*)*cestes* early gave way to the contracted form (*i*)*cez* (but cf. XIII, 83), and the neuter *cel, cest* to *ço* which, when unaccented, appears as *ce*. Whence, by regular phonetic development and certain orthographic adjustments: *celui, ceux*; *cet* and (with loss of final *t* before consonant) *ce, ces*; *celle, celles*; *cette, ces*; and the neuter *ce*. The nominative forms have regularly disappeared (although *cil* is found as late as the sixteenth century), and *celui* (originally a dative) has ousted *cel*; but *cest, cele, ceste* have triumphed over *cestui* (XIV, 75), *celi, cesti* (XI, 64) respectively.

(*I*)*cist* and (*i*)*cil* originally denoted what is close at hand and what is remote respectively, and both could be used either adjectivally or substantivally (cf. XII, 73, 76). But even in O.F. there is a tendency to reserve *cil* for substantival, *cist* for adjectival function, a distinction which was definitely accepted in the seventeenth century.

257. The demonstrative force of the pronouns (forms used substantivally; cf. XIV, 111) gradually weakened, and in order to restore it recourse was had to the adverbs *ci* and *là*, unless the pronoun merely serves as the antecedent of a relative clause or is qualified by a genitive indicating possession (*ceux de mon frère*) or provenance (*Quels vins? Ceux de France*). *Celui* can no longer be separated from the relative (as it was before the time of Vaugelas), except by a partitive genitive (*Ceux de vos amis qui...*). The adjectives (*ce, cet, cette, ces*) maintain their demonstrative force more fully, but here too *ci* (formerly often *ici* XIV, 49) and *là* are added after the substantive to

distinguish what is near and distant. The weakening of the demonstrative force of these adjectives (particularly in O.F.) allows of their being used as practically the equivalent of an article (cf. Mod.F. *ce* 10 *mars*).

258. The neuter *ce* early lost its demonstrative force and, as subject of a verb, became equivalent to the neuter personal pronoun *il* (for older *el*), which it tends more and more to displace. Even before an adjective followed by a clause or by *de* + inf. (*Il est facile de faire cela*), where the rules of grammar require *il est*, modern popular speech shows a preference for *c'est*. Cf. also popular *c'est trois heures* for *il est trois heures*. In O.F. *ce* could be used as the subject of any verb, but in Mod.F. this use is restricted to *être* and a few phrases like *ce me semble, ce peut être*.

259. *C'est* serves to recall or to anticipate the logical subject in such sentences as *Vous avez raison, c'est évident*; *C'est un bon garçon que Jean*. The pleonastic use of *ce* to recall the subject and thus emphasize it (*La raison de sa faillite, c'est son manque de courage*) was rare in O.F. and was less common in the sixteenth and seventeenth centuries than at the present day (but cf. XVI, 1, 18, 83): Vaugelas recommended its use only if the subject was widely separated from the verb. For *c'est* before a pronoun or substantive O.F. occasionally shows the Latin use of a demonstrative pronoun agreeing with the predicate (*Cist n'est pas home, ainz est diable*, Gui de Warewic, 8444). Mod.F. *c'est moi, c'est toi* for O.F. *ce suis je, c'es tu* is due to the analogy of *c'est lui*. In Mod.F. *c'est* is often employed to throw into relief the word or words which it is desired to stress (*C'est vous qui avez raison*).

260. *Ce* was formerly much more widely used as an object (III, 56); as the object of a verb it is now used only if it is the antecedent of a relative pronoun (*Je comprends ce que vous dites*); *ce faisant, pour ce faire* and the like are archaic survivals. After a preposition (XIII, 28) it likewise survives in such archaic expressions as *sur ce*, and between a preposition and *que*: *parce que, en ce que, à ce que, de ce que* (but cf. *pour que, sans que*).

261. To restore the demonstrative value of *ce*, the adverbs *ci* and *là* were added in Mid.F. and eventually became fused with it, whence *ceci* and *cela*, originally denoting what is near and remote respectively. While *ceci* has kept the original force, *cela* has been weakened until it is but little stronger than *ce* and often replaces it. In popular speech the contracted form *ça* is extensively used and takes the place not only of neuter *ce* and *il*, but of personal pronouns (*Ça ne veut pas écouter ses père et mère*).

RELATIVE AND INTERROGATIVE PRONOUNS

262. The general popular tendency to reduce the rôle of the relative pronoun to that of a mere copulative in what is virtually a paratactic structure (see below) led to a simplification of forms in V.L., and ultimately in O.F. to the extensive use of a single form *que* for all purposes. At the same time the relative and interrogative forms coalesced to a large extent. Thus in V.L., QUAE, QUAM were replaced by QUI, QUEM; QUOD by the interrogative form QUID, QUIS by the relative QUI; CUI persisted as the accented oblique form of the relative and as the oblique form of the interrogative.

	Masc. and Fem.		Neuter	
	Relative	Interrogative	Accented	Unaccented
Nom.	*qui*	*qui*		
Obl.	*cui, qui*	*cui, qui*	*quei* > *quoi*	*que*
	que			

Cui was used as a dative or genitive, as the tonic form of the accusative, and after prepositions; but the phonetic confusion with *qui* was complete by the twelfth century, although the spelling *cui* is found as late as the fifteenth (cf. x, 15).

263. The relative was frequently used in O.F. without an antecedent. A survival of this use is to be seen in such constructions as *Amenez qui vous voudrez*; *Je ne sais qui vous voulez dire*. It is in O.F. often the equivalent of modern *quiconque* (IV, 86; XII, 100; cf. *Qui vivra verra*; *Qui m'aime me suive*; also xvii, 23), and this absolute use led to the development of functions such as are served in Mod.F. by *si l'on* (xiii, 20; cf. Mod.F. *Tout vient à point qui sait attendre*) or, when repeated, by *les uns...les autres* (*Ne faisons autre chose qu'apprendre à parler, qui Grec, qui Latin, qui Ebreu*, Du Bellay, *Defence*).

264. *Qui* preceded by a preposition was often used in O.F. when referring to things, and this usage is still found in the seventeenth century (cf. xvi, 50), in spite of the formulation of the modern rule which restricts prep. + *qui* to persons, and prescribes prep. + *lequel* or *quoi* and *dont* for things. It is to be noted that the use of prep. + *qui* referring to persons is declining in Mod.F.

265. The neuter *que* as a nominative gradually gave place to the masc. *qui*, but *que* is found as late as the sixteenth century (*Là son precepteur repetoit ce que avoit esté leu*, Rab. I, 23), and has survived in *advienne que pourra*. *Ce* is now required as an antecedent not only if the relative clause itself is substantival (*Ce que vous dites est vrai*), but if the antecedent of the relative is a sentence (*Il se moque de moi, ce que je ne puis souffrir*). In the latter case *ce* (*ço*) is sometimes used in O.F., but it is not compulsory even in the seventeenth century (cf. also xvi, 4). In certain elliptic uses the neuter *que* is reduced almost to the function of a relative adverb: *que je sache* (= *à ce que je sache*) 'so far as I know'; *Je n'ai que faire de vos dons* 'I would have none of your gifts'; O.F. *faire que sages* (= *faire ce que ferait un homme sage*) 'to act wisely, prudently'; *C'est un bon garçon que* (= *qu'est*) *Jean*; *Qu'est-ce que* (= *qu'est*) *le rhumatisme?*; cf. xiv, 13.

266. The relative adverb *que*, the origin of which is obscure but which is in the main a continuation of QUID—QUOD, was very extensively used in O.F. (iii, 11, etc.) and continues to be so employed in popular speech. It serves to indicate relation pure and simple, and constitutes a slight modification of a purely paratactic structure: *Je vous présente l'ami que je lui ai parlé de vous* is a popular rendering of a still more rudimentary *Je vous présente l'ami; je lui ai parlé de vous*. In the literary language and in correct speech the relative adverb

is still used in expressions of time (*la dernière fois que je vous ai vu*), but even here it is losing ground (*le jour où il partit* for common seventeenth-century *le jour qu'il partit*). It also occurs in phrases such as *C'est à vous que je parle*, beside which we find *C'est à vous à qui je parle* (≠ *C'est vous à qui je parle*); cf. *Et que c'est à sa table à qui l'on rend visite*, Mol. *Mis.* 626.

267. *Quoi* as a relative pronoun has lost considerable ground since the O.F. period (cf. XII, 48; XVI, 54) and is practically confined to such expressions as *Il n'y a pas de quoi; Voici de quoi il s'agit*, and cases where the antecedent is a whole clause or an indefinite substantive, such as *rien, quelque chose* (*Il n'y a rien à quoi je songe plus souvent*). But in quite recent times *quoi* has reappeared in literary usage as a substitute for *lequel* when referring to things (*la chose à quoi je pensais*). In O.F. and even later it could refer to persons as well as things (*Li dus de Bourgoigne de quoi je vous ai parlé*, Joinville, 559; *Les Esseniens de quoy parle Pline*, Mont. II, 8. Examples cited by Sudre, p. 79).

268. *Dont* (< DE UNDE) was originally an adverb of place and is widely employed as such down to the seventeenth century, when its use was restricted to antecedents used figuratively (*la maison dont il est sorti*). As a pronoun it took over many of the functions of the preposition *de* + rel. pron. and of *cui* used as a genitive. Its extension was rapid in the Middle Ages, but since the seventeenth century it has lost ground (cf. *Messieurs les Maréchaux, dont j'ai commandement*, Mol. *Mis.* 751). Among other restrictions one may mention the rule which forbids the use of *dont* when the substantive on which it depends is preceded by a preposition (*l'homme dont j'ai parlé au fils* is not tolerated). If the antecedent is a whole clause, *ce* is now required (cf. *Oui; mais il veut avoir trop d'esprit, dont j'enrage*, Mol. *Mis.* 634).

269. *Où* (< UBI), originally an adverb of place which also came to be used as an adverb of time, shows the same development as *dont* and was used down to the eighteenth century as the equivalent of *à, dans, chez, sur* + rel. pron. referring to persons as well as things (XVII, 34; *Il a trois ou*

quatre fils où son cœur s'intéresse bien tendrement, Sév., III, 73; Sudre, p. 83). It is still used in the combinations *d'où* and *par où* if the antecedent is a whole clause (*D'où je conclus*; *Par où il nous fait savoir*).

270. Interrogative *qui* was used down to the seventeenth century to denote things as well as persons, but in Mod.F. a periphrasis is employed to distinguish things (*qu'est-ce qui*) from persons (*qui est-ce qui* or *qui*). Interrogative neuter *que*, in addition to its use as a direct object (*Que fait-il?*), is still used as the logical subject of impersonal verbs (*Que vous en semble?*; cf. XII, 105) and as the predicate of *être*, *devenir* (*Que sont-ils? Que deviennent-ils?*); *qu'est-ce que* (and the popular *qu'est-ce que c'est que*) for *que* is due to the analogy of *qu'est-ce qui*. Like the Latin neuter pronoun, interrogative *que* is sometimes used adverbially as the equivalent of *à quoi, pour quoi, combien*, particularly in exclamations and rhetorical questions (*Que je suis malheureux! Que n'obéissez-vous?*).

271. Interrogative *quoi*, being the accented form, is used after prepositions, but like the accented personal pronoun (§ 243) was often used as a direct object, particularly before the infinitive and the gerund; such uses are rare in Mod.F. (cf. *Que faire?* beside *Quoi faire?*; *Que ferai-je?* has eliminated *Quoi ferai-je?*). Apart from its use after prepositions (*De quoi s'agit-il?*) it is hardly employed except absolutely, in rhetorical questions and exclamations (*Quoi? Quoi! Quoi de plus beau!*).

272. *Quel* is used as either relative or interrogative in O.F. and follows the adjectival declension Class II. It gradually ceased to be used as a relative, although examples of relative *quel* are to be found in the sixteenth and seventeenth centuries. As an interrogative pronoun it has ceased to be used substantivally since the Renaissance (*Quel est son nom?* but not *Quel vient?*).

273. *Lequel.* When used substantivally, *quel* sometimes took the definite article in O.F. (*le quel*, whence agglutinated *lequel*); *lequel* began to be used adjectivally towards the end of the O.F. period. *Lequel* is not found in the earliest O.F. texts, but it had this advantage over *qui* that it indicated

gender, case, and number more clearly; accordingly it was much favoured in the fifteenth and sixteenth centuries (XIV, 4), being used to reproduce certain Latin constructions, such as the ablative absolute (*Lesquels entrez dedans la maison grande De leur Seigneur, en brief dire leur vient*, Marot, Sudre, p. 80; *Nageoit, une main en l'air, en laquelle tenant un livre transpassoit toute la riviere*, Rab. 1, 23). It was less frequently used in the seventeenth, and since then it has been much restricted: it seldom appears as subject or direct object and it can no longer be used adjectivally. Interrogative *lequel* was used adjectivally or (more commonly) substantivally in the Middle Ages; as an adjective it does not survive the Renaissance (Mod.F. *Lequel des deux?* but not *Lequel livre?*).

INDEFINITE PRONOUNS

274. A certain number of the Latin indefinite pronouns have persisted down to Modern French:

Autre, O.F. *altre* (< ALTERUM), used substantivally and adjectivally from the beginning   Contrary to medieval usage (cf. XIV, 58), *autre* must now be preceded by an article, partitive *de*, or a pronominal adjective. Survivals are: *autre chose* (for older neuter *autre*), *autrefois*, *de temps à autre*. In Mod.F., as in O.F., *autre* can refer to the past (*l'autre jour*), and in popular speech to the future. In the Middle Ages *autre* was also used as a numeral (= *second*). It is regularly opposed, in O.F. as in Mod.F., to *un* in such phrases as *l'un...l'autre*, *l'un et l'autre*, *l'un l'autre* (reciprocal), *les uns ...les autres*. The analogical oblique form *autrui* (cf. *lui*, § 238) is now used only as direct object or after a preposition, but formerly also functioned as a genitive or dative.

Nul (< NULLUM), although itself negative, is accompanied by a pleonastic (analogical) *ne* (*Nuls n'en respondiét*, Rol. 2411). It thus became an alternative for *aucun*, and its use has gradually been restricted until in Mod.F. it is used only in the singular, and as a pronoun only in the masculine (= *per sonne*). The oblique form *nullui* was still used in the sixteenth century.

Tel (< TALEM) was originally inflected like *grand* (§ 187), but early developed an analogical feminine *telle*. With *tel* used adjectivally the indefinite article was originally not essential (cf. *de telle façon, de telle sorte,* and XII, 82; XIV, 85), but has gradually been generalized (*un tel cas,* pl. *de tels cas*). Its use before a substantive in the sense of 'like', 'as for example' results from the ellipsis of the verb *être* or of *que* (*Il s'avança furieux, tel un lion qui cherche sa proie*); cf. also XIV, 57. As a pronoun it is no longer used in the plural (cf. XVI, 57). It was formerly used in combination with other pronouns (*autretel*).

Tout (< *TŌTTUM* for TŌTUM, which supplanted OMNIS), O.F. masc. nom. pl. *tuit* (beside later O.F. *tout*), was used from the beginning substantivally, adjectivally, and adverbially. Adjectival *tout* was formerly used without an accompanying article or pronominal adjective (XIV, 16), and its place with reference to the substantive was not fixed. In Mod.F. it is used in the singular without an article in the sense of 'every', 'each and every' (*Tout homme a sa faiblesse*). The old usage is perpetuated in a large number of more or less set expressions: *à tous égards, de tous côtés, à toutes jambes, toujours* (= *tous jours*), *tous deux* beside more emphatic *tous les deux*. When used adverbially it is sometimes made to agree with a following adjective (§ 212), but not with a substantive (*Il est tout bonté*); the latter is to be distinguished from cases such as *de toute urgence*, where *toute* is an adjective meaning 'highest', 'utmost'.

Other Latin forms persisted in O.F. but have not come down: *alquant* (< ALIQUANTI) 'some', *alque* (ALIQUID) generally used adverbially (*alques*) 'somewhat', *el* (ALIUD) 'something else', *mult* (< MULTI) 'many', *quant* (< QUANTI) 'how many', *tant* (< TANTI) 'so many'.

275. The loss of old forms was made good by new formations.

(*a*) Compound forms:

Aucun (< ALIQUEM + UNUM) preserves its original positive

meaning (VI, 8; XI, 3; XII, 42; XIV, 58) in *d'aucuns* (*d'aucuns prétendent*); but the negative meaning, which results from its constant use in negative sentences, is regular since the sixteenth century. Apart from the case cited, it is no longer used in the plural.

Chacun, O.F. *chascun* < QUISQUE + UNUM influenced by CATA (=κατά) + UNUM (which survives in O.F. as *che(d)un*). *Chacun* ceased to be used as an adjective in the seventeenth century, being replaced by its derivative *chaque* (O.F. *chasque*), which is found as early as the twelfth century. *Chacun* was occasionally used in the plural in O.F. As a pronoun it can still be preceded by the indefinite article in popular speech (*un chacun*), as it was in literary usage down to the eighteenth century. *Chaque* is sometimes used as a pronoun in such expressions as *Ces livres m'ont coûté cinq francs chaque.*

Même, O.F. *me(d)esme* or *me(d)isme* (< *METIPSIMUM from *METIPSE der. from EGOMET IPSE, etc.), is used in French in the original sense 'himself' and also in the sense of IDEM 'the same'. The modern rule requiring that in the sense of 'himself' it should follow the substantive was not formerly observed. The same remark applies to the rule requiring that when used before a substantive in the sense of 'the same' it should be preceded by an article or pronominal adjective (cf. the survivals *en même temps*, *de même qualité*). *Même* can also function as an adverb in the sense of 'even', and as such it often took an adverbial *s* (*mêmes*); this is partly responsible for the hesitation between *même* and *mêmes* (cf. XII, 12; XIV, 1), which has not yet been completely eliminated, in spite of the Decree of 1901 admitting *mêmes* after a substantive or pronoun in the plural.

276. The compound forms of later date have sometimes become completely fused (*quelque, quelconque, quiconque*) although spelling may not indicate the fusion (*quelque chose*); sometimes the constituent parts remain variable (*quelqu'un*).

Quelque dates from the thirteenth century and was at first written as two words; *quel* was perhaps originally an indefinite relative pronoun (*en quel royaume que ce soit*), and with ellipsis of the verb, *quel que* became equivalent to 'whatever' (cf. XII, III), from which the meaning 'some or other', 'some' developed, *quelque* being finally used as a simple adjective. Before a numeral it becomes adverbial and is accordingly invariable (*quelque deux cents hommes*), but was formerly inflected (cf. *tout*). It is also invariable in such expressions as *quelque grand qu'il soit*. This use of *quelque* is modern and is an extension of older *quelque* + substantive + *que* (with pleonastic *que*; XIII, 43) for original *quel* + substantive + *que*, as in *Quel compaignie que tu truisses* (Chemin de Povreté), Nyrop, v, 336. Cf. Mod.F. *quelles que soient vos raisons*.

Quelque chose as an indefinite pronoun dates from the fifteenth century, and since the seventeenth century (Vaugelas) it is treated as a single neuter expression and is therefore masculine. *Quelqu'un* likewise dates from the fifteenth but has never fused completely, both parts being variable. It has gradually displaced *aucun* (cf. § 275).

Quelconque and *quiconque* appear in O.F. as *quel que onques* and *qui que onques*, and on the strength of their frequent occurrence in translations it has been argued that they are Learned formations reproducing QUALISCUNQUE and QUICUNQUE, but there is no need to assume such an influence. *Quelconque* could formerly precede the substantive, and its first element was inflected. *Quiconque* is used as an indefinite pronoun 'anyone whatsoever', or as an indefinite relative 'whoever', for older *qui* (§ 263). In the latter case it may stand as the subject of two verbs (*Quiconque parlera sera puni*) or as the subject of one and the object of another (*Je punirai quiconque parlera*).

Other modern formations are: *n'importe qui, n'importe quel, n'importe quoi, tout le monde*.

277. (*b*) Other indefinite pronouns are formed by using substantives and adjectives with change of function:

On (< HOMO), being originally a substantive, was often preceded by the definite article. Both forms have been preserved, but *l'on* is practically confined to the literary language and its use is governed by euphony: it is employed after *ou, où, si,* to avoid hiatus, and sometimes after *que*; it is avoided if the following word begins with *l* (*si on le voit*). In accordance with its etymology, *on* can only stand as the subject of a sentence, the corresponding oblique form being supplied by *nous, vous, soi* (*Quand on est chez soi*). Contrary to its etymology, *on* can, by syllepsis, be treated as feminine (*On n'est pas toujours belle*) and as a plural (*Quand on est amis il faut se dire la vérité*), but the use of a plural verb (*on répondirent*) has remained confined to dialects (cf. Nyrop, v, 377).

Un, originally a numeral, was frequently used as a pronoun in O.F. and continued to be so used in the sixteenth century (*Comme les Egyptiens, apres leurs festins, faisoient presenter aux assistans une grand'image de la mort par* un *qui leur crioit: Boy et t'esjouy, car, mort, tu seras tel*, Mont. I, 20). It is rare in Mod.F., except in popular speech; *pas un* (=*personne*) was common in the seventeenth century and is still used.

Personne (< PERSONA) came to be used as a pronoun in French, and, owing to its constant use in negative phrases, developed a purely negative value. It kept its original gender down to the seventeenth century, since when it is treated as masc. (*Personne n'est venu*).

Rien (< REM) XIII, 63, also survived as a feminine substantive in the Middle Ages (*por nule rien*). Like *personne*, it has become a negative pronoun (*Rien n'est arrivé*). Cf. the similar use of *chose* (XIII, 64).

Certain (< *CERTANUM der. from CERTUM) is now rarely used substantivally (*certains disent*). As a pronominal adjective it is usually accompanied in Mod.F. by the indefinite article (*un certain renseignement*, pl. *de certains renseignements*) and is to be distinguished from the pure adjective *certain* 'definite', 'conclusive' (*un renseignement certain*).

Plusieurs, O.F. *pluisors* (< L.L. PLURIORES influenced by PLUS), is still used, as in O.F., substantivally and adjectivally (*Plusieurs (hommes) sont arrivés*; cf. x, 64); it has preserved its original uniformity (*plusieurs femmes*).

Maint is of doubtful origin (< MAGNUM + TANTUM?). Extensively used as an adjective in O.F. and also as a substantive in Mid.F., it was described as obsolete by Vaugelas, and has persisted as an archaic and poetic word

C. *VERBS*

278. The Classical Latin verbal system was maintained remarkably well in Vulgar Latin, thanks largely to the fact that the various endings fulfilled a clear, definite and significant function. Phonetic changes had however impaired this clarity to some extent; e.g. AMAVIT and AMABIT, CANTA-(VE)RIM and CANTAREM, SCRIBAM (subjv.) and SCRIBAM (fut.) were confused. New syntactic habits resulting from the general analytic tendency had led to the formation of periphrastic forms (Future and Passive), and the decline of the Classical tradition favoured a general levelling out by analogy and the elimination of anomalies (POSSE, VELLE, ESSE give way to *POTÉRE, *VOLÉRE, *ÉSSERE, etc.).

279. Of the Latin Active Voice the following forms persisted through V.L. into French: the Present, Imperfect, Perfect, Pluperfect of the Indicative; the Present, Pluperfect of the Subjunctive; the Present Imperative, the Present Infinitive, the Present Participle, the Gerund. The Perfect gradually becomes a pure preterite, its function as a perfect being surrendered to a new compound Perfect (HABEO CANTATUM, *j'ai chanté*). The Pluperfect Indicative is found only in the earliest O.F. texts and there fulfils the function of a preterite (II, notes); it is replaced by new compound Pluperfects (HABEBAM CANTATUM, *j'avais chanté*; HABUI CANTATUM, *j'eus chanté*). The Future Indicative survives only in the O.F. future of *estre* (*ier* < ERO, *iers* < ERIS, etc. beside the new forms *estrai, serai*; cf. § 337). The Pluperfect Subjunctive took over the functions of the Imperfect Subjunctive and also of the Perfect Subjunctive, the latter having coalesced with the Future Perfect, from which it differed only in the 1st sing.; new compound forms (*j'aie chanté, j'eusse chanté*) were created. By analogy with the analytic forms of the passive, the verb *être* later came to be used as an auxiliary with reflexive verbs

and certain intransitive verbs (cf. §§ 382–8). The Imperative is maintained only in the 2nd sing. of the present (AMA), the 2nd pl. (AMATE) being replaced by the 2nd pl. pres. ind. (AMATIS > *amez*). Of the Gerund only the ablative in -o survives, and it early tends to be confused with the Present Participle (§ 301 ff.).

280. The synthetic forms of the Passive (AMOR) become rare in V.L. and gradually disappear, with the exception of the Past Participle. They are replaced by analytic forms consisting of the past participle + ESSE on the analogy of the Latin analytic forms (AMATUS SUM, etc.). The Past Participle had given up its past passive meaning[1] in favour of the present passive meaning which it already possessed in certain C.L. constructions. Accordingly, AMOR gives place to AMATUS SUM, AMABAR to AMATUS ERAM, AMATUS SUM to AMATUS FUI, etc. The Deponent verbs are assimilated to the Active (MORIOR, PRECOR are replaced by *MORIO, PRECO), thus completing a movement which had already begun in C.L. The analytic forms have this disadvantage that in the case of verbs expressing a momentary action they do not, in the present, imperfect, and future, render the idea of action (*il est battu* = 'he is beaten', *not* 'he is being beaten'). Accordingly French has had recourse to the indefinite *on* + active voice (*on le bat*) or to the reflexive (*la fenêtre s'ouvre* = 'the window is being opened', whereas *la fenêtre est ouverte* = 'the window is open'). However, in O.F. and as late as the sixteenth century the analytic form was often used where Mod.F. employs *on*.

281. The Future was rendered in V.L. by means of a periphrasis consisting of the pres. ind. of such verbs as VELLE, HABERE, + infinitive. In Gaul HABERE alone persisted in this function. While in V.L. it had not become fused with the infinitive and could precede or follow, French shows from the earliest monuments (I, 5, 7) only forms in which the infinitive has fused with the following contracted forms of HABEO (CANTARE + *AJO > *chanterai*, CANTARE + *AS > *chanteras*, etc.). Parallel with this new future there developed a Future

---

[1] It survives in *mort* and *né* (*il est né* 'he was born'). Cf. also XVI, 71.

Imperfect (Future-in-the-Past or Conditional) composed of the infinitive + contracted forms of the impf. ind. of HABERE (CANTARE + *EAM > *chantereie > chanteroie, chanterais*; cf. § 334). The compound forms *j'aurai chanté* and *j'aurais chanté* are developed in sequence (cf. § 438).

282. The verb-forms which had survived from C.L. underwent in V.L. a series of changes, partly phonetic, partly analogical; the former tending to break down the uniformity of the C.L. system, the latter tending to level out irregularities which were thus created or already existed in C.L. Both may combine to bring about a change of paradigm. Their effect will be examined more in detail in connection with the various tenses, but a few of the more striking V.L. changes may here be mentioned.

283. The 1st sing. pres. ind. of -ĒRE verbs ended in -EO, of some -ĔRE verbs (type CAPIO) in -IO. In V.L. both -EO and -IO became *-jo*, which was maintained in some verbs but reduced to *-o* in others. Those which kept *-jo* tended to be assimilated to -ĪRE verbs in the proportion AUDIO : AUDIRE : : -JO : *-IRE, whence V.L. FODIRE, FUGIRE, CUPIRE, RAPIRE, MORIRE, IMPLIRE, LUCIRE, FLORIRE, etc. Those which reduced *-jo* to *-o* tended to be assimilated to the -ĔRE verbs, whence RESPÓNDERE, RÍDERE, TÓNDERE, MÓRDERE, TÓRQUERE, TÉRGERE, FÚLGERE.

284. The perfect in -UI is found in all four C.L. conjugations, but it was characteristic in the most frequently used verbs of the -ĒRE conjugation and only fairly common in the -ĔRE conjugation. The tendency was therefore to re-model verbs of the latter conjugation in the proportion HABUI : HABĒRE : : -UI : *-ĒRE, whence V.L. SAPUI : SAPĘRE, *CADUI (for CECIDI) : CADĘRE. The same re-modelling gave *POTĘRE (for POSSE), *VOLĘRE (for VELLE). Compounds of FERRE were normalized under the influence of FERIRE, whence *OFFERIRE, *SUFFERIRE.

285. Other analogical changes took place in accentuation. Compound verbs which were still recognized as such were re-composed in V.L., and the accent no longer fell on the

prefix: CÓNTINET > CONTÉNET > *contient*; but CÓLLOCAT > *col-cheț* > *couche*; cf. § 22 (*d*). The alternation of strong forms (accented on the stem) and weak forms (accented on the ending) was to some extent eliminated in V.L. In verbs showing the 1st and 2nd pl. endings '-IMUS, '-ITIS, the accent passed from the stem to the ending under the influence of -ÁMUS, -ÁTIS, -ÉMUS, -ÉTIS, -ÍMUS, -ÍTIS, whence V.L. -ẸMUS, -ẸTIS. FACIMUS and DICIMUS, both frequently used verbs, escaped this levelling process, whence O.F. *faimes*, *dimes*.

286. The levelling tendency is also responsible for the creation of a new conjugation with the accent on the ending throughout the present indicative. This is made possible in a verb like FLORERE by utilizing the inchoative forms FLORESCO, etc., whence a paradigm FLORÉSCO, FLORÉSCIS, FLORÉSCIT, FLORÉMUS, FLORÉTIS, FLORÉSCUNT. The assimilation of many of these verbs to the -IRE class (§ 283) favoured the extension of -ISCO, which soon displaced -ESCO. Similarly a new subjunctive (FLORESCAM) and imperative (FLORESCE) were formed. At a later stage the inchoative suffix -ISC was extended to the 1st and 2nd pl. pres. ind., to the participle-gerund, and to the whole of the impf. ind. Thus arose the inchoative conjugation in -IRE of which the French *finir* class is the continuation. The inchoative meaning had been lost before the end of the V.L. period.

287. The result of these and other changes was to obliterate to some extent the classical distinction of four conjugations on the basis of the infinitive endings: I -ĀRE, II -ĒRE, III -ĔRE, IV -ĪRE. But it should be remembered that even in C.L. this classification failed to cover a host of divergences, quite apart from the so-called irregular, anomalous, and defective verbs. For example, a classification on the basis of the perfect and allied tenses would cut right across the traditional divisions (§ 345). Moreover, the group of verbs of the CAPIO type occupied an ambiguous position between III and IV. Modern French preserves the phonetic equivalents of the four infinitives: -*er* (-ĀRE), -*oir* (-ĒRE), -*re* (-ĔRE), -*ir* (-ĪRE); but they no longer correspond to distinctive series of flexions.

Verbs in *-er* alone present one common and uniform conjugation. Verbs in *-ir* which add *-iss* to the root in the tenses of the present system (type *finir*) constitute a second regular conjugation; but the remaining verbs in *-ir* (about thirty in number), the verbs in *-oir* and in *-re* do not constitute separate conjugations, and one can at most distinguish groups presenting common features. A change of infinitive does not necessarily imply a change of paradigm (e.g. *luire*, § 290), although it may be reflected in analogical re-modelling of certain forms or tenses. Conversely, a change of paradigm (from simple *-ir* to inchoative *-ir*) may leave the form of the infinitive unaffected. Nor must change of paradigm be confused with the creation of a new verb (*tousser* for O.F *toussir* represents, not a change of paradigm, but a new formation from *toux*).

288. The history of the French verbs will therefore be presented in the following pages as the history, not of conjugations, but of forms and tenses, singly or in groups. Their chequered history will show that the fluctuation and conflict between phonetic development and analogical re-modelling already observed continues to the present day, although less striking in the modern period. The alternation of strong and weak forms is normally reflected in corresponding variations in the form of the stem, its vowel developing as a tonic vowel in the former case, and as a countertonic or atonic vowel in the latter. The resulting oscillation between two forms of the stem (*meurs—mourons*) is called Apophony. Further modifications may result from the influence of neighbouring sounds, which vary in the different persons of the same tense or in different tenses of the same verb. Against this has to be set the tendency to consider the stem invariable (seeing that it is the invariable thought-element) and to level out irregularities resulting from phonetic change. Thus O.F. *plourer*, *plourons*, *plourez*, etc. give place to *pleurer*, *pleurons*, *pleurez*, etc. under the influence of the strong forms *pleure*, *pleures*, *pleurent*. A similar associative influence often causes the accent to shift from one syllable to another, one ending

to be substituted for another, or a paradigm to be re-modelled
in whole or in part.

THE INFINITIVE

289. Infinitive in -*er* (< -ĀRE). After a palatal or palatalized
sound, -ARE > -*ier* (JUDICARE > *jugier*, TRACTARE > *traitier*), which
early began to be assimilated to the more numerous -*er*
infinitives, and where it persisted was reduced to -*er* through
the absorption of *i* by the preceding sibilant towards the end
of the Middle Ages (§ 75). The -*er* class remained the most
stable, supported as it was by the more stable and uniform
conjugation. Modern French has preserved none of the O.F.
forms in -*ir*, -*oir*, -*re* for -*er*; such forms were particularly
common in Anglo-Norman. To the -*er* class belong not only
verbs derived from Latin verbs in -ARE (*chanter* < CANTARE)
and from Germanic verbs in -AN, -ŌN, and a few in -JAN
(*guider* for *guier* from wītan, *danser* from dansōn, *gagner*
< *gaaignier* from waidanjan), but also verbs of the following
categories which are still productive: (*a*) Verbs derived from
substantives (*botter*, *draper*). (*b*) A few verbs derived from
adjectives (*aveugler*, *griser*); but later formations of this type
belong to the -*ir* class (*rougir*, *affaiblir*). (*c*) Verbs of foreign
origin (*flirter*, *hâbler*, *stopper*). (*d*) Learned verbs borrowed
from Latin (including those borrowed from Greek through
Latin); the earliest such borrowings of Latin verbs in -ĒRE
-ĚRE appear as -*ir* verbs (*afligir*, *discutir*, *procedir*, *restituir*); but
under the influence of later borrowings, which uniformly give
verbs in -*er* (*assister*, *dissuader*, *instituer*), they too pass into the
-*er* class, with the exception of those which had in the meantime become inchoative (*abolir*, *agir*, *applaudir*, *languir*, *régir*
and compounds of -*vertir*). (*e*) A few accessions from other
classes with change of paradigm (*secouer* for older *secourre*,
tisser for *tistre* (< TEXERE) and *tissir*, *épeler* for *espeldre* and
espelir, *puer* for *puir*, the latter found as late as the seventeenth
century). The following represent, not a change of class, but
the adoption of a doublet of new creation: *sangloter* (formed
on *sanglot*) for *sangloutir*, *tousser* (formed on *toux*) for *toussir*.

290. Infinitive in *-ir* (< -ÏRE, and -ĒRE preceded by a palatal). Besides verbs derived from Latin verbs in -IRE (*dormir* < DORMIRE) and from Germanic verbs in -JAN (*garnir* from warnjan), this class includes: (*a*) Verbs in -ĒRE preceded by a palatal: *gésir* < JACĒRE, *loisir* < LICĒRE, *moisir* < MUCĒRE, *nuisir* < NOCĒRE, *plaisir* < PLACĒRE, *taisir* < TACĒRE; but of these only *gésir* and (as substantives) *plaisir*, *loisir* survive, and the verb *loisir* did not outlive the O.F. period; the remainder have given way to analogical infinitives *nuire*, *plaire*, *taire*, which appear in the twelfth century and are created in the proportion *duit* : *duire* : : *nui(s)t* : *nuire*, *fait* : *faire* : : *plai(s)t*, *tai(s)t* : *plaire*, *taire*. Similarly *luire* replaced *luisir* (< *LUCIRE). (*b*) Verbs in -ĒRE and -ĔRE that passed into the -IRE class in the V.L. period: *fleurir* < *FLORIRE (FLORERE), *emplir* < *IMPLIRE (IMPLERE), *fuir* < *FUGIRE (FUGERE) (§ 283); or in the Gallo-Roman period: *envahir* < *INVADIRE (INVADERE), *trahir* < *TRADIRE (TRADERE). For *offrir* < *OFFERIRE (OFFERRE), *souffrir* < *SUFFERIRE (SUFFERRE), see § 284. (*c*) Such early borrowings of verbs in -ĒRE, -ĔRE as had become inchoative (§ 289). (*d*) Late borrowings from -IRE verbs: *démolir*, *mugir*, *rugir*, etc. (*e*) Most verbs formed from adjectives (§§ 289, 524), some of which replace older verbs in *-ier* (*refroidir*, cf. XIII, 5) and some of which failed to survive (*aveuglir*, *séchir*). (*f*) A few verbs derived from substantives (*brandir*, *croupir*). (*g*) Verbs derived from prep. + subst. (*anéantir*, *aboutir*); cf. § 537. *Tenir* (TENERE) is due to the influence of *venir*. Later accessions from other classes include: *courir* for older *courre*, which has survived as a technical term (*courre le cerf*); *quérir* (and its compounds) for older *querre*; and with change of paradigm: *beneïr* (> *bénir*) for *ben(e)- istre* ≠ *beneï* (§ 369), *étrécir* for *estrecier* ≠ verbs in *-cir*.

291. *-ir* verbs are of two kinds, inchoative and simple (non-inchoative). The former class originally consisted of verbs derived from Latin inchoatives, or from a combination of simple and inchoative (§ 286), and rapidly gained ground at the expense of simple *-ir* verbs. Inchoative verbs never become simple, but the passage from simple to inchoative continues throughout the Middle Ages and is reflected in the medieval hesitation over such verbs as *bénir, croupir, fouir, enfouir, emplir, jouir, nourrir, resplendir, -vertir*, which are now inchoative, and *bouillir* and *partir*, which are now simple. Inchoative forms of *haïr* are rare in the Middle Ages but general since the end of the sixteenth century, except in the sing. of the pres. ind. (§ 321). Traces of former hesitation persist in the case of *saillir*, which is simple in the sense of 'to project' but inchoative in the sense of 'to spurt'; *ressortir*, simple in the sense of 're-emerge', inchoative in the sense of 'be within the province of'; *faillir*, inchoative in the sense of 'go bankrupt'. In many other cases hesitation continued beyond the Renaissance (*tressaillir* still fluctuates in the eighteenth century, but is now simple).

292. Infinitive in *-oir* (<-ĒRE). To this class belong: (*a*) Verbs in -ĒRE except those which in V.L. passed into the -ĔRE class (MÓRDERE, RESPÓNDERE, RÍDERE, TÓNDERE, TÓRQUERE) or into the -ĪRE class (FLORÉRE, etc., cf. § 286), and those in which -ĒRE was preceded by a palatal (§ 290). (*b*) Verbs in -ĔRE that in V.L. passed into the -ĒRE class (SAPÉRE, CADÉRE). (*c*) *POTÉRE (POSSE), *VOLÉRE (VELLE); cf. § 284. (*d*) Verbs in *-ecevoir*, such as *recevoir* for *reçoivre* in the proportion *doit* : *devoir* : : *reçoit* : *recevoir*. Such forms appear as early as the thirteenth century; *falloir* is a later variant of *faillir* (< *FALLIRE for FALLERE), with specialized meaning 'to be necessary', ≠*chaloir, valoir*, etc. in the proportion *chaut* : *chaloir* : : *faut* : *falloir*.

293. Infinitive in *-re* (<'-ĔRE). To this class belong verbs in -ĔRE, except those which in V.L. had joined the -ĒRE or -ĪRE class (see above), and *luire, nuire, plaire, taire* (§ 290), together with *e(s)tre* (< *ESSERE for ESSE). By the loss of unaccented *e*, *r* is brought into contact with the preceding consonant and final *e* persists as a supporting vowel; for the development of the group cons. + *r*, see §§ 100, 102 (*e*). CREDERE > *croire*, PERDERE > *perdre*, COGNOSCERE > *conoistre* > *connaître*; *beivre* (< BIBERE) and *escrivre* (< SCRIBERE) have become *boire, e(s)crire* in the proportion *croit* : *croire* : : *boit* : *boire, lit* : *lire* : : *e(s)crit* : *e(s)crire*; for *reçoivre—recevoir*, see § 292.

294. In O.F. many infinitives presented, beside the etymological form, collateral forms which resulted from various analogical influences, e.g. *cheïr, seïr, veïr,* beside *cheoir, seoir, veoir; rompir* beside *rompre*; cf. also the collateral forms *criembre, criendre, craindre, cremoir, cremir.* Some of these persisted in the sixteenth century, e.g. *nasquir, vainquir, suivir,* formed on the past definite of *naistre, vaincre* (O.F. *veintre*), *suivre*; hesitations which affected the whole paradigm: *couvrir* and *couvrer, recouvrir* and *recouvrer, cueillir* and *cueiller.*

<h2 align="center">SYNTAX OF THE INFINITIVE</h2>

295. The infinitive is a verbal substantive, and its history turns on the varying prominence given to its verbal and its substantival functions respectively. The latter was much more prominent in O.F. than in Mod.F., the infinitive being sometimes used as a pure substantive and supplied with a definite article. Some verbs (*avoir, être, faire*) were used thus from a very early date and became so completely substantival that they were inflected, taking the characteristic *-s* of the nom. sing. (XII, 113). Others retain their verbal force sufficiently to be capable of taking a direct object, although accompanied by the definite article (*al estorm comencier, Rol.* 2413, literally 'at the beginning the battle'). In Mid.F. substantival infinitives are less common and, in spite of an attempt by the poets of the Pléiade to revive them and the favour shown them by Malherbe, Mod.F. shows only such fossilized forms as *un être, des vivres, le savoir, le devoir, le pouvoir, le loisir, le plaisir, le dîner, au sortir, au partir.*

The substantival character of the infinitive is further evidenced by its use as the subject, object or predicate of a verb (*Mentir est honteux; Il semblait avoir entendu; Je désire partir*) and by its use after prepositions.

296. *de* + infinitive was originally the equivalent of the genitive of the gerund (CANTANDI). The original function is clearly seen when the infinitive depends on a substantive or adjective (*le plaisir de voyager, content de vivre*) or takes the place of *de* + substantive (*Il s'abstient de boire = de la boisson; On* *l'accuse d'avoir volɛ = de vol; près de mourir = de la mort*). But gradually the use of *de* + inf. was extended until it came to be little more than the equivalent of English 'to + inf.' or German 'zu + inf.', e.g. when the infinitive is the logical subject (*C'est une honte de mentir*) or direct object (*Je vous conseille de partir*). This development was probably due in part to the common use of *de* + substantive as a genitive of origin (*Chose honteuse est de mensonge = Chose honteuse vient de mensonge*) or as a genitive of reference (*Que tu me consoilles ou d'aventure ou de mervoille!*), which was common in exclamations (*Fils Alexis, de ta dolente mere!* Alexis, 396; *Or du bien faire!* Bodel, *St Nicolas*, 396). The weakening of *de* led to its use as a mere link between the verb and a following infinitive, and before the so-called historic infinitive (*Grenouilles aussitôt de sauter dans les ondes*, La Fontaine, *Fables*, ii, 14). Consequently there has always been considerable hesitation between the use of a pure infinitive, *de* + inf., and *à* + inf.

297. *à* + infinitive was originally the equivalent of the dative of the gerund (CANTANDO) and is generally used after verbs or adjectives implying tendency. In O.F. *à* was much more widely used and tended to become a mere adjunct. Consequently it entered into competition with *de*, before which it continues to give ground down to the present day. *à* + inf. is employed in French to render the Latin supine (FACILE DICTU—*facile à dire*) or the Latin gerundive, and as such develops a passive meaning (*un conseil à suivre*). It is also used independently to denote means, manner, condition (*à en juger, à l'en croire, à vrai dire, à y regarder de près*). Formerly it was also used to denote circumstance, intention or purpose, and seventeenth-century authors favoured it where Mod.F. would require *pour* + inf. (*Je ferai mon possible à bien venger mon père*, Corn. *Le Cid*, 982).

298. The hesitation between *à* + inf. and *de* + inf. has left traces in Mod.F. (after *commencer, continuer, manquer, prendre garde*). Analogical influences and considerations of euphony often favoured one or other preposition (*commencer de* favoured by the analogy of *finir de*; *de* preferred before a vowel in

order to avoid hiatus). The hesitation has sometimes been utilized to distinguish shades of meaning, but this differentiation is not always observed (*commencer à* 'to begin for the first time', *commencer de* 'to begin an action which is not new'; *continuer à* 'to proceed with an action', *continuer de* 'to persist in a course of action'); cf. also xiv, 58, 66. Hesitation between *à* and *de* was particularly common in the sixteenth and seventeenth centuries: *tâcher à* (beside *de*), *essayer à* (beside *de*), *consentir de* (beside *à*), *s'attendre de* (beside *à*). Modern *se plaire à* has displaced seventeenth-century *se plaire de*; *commander de*, sixteenth-century *commander à*.

299. *après* + infinitive. Mod.F. requires the perfect infinitive (*après avoir chanté*). *Après boire*, *après dîner* are survivals of the older usage which allowed the pres. inf. after *après*.

avant + infinitive was fairly common in the sixteenth century, as well as *avant que* + inf. (≠ *avant que* conj.). The latter survived in the seventeenth, but *avant que de* (*de* due to analogy of *de* + inf. after comparative *que*?) was favoured by Vaugelas. *Avant de* was finally adopted in the eighteenth century.

depuis + perfect infinitive is still found in the seventeenth century.

par + infinitive was still commonly used in the seventeenth century to denote means or instrument (*Je rendois mon voyage inutile par être trop court*), but is now used only after *commencer* and *finir*.

pour + infinitive was formerly used not only to denote purpose but cause or concession (*Ah! pour être dévot, je n'en suis pas moins homme*, Mol. *Tart*. 966); the latter use is now possible only with the perfect infinitive (*Je ne le connais pas pour l'avoir vu deux fois*); cf. § 462.

300. Accusative + infinitive. The use of the acc. + inf. construction had been much restricted in V.L., notably after verbs of saying, where a QUOD-clause was preferred. It continued to be favoured, however, if the object of the governing verb was at the same time the subject of the infinitive. With the same restrictions it continued to be used in O.F. Under Latin influence it became general in the sixteenth century

(*Ilz demandoient les cloches leurs estre rendues*, Rab. 1, 18), but its
use was much restricted again in the seventeenth (cf. Haase,
89). It survives, often with passive meaning, in Mod.F. after
verbs of perception (*entendre, sentir, voir*), *laisser, faire* (*Je l'ai
fait venir*). After verbs of saying it is still used if the subject
is a personal pronoun and the infinitive is *être*: *Je le croyais
(être) fini*. After verbs of perception, *laisser*, and *faire*, the dative
is sometimes used to denote the subject of the infinitive (*Je le
lui ai entendu dire*; *Je lui ai fait lire la lettre*). This use of the
dative probably goes back to the L.L. use of the dative with
an active infinitive (*Eos vero ulciscendo multis ad regna caelorum
fecit habere*), which is an extension of the C.L. dative of agent
used with the gerundive or past participle (cf. § 375)

PRESENT PARTICIPLE AND GERUND

301. Of the gerund only the form in -o survived in V.L.,
the other cases being rendered by prep. + inf. Of the present
participle the accusative and the nominative survived, the
latter being re-modelled: *AMANTIS (for AMANS)—AMANTEM.
In G.R. the ending of the First Conjugation (-ANTEM, -ANDO)
was generalized, and displaced -ENTEM, -ENDO, -IENTEM, -IENDO;
but not until after the changes $k^i > iz$, $vj > d\check{z}$ (§ 102 *b, f*):
LUCENTEM > *luisant*, DICENTEM > *disant*, SERVIENTEM > *sergeant*,
which has survived as a subst. With the loss of the final vowel,
-ant results (*-anz* in the nom. sing. and acc. pl. of the present
participle, which therefore conforms to the adjective declension of the *grant* type): *chantant, partant, finissant, bevant, perdant*.

302. The close connection of the present participle-gerund
with the pres. ind. and subjv. results in its being frequently
re-modelled on these tenses, with or without the added support of the infinitive: *ayant* for *avant* (HABENTEM), *pleuvant* for
plouvant, *voyant* for *veant*, *croyant* for *creant* (which survives in
archaic *mécréant*); O.F. *vueillant* (beside *voulant* < VOLENTEM)
survives in *bienveillant, malveillant*; (*as*)*seyant* and (*as*)*soyant*
crowded out (*as*)*seant* (< SEDENTEM), which survives as a substantive and in *bienséant, malséant*. Other verbs in which both

forms survive (one as the pres. part.-gerund, the other in a specialized use which has isolated it from the rest of the verb) are: *pouvant—puissant* (≠*puis, puisse*); *sachant* (≠*sache*) (twelfth century)—*savant* used only as an adj. or subst. since the sixteenth century; *valant—vaillant* (≠*vail, vaille*) now a pure adj. except in *n'avoir pas un sou vaillant*; *en son vivant, sur son séant* are survivals of the O.F. substantival use of the gerund.

303. In *échéant, déchéant, séant, mécréant*, and their derivatives unaccented *e* in hiatus has been maintained and strengthened (cf. § 60); in *méchant* (O.F. *mescheant*) it has been left to its normal fate and has been absorbed by tonic *a*, because here the connection with the verb (*mescheoir*) was early lost sight of, and there was not the same motive for maintaining the verbal stem. The *s* of *lisant, lisent, lise*, etc. for **leant* (<LE-GENTEM), etc. is probably due to the influence of *disant, disent, dise* (§ 301); *prenant* for *prendant* (PRE(H)ENDENTEM) may be due to the influence of *tenant* (§ 321).

SYNTAX OF THE PRESENT PARTICIPLE AND GERUND

304. The C.L. distinction between the syntactic functions of the present participle and the gerund had to a large extent broken down in V.L., the use of the gerund being extended at the expense of the pres. part. In O.F. this movement continued and was facilitated by the identity of form, which became complete when final *s* became mute. Uncertainty in the use of flexional -*s* adds to the difficulty of determining the precise functions of the two forms, but it is clear that the pres. part. in its verbal function continued to give ground before the gerund, notably when the verb is an intransitive verb denoting movement. The gerund was in O.F. used after a variety of prepositions, of which *en* + gerund alone survives; in the sixteenth and seventeenth centuries *en* is still often omitted where Mod.F. requires it (cf. xiv, 113).

The gerund was formerly used more extensively in absolute constructions (xiv, 65; xv *a*, 31), as the complement of a verb (*faire semblant*; cf. xi, 3) or with *aller, venir* as a more graphic variant of simple tenses (iii, 10; v, 3; vi, 22; xvi, 39; xviii *b*,

13; cf. *la somme va en augmentant*). Contrary to Mod.F. usage, O.F. placed the direct object before the gerund (cf. the survival in *chemin faisant*) and did not require that the gerund should refer to the subject of the sentence (XIII, 25); cf. a survival in *L'appétit vient en mangeant*.

305. The present participle, which originally had no distinctive form for the feminine, developed an analogical feminine form in *-e*, found in the twelfth century but not extensively used. Even in the sixteenth and seventeenth centuries there is considerable hesitation, Vaugelas authorizing forms in *-e* only for the pres. part. of intransitive verbs. This hesitation and the confusion of pres. part. and gerund (cf. XIV, 31, 43, 59; XV *a*, 5, 26) were nominally ended by the ruling of the Academy (1679) to the effect that the form in *-ant* should be treated as invariable if it denotes an action, and should vary in number and gender if it denotes a continuous state or quality. But in fact hesitation continues in the eighteenth century. The ruling of the Academy is now observed in literary usage and might be re-worded thus: the gerund, whether accompanied by *en* or not, denotes action and is invariable (*On apprend en lisant*; *Une femme charmant ses auditeurs*); the present participle denotes a state or quality, and, in conformity with its original function, is variable (*une femme charmante*). In such expressions as *une école payante* the real subject is not *école* but an indefinite person or persons, i.e. not 'a paying school' but 'a school where one pays'; similarly *couleur voyante, séance tenante*.

PRESENT INDICATIVE

306.   OLD FRENCH PARADIGMS

chanter	partir	fenir	valeir	beivre
chant	*part*	*fenis*	*vail*	*beif*
chantes	*parz*	*fenis*	*vals*	*beis*
chantet	*part*	*fenist*	*valt*	*beit*
chantons	*partons*	*fenissons*	*valons*	*bevons*
chantez	*partezne*	*fisez*	*valez*	*bevez*
chantent	*partent*	*fenissent*	*valent*	*beivent*

307.   THE ENDINGS

Singular			Plural	
Latin	O.F.		Latin	O.F
-O	—		-AMUS	*-ons*
-(J)O	—		-EMUS -IMUS	
-AS	*-es*		-ATIS	*-ez*
-ES -IS	*-s*		-ETIS -ITIS	
-AT	*-e(t)*		-ANT	*-ent*
-ET -IT	*-t*		-ENT -UNT -(J)UNT	

(1) *-o* persists as a supporting *ə* after a difficult group (*entre, semble, couvre, offre, ouvre, souffre*). Apart from such cases, *-o* disappeared and the first person therefore normally ended in a consonant or an accented vowel or a diphthong. But beginning in the twelfth century, verbs which have *-es*, *-e(t)* in the 2nd and 3rd sing. (i.e. verbs of the *-er* class) also take *-e* in the first person. Forms like *entre*, *semble*, etc. are partly responsible for the extension of this *-e*, but the new 1st sing. is essentially a re-modelling on the analogy of the 2nd and 3rd sing., for not only is *e* added but the preceding consonant is also carried over into the first person (*lef*, *leves*, *leve(t)* give place to *lave*, *laves*, *lave*). Forms without *-e* persist as late as the fifteenth century, when they disappear entirely. All other verbs show *-s* in Mod.F.; this is etymological in verbs whose stem ends in *s* (*crois* < CRESCO, *connais* O.F. *conois* < COGNOSCO, *finis* O.F. *fenis* < FINISCO), and from these *-s*, which came to be considered as the characteristic sign of the 1st sing., was extended by analogy to other verbs (*pars* for *part*, etc.) and was added as such in other tenses as well (see below). This paragogic *-s* first appears in the twelfth century, but the etymological forms without *-s* persist down to the sixteenth (XIV, 40); in the seventeenth they are still employed sporadically (XVII, 9, 21) but thenceforth become the prerogative of poets anxious to rime for the eye as well as for the ear (e.g. *voi*, *sai*, *croi*, in rimes of modern poets). Occasionally *x* appears as an alternative spelling (*vaux, veux*, etc.); cf. § 157.

(2) -AS > -*es*, which persists intact in O.F.; -IS and -ES > -*s*, which combines with a preceding *t* or *d* to give *z* (= ts) later reduced to *s* (*parz* > *pars*), the *d* being sometimes restored in spelling (*perz* > *pers*, orth. *perds*; *renz* > *rens*, orth. *rends*).

(3) -AT > -*eṭ* > -*e*; -IT and -ET > -*t*, which sometimes gives place to -*d* (*tend, coud, moud, prend*), a purely orthographic change due to etymological reaction or the influence of other forms (*tendons, tendez, tendent*, etc.). Similarly the *c* of *vainc* (O.F. *veint*) is due to the generalization of *c* from the re-modelled inf., fut., and past part. (*vaincre, vaincrai, vaincu* for O.F. *veintre, veintrai, vencu*).

(4) The etymological endings are replaced by -*oms*, -*ons*, which are carried over from *soms, sons* (< SUMUS). The latter also appears as *somes* (§ 321), whence the ending -*omes* was sometimes extended by analogy to other verbs.

(5) -ATIS > -*ez*, which was early generalized at the expense of -*eiz* (< -ĒTIS) and -*iz* (< -ĪTIS). After a palatal, -ATIS > -*iez*, which is later reduced through absorption of *i* by the pre-ceding sibilant or by analogy (§ 75); *z* (= ts) is reduced to *s*, which becomes mute, although *z* persists in spelling (§§ 108, 169).

(6) -ANT, -ENT, -UNT[1] alike become -*ent*, which was originally pronounced as spelt, but eventually became mute; *t* is restored in Mod.F. as a liaison-consonant.

308. In Mod.F. the personal endings have to a large ex-tent a purely orthographic value (apart from liaison), -*ons* (= õ) and -*ez* (= ę) alone persisting in the spoken language. Consequently the personal pronouns have become a necessary adjunct for the distinction of persons; they have in fact be-come to a large extent agglutinated and represent a new flexion in place of the old flexion by termination. But even with the help of pronouns the distinction between 3rd sing. and 3rd pl. is possible only if the verb begins with a vowel (il dǫn = *il donne* or *ils donnent*; but *il aime* = ilęm, whereas *ils aimen* = ilzęm). The varying form of the stem sometimes helps to maintain a distinction (*il boit*—*ils boivent, il veut*—*ils veulent*, etc.).

---

[1] The 3rd pl. -IUNT had been completely eliminated by -UNT.

The stem-vowel

309. In accordance with phonetic laws the vowel of the stem developed differently according as the tonic accent fell on the stem (1st, 2nd, 3rd, 6th pers.) or on the ending (4th, 5th pers.), and in the latter case it may disappear entirely if it is counterfinal: *paráulas (parabolas) > *paroles*, while *paraulátis (parabolatis) > *parlez*. The resulting oscillation between two forms of the stem, which is called Apophony, is characteristic of many verbs in O.F., but it has since been eliminated to a large extent by the generalization of one or other of the forms of the stem. The following examples will illustrate this phenomenon.

310. I. Change of vowel: *aim—amons, lef—lavons, truef—trouvons, espeir—esperons, lief—levons, pri—preions, pleur—plourons, suefre—soufrons, apui—apoyons.* In the majority of cases it is the stem of the 1st and 2nd pl. that has been generalized (*je lave, je trouve, j'espère, je lève, je souffre*), but sometimes the reverse has happened (*nous aimons, prions, pleurons, appuyons*). A number of Mod.F. verbs preserve the original apophony: *meurs—mourons, acquiers—acquérons, bois—buvons* (O.F. *bevons*), *veux—voulons, dois—devons, reçois—recevons, viens—venons, tiens—tenons, meus—mouvons, peux—pouvons.* A relic of apophony is to be seen in such forms as *amant* (beside *aime, aimons*, etc.). Occasionally doublets have been created by the generalization of both forms of the stem: *épleuré—éploré*; NECARE and NEGARE by regular phonetic development fell together, giving one verb *neiier* with apophony *ni—neions*, whence through generalization of both forms of the stem the doublet *nier* (with the meaning NEGARE)—*noyer* (with the meaning of NECARE restricted).

311. II. Loss of vowel: *aju(e)* (ADJUTO)—*aidons, desjun(e)* (*DISJEJUNO)—disnons, manju(e)* (MANDUCO)—*manjons, parol(e)—parlons.* The stem of the 1st and 2nd pl. has as a rule been generalized (*parle, mange*); the generalization of both forms has created the doublet *dîner—déjeuner.* Apophony of this type was thus completely eliminated before the sixteenth

century, but the subsequent loss of counterfinal *ə* created a
new series of verbs presenting the same alternation. Orthography preserves *e* throughout, but indicates the apophony
by either doubling the following consonant or employing the
grave accent to distinguish *ę* from *ə*: *appelle—app(e)lons,
cachette—cach(e)tons, achète—ach(e)tons, soulève—soul(e)vons*. Here
too the tendency to generalize one form of the stem re-asserts
itself in popular speech, which, as in the earlier period, prefers
the shortened form (*ach'te, décol'te*), but orthography exercises
a conserving influence. Another type of modern apophony
is that which results from the varying treatment of hiatus-
vowels: *joue* (=žu)—*jouons* (=žwõ), *signifie* (= sin'ifi)—*signi-
fions* (= sin'ifjõ).

312. It sometimes happened that apophony was introduced by analogy into verbs which did not develop it
phonetically. Thus *plei* (PLĬCO)—*pleions* became (under the
influence of *pri* (PRĔCO)—*preions*) *pli—pleions* (>*ployons*),
whence by generalization of both forms of the stem the
modern doublet *plier—ployer*. Similarly *lei* (LĬGO)—*leions* gave
way to *li—leions*, whence, by generalization of the stem form
li-, the modern verb *lier*.

THE FINAL CONSONANT OF THE STEM

313. The varying phonetic conditions in which the final
consonant of the stem finds itself in the different persons
create another form of apophony (cf. the *beivre* paradigm).
This has often been eliminated, partly or entirely, by the
levelling out of one of the forms of the stem. Sometimes this
affects only orthography, while pronunciation preserves the
apophony (cf. the spelling *romps, rompt* ≠ with *rompons*, etc.).

314. (1) By the loss of final *-o* the consonant became final,
with the result that the stem appears in a special form showing
the changes indicated in § 101: *beif—bevons, vif—vivons, serf—
servons, reçoif—recevons, muef—mouvons, plaing—plaignons, prent—
pren(d)ons, rent—rendons*; the loss of the final consonant produces a form of the stem which is identical with that of the
2nd and 3rd sing. (where the consonant regularly disappears

before *s, t*): LEGO > *li,* DEBEO > *DEJO > *dei,* CONDUCO > *condui,* DICO > *di,* VIDEO > *vei,* CREDO > *crei,* RIDEO > *ri.* In all such cases the etymological forms have been replaced by analogical forms in -*s* (cf. § 307). For *estois, suis, vais,* see § 321.

315. The ending -*eo,* -*io* had in V.L. been reduced to -*o* in many verbs (*DORMO, *SENTO, etc., cf. § 283) but persisted in others in the form of -*jo.* A certain number of verbs which in C.L. ended in -*o* joined this category in V.L. (*FALLIO for FALLO, *COLLIO for COLLIGO, etc.). The presence of *j* affected the development of the stem. The resulting apophony is maintained in O.F. but has since been eliminated (with the sole exception of *je puis,* beside analogical *je peux*) by the levelling out of one or other of the two forms which the stem presented:

O.F.	Mod.F.
vail (< VALEO), *vals,* etc.	*je vaux, tu vaux,* etc.
cueil (< *COLLIO for COLLIGO), *cuelz*	*je cueille*
assail (< * -SALIO), *assals*	*j'assaille*
vueil (< *VOLEO), *vuels*	*je veux*
muir (< *MORIO), *muers*	*je meurs*
boil (< BULLIO), *bols*	*je bous*
puis (< *POTEO),[1] *puez*	*je puis (je peux)*
haz (< *HATIO), *hez*	*je hais*
faz (< FACIO), *fais*	*je fais*
oi (< AUDIO), *oz*	—
jail (< *FALLIO), *fals*	*je faux*

In some verbs the levelling out took place in the pre-literary period (JACEO—*gis*). PLACEO, TACEO, NOCEO, LUCEO were remodelled in early O.F.: *plais, tais, nuis, luis* by analogy with the 2nd and 3rd sing. DEBEO > *DEJO > *dei;* SAPIO > *SAJO (≠HABEO > *AJO) > *sai.*

316. (2, 3) The final consonant of the stem, being brought into contact with -*s* or -*t* of the ending, forms a group which develops in accordance with the phonetic laws governing groups of consonants (§ 99): the first may disappear (*vis, vit;*

[1] Cf. § 321.

deis, deit; *sers, sert*; *receis, receit*; *dors, dort*; *escris, escrit*; beside *vif—vivons, dei—devons, serf—servons, receif—recevons, dor(m)— dormons, escri,—escrivons*); final *s* of the stem combines with *-s*, persists before *-t* of the ending, but becomes mute subsequently (*conois, conoist*; *crois, croist*; *nais, naist*; *pais, paist*); for *t, d, +s*, see § 307; *l* or *l' >l >u* (*vaux, vaut*; *bous, bout*; *veux, veut*; *absous, absout*; *faux, faut*; beside *vail—valons*, etc.); *n' > in* (*peins, peint*; *plains, plaint*; *joins, joint*; *crains, craint*; beside *peignons*, etc.); *m > n*, which (like original *n*) is eventually absorbed by the preceding nasal vowel (*rons, ront*; beside *rompons*, etc.). The final consonant of the stem is often restored in spelling: *romps, rompt*; *mets, couds, rends, bats, prends, vends, vêts*.

317. *Cueillir, saillir, assaillir, tressaillir* show a levelling out of the *l'* which originally appeared in the 1st sing. only (*cueil, cuelz, cuelt*). This brought with it the introduction of a supporting *-e* in the 2nd and 3rd sing. (*cueilles, cueille*) which was later extended to the 1st sing. (*cueille*). Such forms as *il assaut, il tressaut* are still used in the seventeenth century but are now extinct. *Saillir* is also conjugated as an inchoative verb (cf. § 291). *Défaillir* shows the same levelling out of *l'* (*défaille*), but *faillir* retains *faux, faut*, beside *faillons, faillez, faillent*.

318. (4, 5, 6) The development of the final consonant of the stem is uniform in the 1st pl., 2nd pl., and 3rd pl., with the following exceptions: (*a*) Palatals show a uniform development in -ĀRE and -ĒRE verbs: COLLOCAMUS > *colchons* (*-ons* being generalized after the change $k^a > t\check{s}$), COLLOCATIS > *colchiez*, COLLOCANT > *colchent*; they disappear before -UNT of -ĒRE and -ĪRE verbs, *-ent* not being generalized until after this change, whence DICUNT > O.F. *dient*, DUCUNT > O.F. *duient*, COQUUNT > O.F. *cuient*; but levelling out of the stem of 1st and 2nd pl. has since taken place, whence *disent, -duisent, cuisent*. (*b*) The fact that the accent fell on the ending in the 1st pl. and 2nd pl., and on the stem in 3rd pl., should in certain cases have produced a varying development of the final consonant: MANDUCĀTIS > *mangiez*, but MANDÚCANT should have given *manduent*; there is however no trace of the latter in French, *mang-* having been levelled out in the pre-literary period. Note that in O.F. *dimes, dites* and *faimes, faites* we have survivals of stem-accented DÍCIMUS, DÍCITIS and FÁCIMUS, FÁCITIS. Beside these forms O.F. also shows analogical *dioms, diez, faions, faiez*; the forms with *-s-* are due to the influence of *disant, diseie, faisant, faiseie*, and appear as early as the thirteenth century. Analogical *disez* and *faisez* survive only in patois or popular speech; but in compounds of *dire*, except *redire* (*redites*), the etymological *-dites* has given way to analogical *-disez* (*médisez, interdisez*, etc.).

319. The stem of verbs in *-oyer, -uyer, -ayer* ends in *j*, which disappeared when the following *ə* became mute, whence the alternation *waj—wa, ẅij—ẅi, ęj—ę* (*envoyons—envoient, ennuyons—ennuyent, payons—payent* or *paient*). In these verbs *y* represented *ij* (*envoyons* = ãvwajõ, older ãnvoijõ), and therefore before *ə* the letter *i* (or in the case of *-ayer* verbs, either *i* or *y*) is retained as part of the graphies *oi* (= wa), *ui* (= ẅi), *ai* or *ay* (= ę). Similarly the *j* which appears in the 1st and 2nd pl. of certain verbs (*croyons, fuyons*, where *y* = *ij*) disappeared in the 3rd pl. when *-ent* became mute, whence krwajõ (*croyons*)— krwa (*croient*), fẅijõ (*fuyons*)—fẅi (*fuient*).

320. Inchoative verbs in *-ir* (*finir* type) originally added *-ISC-* only in the 1st, 2nd, 3rd sing. and 3rd pl., but before the beginning of the O.F. period this was extended to the 1st and 2nd pl. (FINISCO, FINISCIS, FINISCIT, FINISCIMUS, FINISCITIS, FINISCUNT); cf. § 286.

321. The present indicative of the following verbs calls for special comment:

Aller. O.F. *vois, vas, va*(*t*), *alons, alez, vont.* The forms of the 1st, 2nd, 3rd sing. and 3rd pl. represent forms of VADERE, which appear to have developed under the influence of the contracted forms of HABERE (*ai, as, at*). Thus VADO > *VAO, > *vo, which by analogy with *ai* (HABEO) takes *i*, and then paragogic *-s*; *vois* (XIV, 75) gives place to *vais*, which prevails definitely in the seventeenth century. Beside *vais, vois*, a form *va*(*s*) developed by analogy with the 2nd and 3rd sing., and this form was used in the sixteenth and seventeenth centuries (XVIII b, 13); but in spite of Vaugelas' defence of it, *vas* is from the seventeenth century considered a vulgar or dialectal form. Analogical *vais* (2nd sing.) and *vait* (3rd sing.) are found in O.F., the latter being particularly common in the early period; *alons*, *alez* are derived from *ALARE, which is a contraction of AMBULARE resulting from the frequent exclamatory use of AMBULAMUS! (>*ALAMUS!) and AMBULATIS! (>*ALATIS!).

(As)seoir. O.F. *sié, siez (siés), siét, seons, seez, siéent (séent)*. *d* is restored in spelling in *sieds, sied*; hiatus-*j* developed in *seyons, seyez, seyent* (cf. *rire*). The alternative form of the pres. ind. *assois*, etc. is due to generalization of *oi* from the infinitive *seoir*.

Avoir. As a result of their constant proclitic use, HABEO, HABES, HABET were reduced in V.L. to *AJO, *AS, *AT, whence French *ai, as, a(t)*; HABEMUS and HABETIS become, with the usual substitution of endings, *avons, avez*; HABENT, under the influence of SUNT, gave way to *ABUNT, whence *AUNT > *ont*.

Choir (now obsolete) and *déchoir, échoir*. O.F. *chié, chiez (chiés), chiét, cheons, cheez, chiéent (chéent)* have given place to *(dé)chois, chois, choit, choyons, choyez, choient*, under the influence of the infinitive *ch(e)oir*.

Craindre, O.F. *criembre* (< TREMERE + a Celtic verb with the stem *crit-*). O.F. *criem, criens, crient, cremons, cremez, criement*. These forms, together with the infinitive, were re-modelled under the influence of verbs in *-aindre* (<-ÁNGERE), the point of departure being the singular, which offered a close affinity (cf. *plaing, plains, plaint*). Thence the re-modelling was extended to all parts of the verb.

O.F. *ester* (< STARE) develops in the same way as *aler*: *estois* (*ESTAO), *estas, esta(t)* or *estait, estons, estez, estont*.

Être. O.F. *sui, es, est, soms, estes, sont. Sui* for SUM presents a difficulty which M. Fouché (*op. cit.* p. 408) meets by postulating a form *SUJO (< SUM + *AJO < HABEO); in certain dialects, it is argued, the contamination with *AJO took place after SUM had become *so*, whence the dialectal form *soi*.

The final -*s* of *suis* may be due to generalization of -*s* or to the analogy of *puis*. Beside *es*, which represents the countertonic development of *ę*, the tonic form *iés* is also found in O.F. (XII, 75), whence an analogical 2nd pl. *iestes* beside *estes*. SUMUS regularly gives *soms* or, with assimilation of *m*, *sons*; but this form early gave way to *sommes*. The *e* of the latter form may have developed in the first instance as a supporting vowel (whenever a word beginning with a consonant followed), being later generalized (cf. Fouché, p. 410). A third form *esmes*, created on the analogy of *estes*, is also found in O.F. but is comparatively rare.

Haïr (Germ. hatjan). O.F. *hai* (*hé*, *haz*), *hez*, *het*, *haons*, *haez*, *héent*, which by the end of the Middle Ages had given way to forms with *ai* levelled: *hais*, *hais*, *hait*, *hayons*, *hayez*, *haient*. At the same time the tendency to treat the verb as inchoative gave rise to hesitation between *haïs* and *hais*, *haïssons* and *hayons*, etc. In the seventeenth century the modern compromise was arrived at whereby the inchoative forms are accepted throughout the verb, except in the singular of the pres. ind. (*je hais*, *tu hais*, *il hait*, but *nous haïssons*, etc.).

Pouvoir. O.F. *pooir* (< *POTÉRE for POSSE). V.L. POTEO or POSSIO, POTES, POTET, POTEMUS, POTETIS, POTENT; O.F. *puis*, *puez*, *puet*, *poons*, *poeiz*, *pueent*. *Puis* presupposes a V.L. POSSIO (< POSSUM contaminated with *POTEO?); the modern alternative form *peux* is analogical ($\neq$2nd *peux* and 3rd *peut*), dating from about 1500 and persisting in spite of the protests of purists and grammarians. The *v* of Mod.F. *pouvons*, *pouvez*, *peuvent* is probably due to the influence of the infinitive (see below), and begins to appear in the thirteenth century; forms without *v* are still found in the sixteenth century. In the infinitive, when countertonic *o* had become *u* (*pooir* > *puwęr* > *puwar*), it threatened to be assimilated and absorbed by the following *w*. The reaction against this tendency took the form of a differentiation of *w*, which developed a fricative *v* (*puvwa:r*). Two other less satisfactory explanations have been advanced: analogy of *mouvoir*, *mouvons*; *trouver*, *trouvons* and the like, or development of hiatus-*w* between two rounded vowels.

Prendre. O.F. *pren(t), prenz (prens), prent, pren(d)ons, pren(d)ez, pren(d)ent.* Plural forms without *d* are found as early as the *Roland* (*prenent*, l. 2552) but do not completely triumph until the sixteenth century; they are generally ascribed to the influence of *tenons, tenez, tiennent.* In the singular *d* has been restored in modern spelling.

Rire. O.F. *ri, riz, rit, rions, riez, rient,* from which the modern forms have developed regularly, but orthography takes no account of the development of hiatus-*j* (rijõ, riję).

Savoir. O.F. *sai, ses, set, savons, savez, sevent.* In Mod.F. *sai* (= sę) became (sę) by analogy with the 2nd and 3rd sing.; *savent* is due to the analogy of *savons, savez,* and finally ousts *sevent* (< *sapunt) in the fifteenth century.

Suivre. V.L. sequo, sequis, sequit, sequimus, sequitis, sequunt; O.F. *siu, sius, siut, sevons, sevez, sivent.* The O.F. forms show elimination of the palatal element after it had modified tonic *e,* and also vocalization of the labial element of *qu* (= kw) before a consonant or when final (cf. § 103). The metathesis whereby *iu > ui* (*suis,* etc.) was undoubtedly facilitated by the fact that *-u, -us, -ut* constituted an anomaly beside the common endings *-i, -is, -it.* From the resulting *sui(s), suis, suit, ui* was generalized throughout the verb.

PRESENT SUBJUNCTIVE

322.   OLD FRENCH PARADIGMS

chanter	partir	fenir	valeir	beivre
chant	*parte*	*fenisse*	*vaille*	*beive*
chanz	*partes*	*fenisses*	*vailles*	*beives*
chant	*partet*	*fenisset*	*vaillet*	*beivet*
chantons	*partons*	*fenissons*	*vailliens*	*bevons*
chantez	*partez*	*fenissez*	*vailliez*	*bevez*
chantent	*partent*	*fenissent*	*vaillent*	*beivent*

323. THE ENDINGS

Singular		Plural	
Latin	O.F.	Latin	O.F.
-EM	—	-EMUS -AMUS	*-ons*
-(J)AM	*-e*	-(J)AMUS	*-iens*
-ES	*-s*	-ETIS -ATIS	*-ez*
-(J)AS	*-es*	-(J)ATIS	*-iez*
-ET	*-t*	-ENT	*-ent*
-(J)AT	*-e(t)*	-(J)ANT	

The vowel of Latin -EM, -ES, -ET persists as a supporting ə after a group consisting of cons. + liquid or palatal. The O.F. *-e*, *-es*, *-e(t)* were thus the characteristic endings of the subjunctive in all O.F. verbs except those *-er* (-ĀRE) verbs which did not require a supporting ə. The latter were gradually brought into line; this began as early as the twelfth century with the 2nd sing. and 1st sing. The 3rd sing., being more frequently used and supported by other subjunctive forms without *e* (*soit, ait, chantast*, etc.), resisted this levelling tendency much longer. It is not until the second half of the thirteenth century that forms with *-e* in the 1st and 3rd sing. gain the upper hand, and in the 3rd sing. the old forms survive sporadically in the fifteenth and sixteenth centuries—even later in the expression *Dieu te (vous) gard'*, where the apostrophe is unjustifiable (Nyrop, II, § 136). In the 3rd sing. the *-e* of *-et* (< -AT) disappears if the stem ends in *s, r, n*, or *j* (*voist, plaist, puist, curt, taist, ait* < *AJAT, seit* < *SIAT), but it is generally restored by analogy with the 1st and 2nd sing. (*plaise, puisse*); *seit* and *ait*, owing to their more frequent use, have resisted this influence down to the present day.

-EMUS and -AMUS are represented in French by *-ons*, which is due to the analogy of the pres. ind.; but -JAMUS (< -EAMUS and -IAMUS) regularly gave *-iens* (*vailliens, faciens, aiiens, seiiens*, etc.), which was extended by analogy and competed with *-ons* in O.F. The modern *-ions*, which results from a combination of *-ons* and *-iens*, appears as early as the fourteenth century. It triumphed all the more easily as it served to distinguish the subjunctive from the indicative in all verbs.

-ez (< -ATIS) was early generalized at the expense of *-eiz* (< -ĒTIS), but *-eiz* (later *-oiz*) is found sporadically in early texts and survives in certain dialects; *-iez,* which was regular after palatals, was generalized (at the expense of *-ez*) much more slowly than *-ions* (at the expense of *-ons*), and subjunctive forms in *-ez* are found as late as the sixteenth century.

-ent developed as in the indicative (§ 307).

THE STEM

324. The changes in the stem are analogous to those which we have observed in the indicative. Examples of apophony surviving in Mod.F.: *boive—buvions, reçoive—recevions, acquière—acquérions, doive—devions, meuve—mouvions, meure—mourions, tienne—tenions, vienne—venions.* Levelling out has often eliminated apophony, as in the indicative: *pleure—pleurions* for *plourions,* etc.

The modification of the final consonant of the stem before *-s* or *-t* has been eliminated by the development of forms in *-e* (*chante, chantes, chante,* for O.F. *chant, chanz, chant*). The tendency to preserve the same form of the stem as in the present indicative had often interfered with or obliterated the normal development of the final consonant, and had led to the generalization of one or other of the forms of the stem of the indicative: *conoisse,* etc. for **conosche,* etc. (COGNOSCAM); *florisse* for **floresche* (FLORISCAM); the same influence accounts for later re-modellings: *choie* for *chiee, dise* for *die* (cf. XVI, 18), *conduise* for *conduie, prenne* for *prende, doive* for *deie, plaise* for *place, tienne* for *tiegne.*

325. Subjunctive forms in -JAM (< -EAM, -IAM) show a transformation of the stem throughout the tense, similar to that of the 1st sing. pres. ind. in -JO (§ 315): VALEAM > *vaille,* VALEAS > *vailles,* etc.; SALIAM > *saille;* BULLIAM > *bouille;* TENEAM > *tiegne;* VENIAM > *viegne;* *ALIAM > *aille;* SAPIAM > *sache;* FACIAM > *face* > *fasse;* *POSSIAM (< POSSIM + *POTEAM) > *puisse.* The number of such forms had been considerably reduced in V.L. by the substitution of -AM for -JAM (parallel with -O for -JO; cf. § 283): V.L. DORMAM, MENTAM, MORDAM, SERVAM, SORTAM, etc.; but a few new -JAM forms had developed: *COLLIAM (for COLLIGAM) > *cueille*, *FALLIAM (for FALLAM) > *faille*, *VOLEAM (for VELIM) > *vueille*. While the etymological forms of the 1st sing. pres. ind. (*vail, cueil*) were all eliminated with the exception of *puis*, the subjunctive forms (*vaille, cueille*) generally persisted. The stem of the pres. ind. has been generalized in *tenir, venir*, and the stem of the 1st and 2nd pl. pres. ind. has been carried over into the corresponding persons of the subjunctive in *valions, valiez; voulions, vouliez; allions, alliez*. In the compound *prévaloir* the old subjunctive with *l'* (*prévaille*), which was still used in the seventeenth century, has completely disappeared before analogical *prévale*, etc.

BJ and DJ were reduced to J, which appeared as *i* before mute *e*, in DEBEAM > *deie*, HABEAM > *aie*, RIDEAM > *rie*, VIDEAM > *veie*.

In Western dialects and also in Picard, -JAM appears as -*ge* without palatalizing the preceding consonant (*muerge, venge, alge*, etc.); thence the ending spread to other verbs. Subjunctive forms in -*ge* are found in Central French texts down to the fourteenth century, particularly in verbs with stems ending in *l, n, r*: *alge, donge, parolge, prenge, muerge, tienge, vienge*.

326. The following call for special comment:

Aller presented in O.F. three different forms of the subjunctive: *aille, alge*, and *voise*. The latter is modelled on the 1st sing. pres. ind. *vois* (§ 321) and continued in regular use in the sixteenth century.

Donner possessed *doinse* (modelled on 1st sing. pres. ind. *doins*), *donge, doigne* (< *DONIAM) and *done* (Mod.F. *donne*).

Prouver, trouver, and O.F. *rover*, also possessed in O.F. a subjunctive modelled on the 1st sing. pres. ind. (*pruis, truis, ruis*): *pruisse, truisse, ruisse*.

Être. O.F. *seie, seies, seit, seiiens (seiions), seiiez, seient* continue *SIAM for C.L. SIM, etc., with levelling of the stem of the strong forms (*ei*) into the weak. *Seie* > *soie* > *soi*, which in the sixteenth century received paragogic -*s*; *seies* > *soies* > *sois*, the *e* disappearing as in the ending of the impf. ind. For *y* (= *ij*) in *soyons* (swajõ), *soyez*, cf. § 319.

Avoir. O.F. *aie, aies, ait, aiiens* (*aiions*), *aiiez, aient* continue *AJA for C.L. HABEAM, etc., with levelling of the stem of the strong forms (*ai*) into the weak. Beside *ait*, analogical *aie* arose and was commonly used in the sixteenth and early seventeenth centuries. For *y* = *ij* in *ayons* (ejõ), *ayez*, cf. § 319.

Tenir and *venir*. Beside the regular forms *tiegne* (< TENEAM), *viegne* (< VENIAM) (XII, 20; XVI, 68), used as late as the sixteenth century, O.F. also possessed forms in -*ge* (*tienge, vienge*). The modern forms *tienne, vienne*, modelled on the pres. ind., date from the sixteenth century. Similarly *prendre*— *pregne* (XVI, 17), *prenge, prende, prenne*.

Clore. The *s* of the subjunctive forms (*close*, etc.), like the *s* of obsolete indicative forms *closons, closez, closent*, is probably due to the influence of the old sigmatic perfect *closis* (CLAUSISTI), etc. and the fem. of the past participle *close* (CLAUSA).

Verbs in -*oyer*, -*uyer*, -*ayer*; cf. § 319.

IMPERATIVE

327. Of the Latin imperative, the 2nd sing. alone survived in French, the 2nd pl. being rendered by the 2nd pl. pres. ind.

THE ENDINGS

Latin	O.F.	
-A	-*e*	CANTA > *chante*
-E -I	—	VIDE > *voi*
-C	-*i*	FAC > *fai*, DIC > *di*, DUC > *dui*

After cons. + *l*, *r*, the vowels *e*, *i* persist as supporting *ə* (*OPERI > *uevre*, *SUFFERI > *suefre*).

The frequent use of the imperative as an interjection probably accounts for the occasional disappearance of the consonant which became final through the loss of Latin -E, -I

(BIBE > *beif* > *boif* > *boi*, SERVI > *serf* > *ser*) and for the less common disappearance of *ǝ* (< A) : *lais*(*se*), *gar*(*e*).

328. The further evolution of the imperative forms is conditioned by their close association with the 2nd sing. pres. ind. and by the fact that in the 2nd pl. one form served for both ind. and impv. As early as the thirteenth century analogical -*s* appears (*vois, bois, fais, dis, conduis, sers*, etc.); such forms as *voi* (xv, 11), *fai, tien* (iii, 36), etc. still occur in seventeenth-century writers and survive in *voici, voilà*. O.F. imperatives in -*e* take *s* less frequently (*chantes, offres*) and have not preserved it in Mod.F. except before *en* and *y* (*donnes-en à Jean*).

va (< VADE) maintains *a* owing to its constant use as a proclitic before a following infinitive (*va chasser*). The O.F. analogical form *vas* persists (under the influence of *allons-y, allez-y*) before *y* if the latter is closely linked with it: *vas-y*, but *va y mettre ordre*.

SYNTAX OF THE IMPERATIVE

329. The hortative subjunctive was adopted as an imperative of the 3rd sing. and 3rd pl. It could in O.F. be used without the conjunction *que* (xii, 103), but was often preceded by the expletives *car, or, si*. The gradual extension of *que* may be attributed to the fact that the subjunctive is essentially, as its name implies, a subordinate mood, and the hortative subjunctive was therefore assimilated in form to a subordinate clause introduced by *que* (cf. § 399). The use of the subjunctive for the imperative was in O.F. frequently extended from the third person to the 2nd sing. and 1st and 2nd pl. (cf. a similar extension in Latin). The identity of form between *chantez* (ind.) and *chantez* (O.F. subjv.) doubtless facilitated this The subjunctive forms finally triumphed in the verbs *avoir, être, savoir, vouloir*, whence the O.F. imperatives *aies, aiiens, aiiez; soies, soiiens, soiiez; saches, sachiens, sachiez; vueilles, voilliens, voilliez;* -*s* disappeared subsequently in *saches, vueilles, aies*, by analogy with the imperatives of -*er* verbs; but *soies* > *sois* (cf. § 326); *voilliez* was re-modelled on *vueilles*, etc., whence Mod.F. *veuillez*; *sachons* for *sachions*

is due to the influence of the indicative; the remaining forms develop regularly, but there is a tendency to replace *veuille* and *veuillez* by *veux* and *voulez*.

330. In O.F. and as late as the sixteenth century the pronoun subject of the imperative is sometimes expressed (*E! reis celestes, tu nos i fai venir!* Alexis, 335). A negative command addressed to a single person was often expressed in O.F. by means of the infinitive preceded by *ne*: '*Chantecler*', *ce li dist Renart*, '*Ne foïr pas, n'aies regart!*' (*Rom. de Renart*, II, 305). This use of the infinitive has not survived. The modern use of the infinitive, positive and negative, to convey a general instruction or prohibition is probably due to ellipsis: (*on est prié de*) *S'adresser au concierge*, (*je vous prie de*) *Ne pas faire cela*. Various devices are employed to tone down the imperative as occasion demands (*Veuillez me donner ce livre! Voulez-vous me donner ce livre?*). The future is sometimes used, as in O.F. (*Vendredi chair ne mangeras*); often as a strong imperative (*Tu feras ce que je te dis!*).

IMPERFECT INDICATIVE

331.   OLD FRENCH PARADIGMS

chanter	partir	fenir	valeir	beivre
chantoe	parteie	fenisseie	valeie	beveie
chantoes	parteies	fenisseies	valeies	beveies
chantout	parteit	fenisseit	valeit	beveit
chantiiens	partiiens	fenissiiens	valiiens	beviiens
chantiiez	partiiez	fenissiiez	valiiez	beviiez
chantoent	parteient	fenisseient	valeient	beveient

332   THE ENDINGS

Latin		O.F.	Latin		O.F.
-ABAM		-oe	-ABAMUS		-iiens
-EBAM	-IEBAM	-eie > -oie	-EBAMUS	-IEBAMUS	
-ABAS		-oes	-ABATIS		-iiez
-EBAS	-IEBAS	-eies > -oies	-EBATIS	-IEBATIS	
-ABAT		-out	-ABANT		-oent
-EBAT	-IEBAT	-ei(e)t > -oit	-EBANT	-IEBANT	-eient > -oien

-ĒBAM > -ẸA in V.L., whence *eie*, etc., which was the ending of all verbs except those in *-er*.

-ĀBAM persists as -AẠA in V.L., whence on the one hand *eve*, etc., which is characteristic of Eastern dialects, and on the other the development *-aựe > -oựe > -oe, aựes > oựes > oes, -aựent > -oựent > -oent, aựet > oự(e)t > out*, beside which *ot* appears (≠*ot < out <*HABUIT). But at an early date *-eie, -eies, -eit, -eien* were extended to *-er* verbs; the imperfect forms in *-oe* are still found in the thirteenth, and in Anglo-Norman in the fourteenth century.

-ABAMUS, -ABATIS > *-EBAMUS, *-EBATIS (by weakening of A, which is here unaccented), and in common with original -EBAMUS, -EBATIS were reduced to *-EAMUS, *-EATIS, whence O.F. *i-iens, i-iez*. For *i-iens* we find as early as the twelfth century *i-ions* (by analogy with the present), which finally displaces *i-iens* in the fourteenth. These endings were originally disyllabic, but became monosyllabic in the thirteenth century (*-ions, -iez*) and are thenceforth identical with the corresponding endings of the present subjunctive, which were monosyllabic from the beginning. The modern disyllabic pronunciation of *-ions, -iez* after cons. + *l, r* (*ouvri-ons, mettri-ez*) is merely an instance of the general treatment of such a group (*ouvri-er, histri-on*), which dates from the early seventeenth century.

-oie, -oies, -oient, which were originally disyllabic, became monosyllabic when *e* became mute in the course of the Middle Ages; *-eiet* had become contracted to *-eit* much earlier, whence regularly *-oit*. The 1st sing. *-ois* (with paragogic *-s*) appears in the sixteenth century. For the phonetic change *oi > wẹ > ẹ* and the change *oi* to *ai* in orthography, see § 72.

333. The stem remains invariable: the accent being uniformly on the ending, there is no apophony. The verb *être* alone calls for comment.

Être, O.F. *estre*. The Latin imperfect forms ERAM, ERAS, ERAT, ERANT regularly gave O.F. *iere, ieres, ieret, ierent*, or, when unaccented, *ere, eres, eret, erent*, the forms *ieret, eret* being further reduced to *iert, ert* when used proclitically. *Eriens, eriez*, which seldom occur, continue ERAMUS, ERATIS, with the normal termination of the imperfect. This O.F. imperfect is almost entirely eliminated before the end of the thirteenth century by its rival *esteie*, which already appears in the earliest texts, and which is probably taken from STABAM, just as *e(s)tant, e(s)té* are taken from STANDO, STATUM. The fact that the form *estoe (or *esteve), which would represent the normal development of STABAM, never occurs may be explained by pre-literary change to *esteie* (under the influence of *aveie*, or on the model of *metre—meteie*); cf. Fouché, *op. cit.* p. 414. The modern forms develop normally from O.F. *esteie, esteies, estei(e)t, estiiens* (later *estions*), *estiiez* (later *estiez*), *esteient*.

FUTURE AND CONDITIONAL

334. The French future consists of the infinitive + the present indicative of HABEO (§ 281), contracted forms of the latter having become fused with the preceding infinitive in the pre-literary period. In the same way a new tense, the future-in-the-past or conditional, had been created by a combination of the infinitive with contracted forms of the imperfect indicative of HABEO.

THE ENDINGS

	Future			Conditional		
C.L.	V.L.	O.F.		C.L.	V.L.	O.F.
HABEO	AJO	-ai		HABEBAM	ĘA(M)	-eie >-oie
HABES	AS	-as		HABEBAS	ĘAS	-eies > -oies
HABET	AT	-a(t)		HABEBAT	ĘAT	-eit > -oit
HABEMUS	ĘMUS	-ons		HABEBAMUS	JAMUS	-iiens
HABETIS	ĘTIS	-eiz > -oiz		HABEBATIS	JATIS	-iiez
HABENT	AUNT	-ont		HABEBANT	ĘANT	-eient > -oien

For *-ons* replacing *-eins (< -ĘMUS), see § 307.

-ez displaces *-eiz, -oiz* somewhat later (thirteenth century) than in the pres. ind. (§ 307), but the pronunciation *ę* (< *wę* < *oi*) in this tense (as distinct from *ę* in the pres. ind.), which is noted by grammarians in the sixteenth century,

suggests that here the change from -*oiz* to -*ez* was in the first instance orthographic.

The endings of the conditional show the same development as those of the impr. ind.(§ 332).

335. The development of the stem (infinitive) is identical in the future and the conditional. The following remarks on the future therefore apply with equal force to the conditional.

The adjunction of the contracted forms of HABEO, which bear the principal stress, had as a result the reduction of the vowels of the infinitives -ĀRE, -ĒRE, -ĪRE to atonic vowels; accordingly *e* and *i* are normally lost, and *a* is weakened to *ə* (§ 29). But under the influence of the infinitive and of the pres. ind., the future has in many cases been re-modelled and may therefore present forms (*a*) with -*ir* intact (*partirai*) or (*b*) with the stem-vowel of the pres. ind. (*tiendrai, viendrai* for O.F. *tendrai, vendrai*) or of both pres. ind. and infinitive (*boirai* for O.F. *bevrai*); in the latter case the identity of form may result from a re-modelling of both infinitive and future on the pres. ind. (*aimer, aimerai* for O.F. *amer, amerai*), or of the future and pres. ind. on the infinitive (*choirai, choit* for O.F. *cherrai, chiét*), or of all three (*vaincre, vaincrai, vaincs*). The re-modelling of the future on the infinitive may date from pre-literary times (*soffirai*, later *suffirai*; *lirai*; the future of inchoatives; cf. §§ 286, 338). Some of the re-modelled forms disappeared after competing for a time with the regular forms: *voirai* (beside *verrai*) survives only in compounds *pourvoirai, prévoirai*.

336. -ARE verbs. (1) The *ə* which results from unaccented *a* begins to be absorbed by a preceding vowel as early as the thirteenth century and has completely disappeared by the end of the sixteenth (*pri(e)rai, remerci(e)rai*; cf. XVIII *a*, 12). After a diphthong it may still count as a syllable in seventeenth-century poets (*broyerai*). (2) After a single consonant *ə* remained in O.F., with the following exceptions: (*a*) after *r* it was sometimes lost, and such syncopated forms as *durrai*,

demorrai, jurrai exist side by side with the full forms *durerai,
demorerai, jurerai* from the thirteenth until well into the seventeenth century; (*b*) after *n* it disappeared in *don(e)rai, men(e)rai*,
which by assimilation became *dorrai, merrai*; the latter are
still used in the seventeenth century, but then give way to
donnerai, mènerai (re-modelled on the infinitive), which date
from the fifteenth. A third form *derai* or *darai*, rarely used,
goes back to *DARAJO (DARE + HABEO). Since the sixteenth
century *ə* is regularly mute after a single consonant, whence
Mod.F. *appell(e)rai, lèv(e)rai, jett(e)rai, achèt(e)rai, mèn(e)rai,
gèl(e)rai*. (3) After two consonants *ə* is, in accordance with
the 'loi des trois consonnes', pronounced in Mod.F. and
(with few sporadic exceptions) in O.F. The group cons. + *r*
often showed metathesis: *entrerai > enterrai, delivrerai > deliverrai,
mostrerai > mosterrai*; such forms continued to be used between
the twelfth and fifteenth centuries, but under the influence
of the infinitive they gradually disappear before the normal
forms *entrerai*, etc.

Aller derives its future (*irai*) from IRE + HABEO.

Envoyer originally formed its future regularly (*envoyerai*,
whence with loss of *ə*, *envoirai* XIV, 18; XV, 19); but by analogy
with *voir* (*voi* : *verrai* : : *envoi* : *enverrai*) the modern form *enverrai*
arose in the fourteenth and finally triumphed in the seven-
teenth century.

Laisser. O.F. *lairai* (*lairrai, larrai*) beside *laisserai* is not a
contraction but the future of another verb, *laier* (< Germ.
lagan).

337. -ĒRE and -ĔRE verbs. The loss of *e* brought *r* into
contact with the preceding consonant or consonants. The
development of the resulting groups may be summarized as
follows: *n'r, l'r, z'r* (-SERE), *s''r* (-SCERE), *n''r* (-NCERE, -NGERE),
r''r (-RGERE) regularly developed glide-consonants (§ 100):
tendrai, later replaced by *tiendrai* (≠pres. ind.); *valdrai*, later
vaudrai; *co(s)drai*, later *coudrai*; *paroi(s)trai*, later *paraîtrai*;
veintrai, later replaced by *vaincrai*; *plaindrai*; *sourdrai*. *t'r,
d'r* after a vowel > *rr* > *r* (in spelling *rr* is sometimes maintained): *pourrai* (*POTERAJO), *verrai*; O.F. *crerai* (*CREDERAJO),

cherrai (*CADERAJO), *serrai* (*SEDERAJO) have been replaced
by *croirai, choirai,* (*as*)*soirai* or (*as*)*seyerai* or (*as*)*siérai*, which
are forms re-modelled on the infinitive and pres. ind. (but
déchoir preserves the old future *décherrai*). After a consonant
t'r, d'r remain intact: *mettrai, perdrai,* etc. *k'r, g'r* after a
vowel > *r'* > *ir*: *trairai, conduirai, luirai, nuirai, construirai, dirai,*
plairai, tairai (dialectal *plarrai, tarai* or *tarrai*). *r'r* > *rr*: *courrai,*
acquerrai, conquerrai. v'r (Latin P'R, B'R, V'R) remains in O.F.
and generally persists in Mod.F.: *recevrai, devrai, vivrai,* etc.;
but *bevrai* has given place to *boirai* modelled on the infinitive.
*(H)ABERAJO gave rise to the two French forms *aurai* and
avrai; the former developed as the result of the early loss of *e*
when used as an auxiliary (cf. PARAB(O)LA > PARAULA > *parole*),
and definitely displaced normal O.F. *avrai* in the sixteenth
century. *Saura* for *savra* (which disappeared about the same
time) is due to the influence of *aura*.

Être. V.L. evidently possessed a form *ESSERAJO (formed
on *ESSERE for ESSE), of which the regular development is
estrai (III, 46). The development *ESSERAJO > *SERAJO > *serai*
may be explained as due to aphæresis of *es-* in imitation
of those forms of the verb which began with *s* (SUM, etc.). The
future *serai* was from the beginning the most commonly used
form. Alongside of *estrai* and *serai*, the Latin future (ERO)
persisted in O.F. in the form *ier, iers, iert, iermes, ierent*, but
had lost the 2nd pl. and soon fell wholly into disuse. The
collateral forms *er, ers, ert, ermes, erent* show atonic development. Under the influence of the imperfect *ere* (< ERAM), etc.
(cf. § 333), these forms sometimes took a final -*e*.

Faire. *Ferai* (for *fairai) presupposes a form *FARAJO
formed on *FARE. The latter probably represents a reduction
of FACERE used proclitically (e.g. before an infinitive).[1]

338. -IRE verbs. Normally *i* disappears and the resulting
group develops as in -ĒRE, -ĔRE verbs: *vendrai*, since replaced
by *viendrai* (≠pres. ind.), *mourrai, faudrai,* O.F. *eistrai* (inf.
eissir < EXIRE), O.F. *orrai* (*AUDIRAJO); but if cons. + *l, r* precedes, *i* persists in the form of a supporting *ə*: O.F. *ovrerai*,

[1] This use also accounts for the later reduction of *a* to *ə*.

ofrerai, *sofrerai* (whence by metathesis the collateral forms *overrai*, *oferrai*, *soferrai*). But in most cases the regular forms have been replaced by forms re-modelled on the infinitive: *ferirai*, *jouirai*, *haïrai*, *guérirai*, *ouvrirai*, *offrirai*, *souffrirai*. In *cueillerai*, *saillerai*, *bouillerai*, *l'* was restored by analogy with other parts of the verb, and *e* was introduced as a supporting vowel to preserve *l'* intact; but as late as the seventeenth century there was hesitation between these forms and *cueillirai*, *saillirai*, *bouillirai*: *cueillerai* and *bouillirai* have triumphed, while both *saillirai* and *saillerai* persist, the former in the sense 'to spurt', the latter in the sense 'to protrude' (compounds show only -*ir*: *tressaillirai*, *assaillirai*).

In the case of inchoative verbs the re-modelling of the future on the infinitive had taken place in pre-literary times (except *garrai*, *trarrai*, later *guérirai*, *trahirai*), and later accessions to the inchoative class likewise maintain the characteristic vowel *i*: *bénirai*, *croupirai*, *emplirai*, *enfouirai*, *engloutirai*, *nourrirai*, *resplendirai*, -*vertirai*; similarly verbs which formerly hesitated between inchoative and simple (cf. § 291): *dormirai*, *servirai*, *sortirai*, *vêtirai*.

Faillir and its doublet *falloir* have regularly a common future *faudrai*, but *faillirai* is sometimes used as a future of *faillir*.

For the future of *courir*, -*quérir*, *tenir*, infinitives which are not derived from Latin -IRE forms, see § 337.

PAST DEFINITE

The Past Definite continues the Latin perfect, of which there were six types: three in which the tonic accent fell uniformly on the ending (Weak Perfects), three in which the V.L. accent fell on the stem in the first and third person singular and in the third person plural (Strong Perfects).

(a) WEAK PERFECTS

339. In V.L. the perfect in -ĒVI disappeared, leaving weak perfects in -ĀVI and -ĪVI; to these must be added a new weak perfect in -DEDI, created in the V.L. period (cf. § 343).

OLD FRENCH PARADIGMS

chanter	dormir
chantai	*dormi*
chantas	*dormis*
chantat	*dormi(t)*
chantames	*dormimes*
chantastes	*dormistes*
chanterent	*dormirent*

340.   THE ENDINGS

CANTARE C.L.	chanter		DORMIRE C.L.	dormir	
	V.L.	O.F.		V.L.	O.F
-AVI	-AI	*-ai*	-IVI	-II	*-i*
-AVISTI	-ASTI	*-as*	-IVISTI	-ISTI	*-is*
-AVIT	-AUT	*-at*	-IVIT	-IT	*-i(t)*
-AVIMUS	-AMUS	*-ames*	-IVIMUS	-IMUS	*-imes*
-AVISTIS	-ASTIS	*-astes*	-IVISTIS	-ISTIS	*-istes*
-AVERUNT	-ARUNT	*-erent*	-IVERUNT	-IRUNT	*-irent*

The contraction of -AVISTI, -AVISTIS, -AVERUNT to -ASTI, -ASTIS, -ARUNT dates from Classical times and is due mainly to analogy, but perhaps also to the tendency to keep the accent on the characteristic vowel throughout; -AVIMUS and -AVI were reduced considerably later; -AVIT persisted until the end of the V.L. period, when v, being brought into contact with the following consonant, became *u*.

The elimination of v had taken place regularly in -IVI, -IVISTI, -IVIT, -IVISTIS, because here it was preceded and followed by the same vowel; the two *i*'s thus brought into contact combined; -I(V)ERUNT gave place to *-IRUNT through levelling of the characteristic vowel *i*; -IVIMUS was not reduced until the late V.L. period.

341. (1) *-ai* persists as a diphthong, which was reduced in the twelfth century to *ẹ* and before the end of the O.F. period had become *ę*; it is sometimes written *é* as late as the sixteenth and seventeenth centuries.

-is begins to appear for *-i* towards the end of the Middle Ages and triumphs in the seventeenth century; *-s* is here a pure graphy on the analogy of such forms as *mis, pris, fis*, where *-s* is regular.

(2, 3) The loss of final *t* of -AST(I) and the substitution of *at* for *ot (< *AUT) are probably due to the influence of *ai, as, at* (pres. ind. of *avoir* and endings of the new Future); if this be so, *-is* for *-ist* (< -ISTI) might be attributed to analogy with *-as*. In the thirteenth century *t* began to be restored in spelling in *-it* (pronounced in liaison), but not in *-a* (< *-at*).

(4) *-ames, -imes.* Here the final vowel persists in the form of *ǝ* even after the reduction of the group *v'm* which it originally supported: -AV(I)MUS, -IV(I)MUS. The existence of this group (*v'm*) also prevented the passage of tonic *a* to *ãi* (cf. MANU > *main*). The *s* of *-asmes, -ismes*, which appears in the thirteenth century, is a pure graphy due to the influence of *-astes, -istes*, and is perpetuated in Mod.F. by the circumflex accent (*-âmes, -îmes*).

(5) *-astes, -istes* owe their *e* to the influence of *-ames, -imes*, coupled with the tendency to avoid such an anomalous ending as the phonetic development -AST(I)s > *-az* and -IST(I)s > *-iz* would have created.

(6) For *-erent*, we find regularly after a palatal or palatalized consonant *-ierent* (*mangierent, traitierent*), which is later reduced to *-erent* (cf. § 75).

342. All French verbs in *-er* form their past definite in *-ai*, except that the past definite of O.F. *ester* (< STARE) continued *STETUI (C.L. STETI), whence O.F. *estui, esteüs, estut, esteümes, esteüstes, esturent*; and *estoi, estoüs, estout, estoümes, estoüstes, estourent*. Compounds of STARE that were no longer recognized as such formed *-ai* past definites: *cou(s)tai* (*CONSTAVI), *pre(s)tai* (*PRAESTAVI); but *rester* and *arre(s)ter* hesitated between *restui, arre(s)tui*, and *restai, arre(s)tai*.

All verbs in *-ir* now form their past definite in *-is*, whether they continue Latin verbs in -ĪRE with perfect in -ĪVI or originally showed a perfect of a different type (in -SI, in -UI, in -DEDI). The Mod.F. exceptions (which are discussed below) are: *courir, mourir, tenir, venir*, compounds of *quérir*. Certain verbs show hesitation in O.F. between *-ai* and *-is* (*cueillai—cueillis*), but in the majority of cases this hesitation is due to the introduction of dialectal forms.

For those verbs in *-re* which in Mod.F. show past definites in *-is*, see § 354.

343. A new weak perfect arose in V.L. through the transformation of perfects in -DIDIT under the influence of DĔDIT (the reduplicated perfect of DARE), whence V.L. CREDĘ́DI, PERDĘ́DI, etc. Such forms are attested in L.L. texts. By analogy -DĘDIT was early extended to other verbs whose stem ended in *d*; whence V.L. RESPONDĘ́DIT, DEFENDĘ́DIT, CADĘ́DIT, RESPLENDĘ́DIT, etc. The following paradigm indicates their development in O.F.:

V.L.	O.F.
VENDĘ́DI	*vendi*
VEN(DE)DÍSTI	*vendis*
VENDĘ́DIT	*vendiét*
VEN(DE)DÍMUS	*vendimes*
VEN(DE)DÍSTIS	*vendistes*
VENDĘ́(DE)RUNT	*vendiérent*

This form of the perfect was extended to other verbs in the O.F. period (*rompre—rompiét, vivre—vesquiét, cou(s)dre—cosiét*). But under the influence of the remaining persons (*vendi*, etc.) the 3rd sing. and 3rd pl. were re-modelled (*vendit, vendirent*), and such perfects were thus completely assimilated to the weak *-is* class. Subsequently *vesquit* (*vivre*) joined the *-us* class (§§ 348 *c*, 355), whence Mod.F. *vécut*.

(b) Strong perfects

344. The C.L. strong perfects are fairly well maintained in O.F., but (quite apart from regular phonetic changes) they have undergone many analogical transformations. These began in the V.L. period and extend down to Modern French, making their influence felt in varying degrees in the different dialects of the 'langue d'oïl'. In the space at our disposal we can do little more than indicate the more important developments reflected in the modern forms. For a detailed account the reader may consult P. Fouché's *Le verbe français* and the more general treatment in Kr. Nyrop's *Grammaire historique*, Vol. II, both of which we have utilized extensively.

345. Classical Latin presented four types of strong perfects: (1) Perfects in -I (VENI), (2) Perfects in -SI (SCRIPSI), (3) Perfects in -UI (SAPUI), (4) Reduplicated Perfects (MO-MORDI). In V.L. the passage from one type to another is frequent, changes being provoked by analogies of various kinds.

(1) Many -I perfects (and several reduplicated perfects) passed into the -UI class, a new perfect being formed to correspond to the past participle on the analogy of HABUI—HABITUM, RAPUI—RAPTUM, DOCUI—DOCTUM, etc. Thus BIBI, CREDIDI, CECIDI, CUCURRI, FEFELLI, RECEPI, LEGI gave way to *BIBUI, *CREDUI, *CADUI, *CURRUI, *FALLUI, *RECEPUI, *LEGUI, under the influence of BIBITUM, CREDITUM, *CADITUM, *CUR-RITUM, *FALLITUM, RECEPTUM, LECTUM (§ 362). MOVUI is regular, the V of MOVI being a graphy for VU; and by analogy *CO(G)NOVUI, *CREVUI, *PAVUI replaced COGNOVI, CREVI, PAVI (PASCERE). *STETUI for STETI is due to the influence of JACUI, with which it is semantically associated. MORTUUS SUM was rendered by *MORUI, NATUS SUM by *NASCUI. COLLEGI joined the weak -ĪVI class. A few -I perfects joined the weak -DEDI class (*FUNDĘDI for FUDI).

Other -I perfects and reduplicated perfects joined the -SI (sigmatic) class, being re-modelled under the influence (*a*) of the pres. ind.: *ATTANXI, *FRANXI, *PUNXI (under the influence of TANGIT, FRANGIT, PUNGIT) replace ATTIGI, FREGI, PUPUGI; or (*b*) of the past participle: *ELEXI, *MORSI, *OCCISI, *PRE(N)SI, *REDEMPSI, *SESSI (under the influence of ELECTUM, MORSUM, OCCISUM, PREHENSUM, REDEMPTUM, SESSUM) replace ELEGI, MOMORDI, OCCIDI, PREHENDI, REDEMI, SEDI; *QUAESI probably continues the primitive Latin form, which V.L. preserved, while C.L. replaced it by QUAESIVI.

(2) -SI perfects generally persisted.

(3) Of the -UI perfects, a certain number joined the -I class through loss of *w* (< *u* in hiatus) after a group of consonants or a double consonant (cf. § 348), or through loss of *w* by dissimilation after initial *v* (= w): VALUIT > *VALIT, VOLUIT > *VOLIT. TENUI early gave way to *TENI (≠VENI); cf. § 356.

(4) The reduplicated perfects entirely disappeared: some joined the -I, -SI or -UI perfects; PEPENDI, TETENDI joined the weak -DEDI class, *PENDĘDI, *TENDĘDI.

346   OLD FRENCH PARADIGMS

-I PERFECTS		-SI PERFECTS	
Latin	O.F.	Latin	O.F.
VÉNI	*vin*	DÍXI	*dis*
VENÍSTI	*venís*	DIXÍSTI	*desís*
VÉNIT	*vint*	DÍXIT	*dist*
VENÍMUS	*veními*es	DIXÍMUS	*desímes*
VENÍSTIS	*venístes*	DIXÍSTIS	*desístes*
VÉNERUNT	*víndrent*	DÍXERUNT	*dístrent*

-UI PERFECTS			
Latin	O.F.	Latin	O.F.
SÁPUI	*soi*	PARÚI	*parúi*
SAPUÍSTI	*soús*	PARÚISTI	*parús*
SÁPUIT	*sout*	PARÚIT	*parút*
SAPUÍMUS	*soúmes*	PARÚIMUS	*parúmes*
SAPUÍSTIS	*soústes*	PARÚISTIS	*parústes*
SÁPUERUNT	*sourent*	PARÚERUNT	*parúrent*

The Latin forms of VENI, DIXI, SAPUI are here given with their V.L. accentuation, which differed from the Classical in the following respects: the 1st pl. came to be accented on the ending by analogy with the 2nd pl.; the 3rd pl. preserved in V.L. the primitive Latin accentuation '-ERUNT, which C.L. had abandoned for -ÉRUNT (≠-ĒRE); in perfects of the SAPUI type, *w* (< *u* in hiatus) was carried into the 3rd pl. and the accent was thrown back on the preceding syllable. For PARUI, which is here given with its late V.L. (North Gaul) accentuation, see § 348 (c).

347. (1) Final ī disappears regularly, but not until after it has made its influence felt on the vowel of the stem (cf. § 37). Final *s*, which remains regularly in the -SI perfects, is by analogy later extended to the -I perfects (*vins*, etc.).

(2) -ĪSTĪ under the influence of final ī becomes -*is*, the final *t* disappearing by analogy with the weak verbs (§ 341).

(3) -IT. The loss of unaccented *i* brings *t* into contact with the preceding consonant and, thus supported, it remains.

(4) -ĪMUS gives -*imes* (for *-eins*) by analogy with -ISTIS > -*istes*.

(5) -ĪSTIS > -*istes*, with *i* (for *ę*) under the influence of the 2nd sing.; unaccented *e* is maintained by analogy with -*astes*, -*istes* of the weak perfects.

(6) '-ERUNT. Unaccented *e* disappears and the resulting group consonant + *r* develops a glide-consonant.

348. Unaccented *u* in hiatus with following *i*, *e* regularly becomes a semi-consonant *w*, the further development of which may be summarized as follows:

(*a*) After a group of consonants or a double consonant *w* disappeared (cf. §§ 84, 103). The loss of *u* (= *w*) tended to create confusion between the 3rd sing. perf. and the 3rd sing. pres. in forms like CONS(U)IT, *NASC(U)IT, *RUMP(U)IT, *REPENT(U)IT, *VINC(U)IT, *VERT(U)IT; this fact together with the resemblance which these perfects offered in their ending-accented forms with the -DEDI type caused them to be completely assimilated to the latter, whence O.F. *cosiét, nasquiét, repentiét, rompiét, venquiét, vertiét*. They later accompany the -DEDI verbs into the weak -*is* class (§ 343).

(*b*) After a single consonant other than a nasal or a liquid, *w* is either attracted to the preceding accented vowel (§ 350) or combines with a following accented *i* to give *ü* (*so-üs, so-ümes, so-üstes*).

(*c*) After a single nasal or liquid consonant, *w* persists and, under the influence of *fui, fus, fut, fumes, fustes, furent*, is transformed into accented *ü* (type *parui*). Thus arises a new weak perfect with the characteristic vowel *ü*, which is later extended by analogy to other verbs; cf. Fouché, p. 305.

Note that perfects like VOLUI, VALUI, with initial v, had joined the -I class; cf. § 345 (3).

THE STEM

-I AND -SI PERFECTS

349. In the 1st sing., under the influence of final *ī*, the stem-vowel *ę* (< Ĭ or Ē) becomes *i*, which is by analogy extended to the other stem-accented forms (3rd sing. and 3rd pl.), whence *vin, tin, dis, fis* (with analogical *s* for regular *z*), etc. By analogy with such forms and forms like *mis* (< MISI), *quis* appears for *quies (< * QUAESI).

-UI PERFECTS

350. The combination of *w* (in the form of semi-vocalic *ʉ*) with the vowel of the stem, in cases where the latter ended in a single consonant other than nasal or liquid (cf. § 348 *b, c*), gave the following results in the 1st sing.:

$a + ʉ > o$: HABUI > *oi*, PLACUI > *ploi*, SAPUI > *soi*, TACUI > *toi*, *PAVUI > *poi*; but if a palatal precedes, $a + ʉ > e + u > ü$: JACUI > *jui*, *CADUI > *chui*.

$e + ʉ > ü$: DEBUI > *dui*, *STETUI > *estui*.

$o + ʉ > ü$: NOCUI > *nui*, COGNOVI > *conui*; but if *p* precedes, $o + ʉ > o$: POTUI > *poi*.

In the 3rd sing. and 3rd pl. *w* has the same effect on the stem-vowel, but being itself brought into contact with the following consonant (by the loss of the unaccented vowel), it becomes *u* (*out, ourent*; *plout, plourent*; etc.), which is absorbed by a preceding *ü*, whence *jut, jurent*; *dut, durent*; *conut, conurent*; etc. In the weak forms (2nd sing., 1st pl., 2nd pl.) *a* becomes *o* under the influence of following *w* (*so-üs, so-ümes, so-üstes*). *e* and *o* persist (*de-üs* < DEBUISTI, *no-üs* < NOCUISTI).

351. FUI stands apart from the remaining -UI perfects in that the accent falls on the stem throughout, and the resulting uniform *ü* has had an important bearing on the development of the new weak perfect in *-us* (type *parui*, § 348 *c*).

Latin	O.F
FUI	*fui*
FUISTI	*fus*
FUIT	*fut*
FUIMUS	*fumes*
FUISTIS	*fustes*
FUERUNT	*furent*

Later the 1st sing. *fui* gave place to analogical *fus*. The collateral O.F. forms *feüs*, etc. are due to the influence of the perfect of *avoir*: *eüs*, etc. for older *oüs*, etc. (§ 350).

352. The following classified list contains the commoner strong perfects as they survived in O.F.

I. -I perfects:

voir—vi(s), ve(d)is, vit, ve(d)imes, ve(d)istes, vi(d)rent.

tenir, which in V.L. passed from the -UI to the -I class (§ 345), is conjugated like *venir*.

faire—fis, fesis, fist, fesimes, fesistes, firent.

II. -SI perfects:

ceindre—ceins, ceinsis, ceinst, ceinsimes, ceinsistes, ceinstrent. Similarly *plaindre, joindre, esteindre, feindre, peindre, teindre, ataindre—atains* (< *ATTANXI for ATTIGI; § 345), *fraindre—frains* (< *FRANXI for FREGI; § 345), *poindre—poins* (< *PUNXI for PUPUGI; § 345).

(con)duire—duis, duisis, duist, duisimes, duisistes, duistrent. Similarly all compounds of *duire*, compounds of *-struire* (*construisis, destruisis*, etc.), *cuire—cuis, tordre—tors, (re)soldre—sols* (< *SOLSI for SOLUI), *mordre—mors* (< *MORSI for MOMORDI), *(con)clure—(con)clus.*

prendre (the V.L. perfect of which was *PRESI for PREHENDI; cf. § 345 (1))—*pris, presis, prist, presimes, presistes, pristrent.* Similarly *metre—mis, rire—ris, seoir—sis* (< *SESSI for SEDI ≠ SESSUM; § 345), *escrire—escris, querre (quérir)—quis.*

Verbs which have disappeared or survive as archaisms in Mod.F.: *traire—trais, ardoir—ars, clore—clos, despire—despis, raembre—raens, espardre—espars, (re)manoir (maindre)—(re)més, terdre—ters, rere—res, occire—occis*

III. -UI perfects:

savoir type: *avoir—oi, plaisir (plaire)—ploi, taisir (taire)—toi, pooir (pouvoir)—poi, paistre—poi* (< *PAVUI for PAVI).

devoir—dui, deüs, dut, deümes, deüstes, durent. Similarly *boivre— bui, reçoivre (recevoir)—reçui, lire—lui* (< *LEGUI for LEGI), *gésir— jui, ester—estui* (< *STETUI for STETI), *croire—crui* (< *CREDUI for CREDIDI), *croistre—crui* (< *CREVUI for CREVI).

nuisir (nuire)—nui (<NOCUI), *noüs, nut, noümes, noüstes, nurent.* Similarly *mouvoir—mui, conoistre—conui, plouvoir—plui,* and the O.F. impersonal verb *estouvoir—estut* 'it was necessary'.

paroir type: *courre (courir)—courui, moldre—moului, mourir— mourui, douloir—doului.* Cf. § 348 (c).

For *estre—fui,* see § 351.

LATER DEVELOPMENT OF THE STRONG PERFECTS

-I AND -SI PERFECTS

353. Under the influence of *virent* and *firent,* the 3rd pl. forms in *-istrent* give way to forms in *-irent,* the latter triumphing in the sixteenth century: *assirent, dirent, mirent,* etc.

Under the influence of *veïs* (< *veḍis* < VIDISTI), *veïmes, veïstes,* there arose early in the twelfth century, beside *fesis, fesimes, fesistes,* forms without *s: feïs, feïmes, feïstes;* and somewhat later the same influence caused the elimination of *s* in the *-si* perfects, whence *deïs, deïmes, deïstes,* etc., which became general in the thirteenth century. The reduction of unaccented *e* in hiatus gave a perfect with the accent uniformly on the stem: *dis, dis, di(s)t, di(s)mes* (with *s ≠ distes*), *di(s)tes, dirent,* although *e* is often maintained in spelling as late as the sixteenth century. Similarly developed *mis, pris, (ac)quis, (con)quis, ris, (as)sis.*

This levelling out, which was in its effect a generalization of the strong form of the stem, was extended to *vins* and *tins* including the elimination at a later date of *d* in the 3rd pl.; *vinrent* and *tinrent* do not, however, completely displace *vindrent* and *tindrent* until the end of the seventeenth century.

354. In other verbs (generally less used) the influence of perfects of the -īvī class facilitated the generalization of weak (ending-accented) forms, the result being a weak perfect identical with the -īvī (*dormir*) type: *condui, conduist, conduistrent* are re-modelled on *conduisis, conduisimes, conduisistes*. This applies to all verbs in -*uire*: *cuis(is), déduis(is), séduis(is), réduis(is), construis(is), détruis(is), luis(is), nuis(is)*, etc. Where such verbs presented a stem at variance with that of the pres. ind., the generalization of the weak form was accompanied by a re-modelling of the stem on that of the weak forms of the pres. ind. (*dormons, dormez*) and of other tenses, again on the analogy of the -īvī (*dormir*) type, which presents the same stem in the perfect as in the present. This applies to verbs in -*eindre*, -*aindre*, -*oindre*, -*ondre*, -*ordre*: *ceignis, peignis, feignis, teignis, éteignis, atteignis, étreignis, enfreignis, plaignis, joignis, oignis, pondis, tordis, mordis*, for O.F. perfects *ceins, peins*, etc.; cf. § 352; also to *crembre* (Mod.F. *craindre*)—*craignis* for O.F. *crens*, and to *écrire*—*écrivis* for O.F. *escris*.

conclus and *exclus* joined the weak perfects in -*u* (type *parus*).

resous, absous, dissous were re-modelled under the influence of the past participles *résolu, absolu, dissolu*, whence *résolus, absolus, dissolus*, of which the two latter have fallen into disuse.

-UI PERFECTS

355. The weak forms show weakening of pre-tonic *o, e* in hiatus to *ə*, and the latter is subsequently absorbed by the following *ü*: *soüs > seüs > sus, soümes > seümes > sûmes, soüstes > seüstes > sûtes*; note that the perfect of *avoir* keeps the spelling *u* (e.g. *eûmes* = ü:m). By analogy *ü* is introduced in the 3rd sing. and 3rd pl. of the SAPUI—*soi* type, whence *sut, surent*; *(e)ut, (e)urent*; and the 1st sing. is re-modelled on the 2nd and 3rd sing. (with final *s* on the analogy of the -*si* perfects), whence *sus, (e)us* for older *soi, oi*, etc. In the 1st pl. -*s*- is introduced by analogy with the 2nd pl. (*susmes*, Mod.F.

sûmes ≠ *sustes*, Mod.F. *sûtes*). The result is a perfect accented on the stem throughout and presenting the characteristic vowel *ü*: *sus*, *(e)us*, *plus*, *tus*, *pus*, *dus*, *bus*, *reçus*, *lus*, *crus*, *crûs* (with circumflex accent to distinguish it from *crus*), *mus*, *connus*, *plus*, and the obsolete forms *pus* (*paître*) and *jus* (*gésir*).

With the substitution of *nuire* for *nuisir*, the perfect of this verb was re-modelled on the analogy of verbs in -*uire*: *nuisis*, *nuisis*, etc. for O.F. *nuis*, *nuisis*, etc.

For *na(s)quis, vainquis, repentis, rompis, -vertis, cousis*, see § 343; *vesquis* > *ve(s)cus* ≠ the past participle *ve(s)cu*.

356. *Vouloir*. The perfect of this verb illustrates most adequately the multiplicity of analogical changes in the evolution of strong perfects. The reduction of *ui* to *i* (§ 345 (3)) led to the following paradigm (with *o* levelled out): *voil* (< *VOLI*[1]), *volis*, *volt*, *volimes*, *volistes*, *voldrent*, whence with re-modelling of the strong forms on the weak: *volis*, *volis*, *volit*, *volimes*, *volistes*, *volirent*. Beside these there existed a sigmatic perfect (*VOLSI): *vols*, *volsis*, *volst*, *volsimes*, *volsistes*, *volstrent*, whence with levelling: *volsis*, *volsis*, *volsit*, *volsimes*, *volsistes*, *volsirent*. The sigmatic *vols*, *volsis*, etc. was the form most commonly used in the later Middle Ages, but all four of these O.F. perfects gave way in the sixteenth century to the modern *voulus*, etc., which is a re-modelling (dating from the fourteenth century) of *voil*, *volis*, *volt*, etc. under the influence of the past participle *voulu*.

Valoir. The reduction of VALUI to *VALI (§ 345 (3)) should have given a paradigm *vail*, *valis*, etc., but O.F. offers *valui* (later *valus*), *valus*, *valut*, *valumes*, *valustes*, *valurent*, which is probably due to the analogy of *chaloir* and other verbs of the *paroir* type.

Lire. The sigmatic perfect *lis* (< *LEXI), *lesis*, etc. is displaced in the fifteenth century by *lus*, *lus*, *lut*, *lu(s)mes*, *lu(s)tes*, *urent*, which goes back to *LEGUI; cf. § 345 (1). Similarly *élire*.

---

[1] The change *VOLI > *voil* is irregular, unless we postulate an intermediate stage *voli̯* resulting from the use of *voli* before a word beginning with a vowel (Fouché, p. 271).

357. The aspect and constitution of the strong perfects have thus been completely altered: the alternation of strong and weak forms has been eliminated, leaving in Modern French either perfects with a characteristic stem-vowel uniformly accented (*acquis, assis, eus, bus,* etc.) or weak perfects of the *-us* and *-is* types (*résolus, conclus, conduisis,* etc.).

IMPERFECT SUBJUNCTIVE

The Latin imperfect subjunctive (CANTAREM) disappeared, and its functions were taken over by the Pluperfect Subjunctive (CANTAVISSEM).

358.   OLD FRENCH PARADIGMS

Latin	O.F.	Latin	O.F.
CANTA(VI)SSEM	*chantasse*	DORMI(VI)SSEM	*dormisse*
CANTA(VI)SSES	*chantasses*	DORMI(VI)SSES	*dormisses*
CANTA(VI)SSET	*chantast*	DORMI(VI)SSET	*dormist*
CANTA(VI)SSEMUS	*chantissons*	DORMI(VI)SSEMUS	*dormissons*
CANTA(VI)SSETIS	*chantisseiz*	DORMI(VI)SSETIS	*dormisseiz*
CANTA(VI)SSENT	*chantassent*	DORMI(VI)SSENT	*dormissent*

THE ENDINGS

359. The impf. subjv. endings of verbs with -DEDI perfects do not differ from those of *dormir*. Normally they should have given forms in *-esse*: *PERDEDISSEM (for C.L. PERDIDISSEM) >perdesse*; *-isse* is due to the influence of verbs of the *dormir* type. The same influence accounts for the *i* of impf. subjunctives corresponding to strong -I and -SI perfects: *fesisse* (FECĬSSEM), *desisse* (DIXĬSSEM).

The impf. subjv. of verbs with strong -UI perfects shows the same fusion of *u* with following accented *i* as in the perfect (§ 348 *b*), whence the paradigm *parusse, parusses, parust, parussons, parusseiz, parussent.*

The contracted forms in -ASSEM, -ISSEM date from Classical times.

The preservation of unaccented *e* in the 2nd sing. is due to the tendency to avoid the fusion of flexional *s* with the preceding *s*, and it was carried thence into the 1st sing. by analogy, on the model of the pres. subjv. *-e* (< -AM) beside *-es* (< -AS).

Analogical *-ons* (§ 307) appears from the beginning of the O.F. period; but beside it *-iens* is found in the twelfth century (cf. x, 30), and later *-ions*, which triumphs in the fifteenth (cf. § 323); *-eiz* (later *-oiz*) gives place to *-ez* and finally *-iez*, as in the pres. subjv. (§ 323)

The *i* of *-issons*, *-isseiz* (< -A(VI)SSEMUS, -A(VI)SSETIS) is difficult to explain. M. Fouché (p. 332) assumes a weakening of *a* to *e*, followed by dissimilation *e—ę > i—ę* (CANTASSEMUS > *CANTESSĘMUS > *chantisseins—chantissons*); but there seems to be no parallel for such a dissimilation of counterfinal *ə* (< A) before tonic *ę*. Occasionally *i* appears by analogy in other persons than the 1st pl. and 2nd pl. in the fifteenth and sixteenth centuries. Levelling out of the characteristic vowel *a* gave *-assions*, *-assiez*, which first appear about 1500 but do not finally triumph until the beginning of the seventeenth century.

THE STEM

360. The stem of the impf. subjv. shows the same form as the perfect indicative (the weak form of the stem in the case of O.F. strong perfects) and shares its later transformations: O.F. *veïsse*, *venisse*, *tenisse*, *presisse*, *conduisisse*, *plainsisse*, *desisse*, *fesisse*, *oüsse*, *deüsse*, *coneüsse*, *parusse* (beside perf. 2nd sing. *veïs*, etc.) give place to Mod.F. *visse*, *vinsse*, *tinsse*, *prisse*, *conduisisse*, *plaignisse*, *disse*, *fisse*, *eusse*, *dusse*, *connusse*, *parusse* (beside *vis*, *vins*, *tins*, etc.).

To *voil* (*volis*), *vols* (*volsis*) correspond the subjunctives *volisse*, *volsisse* respectively, both replaced in Mod.F. by *voulusse*.

PAST PARTICIPLE

361. Classical Latin possessed strong forms in -SUM, -TUM and weak forms in -ĀTUM, -ĒTUM, -ĪTUM, -ŪTUM. Vulgar Latin shows the same types, with the exception of -ĒTUM, which disappeared together with the verbs in question or their

passage to the -ĪRE class : COMPLERE gives place to *COMPLIRE, whence *COMPLÍTU (> (ac)compli) for COMPLÉTUM. But analogical re-modellings had completely altered the original distribution and had created many collateral forms.[1]

VULGAR LATIN CHANGES

362. -SUM received accessions from the -TUM class:

C.L.	V.L.	O.F.
ABSCONDITUM	ABSCONSU	*ascons*
MONITUM	MONSU	*(se)mons* (cf. Mod.F. *semonce*)
PERDITUM	PERSU	*pers*
POSITUM	POSU	*pos*
QUAESITUM	QUAESU	*quis* (Mod.F. *acquis, requis*)
SURRECTUM	SURSU	*sors* (cf. Mod.F. *ressource, source*)
TORTUM	TORSU	*tors* (Mod.F. *fil tors, soie torse*)

and from the -UTUM class:

SOLUTUM	SOLSU	*sols* (cf. § 370)
VOLUTUM	VOLSU	*vols, vous* (cf. Mod.F. *voussure, voussoir*)

Losses consist in re-modellings in -ĪTUM and -ĬTUM (-ŪTUM).

-TUM received a number of accessions, thanks to re-modellings under the influence of those -ĒRE, -ĔRE verbs which had participles in '-ĬTUM (HABERE—HABITUM, CREDERE —CREDITUM).

C.L.	V.L.	French fossilized forms
FALSUM	FÁLLITU	*faute, défaut*
FISSUM	FÍNDITU	*fente*
MOTUM	MÓVITU	*meute*
PENSUM	PÉNDITU	*pente*
TENTUM	TÉNDITU	*tente*

The new forms *FALLITU, etc. were later replaced by analogical re-modellings in -ÚTU(M): *fallu*, etc. A number of

---

[1] For the following account (§§ 362–70) we have drawn extensively upon Fouché, pp. 345–76.

-TUM forms passed to the -ĪTUM, -SUM classes, or directly to the
-ŪTUM class.

363. -ĀTUM presents no gains or losses in V.L.

-ĪTUM. The number of -ĪTUM forms was greatly increased
by re-modelling (on the infinitive) of the past participles of
almost all those -ĪRE verbs which presented forms in -TUM:
SALTUM > *SALÍTU formed on SALIRE; or in -SUM: SENSUM
> *SENTÍTU on SENTIRE, VERSUM > *VERTÍTU on *VERTIRE.
COLLECTUM joined this class as the result of the re-modelling
of COLLIGERE (§ 315), whence *cueillir—cueilli*. VESTĪTUM joined
the -UTUM class.

-ŪTUM, which in C.L. was confined to verbs whose stem
ended in U (CONSUERE, etc.), was extended to a large number
of verbs with participles in -SUM and -TUM. The re-modelling
began with those verbs which had -UI perfects (or developed
them in V.L.), in the proportion CONSUI : CONSUTUM : : -UI :
*-UTUM. The first of the -UI verbs to be affected were those
which presented a past participle in -ĬTUM, whence *DEBÚTU,
*HABÚTU, *MOLÚTU, *PARÚTU, *PLACÚTU, *BIBÚTU, *VALÚTU,
*NOCÚTU; or had developed it in the Vulgar Latin period
(§ 362): *FALLÚTU, *MOVÚTU, *CURRÚTU, *JACÚTU, *PLO-
VÚTU, *VINCÚTU, *VISCÚTU, and also *CONOVÚTU for COG-
NITUM; whence the French forms *d(e)u, (e)u, moulu, paru,
pl(e)u, b(e)u, valu*, O.F. *n(e)u, fallu, m(e)u, couru*, O.F. *j(e)u,
pl(e)u, vencu, ve(s)cu, conn(e)u* respectively. These were followed by other -UI verbs: *LEGÚTU (for LECTUM), *RECEPÚTU
(RECEPTUM), *RUMPÚTU (RUPTUM), and *TENÚTU (TENTUM)
(under the influence of which *VENÚTU for VENTUM was
created), including some which had no past participle in
C.L.: *POTÚTU, *SAPÚTU, *VOLÚTU. Thus arose the French
forms *l(e)u, rec(e)u, rompu, tenu, venu, p(e)u, s(e)u, voulu*. But
once begun, the movement carried with it past participles in
-ĬTUM (primary or secondary) which did not correspond to -UI
perfects: *PERDÚTU, *VENDÚTU, *EXÚTU; and *VIDÚTU (for
*VIDĬTU for VISUM), *DESCENDÚTU, *FERÚTU, *RENDÚTU, *DE-
FENDÚTU, *FINDÚTU, *FUNDÚTU, *PENDÚTU, *RESPONDÚTU,
*TENDÚTU, *TONDÚTU; whence French *perdu, vendu*, O.F. *eissu*

(and *issu*, cf. Mod.F. *issue*), *v(e)u, descendu, feru, rendu, defendu, fendu, fondu, pendu, re(s)pondu, tendu, tondu*.

The original forms often persisted alongside of the new collateral forms, but, as they tended to appear anomalous, they were gradually deprived of their verbal function and either disappeared or survived only as adjectives or substantives (cf. § 371).

The creation of new analogical forms continues in the O.F. period, and in popular speech to the present day; but since the seventeenth century the literary language presents few hesitations. The development of the various types may be briefly summarized as follows.

364. -ATUM > -*éṭ* > -*é*, or after a palatal > -*iéṭ* > -*ié*, which is reduced during the Mid.F. period to -*é* (*traitié* > *traité*, *mangié* > *mangé*). Modern French shows no re-modellings in -*é*, but the number of -*é* forms has been greatly increased by additions to the verbs in -*er* (§ 289): *epelé, grondé, pué, sangloté, secoué, toussé, tissé,* and *distribué, affligé*; such forms are not re-modellings, but regular forms corresponding to new -*er* verbs. *Cueillir* and a few other verbs show collateral forms in -*é*, which were used sporadically in the sixteenth and seventeenth centuries. On the other hand *recouvrer* hesitated (under the influence of *recouvrir*) between *recouvert* and *recouvré*, from the fifteenth to the end of the seventeenth century.

365. -ĪTUM > -*iṭ* > -*i*. Examples: *senti, accompli, fini, cueilli*. Such re-modelled forms as *ouvri, offri*, dating from O.F., have not survived, although still used in the sixteenth century (*batti*).

366. -ŪTUM > -*uṭ* > -*u*. The participles in -*u* gradually ousted the collateral forms, e.g. *couru, venu, tenu, fondu* alone survive in French; *ardu, rompu, élu* did not displace *ars, rout, e(s)lit* until the sixteenth century, while *tordu, mordu* triumphed over *tors, mors* in the seventeenth. On the other hand, *craint, né, nui, resplendi, suivi, -verti, repenti* eliminated the collateral -*u* forms *cremu, nascu, neü, resplendu, seü, -vertu, repentu*, before the sixteenth century. Re-modellings in -*u* dating from the O.F.

period have not as a rule survived (*prendu*), or at least only
to the sixteenth or seventeenth century (*sentu, mouru*).

367. The elimination of the final consonant of the stem
(if that consonant was intervocal; cf. § 98) before -*u* and the
weakening of the preceding vowel produced *e-ü* forms (*SAPÚTU
> *se-u*, *LEGÚTU > *le-u*, *BIBÚTU > *be-u*, *PLACÚTU > *ple-u*)
which persist as such in O.F., but are reduced in Mid.F.
(cf. § 61). The contraction was generally noted by a circumflex accent, but this is now only used in *mû* < *meu* < *MOVÚTU,
crû < *creu* < *CREVÚTU, *dû* < *deu* < *DEBÚTU; the accent here
serves to distinguish *crû*, *dû* from *cru* (p.p. of *croire*), *du*, and is
therefore not used in the feminines *crue*, *due*, and also in *mue*;
the compounds show inconsistency: *accrû*, *décrû*, *redû*, but *indu*,
ému, *promu*. Note also that *crû* used as a substantive does not
take the accent (*de son propre cru*).

In spelling, *e* persisted long after it had ceased to have any
phonetic value, and this led to an artificial restoration of the
disyllabic pronunciation (*e-ü*) in the sixteenth century and
consequent hesitation between *ü* and *e-ü* well into the seventeenth century. Only in the past participle of *avoir*, *eu* (= ü),
has the old spelling been maintained in Mod.F.

368. -TUM > -*t* and -SUM > -*s*. When unsupported, *t* early
became mute: NATUM > *nét* > *né*, but NATUS > O.F. *nez*; STATUM
> *e(s)té*. When supported (in Latin or Romance), *t* persists
in O.F.; but by the sixteenth century both *t* and *s* had become
mute in the masculine, while they remained in the feminine,
where they had been protected by *e* (now mute; cf. §§ 62–4):
conduit—conduite, *mis—mise*. Certain forms show this loss of the
final consonant in spelling and therefore appear in Mod.F.
in the guise of -*i* participles: *ri(s)*, *suffi(t)*, *lui(t)*, *nui(t)*;[1] they
are all intransitive verbs conjugated with *avoir* and there-
fore never used in the feminine, which would account for
their readiness to drop a meaningless consonant and join the
-*i* class. In other participles the existence of feminine forms

---

[1] When *luisir*, *nuisir* gave way to *luire*, *nuire* (§ 290) the participles *luit*,
nuit (for O.F. *luisi*, *neü*) were created under the influence of verbs in
-*uire* (*conduire—conduit*).

prevents such an assimilation; but *conclus*, *exclus* became *conclu*, *exclu*, in spite of the feminine forms *concluse*, *excluse*, which were still used in the eighteenth century; for this change the influence of the infinitives *conclure*, *exclure* and the analogy of *valu*, etc. are doubtless responsible; *exclus*, *excluse*, *inclus*, *incluse* survive as adjectives, also *perclus*, *percluse*; *reclus* remained unaffected.

369. -ECTUM and -ĬCTUM regularly gave -*eit*, later -*oit* (COLLECTUM > *coilleit*, BENEDĬCTUM > *bene(d)eit*, MALEDĬCTUM > *male-(d)eit*), which came to be considered as a participial suffix in O.F. and led to such re-modellings as *cheoit* (beside *cheü* < *CADÚTU). None of the latter survived, except as fossilized forms: *benoît* (dial. *benêt*) < *bene(d)eit*, and *cueillette*, which (with change of suffix) continues *coilleite*, *cueilloite*. Similarly DĬCTUM should have given *deit, but under the influence of the infinitive we have *dit*, also *maudit* (for O.F. *male(d)eit*, *maleoit*); *béni—e* is a new formation on the inf. *bénir*; *bénit—e*, now only used as an adjective (*pain bénit*, *eau bénite*), either continues *BENEDĬCTUM (with ī by analogy with the infinitive) or arose when *bénir* (for O.F. *beneïstre*) developed a collateral *benire* (≠*maudire*), a form which is still found in the seventeenth century.

370. The conflict between *sous* (*SOLSU), *solu* (SOLUTUM), and *sout* (*SOLTU) is still reflected in the verbs *résoudre*: p.p. *résolu—e* beside *résous* (used as a technical term in chemistry, etc.); *dissoudre*: p.p. *dissous*, *dissoute*; *absoudre*: p.p. *absous*, *absoute*; *dissolu* and *absolu* survive only as adjectives.

371. The number of strong forms thus shows a steady decline, beginning in V.L. and continuing down to the seventeenth century. Some have disappeared since O.F., together with the verbs to which they belonged: *occis* (*occire*), *ters* (*terdre*), *raent* (*raembre*), *tolt* (*toldre*, *tollir*); others have given way to re-modelled forms: *mors*, *tors*, etc. (§ 366). Many survived in the form of substantives (masc. or fem.) or adjectives; to those already mentioned the following may be added: BIBITUM—O.F. *boite* 'drink'; COGNITUM—O.F. *cointe* (whence Engl. *quaint*) 'knowing', 'well-prepared', 'dainty'; CONFUSUM—*confus*; CURSUM—*cours, concours, recours, secours*; DEBITUM—*dette*; DEFENSUM—*défens, défense*; DISPENSUM—*dépens, dépense*; ELECTUM—*élite*; FALSUM—*faux*; FISSUM—*fesse*; FUGITUM—*fuite*; *FUNDITU—*fonte*; (MALE) HABITUM—*malade*; *IMPLICITU—*emplette* (O.F. *empleite*); MISSUM—*mets* (O.F. *mes*); MORSUM—*mors, remords*; OFFENSUM—*offense*; PERDITUM—*perte*; PLACITUM—*plaid*; PRAEPOSITUM—*prévôt*; QUAESTUM—*acquêt, buête, conquête, requête*; RASUM—*rez* in *rez-de-chaussée*, etc.; RECEPTUM—*recette*; *RENDITU—*rente*; REPOSITUM—O.F. *repost* 'hidden'; RESPONSUM—*répons, réponse*; RUPTUM—*route, déroute*; *SEQUITU—*suite*; SPARSUM—*épars*; SUCCUSSUM—*secousse, re(s)cousse*; TENSUM—*toise*; *TONDITU—*tonte*; TORTUM—*tort*; VENDITUM—*vente*; *VOLTU—*voûte*.

SYNTAX OF THE PAST PARTICIPLE

372. In Latin the past participle is purely adjectival and always agrees with the substantive which it modifies. It continues to be so treated in French if it is used adjectivally (*une occasion perdue*; *Il la trouva accablée*). Similarly, in absolute constructions (*La nuit venue, il partit*), which were formerly used much more freely and, under Latin influence,[1] enjoyed great popularity in the sixteenth century (XIV, 2, 7, 58, 68). Such constructions could formerly be preceded by a preposition (*avant la nuit venue*). Similarly, *excepté, ci-inclus, ci-joint* agree if they follow the substantive (*la lettre ci-jointe*); but if they precede, they become practically equivalent to adverbs or prepositions and are therefore invariable (*excepté ses amis*; *Vous trouverez ci-joint la lettre*).

373. In compound tenses formed with *être*, the past participle regularly agrees with the subject, as in Latin. In O.F. it was sometimes treated as invariable (X, 61), particularly if the subject followed, *être* + participle being treated as

---

[1] Latin influence is also responsible for the use of the participle as the equivalent of a clause, as in XVII, 27. Cf. also the following bold use of the absolute construction: *Aux murs miroitaient des armes de toute provenance:...un casque de soldat prussien que le comte me montra, presque aussitôt entrés*, Bourget, *Le Disciple*.

a unit, the equivalent of a simple tense. For a similar reason the absolute *étant donné* remains invariable (*étant donné ces conditions*).

374. When conjugated with *avoir* the past participle originally agreed with the direct object (III, 41, 42; IV, 80; VI, 62), as in Latin (HABEO LITTERAS SCRIPTAS); but with the weakening of *avoir* to the function of a mere auxiliary, *avoir* + participle became the equivalent of a simple tense, and the passive meaning of the past participle became obliterated. Hence a tendency to leave the participle invariable, which is observable in the twelfth century and becomes more general in the thirteenth. Latin influence may have had a share in maintaining agreement, which remained the rule when the direct object preceded (*J'ai la vérité entendue*). Out of the confusion and hesitation which obtain down to the eighteenth century (cf. xv *b*, 2), two tendencies emerge, one to leave the participle invariable if the direct object follows, the other to make it agree if the direct object precedes. In the seventeenth century the question was much debated, but there was general agreement to leave the participle invariable if another word followed. The modern rule requiring agreement with the direct object if the latter precedes was adopted in the eighteenth century.[1]

375. If the participle is followed by an infinitive, agreement with the direct object is the rule in O.F. (*Je l'ai faite venir*; cf. IV, 98); but here, too, hesitation exists and continues in the seventeenth century (cf. also xv *b*, 9). The modern rules which make *fait* always invariable, and the participles of other verbs invariable if the object is the object of the infinitive (*La chanson que j'ai entendu chanter*), are due to a modern interpretation of the infinitive as active in meaning instead of passive (as it was in O.F.; cf. § 300).

376. The past participle of pronominal verbs agreed with the subject down to the seventeenth century, when, *être* being interpreted as a variant of *avoir*, the past participle was made

[1] It had been formulated as early as the sixteenth century by Marot and Ramus; cf. Sneyders de Vogel, § 287 ff.

to agree with the preceding direct object (*Elle s'est coupée*; but *Elle s'est coupé la main*). The rule becomes illogical in cases like *Elle s'est écriée*; *Ils se sont plaints*; where *se* is the grammatical, but not the logical, direct object, *s'écrier* and *se plaindre* not being 'reflexive' verbs (cf. § 384 ff.).

The past participle of impersonal verbs (with few exceptions) and of intransitive verbs (unless used transitively: *la vie que j'ai vécue*) has always been invariable.

377. It should be noted that in many cases the question of agreement affects spelling and versification only (*vu—vue, fini—finie*). In the remaining cases the spoken language shows much fluctuation, the tendency to leave the participle invariable being counteracted by the influence of the schoolmaster and of the written word.

CONCORD

378. Exceptions to the rule that the verb agrees with its subject in person and number are due to attraction or syllepsis. Such forms as *j'avons* are now confined to patois, but formerly had a wide currency. O.F. *ce suis je, ce sommes nous*, in which *ce* is the predicate, gave way in the sixteenth century to *c'est moi, c'est nous*, because *ce* had come to be regarded as the subject of an impersonal expression *c'est* (*c'est il*; *c'est lui*; *c'est raison*). *Ce sont* was in certain cases allowed by seventeenth-century grammarians, but even here the force of analogy has gradually broken down their artificial rules: *c'est*, which had continued to be used in popular speech, has now received official sanction, whether before a plural pronoun or substantive (*C'est eux*).

379. The rule requiring the agreement in person (and number) of the verb in a relative clause with its antecedent was often violated in medieval practice and as late as the eighteenth century. In some cases hesitation persists to the present day. Such constructions as *Je ne vois plus que vous qui la puisse défendre* (cf. § 411) represent the triumph over formal rules of a feeling that the antecedent is not really *vous* but

a generic '*personne*' implied in *Je ne vois plus* (cf. Sneyders de Vogel, § 187). In literary usage the formal rule is now observed; but if the antecedent is followed by a complement or predicative adjective, there is often hesitation: *Vous êtes les seuls qui soyez (soient) arrivés.*

380. If the subject is a collective noun, the verb is often in the plural in medieval usage (*la gent dient*); cf. x, 91; xi, 52. In Mod.F. the formal rule requiring the singular gives rise to hesitation only if the substantive is followed by a plural complement (*la foule des gens*), and the usual practice is to use the singular if the notion of collectivity is uppermost in the mind, otherwise the plural; but by an official dispensation (1901) the plural is allowed in all cases. Contrary to seventeenth-century practice, the plural is now compulsory after *la plupart des*.

381. After a compound subject Mod.F. requires, with few exceptions, the plural of the verb; but as late as the eighteenth century agreement with the nearest substantive was tolerated if the several substantives are linked by *et*. If they are linked by *comme, ainsi que, ni, avec,* the verb may now always be in the plural (as it was in the seventeenth century), the subtle distinctions of grammarians having been disowned by the Decree of 1901.

TRANSITIVE AND INTRANSITIVE VERBS

382. The distinction between Transitive verbs (those which take a direct object) and Intransitive verbs (those which take an indirect object or no object) is a purely formal one. It does not reflect a difference in the notion conveyed, but (*a*) linguistic habits, (*b*) the point of view from which the action is regarded. It follows that, as linguistic habits change, so a verb may pass from one class to the other, and that at a given period the same verb may be used transitively and intransitively. Thus *délibérer, consentir, jouir* were used transitively down to the seventeenth century, but are now intransitive. Conversely *assister, contredire, fuir, regarder* (but *y regarder*)

have in Modern French become transitive. The change is sometimes due to analogy. Thus *ressembler quelqu'un* > *ressembler à quelqu'un* ≠ *être semblable à*. The fact that proclitic *vous, nous, me, te*, etc. do not permit of a distinction between accusative and dative and that *lui, cui*, etc. were formerly used both as accusative and dative may have helped to cause hesitation. But often the change is due simply to a new way of conceiving the action, when both uses may persist: *croire qqn., croire à qqn., croire en qqn.*; *aider à qqn.*, which was common even as late as the seventeenth century, is now possible only if a prepositional infinitive follows (*aider à qqn. à faire qqch.*), otherwise *aider qqn.* is used; *prier à qqn., servir à qqn., survivre qqn.* did not outlive the seventeenth century; cf. also XIV, 18.

383. Such fluctuations are different in kind from the derived functions presented by the absolute use of a transitive verb (*Il écrivait*), or the factitive use of intransitive verbs (*arrêter*, originally intransitive, becomes *arrêter* v.tr. 'to cause to halt'). Intransitive verbs frequently become transitive in form without change of meaning when they are followed by an accusative denoting the cause of the action (*Je pleure la mort d'un ami*), the place where it happens (*courir les rues*), or repeating the notion conveyed by the verb (*vivre sa vie*). Some verbs have developed a variety of uses (*Il descend; Il descend l'escalier; Descendez-moi ces bagages! L'avion a été descendu*). *Apprendre* 'to apprehend', 'to learn', a transitive verb, used factitively, became *apprendre* 'to cause to learn', 'to teach' (*Oiseaux qu'ils ont appris à chanter*, Vaugelas, *Q.Q.* VIII, 9; Sudre, p. 94), whence the passive *être appris* (*Singulierement, estoit aprins à saulter hastivement d'un cheval sus l'aultre*, Rab. I, 23), which has survived in *bien appris, mal appris*; *apprendre qqn., apprendre qqn. à faire qqch.* are common in the seventeenth century, but have given way to *apprendre qqch. à qqn., apprendre à qqn. à faire qqch.* Montaigne's *Qui apprendroit les hommes à mourir, leur apprendroit à vivre* (I, 20) may be taken as characteristic of a common sixteenth-century hesitation between transitive and intransitive use of verbs.[1]

[1] Cf. Nyrop, VI, §§ 184–9; Sneyders de Vogel, §§ 192–9.

PRONOMINAL VERBS

384. Of the pronominal verbs (constructed with a reflexive pronoun) some are genuine reflexives, i.e. the subject is at the same time the object (direct or indirect) of the action denoted by the verb: *Je me couche*; *Il se tue*. The Latin pronominal verbs were all of this type; but, if the subject was an inanimate object or the verb abstract, their reflexive force was hardly apparent and they tended to acquire a purely neuter value (SE MUTARE). In time, the reflexive pronoun came to be considered as a mere adjunct of the verb, serving at most to establish a closer connection between subject and verb, and giving more subjective force to the action. It was therefore natural that the reflexive pronoun should be employed to serve a similar function with neuter verbs, and we find it so used from the beginning of the O.F. period: *Charles se gist* (*Rol.* 2513); *Charles se dort* (*Rol.* 718); *Et les oiseaux qui se crïent* (*Auc. et Nic.* 5, 13); IV, 86. This optional use of the reflexive pronoun was still common in the sixteenth century, and in the seventeenth there is still hesitation between *apparaître* and *s'apparaître*, *disparaître* and *se disparaître*, *éclater de rire* and *s'éclater de rire*; *approcher* alone preserves it in Mod.F. In other cases the language has utilized the hesitation to make a slight distinction in meaning: *jouer—se jouer*, *rire—se rire*, *avancer—s'avancer*, *mourir—se mourir*; or has accepted the pronominal form: *s'évanouir*, *s'affaiblir*, *s'écrier*, *s'écrouler*, *se taire*, *s'endormir*; or more commonly has dropped the reflexive pronoun. In a number of verbs the reflexive pronoun has been maintained before *en* only: *s'en aller*, *s'enfuir*, *s'en retourner* (note *se retourner* = 'to turn round'), *s'en revenir*, *s'envoler*. In popular speech and in many patois the medieval usage is to a large extent maintained. This purely formal use of the reflexive pronoun has been extended by analogy to certain transitive verbs: *s'apercevoir*, *s'aviser*, *se moquer*.

385. The optional use of the pronoun with neuter verbs led in O.F. to a parallel optional suppression of the pronoun

with genuine reflexive verbs. This is still found after modal auxiliaries; in more or less fixed locutions (*faire taire, envoyer promener*) the pronoun is suppressed, but generally the tendency is to use it.

386. Certain pronominal verbs show the use of the reflexive pronoun as a dative of interest (*s'imaginer, se figurer, se rappeler qqch., se permettre*); in some it can be used either as a dative or as an accusative: *Elle s'est coupé la main—Elle s'est coupée; Elle s'est caché la figure—Elle s'est cachée.*

387. The readiness with which the pronominal form acquires a purely passive meaning is evidenced by the use in Latin of both the analytic passive (MUTATUM EST) and the pronominal forms (SE MUTAVIT) to render the neuter idea 'it has changed'. In French the pronominal form does not appear to have been used to render the passive before the fourteenth century. Its rapid extension in the sixteenth may be due in part to Italian influence. Since the seventeenth century it has been much restricted and is now only employed with an inanimate subject: *Le livre ne s'est pas retrouvé = Le livre n'a pas été retrouvé*; but *La jeune fille ne s'est pas retrouvée* can no longer be used as the equivalent of *La jeune fille n'a pas été retrouvée.*

388. The compound tenses of pronominal verbs are formed with *être*, but in O.F., as in modern popular speech, *avoir* is common. The use of *avoir* with a genuine reflexive is logically justified: O.F. *je m'ai levé* (literally 'I have raised myself') being exactly parallel to *j'ai levé la main* ('I have raised my hand'), but beside *je m'ai levé* we find *je suis levé* (which continues Latin LEVATUS SUM), and with analogical introduction of the pronoun, *je me suis levé*. The eventual triumph of the latter over *je m'ai levé* as the perfect of *se lever* was facilitated by the development of a purely neuter meaning (*se lever* = 'to get up'); *je suis levé* came to denote only the passive 'I am raised' or a state 'I am up'.[1]

---

[1] Cf. Sneyders de Vogel, §§ 152–74.

IMPERSONAL VERBS

389. French inherited the impersonal verb from Latin and preserves the liberty to employ personal verbs impersonally (*Il arrive des accidents*), and conversely to employ impersonal verbs personally, by giving them a factitive meaning (*Il tonne contre ses ennemis*). The impersonal use of the passive of neuter verbs (ITUR) was continued in O.F. but has practically died out, although transitive verbs may still be used in this way (*Il est dit*). Similarly Mod.F. continues to use pronominal verbs impersonally (*Il se trouve*). Contrary to Latin usage, a construction like *Il pleut des balles* (grammatically impersonal but logically personal) may be turned into *Des balles pleuvent.* (grammatically and logically personal); cf. xi, 6.

390. The stock of impersonal verbs varies at different periods of the language; they are now less numerous than formerly. Of the Latin verbs denoting natural phenomena, the majority have survived (*il pleut*—PLUIT), and losses have been more than made good by the development of *il fait*, which is used in O.F. to denote weather conditions (*Et al maitin fist mult bel jor et mult cler*, Villehardouin, 78) and is gradually extended to denote other phenomena.

391. Other impersonal verbs have been less stable: many do not persist in French (PUDET, etc.), others did not survive the O.F. period (*loist* < LICET). Unless they are used personally (see above), they require a complement (substantive, infinitive or clause), which, although it may logically appear as the subject, is grammatically the direct object; and therefore the oblique case is the rule in O.F.: *Il nen i at ne veie ne sentier* (obl.), *Rol.* 2399. With the loss of case distinctions the complement comes to be regarded as the subject: *Il y a des hommes* is felt to be logically on the same footing as *Des hommes existent*; cf. Engl. 'there *are* men'.

392. There has been considerable variation in the impersonal use of personal verbs: *douloir, afferir* (cf. xi, 3), *apparoir* become purely impersonal in the sixteenth century (*duelt, affiert, apert*) and do not survive in Mod.F., whereas *déplaire, ennuyer, fâcher* and other verbs show hesitation in the seventeenth; *souvenir* still preserves the hesitation between *je me souviens de* and *il me souvient de* (now obsolescent). Certain French creations such as *pert, apert, chaut* 'it matters' (XIII, 7, 23) have not survived, except as archaisms; *convient* has been partly, O.F. *estuet* (< STUPET) 'it is necessary' completely eliminated by *il faut* (< FALLIT), which from the meaning 'it is lacking', 'it is needful' developed the modern meaning 'it is necessary' (found as early as the twelfth century; cf. XIII, 11, 94). The impersonal use of *avoir* dates from V.L., whether in the sense of 'there is, there are' or 'ago' (*il y a dix jours*). As late as the sixteenth century (and sporadically in the seventeenth) the use of *il* and *y* is optional (*Set anz at pleins qu'en Espaigne venimes* (*Rol.* 197); *Voilà ce que* (*je devais vous avoir écrit il a longtemps*, Voiture; Haase, 10, 1 The older usage is reflected in archaic *naguère* (*n'a guère* = *il n'y a guère*), *pieça* (= *piece a*). The impersonal use of *être* in the sense of *il y a* (*Il est un Dieu*) dates from O.F. (cf. XVI, 68), but is now little more than a literary variant (*Il est des beautés qui échappent à l'artiste*).

393. The pronoun *il*, which in Mod.F. figures as the grammatical subject of impersonal verbs, was regularly omitted in O.F. It gradually came to be used by analogy with personal verbs (§ 240); but it is far from universal in the sixteenth and seventeenth centuries, and often preserves its demonstrative force, being the equivalent of Mod.F. *cela* (XVI, 21). A few expressions, such as *à Dieu ne plaise, n'importe, naguère*, represent survivals of former usage.

MOOD

394. French inherited from Latin the parallel series of verbal forms which we call the Indicative and Subjunctive,[1] but the use it makes of them presents a number of striking deviations from C.L. practice. The general significance of these series of forms (moods) has, however, remained the

[1] For the Infinitive and Imperative, see §§ 295-300, 329-30.

same. The Indicative is the objective mood and is employed for an objective statement of fact (whether positive or negative) or for a direct question. The Subjunctive is the subjective mood and is employed to convey the attitude of the speaker: something of himself is introduced into the statement (or question), which is put forward, not as something absolute, but as dependent upon the thoughts or feelings of the speaker; he presents the action denoted by the verb as something unfulfilled, possible, probable, hypothetical, desirable, or states it in an attenuated (polite) form. The Subjunctive may therefore with some justice be called the contingent or prospective mood. But, as applied to human speech 'subjective' and 'objective' are relative terms, and correspond largely to a difference of degree. Thus, in a sentence like *Voilà un livre qui est intéressant*, the relative clause is purely descriptive, and yet the speaker identifies himself with the statement to the extent of putting it forward as being in his opinion correct. On the other hand, if he says *Donnez-moi un livre qui soit intéressant*, the qualification attached to the book is put forward as something desired or demanded by the speaker (cf. § 411). Between the two we can imagine a whole series of gradations in degree and in kind, some of which might be rendered by the addition of *peut-être, probablement, à mon avis*, others by a mere inflection of the voice. We must therefore recognize, on the one hand, that the Indicative is never purely objective, and, on the other, that the Subjunctive is but one of a number of devices employed by the language to indicate the attitude of the speaker. Further, no language possesses the necessary formal devices for rendering accurately each one of the gradations referred to, and in practice one device is often employed to render a whole series. This is pre-eminently true of the two linguistic devices (series of flexional forms) which we call the Indicative and the Subjunctive.

395. The second consideration to be borne in mind is that in the course of time new habits of thought, a change in attitude, phonetic and analogical changes, outside influences

(such as the influence of Latin on French), may bring about a change in the functions assigned to such devices as the indicative and subjunctive moods. Thus the subjunctive of indirect discourse falls into disuse in V.L., and it is no longer considered essential to indicate by a change of mood such a purely intellectual relation as that of the speaker to reported speech. It is quite in accord with the analytical tendency observable in V.L. and the Romance languages that analytical constructions composed of DEBERE or POSSE + infinitive should be preferred in many cases to the subjunctive flexions. Or again, the distinction which is made in O.F. between a substantival clause embodying a statement (*Je dis qu'il est venu*) and an opinion (*Je crois qu'il soit venu*) is now no longer reflected in a difference of mood. This may be partly due to an abandonment of what are considered superfluous distinctions, or to analogy; but it is in the main accounted for by the fact that the dependent clause has become more completely subordinated to the main verb and that the distinction is held to be quite adequately indicated by the meaning of *je dis* and *je crois* respectively. The O.F. fondness for the paratactic structure (*Guardez de nos ne tornez lo corage*, *Rol.* 650; *Ne poet muder n'en plort*, *Rol.* 2517; also II, 10; IV, 7, 67) made the subjunctive a practical necessity and often accounts for its use where from the Mod.F. point of view we might not consider it called for.

396. Furthermore, phonetic evolution and analogical influences have in many cases obliterated the distinction between the Mod.F. indicative and subjunctive (*je donne, tu donnes, il donne, ils donnent*, and the like). Consequently the subjunctive is incapable of fulfilling the functions it served in Latin and to a large extent in O.F., and it is fast falling into disuse in popular speech.

397. The literary language naturally maintains more fully the use of the subjunctive. It utilizes it for maintaining distinctions of meaning and mood that are not felt to be necessary in popular speech or are rendered by other devices. Consequently there is a certain artificiality about the sub-

junctive; it owes its continued vitality in some measure to the conscious endeavour to write 'correctly', or to the efforts of grammarians and teachers. As the latter have evolved rules of the type 'the subjunctive is used after verbs of wishing' or 'the subjunctive is used after verbs of saying and thinking used negatively, unless the statement is accepted as a fact', it is not surprising that the use of the subjunctive has become largely formalized and that it is employed much less *naturally* than in O.F. Analogical extension of the subjunctive is therefore more common in the modern period; its optional use having practically disappeared, the language has lost in expressiveness in this particular direction. The literary language reflects the popular tendency to make over the traditional functions of the subjunctive to modal verbs (*devoir, pouvoir*) accompanied by the infinitive, or to various tenses of the indicative. In particular, the future-in-the-past has developed a modal value which is being used more and more.

398. In the following pages we shall indicate briefly some of the more striking changes in the use of the subjunctive, grouped under the traditional headings. It will be seen that the most notable development is the more and more complete subordination of the dependent clause, and a consequent tendency to make its verb reflect the attitude of the speaker, not directly, but indirectly through the principal verb or through the conjunction. In spite of this tendency, the older and more natural uses survive, often branded as exceptions: compare *J'admets que cela est vrai* 'It is true, I admit it' with *J'admets que cela soit vrai* 'Let it be true, I am willing to assume it'. The grammarian who considers such cases empirically will say that if the verb is used in one sense it takes the subjunctive, if used in another it takes the indicative. It would be more correct to say that the subjunctive has invested the principal verb with a new meaning, or stresses certain of its meanings to the exclusion of others. Compare the following passage from Mme de Sévigné (IV, 3), quoted by L. Sudre (p. 125): *Ils crioient qu'on les menât au combat; qu'ils vouloient venger la mort de leur père...; qu'avec lui ils ne craignoient*

*rien, mais qu'ils vengeroient bien sa mort; qu'on les laissât faire,
qu'ils étoient furieux et qu'on les menât au combat.*

Similarly, the use of the subjunctive in an independent
sentence as a direct reflection of the mood of the speaker has
progressively declined, being now restricted practically to the
jussive; and it is significant that it is in form brought into
line with dependent clauses (*qu'il vienne*), even being explained
in some school grammars as an elliptical expression—an
interesting sign of the decline of the subjunctive.

INDEPENDENT SENTENCES

399. The indicative continues to be used for objective
statement of real facts (positive and negative) and direct
questions.

The subjunctive has steadily lost ground since C.L. The
hortative or jussive subjunctive survives in the form of an
imperative of the third person (§ 329). The optative subjunctive was used in O.F. as in Latin, the present denoting
a realizable wish (IV, 48–50), the imperfect and pluperfect
an unrealizable wish; but since the seventeenth century it is
essentially a literary form; *que* has become compulsory in the
third person, except in certain fixed locutions (*Vive le roi!*)
and in optative phrases introduced by *pouvoir* (*Puisse-t-il
réussir*) or of the type *Plût à Dieu qu'il en fût ainsi!* In the
first and second persons the optative subjunctive has become
restricted practically to the last two cases mentioned (*Puissé-je
le revoir! Fussions-nous sûrs de le revoir!*). The concessive subjunctive survives in *soit* 'so be it', *advienne que pourra*; it was
common in O.F. (*Voeillet o non, desoz cez vals s'en fuit*, Rol.
2043).

400. The Latin 'subjunctive of modesty' survives in *je ne
sache* (*Je ne sache rien de si beau*), but is normally rendered
in Mod.F. by the conditional, as is also the potential subjunctive: *Je ne dirais pas que c'est plus beau*; *Je ne saurais répondre
à cette question*; *On aurait cru qu'il faisait jour*. Historically
such uses of the conditional represent a development of the
conditional sentence, the protasis being understood. For the

mood of the verb in the apodosis of conditional sentences, see §§ 422–6.

DEPENDENT CLAUSES
SUBSTANTIVAL

401. After verbs of declaring and believing. In O.F. the mood used in a substantival clause is determined by the attitude taken up by the speaker. If he presents the statement as certain, the indicative is used; if he wishes to imply contingency, the subjunctive. Consequently the indicative was normal after verbs of declaring, the subjunctive after verbs of believing. But as verbs of declaring and believing may be used with varying degrees of positive or negative meaning, this rule was anything but hard and fast. The resulting hesitation is still to be observed in the case of *admettre* and *supposer* (*Je suppose qu'il viendra demain*; *Supposons qu'il vienne demain*). When used negatively, interrogatively or with a condition implied, both types of verbs were regularly followed by the subjunctive. Modern usage is due partly to analogical levelling, partly to a desire to eliminate as being irregular those fluctuations which in O.F. represented real distinctions. Mod.F. therefore employs the same mood in *Je dis que cela est vrai* as in *Je pense que cela est vrai* (cf. *La plus belle des deux, je crois que ce soit l'autre*, Corn. *Menteur*, I, 4—condemned as a mistake by Voltaire), but nevertheless allows logic to prescribe the indicative to denote a certain fact after a verb of saying or thinking used interrogatively or negatively (*Vous a-t-on dit qu'il était là?*).

402. Verbs of saying and thinking which are definitely negative (*nier*, *douter*) regularly take the subjunctive. When such verbs are used negatively they are equivalent to an affirmation and regularly take the indicative in O.F., but as the form is negative (*Je ne doute pas*), the subjunctive preceded by an expletive *ne* is also used on the model of Latin NON DUBITO QUIN (*Je ne doute pas qu'il ne vienne*).

403. Verbs implying the intervention of the will (*vouloir*, *demander*, *conseiller*) regularly take the subjunctive in O.F. as in Mod.F.; but after verbs implying decision (*résoudre, décider*) the indicative (fut. or fut.-in-the-past) is used, if the emphasis is on the decision, as distinct from the attitude of the speaker (*J'ai décidé qu'il partira demain*; but *J'entends qu'il parte*).

404. Verbs of feeling hesitated in O.F. between the indicative (if the dependent clause is looked upon as expressing a fact) and the subjunctive (if the subjective element is prominent). Similarly, verbs of fearing continued to be followed by the indicative (fut. or fut.-in-the-past) as late as the seventeenth century in cases where they are virtually equivalent to a declaratory verb: *J'ay grand peur que toute ceste entreprinse sera semblable à la farce du pot au lait*, Rabelais; Sudre, p. 126.

405. After impersonal expressions denoting certainty or probability (*il est certain, il est probable*), the verb of the substantival clause, which is the logical subject, is treated in the same way as after verbs of saying and thinking. The O.F. hesitation is preserved after *il semble*, the indicative implying that the speaker regards the dependent clause as expressing a fact.

406. After other impersonal expressions (denoting necessity, possibility, etc.) the subjunctive has always been the rule, but down to the eighteenth century exceptions are common. Thus *il se peut, il est possible, il suffit* are frequently followed by the indicative in seventeenth-century authors: *Il se peut que son intention n'a pas été mauvaise* (G. de Balzac); *Est-il possible que vous serez toujours embéguiné?* (Mol.); *Ne vous suffit-il pas que je l'ai condamné?* (Rac.); cited by Haase, 81 (*a*), 79.

407. After *ce n'est pas que* the subjunctive is regularly used because the substantival clause is not presented objectively: *Ce n'est pas que de tels accidents soient rares* 'It is not as though such accidents were rare'; but after *n'est-ce pas que* the question is more or less rhetorical and the answer 'Yes' is expected: *N'est-ce pas que de tels accidents sont rares?* 'Such accidents are rare, are they not?'; *est-ce que* has come to be a mere periphrastic device for the formulation of direct questions (without inversion) and therefore takes the indicative.

408. It often happens in O.F. and in Mod.F. that a dependent clause which normally shows the indicative takes the subjunctive if it precedes the main clause, the reason being that the speaker does not commit himself as to its reality or otherwise and reserves his decision for the following main clause: *Qu'il ait mérité sa disgrâce, je le sais, j'en suis sûr*, etc.

409. Indirect questions. The subjunctive, which was the rule in indirect questions in C.L., gradually gives place to the indicative in L.L. and survives in O.F. only if it reflects the feeling or wish of the speaker, sometimes if nothing more than deliberation in his mind is implied (*'Deus!' dist li quens, 'or ne sai jo que face'*, *Rol.* 1982). In the sixteenth century the subjunctive is still fairly common in such cases, and the influence of Latin undoubtedly helped to maintain and temporarily to extend it (*Platon ne scait en quel rang il les doibve colloquer*, Rabelais; Sudre, p. 128); but since then it is no longer used in genuine indirect questions.

ADJECTIVAL

410. Relative clauses are either explanatory (non-defining) or attributive (defining). Explanatory relative clauses are in the nature of intercalations and can be omitted without destroying the general meaning of the sentence. Syntactically they are on the same footing as co-ordinated clauses and the verb is therefore regularly in the indicative.[1] Logically the relative clause may be the equivalent of a main clause (*Mon ami, que j'attends, n'est pas arrivé*) or of an adverbial clause (*Mon ami, qui m'avait promis de venir, n'est pas arrivé*). Similarly the verb of a relative clause referring to the whole of a preceding sentence is in the indicative (*Il m'avait promis de venir, ce qu'il a oublié*).

411. The normal function of an attributive relative clause is to define the antecedent in the same way as an attributive adjective would define it, in which case the indicative is used.

---

[1] In O.F. the subjunctive is occasionally used in clauses of this type in the same way as in a main clause (§ 399): *'Dieu vous en oie, sire'*, *dist Aimeris, 'Qui me croisse barnage'*; quoted by Sneyders de Vogel, § 227.

But the relative clause is often utilized to give expression
at the same time to some idea or feeling of the speaker, with
the result that the qualification it embodies is put forward
as something contingent (§ 394), in which case the subjunctive
is employed. Under the latter head are to be included those
relative clauses which are commonly described as virtually
final, consecutive or concessive (*Je cherche un moyen qui soit sûr*
and the like), but it will be observed that the purpose, result
or concession is not logically dependent upon the grammatical antecedent. *Donnez-moi un livre qui soit intéressant* does
not signify 'Give me a book so that it may be interesting', but
rather 'Give me a book, but I demand (or wish) that it shall
be interesting'. The difference between *Donnez-moi un livre
intéressant* and *Donnez-moi un livre qui soit intéressant* lies in the
introduction of the personal element implied in the subjunctive. The introduction of this personal and contingent element
may be induced by the form in which the antecedent is
presented, e.g. it may form part of a negation, a question, a
hypothesis, a command (*Je ne vois personne qui puisse nous
aider*; *Y a-t-il quelqu'un qui puisse nous aider?*; cf. XIV, 21). The
same effect is produced by an adjective in the superlative
(*C'est le meilleur moyen qu'on puisse trouver*), and occasionally
by the positive form, if the adjective implies the exercise of
the speaker's opinion or judgment (*le seul homme que j'aie vu*;
la dernière édition qui soit parue). Similarly seventeenth-century
authors employ the subjunctive after *tout* (*Anvers...surpasse
toutes les autres villes que j'aie vues*, Regn.; Haase, 75).

412. Latin made a wide use of the subjunctive in relative
clauses of the above types, but it was not compulsory. Modern
French shows a more consistent use of the subjunctive; but
in the Middle Ages it was not completely normalized, and
the subjunctive preserved to a fuller extent its real significance.
Thus it is sometimes used in O.F. with a definite antecedent.
In the following example quoted by Sudre (p. 128): *Quatre
homes i tramist armez Qui lui alassent decoler* (Saint Léger, 37)
the idea of purpose embraces the whole of the sentence, but
this idea is rendered merely by employing the subjunctive

in the relative clause. On the other hand the indicative was sometimes used where Mod.F. requires the subjunctive, and examples are found as late as the seventeenth century: *Je vous souhaiterais une femme de chambre qui ne sait pas bien peigner* (La Rochefoucauld; Haase, 75). Here the optional use of the indicative has enabled the writer to eliminate the personal or contingent element and to make the clause strictly equivalent to an attributive adjective.

413. After the superlative there has always been hesitation. O.F. prefers the indicative (*Cons fut de Rome, des melz ki dunc i erent*, Alexis, 17; *Et leur mist couronnes d'or les milleurs que il avoit*, Asenath, p. 11). If the superlative idea is prominent, the subjunctive is used; if it is secondary, the indicative. This rather subtle distinction is not always observed, and the consequent hesitation has been officially ended in modern literary usage in favour of the subjunctive; but popular speech prefers the indicative, and it is often used by modern authors. Seventeenth-century writers show a marked predilection for the conditional (*la plus grande marque que je vous saurais jamais rendre*, Voiture, and further examples in Haase, 75, 3).

ADVERBIAL

414. Here, too, the subjunctive is revealed as the subjective, contingent or prospective mood. Consequently it has always been used in final clauses, while the indicative is reserved for local clauses. In other adverbial clauses the choice of mood depends upon the degree to which the subjective element is present and stressed.

TEMPORAL CLAUSES

415. The indicative has been the rule from the beginning, except when the action denoted by the verb is conceived of as being contingent or prospective, i.e. normally after *avant que* (O.F. *ainz que* and other equivalents) and *jusqu'à ce que* (O.F. *jusque, tresque*). After *jusqu'à ce que*, but not after *avant que*, Mod.F. has preserved the O.F. use of the indicative when referring to an action already accomplished and therefore

not contingent (*Il resta là, jusqu'à ce que son maître vint le trouver*).
In O.F., and as late as the sixteenth century, the future or
future-in-the-past is sometimes used to render the prospective
or contingent action where Mod.F. requires the subjunctive
(*Jusques à ce qu'il aura deffait tout*, Cent Nouv.; Sudre, p. 131).

CAUSAL CLAUSES

416. The verb is regularly in the indicative in O.F., as in
Mod.F., if the cause is presented objectively. The use of the
subjunctive after *comme*, which is frequent in late Mid.F. and
is due to Latin influence (CUM + subjv.), disappears in the
seventeenth century. If the cause is presented as unreal the
subjunctive is used (*Non que je le veuille* 'it is not as though
I wished it').

CONCESSIVE CLAUSES

417. The C.L. distinction of mood disappeared together
with the concessive conjunctions, and O.F. employs the subjunctive with or without *que* (*Veuille ou non*; XVI, 93; XIII, 19).
But here, too, the insistence upon the thing conceded as a
fact induced the use of the indicative (XIII, 58), and this
distinction was defended by Malherbe. It has survived only
in the case of *tout...que* + ind. denoting an objective fact
(*tout mauvais qu'il est*), as opposed to *si...que* + subjv. to denote
a hypothetical assertion (*si mauvais qu'il soit*). Elsewhere the
subjunctive has been generalized, and no distinction is now
made between 'although it is' and 'although it may be'
(*quoiqu'il soit*). Popular speech, however, continues to use the
indicative.

418. The concession may bear upon one member of the
sentence. To meet this case French has extended the use of
que preceded by a pronoun or adverb: *qui que, quoi que, quel
que, quelque...que, tant que, où que* (*Qui que vous soyez*); cf. § 276.

419. The concessive subjunctive without a conjunction
survives in the inverted expressions *fût-il, eût-il, dût-il* and the
like, which denote a hypothetical concession (*Dût-il m'en
coûter cent fois plus, je le ferais encore*). Two concessive clauses

presented as alternatives are now introduced by *que* or *soit que* (*Qu'il soit bon, qu'il soit mauvais, je n'en veux pas*), but did not formerly require a conjunction (*Mais soit cette croyance ou fausse ou véritable*, Corneille; Sudre, p. 136).

420. The modal value which the future-in-the-past developed (§§ 438–9) has here, too, led to the partial elimination of the subjunctive, and it is used after *quand* or *quand même*: *Quand (même) ce serait vrai, il ne faudrait pas l'avouer*, or without a conjunction (the main clause being introduced by a virtually consecutive *que*): *Et je vous promettrais mille fois le contraire, Que je ne serais pas en pouvoir de le faire*, Mol. *Mis.* 454.

CONSECUTIVE CLAUSES

421. Modern French continues the O.F. distinction between the result presented as an accomplished fact or a logical consequence (indicative) and the result envisaged as contingent or prospective (subjunctive as in xv, 6, rarely the future indicative): *Il est si fatigué qu'il ne peut plus travailler; Faites en sorte qu'on ne vous voie pas; Je ferai en sorte qu'il ne l'oubliera pas*. After *si, tant*, O.F. often omitted the conjunction *que*: *L'emperedor tant li donez aveir, Franceis n'i ait ki toz ne s'en merveilt*, *Rol.* 570.

CONDITIONAL CLAUSES

Conditional clauses are usually introduced by *si*. They may be classified under the following headings:

422. A. NOTHING IMPLIED AS TO THE REALITY OF THE CONDITION. Here the indicative is the rule, as in Latin; but if there are two conditional clauses, the second often appears as contingent upon the first; accordingly its verb is generally in the subjunctive in O.F. and the repetition of *si* (or the alternative use of *que*) is not compulsory: *Se il se muevent et il me soit conté, Perdu avrez mon cuer et m'amisté*, Gaydon, 668. In Mod.F., unless *si* is repeated, *que* + subjv. is compulsory: *S'il vient et qu'il me voie*.

423. B. THE CONDITION PRESENTED AS HYPOTHETICAL OR CONTRARY TO FACT. The formal distinction which was made in

C.L. between the hypothetical or contingent condition (pres. subjv. or perf. subjv.) and the contrary-to-fact condition (impf. subjv. or ppf. subjv.) did not survive in French. The imperfect subjunctive having disappeared, the pluperfect subjunctive took over its functions and therefore had a two-fold meaning: *S'il eust, il donast* (Type I) = 'if he had he would give' and 'if he had had he would have given'. This ambiguity was overcome by the use, as early as the eleventh century, of an analytic pluperfect: *S'il eust eu, il eust doné* (Type II), the simple forms *eu(s)t* and *dona(s)t* continuing to be used as pure imperfect subjunctives, whence the types *S'il eût eu, il donnât* (Type III) and *S'il eût, il eût donné* (Type IV). As in other cases (§§ 413, 420), the conditional (future-in-the-past) tended to usurp the function of the subjunctive, and it appears in the apodosis (rarely in the protasis), whence the type *S'il eût, il donnerait* (Type V). The conditional in the apodosis brought with it the use of the imperfect indicative in the protasis: *S'il avait, il donnerait* (Type VI) and similarly *S'il avait eu, il aurait donné*. The imperfect indicative is some-times used for the compound tense in the apodosis of this type in order to give greater vividness to the action (*S'il avait résisté, il mourait* 'if he had resisted he was as good as dying'. The pluperfect (or imperfect) indicative in the protasis is sometimes combined with the pluperfect (or imperfect) subjunctive in the apodosis: *S'il avait eu, il eût donné* (Type VII) and very rarely *S'il avait, il donnât*.

424. Of the above seven types, which do not exhaust all the possible combinations, but may be taken as representa-tive, those which show the subjunctive continue to be used as late as the seventeenth century. They have disappeared from the spoken language with the subsequent elimination of the imperfect subjunctive (§ 441). In the literary language the pluperfect subjunctive alone continues to be used (in con-structions of Type II). Type VI, which is found as early as twelfth century, is the normal construction employed the in present-day French.

425. As already indicated, the conditional (future-in-the-

past) does not normally appear in the protasis of a genuine conditional sentence, but examples of its use are to be found in O.F. and in seventeenth-century writers (*S'ils auraient aime ces promesses... leur témoignage n'eût pas eu de force*, Pascal; Haase, p. 103), and it is common in popular speech and dialects. Other apparent exceptions are to be attributed to the special use of the conditional as an attenuated present (§ 439) (*Le diable m'emporte si je l'aurais deviné*, Regn.; *ib.*) or to the fact that the conditional itself depends upon a second implied condition (*Frappe, ou si tu le crois indigne de tes coups,...Ou si d'un sang trop vil ta main serait trempée...*, Racine; Tobler, *Verm. Beitr.* III, p. 60).

426. Conditional clauses embodying a wish regularly take the subjunctive. They are introduced in Latin by the conjunctions DUM, MODO, DUMMODO, in French by *pourvu que* (O.F. *por que, poruec que, por ço que, por tant que*): *J'y consens, pourvu qu'il n'y revienne pas.* Similarly, the subjunctive is regularly employed after *sans que, à moins que* (Latin NISI): *Ne dites rien sans qu'il vous le permette*; in O.F. *se* (*si*) with a following negative is sometimes used in such a case (*S'en ma mercit ne se colzt a mes piez E ne guerpisset la lei de chrestiiens, Jo li toldrai la corone del chief, Rol.* 2682), a construction which persists in the sixteenth century (*Je ne viendray pas si vostre pere n'y soit*, Palissy; S. de V. 239). The optional use of the indicative after *à condition que* results from the fact that *condition* has not entirely lost its substantival force and that the clause may therefore be treated as a *que*-clause depending on *condition* (*Je vous pardonne à condition que vous ne le ferez plus*). On the other hand, *en cas que* has become completely fused and is regularly followed by the subjunctive (*En cas que vous soyez occupé, je ne vous le demanderai pas*).

COMPARATIVE CLAUSES[1]

427. The indicative has always been the rule in comparisons of equality and in those comparisons of inequality which leave no doubt as to the reality of the second term (*Il es,*

[1] Cf. §§ 217, 455.

plus riche que je n'avais cru). If the case is envisaged as hypo-thetical, O.F. continues the Latin use of the subjunctive (II, 17).

428. The French equivalent of Latin QUAM UT is *que que*, and this is sometimes found in O.F. (*J'aimeroie mieus qu'un Escos venist d'Escoce et gouvernast le pueple dou roiaume...que que tu le gouvernasses malapertement*, Joinv. 21; S. de V. 251), but the cacophonous repetition of *que* is generally avoided. The second *que* is sometimes omitted, just as UT was sometimes dispensed with in Latin (II, 17; VII *b*, 19; *Miex amasse estre d'un pié manc, Que tu eüsses marremens*, Renart, II, 325), or *non pas, non point, pas*, or *point* are intercalated (*Il arrive bien plus souvent qu'on admire trop que non pas qu'on admire trop peu*, Des-cartes; Haase, 103 *a*). Both of these constructions are com-mon in the seventeenth century, and the former is still found; but Mod.F. prefers the alternative construction with the infinitive (*Il nous arrive bien plus souvent d'admirer trop que d'admirer trop peu*).

429. In comparisons of equality, *comme* regularly intro-duced the dependent clause; but *que* has gradually supplanted it, *comme* being confined to cases where there is no correlative adverb (*aussi, si*) in the main clause: *Il est bien aussi riche que vous croyez; Il n'est pas si* (or *aussi*) *riche que vous croyez; Il sera aussi patient que vous voudrez*. A clause introduced by *comme si* is virtually conditional (the apodosis being implied), and accordingly the subjunctive is often found (*A l'iglise se fist porter Cume s'il ne peust aler*, Wace, *Roman de Rou*, 604; cf. III, 48); in Mod.F. only the pluperfect (*Il était abattu, comme s'il eût essuyé un refus*).

430. For Mod.F. *plus...plus* 'the more...the more', older usage presents a number of variants which do not survive the seventeenth century: *plus...et plus, (cum) plus...(tant) plus, d'autant plus que...tant plus, tant plus...tant plus* (XI, 5; *Tant plus le vois et plus m'assotte*, Pathelin, 209).

TENSE

PRESENT INDICATIVE

431. The present indicative is used substantially as in
Latin. The so-called Historic Present was not subject to the
same restrictions in the older periods of the language as
obtain in Mod.F. (VI, 43; X, 94; XIV, 87, 102). As late as
the seventeenth century one finds examples of the intermingling of the present and past tenses in the same sentence
(cf. Haase, 65).

To denote a future action C.L. rarely employed the present,
but in V.L. it would appear to have usurped for a time the
functions of the future. In O.F. it is used of a more remote
future than would be possible in Mod.F.

PAST DEFINITE, PAST INDEFINITE, IMPERFECT

432. The Latin perfect served a double function in C.L.,
that of a preterite or past historic and that of a present
perfect. It survives in Mod.F. as the Past Definite with the
former function. The latter function is in French taken over
by a new compound perfect, the Past Indefinite (*j'ai chanté*).
The point of departure of the type *j'ai chanté* is the Latin construction HABEO + past participle (HABEO LITTERAS SCRIPTAS),
in which the past participle is still adjectival and HABERE
preserves its full meaning. But even in C.L. this construction
had already begun to develop a temporal significance. A slight
change in the point of view from which the statement is
regarded sufficed to change the force of HABEO LITTERAS
SCRIPTAS from 'I have the letter [which is] written' to 'I have
written the letter'. From denoting a state, the construction
came to denote the action which produced the state. The
meaning of HABERE was lost sight of, and it was reduced to the
rôle of an auxiliary, the participle being so closely linked
with it that the two together are the equivalent of a simple
tense, a present perfect. Such was its meaning in O.F., but
its origin was still reflected in the tendency to make the

participle agree with the direct object regardless of the position of the latter (§ 374): *Li emperere s'est culcét en un pret,...si at vestut sun blanc osberc* (IV, 91) 'and he has his white halberk on'. Yet even in O.F. it began to develop a purely preterite meaning, as can be seen from the first verb in the example just quoted. The new perfect (Past Indefinite) was thereby brought into line with the Past Definite, which had inherited the preterite meaning of the Latin perfect. But the use of the Past Definite had in the meantime been extended to cover some of the functions which are the natural domain of the Imperfect, and it therefore occupied an ambiguous position between two tenses that had the advantage of presenting none of the formal anomalies of the Past Definite.

433. The result of these developments has been the progressive elimination of the Past Definite (*je chantai*). In the spoken language its preterite functions have been completely taken over by the Past Indefinite (*j'ai chanté*) and its descriptive functions by the Imperfect (*je chantais*). The Past Definite survives in the speech of certain outlying provinces only. In the written language the Past Definite continues to lose ground and tends more and more to be used only in the third person, the Past Indefinite taking its place in the first and second persons. The Past Indefinite is used whenever the past action is closely connected with the present state: *Il a habité Paris pendant deux ans*; the action is completed, but the connection with the present state lies in the implication that the action is recent and that the person in question does not live in Paris now. On the other hand *Il habita Paris pendant deux ans* contains no such implication and there is no connection whatever with the present state. Therefore the sentence 'He went there twice this week' would be rendered by *Il y est allé deux fois cette semaine* and not by *Il y alla deux fois cette semaine*.

434. The Past Definite has thus lost more than all the ground it had usurped in O.F. at the expense of the Imperfect. Modern French writers tend more and more to use the Imperfect, where one might, according to the formal rules of grammar, expect the Past Definite; in their hands the Imperfect often becomes an artistic device for presenting a past action more graphically, as something actually going on before the mind's eye. This development is part of a wider change in outlook: the modern tendency to envisage the past as a scene or a picture, whereas to the medieval mind it appeared above all as action. We may say that, broadly speaking, Mod.F. prefers the static tense (Imperfect), while O.F. preferred the dynamic (Past Definite). Modern French employs the Past Definite only to denote an action or series of actions presented as having happened at a given time in the past, the Imperfect to describe an action or series of actions in progress at a given time in the past. Old French differs from Mod.F. above all in its tendency to present in the former way what Mod.F. normally presents in the latter.

435. The redistribution of the functions of the three tenses under consideration is in its broad outlines completed by the end of the sixteenth century. Since then grammarians have defined them with greater precision, but the spoken language carries on the analogical levelling out and generalization of analytic constructions. The written language, partly impelled by the desire to achieve greater expressiveness, partly under the influence of popular speech, shows at the present day a growing restiveness under the yoke of formal rules.

PLUPERFECT INDICATIVE

436. The Latin pluperfect falls a victim to a progressive obliteration of its original meaning to that of a mere perfect. This process had begun in Latin and is completed by the time we reach the earliest O.F. texts, where the pluperfect is occasionally used, and always as a past historic tense (cf. II, notes). New compound forms take its place: HABEBAM CANTATUM (*j'avais chanté*) and HABUI CANTATUM (*j'eus chanté*) corresponding to the Imperfect and Past Definite respectively. As in the case of the simple tenses, O.F. differs from Mod.F. by its tendency to employ the form *j'eus chanté* (Passé Antérieur); this is now confined to the literary language, and is

compulsory in the temporal clause if the principal verb is in the Past Definite (*Quand il eut fini son travail, il partit*). In the spoken language it has been displaced by the so-called Parfait Surcomposé (*j'ai eu chanté*), which first appears in Mid.F. and becomes general in the sixteenth century; since then it has gradually forced its way into the written language, but it is always associated with a familiar style. The pluperfec subjunctive *j'eusse chanté* is similarly rendered by *j'aie eu chanté*.

FUTURE AND FUTURE PERFECT

437. As has been pointed out, the Latin future gave place in V.L. to a new periphrastic form consisting of the inf. + pres. ind. of HABERE. Similarly, a new compound was formed to fulfil the function of the future perfect (*j'aurai chanté*). An analogous periphrasis consisting of pres. ind. of *aller* + inf is frequently employed to denote a near future (*Je vais partir demain*). The future describes an action as future in relation to the present; but its temporal meaning may be partly obliterated, and it may therefore be used to postulate an action as a concession (*Il dira tout ce qu'il voudra, personne ne le croira*), or as a supposition (*Pourquoi ne vient-il pas? Il sera malade*). The future perfect may be similarly employed (*Il se promène devant sa porte: il aura oublié sa clef*). The future may also be used to express a peremptory command (*Tu rentreras avant sept heures!*).

FUTURE-IN-THE-PAST AND FUTURE-PERFECT-IN-THE-PAST

438. These forms are parallel to the Future and the Future Perfect and describe, respectively, an action which is future in relation to the past (*je chanterais*), and an action anterior to another action which is future in relation to the past (*j'aurais chanté*). In the same way as the temporal meaning of the future may be obliterated (§ 437), so the future-in-the-past may be employed to describe an action as contingent or hypothetical, and it is to this modal use that it owes its

alternative name, the Conditional (*Je le ferais, si je pouvais*). The modal use dates from V.L., when the infinitive and HABERE had not yet completely fused, when HABERE maintained much of its original force and was practically equivalent to DEBERE (cf. Engl. 'I have to admit'). The obliteration of the temporal meaning, and the consequent use of the form *chanterais* (CANTARE + HABEBAM) to denote an action as contingent or hypothetical in relation to the present or future, is analogous to the temporal shifting already noted in connection with the Latin pluperfect subjunctive (§§ 279, 423).

439. The condition upon which the action denoted by the future-in-the-past is contingent may be expressed by a *si*-clause or its equivalent (§§ 422–6), or it may be merely implied (*Vous me demandez mon avis; eh bien! je ferais comme vous*). Similarly, the conditional may serve merely to indicate that the action is uncertain, or that the statement is not advanced on the speaker's responsibility (*D'après les journaux le ministre aurait exprimé sa satisfaction*), or qualified by some reservation in the mind of the speaker or a desire to tone it down (*Je ne dirais pas que vous ayez raison*); cf. *je pourrais* 'I might', *je devrais* 'I should', *je voudrais* 'I should like to', and the common use of the conditional of *savoir* (*Je ne saurais vous remercier assez* 'I don't know how to thank you enough'; *Il ne saurait être question de rendre cet argent* 'One could not think of returning the money'). Cf. also §§ 397, 400, 404, 413, 420.

TENSES OF THE SUBJUNCTIVE

440. To replace the Latin perfect subjunctive a new compound form was created (*j'aie chanté*), which is found in the earliest O.F. texts. The pluperfect subjunctive supplanted the imperfect. For a time it preserved its original function as well (§ 423), but this has been taken over by a new compound form (*j'eusse chanté*). For the use of these tenses and of the present subjunctive in the main clause and in conditional sentences, see §§ 399–400, 421–6. After verbs followed by *que* + subjv., the rule governing the sequence of tenses is: the pres. subjv. and perf. subjv. (*j'aie chanté*) are used in the

dependent clause if the principal verb is in the present, future, or past indefinite; the imperf. subjv. (*je chantasse*) and the ppf. subjv. (*j'eusse chanté*) are used in the dependent clause if the principal verb is in the imperfect, the past definite, the conditional, or the pluperfect.

441. The elimination of the past definite (§§ 433–4) brought with it the elimination of the impf. subjv. and ppf. subjv., and they are no longer used in the spoken language: the former is replaced by the present, the latter by the perfect (*j'aie chanté*) or the new compound form *j'aie eu chanté* (cf. § 436). Even in the literary language the impf. and ppf. subjv. are fast falling into disuse. Various factors contribute to this decline: the endings of the 1st and 2nd pl. stand apart as the only disyllabic endings; *-assions*, *-assiez* are felt to be cacophonous (*chassassions*, *arrachassions*, etc.); *-issions*, *-issiez* do not permit distinction between the impf. ind., impf. and pres subjv. of inchoative verbs (*finissions*, *finissiez*). The result is that the 1st and 2nd pl. of the impf. subjv. are generally avoided, and in the case of *-er* verbs the only form regularly employed is the 3rd sing. (*chantât*).

D. *ADVERBS*

442. In spite of extensive losses, a large number of Latin adverbs have persisted in French: *ailleurs* (? < ALIORSUM), *en* (< INDE), *hier* (< HERI), *là* (< ILLAC), *où* (< UBI), *quand* (< QUANDO), *tant* (< TANTUM), *tard* (< TARDE), *très* (< TRANS), *y* (< IBI). Others were still in use in the O.F. period: *es* or *ais* or *eis* (< ECCE), *hui* (< HODIE) preserved in *aujourd'hui*, *ja* (< JAM) preserved in *déjà* and *jadis*, *jus* (< DEORSUM under the influence of SU(R)SUM > *sus*), *main* (< MANE) preserved in *demain*, *mais* (< MAGIS) (XI, 16) preserved in *jamais*, *moult* (< MULTUM), *ont* (< UNDE) preserved in *dont* (XI, 15), *par* (< PER) 'very', *pruef* (< PROPE), *riere* (< RETRO) preserved in *arrière* and *derrière*, *sez* (< SATIS) preserved in *assez*, *si* (< SIC) preserved in *ainsi* and *aussi*.

443. The final *s*, which is etymological in many adverbs, came to be regarded as a distinctive adverbial ending and was extended by analogy to others: *jadis* (JAM DIU), *loin*, O.F. *loinz* (LONGE), *tandis* (TAM DIU), *volontiers* (VOLUNTARIE). In O.F. both forms often existed side by side: *onques* and *onque* (< UNQUAM), *nonques* and *nonque* (< NUNQUAM), *or(e)s* (whence *lors*, *alors*) and *or(e)* (< AD HORAM), *rien* and *riens* (XII, 114).

444. To replace adverbs which did not survive, and to meet new needs, a variety of new creations were resorted to. A common device consists in the adverbial use of adjectives: *peu* (< PAUCUM), *voir(e)* (< VERA); *chanter faux, parler haut*, etc. Borrowing is rare: *guère* (Germ. weigaro), O.F. *trop* 'very', 'rather' (Germ. *þorp* 'conglomeration'; cf. Engl. 'thorpe').

445. Composition has remained one of the most fruitful sources. The fusion is complete in the earlier formations (see above): *assez* (< AD SATIS), *dans* (*de + ens* or *enz* < INTUS), *dont* (< DE UNDE), *ensemble* (< IN SIMUL), *ici* (< ECCE HIC), *oui*, O.F. *oïl* (< HOC ILLE), *cependant, dedans, désormais, dessus, dessous, maintenant.* Later compound forms do not necessarily fuse: *de près, au-dessous, nulle part, sur-le-champ, sans doute, peut-être*, and are often more accurately described as adverbial phrases: *tête-à-tête, vis-à-vis.*

446. Most numerous are new formations in *-ment*, which persists as a productive suffix, and as such is sometimes added to substantives (*bêtement, diablement*), or even to an adverb (*mesmement*, XIII, 13; *comment*, der. of *comme*). Originally it was a substantive (abl. sing. of MENS) which formed a compound with the preceding feminine adjective in the same case: BONA MENTE 'in a good manner', cf. English formations in *-wise* (*likewise*, etc.). Adjectives which did not originally possess a feminine form in *-e* (§§ 187, 189) show assimilation of the final consonant to the following *m*: *for(t)ment, grie(f)ment, grammment, loyaument*. With the development of an analogical feminine (*forte*, etc.), such forms began to be re-modelled; they had by the end of the sixteenth century disappeared, with the exception of adverbs formed from adjectives in *-ant* and

-ent, whether originally uni-form (*élégamment, constamment, prudemment, savamment*) or bi-form (*violemment* for *violentement* < VIOLENTA MENTE); but *lentement* (< LENTA MENTE) has resisted the levelling tendency; *présentement* and *véhémentement* are analogical creations; *gentiment* for *gentilment* is perhaps due to the analogy of *joliment* (see below).

447. Adjectives which possessed a distinctive form for the feminine regularly gave adverbs in *-ement*. The feminine *e* early became mute after a vowel (*joli(e)ment, hardi(e)ment, vrai(e)ment*), its loss being often indicated by a circumflex accent (*dûment, crûment*; cf. § 367); there is still hesitation in spelling between *gaiement* and *gaîment, nuement* and *nûment*. In this way *-eement* (*aiséement, séparéement*) regularly gave *-ément* in Mod.F., whence by analogy new forms in *-ément* for etymological *-ement* (*confusément, profondément, obscurément*). Apart from such re-modellings, *e* persists if a consonant precedes: *bonnement, faussement, heureusement, nouvellement*; *brièvement* shows the old form of the adjective *br(i)ef, br(i)ève*; for *traîtreusement* beside *traître*, see § 204.

448. Adverbs form their comparative in the same way as adjectives (§ 214). The following synthetic forms have survived: *mieux* (< MĔLIUS), *moins* (< MĬNUS), *pis* (< PĒJUS) beside *plus mal, plus* (< PLŪS).

For the place of the adverb in the sentence, see § 488.

NEGATION

449. French inherited from Latin the negative NON and the compound forms NEC (NEQUE) > *ne*, Mod.F. *ni*; NUNQUAM (NE + UNQUAM) > O.F. *nonque(s)* (II, 13). In French, *non* appears in two forms, accented *non* and unaccented *ne*. The alternative unaccented form *nen*, which is sometimes used in O.F., but only before a vowel (III, 38; V, 42), has not survived, except in *nenni* (NON ILLE); cf. *oui*, O.F. *oïl* (< HOC ILLE).

450. The accented form *non* was employed in O.F. before finite parts of the verb (particularly of *être, avoir, faire*), and in Mid.F. was very common before the infinitive and present participle (whence *nonchalant*, and Learned *nonobstant*). In reply to a question the use of *non* is elliptical: *Le ferez-vous demain? Non (ferai)*; cf. XII, 69, 73. It is also used to negative one of the elements of a sentence: *Il parle de son frère et non de vous; Il l'a entrepris non sans succès*. Other survivals of the former wide use of *non* are *sinon, non que, non plus, non pas*; it also figures as a prefix in *non-sens, non-conformité*, and the like.

451. Originally *ne* was used without an accompanying particle (*pas, point*, etc.),[1] but very early it began to be strengthened by the addition of a substantive or an adverb: *pas* (< PASSUM), *point* (< PUNCTUM), *mie* (< MICA), *goutte* (< GUTTA), *guère* (Germ. w e i g a r o), *rien* (< REM), *mais* (< MAGIS), *jamais* (*ja* + *mais*), *plus* (< PLUS), *aucun, mot, personne*. The particles *goutte* and *mie* were formerly used much more extensively, but were already losing ground in the seventeenth century; *goutte* survives, but is considered familiar and is practically confined to *je n'y vois goutte*. By the fifteenth century *pas* and *point* had become recognized as the normal negative particles. In O.F. many other words were similarly employed: *âme, bouton, chose, denier, grain, neient*, etc.; cf. the Mod.F. *On ne voit âme qui vive* = *On ne voit personne*.

452. The constant use of these words as negative particles resulted in a weakening of their meaning and in their extension (e.g. PASSUM 'a pace' with verbs other than verbs of motion), and gradually they came to be invested with a negative meaning;[2] *ne*, being a mere proclitic and incapable of bearing a stress, is correspondingly weakened and tends to be omitted as unessential. In popular speech its omission has become almost the rule. In the literary language it is omitted only in replies to questions (*L'avez-vous vu? Pas encore* or *Jamais*), in exclamatory or elliptical phrases (*Pas de bruit! Point d'affaires*), sometimes in questions (*Vient-il pas?*); but its omission was formerly common in conditional sentences and indirect questions (xv *b*, 4).

453. The constant use of *ne* before the verb, even if it is another word in the sentence that is negatived, caused it to

---

[1] Cf. Montaigne's addition of *point* in Extr. XVI, 6.
[2] Similarly *aucunement*, still positive in XVI, 3.

be used pleonastically with *nul* and *ni* (O.F. *ne* < NEC). Accordingly *nul* is reduced to the same rôle as *personne, aucun*, and in O.F. is sometimes used with positive meaning (XVI, 21). Similarly O.F. *neïs, nes* or *nis* (< NEC IPSE) often means 'even'. In O.F., *ni* generally appears in the weakened form *ne* (II, 7–8; IV, 58; XII, 23), which is still occasionally used in the seventeenth century (*ne plus ne moins*). It was formerly used much more extensively, but seldom with full negative force unless accompanied by *ne* (< NON); cf. XI, 15, 86. In fact, whereas NEC = ET NON, *ni* became almost the equivalent of *et* or *ou* and was often used in O.F. where Mod.F. employs *et* or *ou*: *Plus est isnels qued esperviers n'aronde* (*Rol.* 1535); *N'i remandrat ja porte ne postiz en estant,... tant seit forz ne pesanz* (*Voyage de Ch.* 475); *Elle écouta son arrêt sans frayeur ni sans faiblesse* (Mme de Sévigné; Haase, 140).

454. In spite of the generalization of the negative complementary particle, Mod.F. still makes a fairly extensive use of the simple *ne*: (*a*) in fixed locutions (*À Dieu ne plaise*; *N'importe*; *Il n'est pire eau que l'eau qui dort*) or verbal constructions of the type *n'avoir garde, n'avoir cure*; (*b*) optionally with *cesser* + inf. (*Il ne cesse de parler*), with *oser, savoir, pouvoir*; (*c*) with restrictive *que* (*Il n'a que deux livres*), which is originally comparative 'not more than two books', whence 'only two books' (cf. XVI, 1), the negative 'not only' being rendered by the insertion of *pas* (*Il n'a pas que deux livres*); (*d*) after exclamatory *qui* or *que* (*Que n'est-il venu!*; *Qui ne voit la raison de tout cela!*); (*e*) often in subordinate clauses introduced by conditional *si*, final *que*, or depending upon a negative, or expressing a condition by inversion (*Je n'ai pas d'amis qui ne soient les vôtres*; *N'eût été la guerre* 'had it not been for the war').

455. In a different category are the many uses of so-called expletive *ne*, introduced because of the negative idea which is implied and obtrudes upon the attention of the speaker. Expletive *ne* is the result of semantic contamination and is, from the syntactic point of view, pleonastic or illogical. In comparative clauses of inequality, such as *Il est plus riche que vous ne croyez*, the presence of *ne* is due to the negative idea 'you do not realize how rich he is'; cf. also the older use of *non pas* in such phrases (§ 428); popular speech tends to omit this *ne*, and its use has been made optional by the Decree of 1901. After verbs of fearing the presence of *ne* is due to the wish that what is feared may not happen (*Je crains que vous ne soyez dérangé*); there has always been much hesitation in the use of this *ne*, and while grammarians demand its use, popular speech generally dispenses with it; the Decree of 1901 made it optional. Similar hesitation obtains after *empêcher*, *éviter*, formerly also *défendre*, after verbs of negation or doubt used negatively (*Je ne doute pas que vous n'ayez fait votre possible*), and after *il s'en faut, avant que, à moins que*.

The place of the negative complementary particle

456. Normally the particle follows the verb. In the compound tenses it comes between the auxiliary and the past participle (except *personne* and *aucun*), but this order was not yet fixed in the seventeenth century. Both *ne* and the particle (except *personne* and *aucun*) precede the infinitive (*ne pas le faire*), but in the seventeenth century this was not yet the rule: if a personal pronoun preceded, the word-order *ne le faire pas* (cf. also XVI, 85), and still more commonly *ne le pas faire*, was observed; generally, the particle could come after the infinitive more freely than in Mod.F. The particle was frequently placed at the beginning of the sentence in medieval usage, particularly if the subject is unexpressed (XIV, 63; cf. the Mod.F. survival *Pas n'est besoin*); *jamais* can still precede *ne* for emphasis (*Jamais je n'ai vu un homme si bête*). *Personne, rien, pas un*, etc., can, as indefinite pronouns, stand as subjects of the verb and precede *ne*: *Personne* (or *Pas un*) *n'est arrivé*.

E. *PREPOSITIONS*

457. The important rôle played by prepositions in Mod.F., as compared with C.L., is largely the result of the general analytical trend of the language. Syntactic relations which are now rendered by means of prepositions were in Latin rendered by means of case-endings. But even in Latin prepositions were often employed to make the syntactic relations more explicit. With the reduction of the Latin cases to two, subject case and oblique case, prepositions became a practical necessity (cf. § 173). The function of the genitive is generally served by *de* + oblique case, that of the dative by *à* + oblique case; most of the functions of the ablative are taken over by *de*, but some are shared with other prepositions: *par, avec* to denote the instrument; *à, en, avec,* manner; *à, dans,* place. The frequent use of *de* and *à* as the equivalent of case flexions and their consequent loss of explicitness have caused them to give way often to new and more explicit formations (*à cause de, au moyen de, de la part de*). The tendency to replace the simple prepositions by a compound form or prepositional phrase persists from Latin down to the present day (see below). In addition to the extension in meaning and function of existing prepositions and the formation of new ones by composition, the commonest form of creation (which French inherited from Latin) consists in the prepositional use of adverbs, adjectives, substantives, and participles.

458. Of the Latin prepositions some have persisted in French with very little change of meaning or function (SINE > *sans*), others show restriction (ULTRA > *outre*, SUPER or SUPRA > *sur*) or extension of meaning (AD > *à*, DE > *de*). A preposition may fall into disuse because its functions are fulfilled by another which is more frequently used (*joste, estre*), more expressive (*entre*), or less exposed to homonymic confusion (*od, en*). A certain number of Latin prepositions did not persist in French (CORAM, PROPTER, etc.), others did not survive the Middle Ages: *estre* (< EXTRA), *joste* (< JUXTA) and its compound *dejoste* were rare even in O.F.; *od* or *o* (< APUD) (IV, 3, 9) 'with', 'near', 'at', survives in modern patois, but disappeared from literary usage towards the end of the fifteenth century, being replaced by *à, avec, chez*; *très* (< TRANS) 'beyond', 'behind', has survived only as an adverb, while *detrès* has completely disappeared; ANTE survives only in compounds

(*avant* < AB ANTE) and in the O.F. derivative *ainz, einz, ains*
(< *ANTIUS), an adverb which came to be used as a preposition and as a conjunction, but has since been replaced by
avant, devant; POST is similarly represented by a derivative
puis (< *POSTIUS for POSTEA), which could be used as a
preposition in O.F. (*puis cel temps*), the compound form *depuis*
being still used as either preposition or adverb; EX survives
in the compound *dès* (< DE EX).

The following have survived in Mod.F.:

459. *entre* (< INTER), less widely used than formerly, was
commonly employed in O.F. in combination with *et*: *entre...et*
'both...and', and was often used in the seventeenth century
where Mod.F. requires *d'entre* (*lequel entre vous*). It has given
ground before *parmi*.

selon probably resulted from the contamination of *se-on*
(< SECUNDUM) + *lonc* (< LONGUM); both *son* and *lonc* were used
in O.F. with the meaning 'along', 'alongside of'.

outre (< ULTRA) 'beyond' is no longer used in a locative
sense, except in set expressions (*outre mer, outre mesure*).

sur for O.F. *sour(e)* (< SUPER or SUPRA) shows the con-
taminating influence of *sus* (< SURSUM). The meaning 'above'
has been taken over almost completely by *au-dessus de*. O.F.
also possessed a compound form *desur* (x, 69).

460. *à* (< AD) inherited most of the functions of Latin AD
and of the dative case. It further inherited some of the
functions of AB, with which AD had been confused in V.L.
Its use was further extended by analogy until it came to
denote a whole range of notions (attribute: *un verre à pied*;
manner or measure: *à la française, à cinq pour cent*; purpose:
la boîte aux lettres), some of which are very remote from the
original notion expressed by AD, viz. tendency, direction,
goal, objective. It has encroached upon the domain of other
prepositions, such as *od* (< APUD). On the other hand it has,
since the Middle Ages, given ground somewhat before other
more expressive and more explicit prepositions: *avec* to denote
means, instrument; *dans, en, sur* to indicate direction or
place; and it has been suppressed in certain expressions of

time: *cette fois, ce soir,* and the like. It is still used in popular speech to denote possession (*le livre à Jean*), but this use is found in literary usage only in predicative expressions, such as *Ce livre est à Jean,* or with personal pronouns to strengthen a possessive (*son livre à lui*). Before names of towns O.F. preferred *en* to *à* (*en Costentinoble*). For the use of *à* before an infinitive, see §§ 297–8.

461. *de* (< DE) originally denoted the point of departure of a movement and allied notions (origin, cause, manner); but before the end of the V.L. period its extension at the expense of AB and EX, and its use for the genitive (and to a large extent for the ablative), had made it the commonest preposition. Further, the extension of *de* as a partitive genitive led to the creation of the partitive article (§§ 230–5). From the use of *de* for the Latin ablative of means or instrument there developed its use to denote the agent in passive constructions (*un homme aimé de tout le monde*); in Mod.F., *de* has in this latter use lost a certain amount of ground to *par*. *De* further replaces the ablative of measure after comparative expressions (cf. § 217) and is used in this sense in a variety of expressions (*plus grand de la moitié; haut de six pieds*). It continues to be used with the meaning 'concerning' (cf. XII, 86), and has been much extended, particularly after verbs; the many cases in which *de* is used in O.F. (and sometimes in Mod.F.) before substantives and pronouns without any specific meaning may be explained as a weakening of this function (*De sa mort est granz damages* 'Alas for his death!'; XIV, 12; XVI, 90; *Ce que c'est que de nous!*); in O.F. it was often used in exclamatory phrases (*Filz Alexis! de ta dolente medre!* Alexis, 396). For the prodigious extension of *de* before the infinitive, see §§ 296, 298.

462. *par* (< PER). We have already noted the growing use of *par* to denote the agent in passive constructions. The allied meanings of cause and manner (*Il a péché par ignorance; Il m'a sommé par lettre*) are now less frequently rendered by *par* than in the seventeenth century. In the locative sense 'through', 'across', 'throughout', *par* has gradually lost ground to more

expressive compound forms (*à travers, partout dans*), but is still commonly used to indicate direction (*Par où a-t-il passé? Il a sauté par la fenêtre*). As a temporal preposition it has been practically eliminated in Mod.F. by *pendant* and *durant*, but is still used in expressions descriptive of the weather (*par la pluie; par un beau jour d'été*).

pour (< *POR for PRO under the influence of PER) has been extended to denote purpose, motive, destination, whence also cause (*C'est pour cela qu'il pleure; Je le connais pour l'avoir pratiqué*). In the latter sense it was formerly employed much more extensively (IX, 22; XIII, 27) and prefixed to the pres. inf. (XVI, 22) no less than the perfect, and in the conjunction *pour ce que* (for modern *parce que*). It was also widely used with concessive force (*Pour grands que soient les rois, ils sont ce que nous sommes*, Corn. *Le Cid*, 157). The Latin locative use has not survived.

463. *en* (< IN). This preposition, which was one of the commonest in Latin, has lost ground almost continuously in French. The Latin meaning 'upon' persisted in O.F., but survives in Mod.F. only in set expressions (*casque en tête*). The distinction between *en huit jours* and *dans huit jours* 'at the end of eight days' is modern; O.F. used *en* to express both notions. The chief reason for the progressive elimination of *en* in favour of *dans* (and in a lesser degree of other prepositions, *à, par,* etc.) lies in the fact that it combined with the definite article (*en le > eu, ou* and *en les > els > ès*). Towards the end of the Middle Ages *ou* began to be confused with *au*, and consequently also *ès* with *aux*; *en* ceased to be employed with *le, les,* and was replaced by *dans* (cf. § 139). It survives with a variety of meanings, in expressions which have become more or less fixed and show the older tendency to omit the definite article (§ 225) after prepositions: *en France, en considération de, mettre en morceaux, en français, se mettre en colère, fertile en suggestions,* and the like. The use of *en* in the sense of 'in the manner of', 'in the capacity of', dates from Late Latin and has been much extended in Mod.F., often replacing the older use of a predicative substantive: *Il parle en artiste; Je vous conseille en ami.*

464. New prepositions created by the utilization of adverbs: *sous* (< SUBTUS), whence the compound *dessous* (XII, 80); *enz* (< INTUS); of adjectives: *sauf* (< SALVUM), originally inflected; *long* (< LONGUM) 'beside', 'alongside of', replaced by *le long de, près de, à côté de*; *tout* (< * TŌTTUM) and *atout* (XI, 50) 'with'; of participles: *pendant, vu, excepté*, some of which were already used prepositionally in Latin; *vers* (< VERSUM, p.p. of VERTERE), whence *devers, envers*; *près* (< PRESSUM), *après* (< AD PRESSUM); more rarely of substantives: *chez*, O.F. *chies(e)* (< CASA); O.F. *lez* (< LATUS), surviving in *Plessis-les-Tours* and the like; *fors* (< FORIS used adverbially in Latin), which, together with *defors*, survives in Eastern dialects. *Hors* is derived from *dehors*, which represents an irregular development of L.L. DEFORIS, presumably by the loss of *f* and the introduction of a hiatus-*h*.

465. As has already been indicated, many new prepositions were created by composition. The fusion is sometimes complete: AB ANTE > *avant* (*devant, de devant*), DE INTUS > *denz* > *dans* (*dedans*), DE USQUE > *jusque* (*jusqu'à*), DE RETRO > *derrière*, MALUM GRATUM > *malgré*, AB HOC > *avuec* > *avec*; later formations: *encontre* (now only found in *à l'encontre de*), *parmi, envers, depuis*; O.F. *devers* (X, 55), *emprés, endroit* (X, 77), *ensemble, enmi, amont, contremont* (X, 75), *contreval, entour, environ*. Many prepositional phrases were created later and do not show fusion: *en dehors de, vis-à-vis de, hors de, en face de, par rapport à, au-delà de*.

F. CONJUNCTIONS

466. Of the vast number of Latin conjunctions, very few have survived in French: ET > *e*, now written *et*; AUT > *ou*; NEC > *ne*, replaced in the sixteenth century by *ni* (cf. § 453); SI > *se*, replaced by *si* (cf. § 134), usually conditional, but capable of developing causal or concessive force (*S'il est juste, il n'en est pas moins dur; S'il le demande, ce n'est pas une raison pour le lui donner*), and in popular speech often strengthened by the addition of *que*; QUANDO > *quant*, now written *quand*, originally an interrogative adverb, but used already in Latin as a temporal or causal conjunction, and continued to be so used in O.F. (III, 55; XII, 33). In Mod.F. *quand* has lost its causal function, but has on the other hand come to be used (with the conditional in both clauses) concessively, often reinforced by *même*: *Quand (même) j'en devrais mourir, je le ferais encore.*

467. The following Latin adverbs have similarly come to be used as conjunctions:

*ANTIUS (formed on ANTE) > O.F. *ainz* 'sooner', 'rather', with inversion (*ainz venist le soir*).

MAGIS > *mais* O.F. 'rather', 'but', Mod.F. 'but'.

QUARE > *car* 'wherefore', 'for', also employed in O.F. as an intensive particle to reinforce a command (*Car cheval-chiez!*) or a wish (v, 22; *Car oüsses parlé* 'Would that you might have spoken').

SIC > *si* 'so', 'and so', 'and', very common in O.F. as a co-ordinating conjunction (II, 24; III, 13).

DUM + TUNC > *donc*, originally temporal.

QUOMODO > *comme* (O.F. *come, com*), originally comparative; but under the influence of Latin CUM, it has come to be used as a temporal and causal conjunction. It was formerly extensively used as an interrogative adverb (XVI, 84) and to introduce a substantival clause, but has gradually been supplanted by *comment*, and survives as an adverb of intensity (*Comme c'est beau!*). In comparative clauses of equality it has since O.F. been displaced by *que*, except when there is no correlative in the principal clause. It has similarly given way to *que* in various combinations such as *tandis comme, sitôt comme. Comme si* and *comme* appear from the beginning as the equivalent of Latin QUASI (III, 48). *Comme* is sometimes used as a co-ordinating conjunction equivalent to *et* (cf. the similar use of *ainsi que*).

468. Later formations include the use of *soit, savoir*, and such compounds as *sinon* (O.F. *se non*, the two elements being separable), *néan(t)moins* (a rendering of NIHILOMINUS), *toute-ois* (O.F. *toutes voies, toute voie*; VI, I), *pourtant, pour cela, partanti, par quoi, cependant* (cf. older *ce non obstant*, XIII, 31); *auss*

(ALIUD SIC), originally comparative, came to be used as a copulative, and when introducing a sentence (with inverted word-order) serves as a causal conjunction (= *ainsi*). But the majority of French conjunctions are formed by the combination of an adverb, preposition or prep. + subst. with *que*.

469. The origin of *que* is a much debated question.[1] It is perhaps correct to describe it as in the main a continuation of QUOD, the use of which was much extended in V.L. at the expense of UT, and particularly in the form of QUOD-clauses replacing the Latin acc. + inf. There took place at the same time an extension and a weakening in the meaning of the conjunction, and confusion with QUIA, QUEM, QUID. The result is that in O.F. *que* appears as a universal conjunction which often serves merely as an indication that what follows is subordinate to what precedes. The precise nature of the subordination was indicated, as in popular or primitive languages generally, by the mood of the dependent verb or by such auxiliary devices as variations of pitch and stress, pauses, and gestures. The development of O.F. as a literary language brought with it a change from this largely paratactic structure to a highly developed syntactic structure, in which the relation between the principal and the dependent clause is indicated more precisely by formal devices, viz. a series of conjunctions capable of rendering a whole range of fine distinctions. The wide choice of conjunctions that is characteristic of C.L., as of literary languages in general, had thus to be re-created in French, and this was done by defining more clearly the force of *que*, which had in the meantime become confused with the relative adverb *que* (§ 266).

470. The conjunction has thus become an important syntactic device, and the rôle of other devices, particularly the subjunctive (cf. § 398), has been correspondingly reduced. The following list may serve to illustrate the wealth of new creations that French has at its disposal. It will be observed

---

[1] J. Jeanjaquet, *Recherches sur l'origine de la conjonction* que *et des formes romanes équivalentes*, Neuchâtel, 1894; R. L. Græme Ritchie, *Recherches sur la syntaxe de la conjonction* que *dans l'ancien français*, Paris, 1907.

that some conjunctions have in the course of time passed
from one category to another (*puis que*, originally temporal,
becomes causal) or serve a multiple function (*sans que*, concessive, conditional, consecutive); many have been abandoned
after a long period of use.

471. Temporal: *pendant que, lorsque, alors que, avant que,
aussi longtemps que, après que, dès que, aussitôt que*; *jusqu'à ce que*
is already common in the sixteenth century and has displaced
older *jusques, en jusques, jusques que*; *tant que* continued to be
used in the sense 'until' as late as the seventeenth century
(cf. XIV, 30); *tandis que* (O.F. also *tandis come*), originally
purely temporal (XI, 56), came to denote opposition (='whereas'),[1] but of recent years has come to be used more and more
in a purely temporal sense, to the disadvantage of *pendant que*;
puisque, originally temporal, early developed a causal meaning,
which alone persisted, while *depuis que* (for older *dès puis que*)
is temporal. A large number of conjunctions current in O.F.
have disappeared—'while': *endementiers que, entrues que, en ce
que, que que, quoi que, ainsi com, si com, où que*; 'as long as':
pour tant que, tant com; 'before': *ainz que, ançois que, premier que,
primes que. Aussitôt que* and *sitôt que* have replaced older *si tost
comme* (XII, 91), *tantost comme*, and O.F. *lues que, ainsi comme,
ainsi que, manois que*; *soudain que, incontinent que, subit que* were
still used in the sixteenth century, *d'abord que, désormais que,
dès lors que* in the seventeenth; *devant que* and *cependant que* are
now obsolete, but were still common in the seventeenth
century.

472. Causal: *vu que, attendu que, d'autant que, de ce que, en ce
que, puisque* (§ 471); *parce que*, which originally denoted means
and was rare in O.F., became confused with *pour ce que*
(XI, 18, 36, 74) and has displaced it since the seventeenth
century. O.F. possessed also *pour que, pour tant que*, which with
later formations, *à cause que, considéré que, d'autant que* (XVI, 2,
59), continued to be used in the sixteenth century.

473. Final: *pour que, afin que, à cette fin que*; O.F. possessed
pour ce que, à ce que, à la fin que, à celle fin que (which by popular

[1] *là où*, originally locative, came to be used similarly (cf. XVI, 35).

confusion became in the sixteenth century *à seule fin que*);
'lest' was rendered in O.F. by *pour peur que*, since replaced
by *de peur que* (seventeenth century also *peur que*) and *de
crainte que*.

474. Concessive: concessive clauses may be introduced
by indefinite relative pronouns (interrog. pron. or adv. + *que*:
qui que, quoi que, où que, etc.) or by *tout...que, si...que,
pour...que*; or, if the concession applies to the whole clause,
by *quoique, bien que, pour peu que, encore que, nonobstant que,
soit que*. O.F. often employed the subjunctive alone or reinforced by such words as *tant, tout, bien, encore*, whence ultimately the conjunctions *bien que*, etc. *Bien que* has eliminated
older *combien que* (common in the sixteenth century and still
used in the seventeenth century), which, like *quoique*, was
originally intensive (= 'however much'); cf. IX, 1; XIII, 58.
Malgré que, as the equivalent of *bien que*, is a popular feature
which is making its way into literature. The concessive *soit*,
reinforced by *ja* (<JAM), gave rise to a compound form
ja soit que (commonly written *jasoit que* or *jaçoit que*), which
was still used in the seventeenth century; cf. English 'be he
never so bold'.

475. Conditional: *à moins que, sans que, pourvu que, à condition que, au cas que, en cas que, pour peu que, sauf que, loin que,
outre que, au lieu que, hormis que, posé que, supposé que*; O.F.
fors (ce) que, fors tant que, pour ce que, pour que, mais que (VI, 118),
par ainsi que.

476. Consecutive: *de sorte que, en sorte que, de façon que*. The
two elements of consecutive conjunctions have fused much
less completely: *que* often retains its consecutive force while
the adverb or its equivalent serves as a correlative (*Il est si
fatigué qu'il ne peut plus marcher*; similarly *tant...que, tel...que,
assez...pour que, trop...pour que*). If the two elements become
permanently linked the meaning of the adverb or adverbial
expression is naturally weakened (*de sorte que, de façon que,
si bien que, sans que, de manière que*). Similarly, *si que* came to
be used in O.F. as the equivalent of a simple consecutive
que; *tellement que* has since the seventeenth century recovered

its original intensive force (cf. xv *a*, 24). *De mode que* is a sixteenth-century creation under Italian and Spanish influence, and it did not survive the seventeenth century.

477. While the simple *que* has thus ceased to be the universal conjunction it once was, it is still extensively used, not only as an adverbial pronoun (*Il y a deux semaines qu'il est parti*; *C'est à vous que je parle*; *au moment que*; cf. § 266), but as the usual conjunction introducing a substantival clause (including elliptical *que oui, que non*), and as a final conjunction after the imperative (xiv, 56) with a tendency to become temporal (*Attendez que je sois revenu*). It is causal after a question (*Que voulez-vous que vous me tourmentez ainsi?*) or after *non, ce n'est pas, c'est* (*Il ne comprend pas; c'est qu'il est sourd*), consecutive after a negative main clause (*Il n'ouvre jamais la bouche qu'il ne dise une sottise*). We have already noticed its use in concessive clauses of the type *Je le jurerais qu'il ne le croirait pas* (§ 420). It has gradually become obligatory before an optative or jussive subjunctive in an independent sentence (§§ 329, 399). For the use of *que* (= QUAM) in comparative clauses of equality, after a comparative of inequality (except before a numeral), and for *que que*, see §§ 217, 427–30.

478. Contrary to O.F. usage, *que* is employed in Mod.F. to introduce the second of two parallel subordinate clauses. At first this served to avoid repetition of compound conjunctions embodying *que* (*Il ne veut pas partir parce qu'il n'a pas vu le commandant et qu'il lui faut des renseignements*; cf. also xvi, 5, 97), but later of *quand* and *comme*. In the case of *si* its introduction was facilitated by the fact that *que* + subjv. was an alternative method of expressing a condition (*s'il vient et que je sois parti*); cf. § 422.

479. In popular speech and in patois *que* (both as relative adverb and as conjunction) continues to be used much more extensively and often pleonastically (§ 266). The excessive use of *que* was condemned by seventeenth-century grammarians and purists, but is common in classical writers, particularly in Molière. Such passages as the following, with its repetition of *que* (rel. pron., rel. adv., conj.), have some-

times been condemned as jargon but are more correctly described as characteristic of popular or careless speech:

> Qu'est-ce que cette instance a dû vous faire entendre,
> Que l'intérêt qu'en vous on s'avise de prendre,
> Et l'ennui qu'on auroit que ce nœud qu'on résout
> Vînt partager du moins un cœur que l'on veut tout.
>
> (*Tartuffe*, 1433–6.)

480. The practice of introducing *ce* (*ço*) in the main clause as a correlative of the substantival conjunction *que* (*Quant ço veit Guenles qu'ore s'en rit Rodlanz, Rol.* 303) led to the use of *ce que* as a variant of *que* (*Et ce que je vos voi plorer Me fet grant mal et grant enui*, Chrétien, *Erec*, 2762). While this is no longer used, *de ce que* with indicative is often employed after verbs of feeling as an alternative to *que* + subjv. (*Je m'étonne de ce que vous êtes venu* beside *Je m'étonne que vous soyez venu*) and after verbs constructed with *de* (*Je vous remercie de ce que vous êtes venu*), and in popular speech is widely used as an equivalent of *que*; cf. the examples from seventeenth-century writers quoted by Brunot, IV, 1080.

481. By a similar development *à ce que* is not only used after verbs constructed with *à* (*consentir, s'exposer, s'attendre*; but cf. XVI, 92), but in popular speech tends to supplant *que* after such verbs as *demander, chercher*. This is a modern use, and, although it tends to suggest the idea of purpose, it is distinct from the sixteenth-century use of final *à ce que*.

482. The omission of *que*, which is common in O.F., as is to be expected of a language still largely paratactic (*Respont Rodlanz:...'Ço set hom bien n'ai cure de manace'*, *Rol.* 293), is no longer tolerated.

G. *WORD-ORDER*

483. The comparative fixity of Modern French word-order offers a marked contrast with the flexibility of Latin. The former is an analytic language, the latter synthetic; that is to say, the process of analysis by which a concept is translated into terms of speech (cf. § 16) is much more com-

plete in the case of French. The relations between the elements
of a sentence are patently revealed to the hearer or reader,
partly by the use of prepositions, partly by a logical order
(Subject + Verb + Object). The development of the highly
analytical Modern French structure with its logical word-
order has sometimes been taken to reveal the rational trend
of the French mind; but it must be remembered that it
represents the culmination of a movement which had begun
in V.L. and was in part due to the decay of the Latin flexional
system. The subsequent breakdown of the O.F. two-case
system made the logical word-order in most cases a practical
necessity; the force of analogy and the logically-minded
grammarians did the rest. But as language is never entirely
logical (i.e. a purely analytical presentation of man's thoughts),
word-order always presents a certain amount of fluctuation.
Thus, at all periods of the language we must allow for variations ranging from the direct rendering of the speaker's
emotions in disjointed utterance to normal ordered discourse.
And even the latter is not the same in popular speech as in
the literary usage. The literary language is always inclined
to cling to tradition, and we find that Modern French preserves, not only archaic expressions embodying an older
word-order, but certain general 'illogical' features which
have an historical explanation. Popular speech, on the other
hand, reveals a much closer adherence to the logical word-
order.

484. Word-order has thus come to fulfil a very important
syntactic function in Modern French, and as a result it can
no longer be utilized, except in a very limited degree, to
bring into prominence certain elements of the sentence.
Nevertheless, while logic can be said to determine the word-
order of Modern French, the possibility of securing stylistic
effects has not been lost, and modifications of the logical word-
order are often induced by the characteristic rhythm of
Modern French (cf. §§ 145–50). The order Subject + Verb
+ Object is not often affected (cf. § 486), but the place of
adverbial adjuncts, the order as between direct object and

indirect object, the place of the attributive adjective, are generally determined by considerations of rhythm; the latter may become imperative, and therefore in effect syntactic rules (e.g. the place of pronoun objects; cf. § 249). Where neither logic nor rhythm determines word-order, the freedom which the language enjoys has sometimes been utilized to make semantic distinctions (e.g. in the position of the attributive adjective; cf. § 218). Quite apart from the latitude which poets, particularly of the Classical School, allow themselves, one may therefore speak of permissive as against obligatory modifications of the logical word-order. The artistic use of the former characterizes the stylist; the observance of the latter is imposed partly by inherited tradition, partly by French speech rhythm. It is impossible to vary the order of a simple phrase like *Je le dis* with a view to emphasizing any one of its three elements, nor is it possible to violate normal speech rhythm by bringing a strong stress to bear upon *je* or *le*. One cannot render '*I* say it' by stressing *Je*; one must say *Moi, je le dis* or *C'est moi qui le dis*. Similarly, one may give prominence to the direct object in *J'ai vu cet homme* by placing *cet homme* first, but only on condition that it is set apart and a complete sentence *je l'ai vu* formed independently of it (*Cet homme, je l'ai vu*).

485. The fundamental change in word-order from Latin to Modern French therefore consists in its rise as a syntactic device and its decline as a stylistic device. Old French occupies a position midway between Latin and Modern French; to judge from literary works alone, the comparative flexibility of Old French is striking, but in spite of the many liberties which the two-case system permitted, the logical order Subject + Verb + Object was already normal, and in popular speech perhaps general.

486. Modern French literary usage preserves the following relics of former liberties:

(*a*) If the subject is a substantive and the verb is intransitive, inversion may be employed to give greater prominence to the verb: *Restent les motifs de cette démarche*.

(*b*) Inversion is now obligatory in intercalated phrases of the type *dit-il, s'écria-t-il*. This rule is not observed in popular speech.

(*c*) Inversion of verb and personal pronoun subject is the rule if the sentence begins with *à peine, peut-être, en vain, aussi* (in the sense of 'therefore', 'accordingly'), *toujours* (adversative). This is a survival of the O.F. rule requiring inversion whenever the sentence began with an adverb or an adverbial adjunct. This type of inversion was probably due to Germanic influence (cf. its survival in Modern German); it became optional in Mid.F. but is still common in the sixteenth century, since when it has ceased to be optional. If the subject is a substantive, it precedes the verb, but is repeated in the form of a pronoun after the verb: *Peut-être cet homme n'avait-il pas compris*.

(*d*) A similar survival is to be seen in the inversion of subject and verb in a subordinate clause: *Il me montra le livre que lui avait donné son ami*; *L'ambassadeur était sur le point de partir, quand arrivèrent les délégués*.

(*e*) If the direct object comes first, Mod.F. does not tolerate inversion and requires the repetition of the object in the form of a personal pronoun: *Cet homme, je l'ai vu*. In O.F., inversion was common (XI, 2, 29), survives in Mid.F. (XIII, 13), and is frequently employed by Rabelais (XIV, 115).

(*f*) Old French inversion in sentences beginning with a predicative adjective or substantive has survived in Mod.F., but since the sixteenth century the adjective rarely stands at the head of the sentence (*Tel est mon avis*), except in rhetorical style (*Grande fut ma surprise*).

(*g*) Inversion is still found in certain optative expressions (*Vive le roi!*), but was much more common in such constructions as late as the seventeenth century.

487. French relies primarily upon intonation as an interrogative device (*Notre ami vient?*), and popular speech generally dispenses with the auxiliary device of inversion. The latter developed in O.F. and was applied uniformly, whether the subject was a substantive or a pronoun. Inversion with a substantive is now possible only if the sentence begins with an interrogative expression: *Que dit ton frère? D'où vient ce bruit? À quelle heure arrive le courrier?* In other cases the substantive is placed first and repeated in the form of a pronoun after the verb: *Notre ami vient-il?* This construction is found as early as the twelfth century and becomes usual in Mid.F. From the sixteenth century onwards *est-ce que* came to be used as an alternative device to inversion (§ 407).

488. The place of the predicate, the direct object, the indirect object, the adverb, was much less fixed in O.F. than in Mod.F. The predicate could be placed at the beginning of the sentence or between the subject and the verb. The direct object could, as we have seen, precede the verb in O.F. without a following pronoun; it could also come between the subject and the verb, but this licence disappeared with the loss of case distinctions (but cf. *sans coup férir, sans mot dire*). With regard to the indirect object and adverbial adjuncts, French preserves only a fraction of its former flexibility (cf. xiv, 55, 87). In Mod.F. they usually follow. Normally the direct object precedes the indirect, but considerations of rhythm often induce a deviation from this rule: the general practice is to place the shorter object first (*J'ai demandé ce livre à mon ami*, but *J'ai demandé à mon ami la raison de cette démarche*). If the adverb precedes, it no longer brings with it inversion, except in the cases mentioned above (but cf. *Ainsi soit-il*). The place of the negative particles (*pas, point*) was formerly much less fixed: they could precede *ne* and could be more widely separated from *ne* than is now possible (cf. the survival in *Pas n'est besoin*; cf. also § 456). Similarly, *plus* in a comparative clause could formerly be separated from the adjective (*Plus est grand que vous ne croyez*), or follow (*Grand est plus que vous ne croyez*).

489. In compound tenses the auxiliary could formerly be separated from the participle, not only (as in Mod.F.) by adverbs which have become weakened in meaning or stress (*Je vous l'avais bien dit*; *Il n'est pas encore venu*), but by the direct object (*Mais ayant de vos fils les grands cœurs découverts*,

Malherbe; Sudre, p. 227; cf. also XVII, 42) or the subject (now only with pronouns: *Qu'a-t-il dit?*): *Messe e matines at li reis escoltét, Rol.* 670. The same liberty obtained in the case of modal verb + inf. (§§ 249, 300).

For the place of attributive adjectives and of pronoun objects, see §§ 218, 249. Further details will be found in §§ 145–50, 243–4, 257, 275, 372–7, 399, 456, 539.

Chapter VI

VOCABULARY

A. *GENERAL*

490. A word may be defined as an articulated sound or group of sounds recognized as a unit in virtue of the idea it conveys or the function it fulfils in speech-activity.[1] Those words which are used to modify meaning or which serve a functional purpose are dealt with in the chapter on Morphology and Syntax. They include all words whose primary function it is to indicate the relation between the members of a phrase or sentence (prepositions and conjunctions), to define the substantive to which they are attached (articles and pronominal adjectives) or to replace it (pronouns), or to serve some other morphological or syntactic purpose (auxiliary verbs, adverbs, numerals). The present chapter is therefore concerned only with substantives, adjectives, verbs, and interjections. Such a division of the field, like the customary distinction of 'parts of speech', may be criticized on theoretical grounds[2] and it is undertaken merely for convenience and clearness in exposition.

491. Confining our attention for the present to substantives, adjectives, verbs, and interjections, we find that each word is a conventional symbol corresponding to a certain idea or to alternative ideas which the speaker or writer wishes to evoke in the mind of the hearer or reader. In the economy of human speech, the latter is guided in the interpretation of the symbol by the context or by auxiliary devices such as intonation. The alternative ideas may be closely related or

---

[1] In connected speech the recognition of a word as a unit may be very hazy or may disappear, and it is far from possessing in all cases the clearly defined individuality conferred upon it by the written or printed symbol.

[2] Cf. what is said in §§ 541–2 on derivation by change of function.

very widely separated (cf. § 543 ff.). The symbol itself may represent the fusion of two forms which, although originally distinct, have by the process of phonetic evolution become homophonous (*louer* < LAUDARE and *louer* < LOCARE). From the phonetic point of view such a symbol counts as a single word, whether it appears as such in spelling (*louer*) or nto (*pain, peins, peint, pin*). We may therefore study the vocabulary of a language from the point of view of the symbols it employs and proceed to consider the meanings it attributes to them, or we may take the ideas as our point of departure and examine how the language renders them. The latter procedure has much to commend it, and M. Brunot[1] and others have shown how fruitful it can be; but the former line of approach still presents definite practical advantages which cannot be ignored. Similar considerations govern the somewhat arbitrary treatment in separate sections of the two aspects: form and meaning. Such artificial divisions are inevitable if we wish to present in analytical form what is in effect a synthesis of psychological and physical elements, in which cultural, social, and political conditions, and, to a lesser degree, individual caprice or creative activity play a part.

492. The changing conditions and varying needs which a language is called upon to meet, and the wear and tear to which as an instrument it is subject, imply a constant change in vocabulary: formation or borrowing of new words; discarding or loss of old words; extension, restriction, or shifting of the meanings and functions of existing words. But before proceeding to discuss the changes which the vocabulary of the French language has undergone, it is necessary to examine the hereditary stock which French took over from Latin. The expression 'took over' implies a break in continuity which did not exist, and while we may from the phonetic point of view consider the French language as dating from the time when the Latin spoken in Northern Gaul began to develop features differentiating it from the types of Latin spoken in the rest of the Empire, we shall for present purposes quite

[1] *La Pensée et la Langue.*

arbitrarily define the hereditary stock as consisting of those words (whether of Latin or non-Latin origin) which Vulgar Latin possessed at the time of its introduction into Gaul. Having characterized this hereditary stock, we may proceed to consider its evolution, always remembering that in the early stages this evolution is often common to the greater part of the Latin-speaking world.

493. A comparison of the vocabulary of Vulgar Latin with that of Classical Latin reveals the same relation as that which subsists between any popular speech and its literary counterpart. On the one hand, many words of a literary character remained confined to Classical Latin, and the wealth of synonyms at the disposal of Classical writers was in every-day language reduced to the bare essentials: thus AEQUOR, TERGUM, VULNUS do not appear to have been used, while ALTER, FORTIS, GRANDIS survived at the expense of ALIUS, VALIDUS, MAGNUS. On the other hand, technical terms connected with various trades and occupations (APIARIUM, BATT(U)ALIA, BIS-ACUTUM, SPATHA), vulgarisms (BASSUS, BATT(U)ERE, BOTELLUS, GABATA, GLUTO, TATA), and picturesque or metaphorical terms (CARRICARE, EXAGIUM, IMPEDICARE, SANGUISUGA, MANDUCARE, TESTA) abounded in Vulgar Latin and only occasionally found their way into literature. With the decline in culture the difference was accentuated, and it receives a special significance from the fact that Latin was largely propagated in the various parts of the Empire by the lower classes. Throughout the period of romanization of Gaul the vocabulary of Vulgar Latin continued to change. Among the factors which contributed to modify it were the spread of Christianity, the direct contact with foreign peoples, and the changed conditions of life in general. Thus the primitive stock itself had by the end of the fifth century already undergone many of the changes and adaptations which we find again in the subsequent history of the language, and we may therefore conveniently group them with later changes under their respective headings.

B. *BORROWED WORDS*

494. The borrowing of words may result from the importation of a new or exotic object, in which case the name it bears in the country of origin or in the country through which it is transmitted is generally adopted. But where borrowing is at all extensive, it results from a deficiency in the native vocabulary, coupled with a temporary cultural superiority in one or more fields on the part of the nation from whose language the deficiency is made good. The demand is created by changes in political and social conditions, in pursuits, interests and tastes, which require a new terminology. Where such changes are due to the example or influence of a foreign nation, it is natural that the supply of new words should be drawn from the same source. The result is generally an excess of borrowings, which may lead to the elimination of native words and to a temporary distortion of the vocabulary. The language will of its own accord make the necessary adjustment and discard in the long run what is superfluous; except in very favourable circumstances, the patriotic efforts of purists to stem the influx are of little moment.[1] The same may be said of borrowings which are dictated by personal caprice or mere affectation. We shall leave out of account such temporary or personal borrowings and concentrate upon words which have been retained.

LOW LATIN AND CLASSICAL LATIN

495. Vulgar Latin as a purely popular idiom possessed a vocabulary quite inadequate to meet the changed conditions resulting from the introduction of Christianity and, at a later date, from the revival of interest in literature, philosophy, and science. It was natural that from the beginning this deficiency should be made good by drawing upon the resources of written Latin (Low Latin), which continued to use a host of Classical

[1] This has been well brought out by B. H. Wind, *Les mots italiens introduits en français au XVIe siècle*, Deventer, 1928.

Latin terms unknown to the vulgar, and had even added to that store, partly by derivation and analogical creation, partly by borrowing from Greek (cf. § 502). The clerks, who alone continued to write and to speak Latin, were in a sense bilingual and inevitably transposed words from one medium to the other.

496. The earliest borrowings from written Latin are consequent upon the introduction of Christianity. Such words as *crestiien, eglise, prestre* (cf. § 500), although their form alone would indicate a later borrowing, must have been introduced along with the new religion. The use of the vulgar tongue in sermons is responsible for a further influx (*angele, apostele* or *apostolie, virgene*, etc.), but extensive borrowing first set in with the use of the vulgar tongue for literary purposes. The earliest works in the vernacular were of a religious or edifying character and composed by clerks who drew upon Latin to fill the gaps in the vocabulary of the vernacular. A distinction must, however, be drawn between mere Latinizing in spelling or vocabulary and genuine borrowing. Thus the sequence of *Eulalia* (*ca.* 880) offers a number of Latinisms (*Eulalia, anima, rex, in, Christus, post, clementia*), some of which are popular words clothed in a Latin orthography, but also shows a large number of borrowings (*menestier, domnizelle*(?), *colomb, conselliers, christiien, element, empedementz, figure, virginitét*). Similarly in the *Vie de Saint Alexis* (eleventh century) one finds a relatively high percentage of borrowings. The fact that the early literary monuments are generally based upon Latin originals would account in part for such borrowings, but the chief reason is the purely practical one of a deficiency in the popular vocabulary. Translations, such as the Oxford Psalter and the Cambridge Psalter, naturally show a much higher percentage. Not only in such works of edification, but in lapidaries and other early secular writings, the borrowed element is of ecclesiastical origin or was introduced by clerks, the sole persons possessed of culture and a knowledge of Latin. Twelfth-century French already possessed the juridical and political terms *cense, criminel, defense, duc, heriter,* *justice, noble, sceptre, testimonie*; terms of animal-lore, astronomy, etc., *scorpïon, embolisme, kalendier, moment, zone, ametiste, cristal, topaze*; scholastic terms, *allegorie, ancïen, argument,* etc. More varied in character are the borrowed words in the 'chansons de geste'. According to Berger,[1] who counts only words borrowed after 800, the *Chanson de Roland* contains 112, the *Couronnement Louis* 100, and the *Charroi de Nîmes* 52.

497. Borrowings from Low Latin (ecclesiastic, scholastic or legal) continued throughout the thirteenth century. Texts of this period first show such words as *accusation, avaricieux, discerner, excessif, praticien, transitoire*. But previous borrowings are as nothing compared with the transposition in bulk of Latin words in the fourteenth century, henceforth drawn for the most part from Classical Latin. The revival of learned studies and the activity of translators are contributory causes, but the real explanation lies in the fact that French literature undergoes a profound change. It is now taken seriously, new genres are developed and great store is set by learning, Classical Latin literature being at the same time the model and the repository. It is often the work of men who write and speak Latin and, owing to daily converse with Latin authors, think in Latin while writing French. Borrowing from Low Latin continues to some extent, facilitated by the use of both French and Latin in different branches of law and administration. Borrowings at this date are of the most varied character, but may be characterized as being of a rather more bookish character than hitherto. Consequently, many have never become popular, and others have penetrated very slowly into general literary use and thence into popular speech (*abus, decence, anatomie, atrocité, diversion, perplexe, interminable, defectif, emanciper*).[2]

498. Borrowing from Latin continues unchecked in the fifteenth century, accelerated by the first stirrings of the Renaissance and culminating in the absurd Latinized French

---

[1] *Op. cit.* p. 21; cf. Gaston Paris, *op. cit.*

[2] These examples are taken from the extensive lists given by Brunot, I, pp. 514–25.

of the 'escumeurs de Latin' ridiculed by du Bellay. The cult
of Latinism as a literary ornament reached its climax in the
school of the Grands Rhétoriqueurs, but continued to find
its adepts throughout the sixteenth century. From the point
of view of vocabulary this century is important in that the
sciences began to develop their own special vocabularies,
made up largely of Latin and Greek borrowings and formations, some of which passed into the literary language (*cadavre*,
ligament, *semestre*, *structure*, *véhicule*; *épithète*, *hypothèse*, *hiéroglyphe*, *symptôme*, *symptomatique*). The seventeenth century
frowned upon such neologisms, but they found their cham-
pions even in that age (cf. Brunot, IV, i, pp. 446-9). With
the advance of the various sciences in the eighteenth century
and the popularization of certain of them, more and more
technical words find their way into literature. Since the
beginning of the nineteenth century the number of such
words has gone on increasing, beginning with the Romantic
writers, who championed the 'mot propre', and accelerated
by the progress of science and industry, the spread of education, and the activity of the press. Compared with such
borrowings through the technical vocabularies of the various
sciences, the number of words borrowed directly by the
literary language is small. The eighteenth century with its
tendency to abstraction is responsible for a number of accessions (*agglomération*, *cohésion*, *cynisme*, *natation*). The nineteenth
century and our own are notable for the extravagant use made,
particularly by politicians, journalists, and administrators, of
the borrowed words already existing in the language.[1]

THE TREATMENT OF WORDS BORROWED
FROM LATIN

499. The general rule is that a borrowed word undergoes
those phonetic changes which supervened after its introduction into the language and is not affected by changes which
had been completed before that date. Therefore words bor-

---

[1] For the extensive use made of Learned suffixes, see § 529.

rowed from written Latin during the V.L. period would not be distinguishable from Popular words, and it would appear a simple matter to arrange later borrowings in chronological order. But a number of factors have intervened to obscure the issue, and it is necessary to study the circumstances in which a particular word was introduced and the manner in which it was propagated.

500. The first circumstance to be noted is that the earliest borrowings were oral and not written, and when one bears in mind that the clerks carried into their pronunciation o Latin many of the features of the vulgar tongue, it is clear that a word may be borrowed after the completion of a sound-change and yet appear to have been subjected to it. No one will contend, for example, that *charité* (CARITATEM) was borrowed before *c* followed by *a* had become *ch*, and yet Latin *c* is here rendered by *ch*. The Carolingian reforms went some way towards restoring Classical pronunciation of written Latin, so that words borrowed after that date are more easily recognized; but even their chronology is difficult to establish. Firstly, the reforms did not completely eradicate such popular pronunciations as *c = ts* before *e*, *i* and *c = tš* before *a*. Our knowledge of the medieval pronunciation of Latin is very imperfect; and yet it is a factor which has to be reckoned with throughout the history of borrowings from Latin, accounting as it does for such features as the rendering of Latin short *u* by *ü*: *tube* (TŬBA), *cumuler* (CŬMŬLARE), etc. Secondly, post-Carolingian borrowings are no longer made by word of mouth, but direct from written Latin, and they are Learned in a narrower sense of the term. They continue, however, to be borrowed from Low Latin down to the end of the thirteenth century; after that date from Classical Latin, and less frequently from Low Latin. Thirdly, the existence of the Latin word alongside of the Learned borrowing (often in the linguistic equipment of the same individual) may exercise a retarding influence on the development of the latter, which would not be caught up in the popular stream and would therefore be made to appear a later borrowing than it in

fact is. This is undoubtedly true of such words as *angele,
esperit, virgene, crestiien, prestre, eglise*. Fourthly, the same word
may be re-borrowed at various dates. We get in this way,
in addition to etymological doublets consisting of a Popular
form and a Learned form (*meuble—mobile*), doublets consisting of an early borrowed word and a late borrowed word
(*frêle—fragile*); if the phonetic interval is slight, the former
may be eliminated by the latter (*soutil, vitaille* give way to
subtil, victuaille; cf. § 574). Fifthly, what appear to be Learned
words may in certain cases be Popular words re-modelled
under the influence of the Latin form. Thus, *bisaïeul, instruire,
instrument, suffire* have replaced *besaïeul, enstruire, estrument,
soufire*. That is to say, it is sometimes difficult to draw the
line between mere Learned influence and outright borrowing, just as in early monuments it is difficult to distinguish
between Latinisms, Latinized spellings, and Learned borrowings; cf. §§ 152–3, 496.

501. The form of a word may therefore lead to a wrong
conclusion or may even fail to reveal the fact that the word
is borrowed (*montrer, évêque*). Hence the dating of pre-literary
borrowings is a delicate operation and must be undertaken
with due regard to the meaning of the word and the circumstances which account for the borrowing. They can, as a
rule, be distinguished from later borrowings by the fact that
they follow Popular words in maintaining the accent on the
same syllable as in Latin, though not sharing all their phonetic
changes (*âme, ange, apôtre, chanoine, prêtre, moine*).[1] Later borrowings either keep the Latin form (*cirrus, nimbus, pensum*
(= pĕsǫm), *rictus, examen*) or are adapted, generally by giving
them a French termination (*correctif, différent, habitude, légume,
iuriste*). For the dating of such Learned forms the first occurrence in a text furnishes a provisional *terminus ante quem*,
but leaves open the question of its currency at the time

---

[1] An exception must be made in favour of Latin formulae adopted
at various periods without change, except for a shifting of accent or such
alterations as had taken place in Low Latin (*ave, cancan, déficit, ergo,
item, rogaton*).

and the possibility of its being found ultimately in a still earlier text.

GREEK

502. The Greek element in the vocabulary of Modern French is only to a slight extent the result of direct borrowing, the bulk of it having come to French through Latin. The majority of the Greek words used by Classical writers were of a learned and literary character and never found currency in Vulgar Latin. Some of them passed into Low Latin and thence into French, others directly from Classical Latin to French at a later date. A considerable number of ecclesiastical terms: *église* < ECCLESIA (ἐκκλησία), *évêque* < EPISCOPUM (ἐπίσκοπος), *ange* < *ángele* < ANGELUM (ἄγγελος), and a few miscellaneous terms such as *coup* < COLAPHUM (κόλᾰφος), *corde* < CHORDA (χορδή), were adopted by Low Latin in the V.L. period and passed thence into the vulgar tongue. Direct borrowing, by word of mouth, was rare in this period. The Crusades resulted in a number of borrowings, some of which appear to have been made directly (*boutique, chaland, dromond*), others through Low Latin (*besant, endive*) or through Italian (*fanal, golfe, page, riz*). The revival of Hellenistic studies in the sixteenth century resulted in the transposition of numerous Greek words by such enthusiasts as Rabelais, but very few of their borrowings were adopted (*anagramme, athée, enthousiasme*). The bulk of the Greek element that makes its appearance at this time and later is either adopted from Latin (*stratagème, épithète, sympathie*) or filters into the literary language through the technical vocabularies of the sciences (*symptôme, hygiène, rhomboïde*). Since the sixteenth century Greek has furnished the sciences (particularly medicine and chemistry), and to some extent industry, with the greater part of their technical vocabulary, not so much in the form of ready-made words as of elements which are freely utilized for new creations (*chronomètre, laryngoscope, photographe, télégramme, téléphone*). These are not always made with a sure

linguistic perception and result in such Graeco-Latin and
Graeco-French hybrids as *centimètre*; *bureaucratie, cartographie.*

What has been said in §§ 499–501 applies to Greek words
that have passed through Latin, the earliest borrowings
developing like Popular, the later like Learned words. The
rendering of Greek words in Latin varies according to (*a*) the
date of their introduction (κάμηλος—V.L. KAMĘLU > O.F.
chemeil is early, while ταπήτιον—V.L. TAPPÍTJU > *tapis* is in
accordance with the late Greek pronunciation of η as *i*),
(*b*) the manner of their transmission, literary or oral: φ, θ, χ
appear as PH, TH, CH respectively in C.L. but, with loss of
the aspirate quality, as P, T, K in V.L. (and in archaic Latin):
CÓLAPHUS (κόλαφος)—V.L. KOLPU > *coup*, CATHÉDRA (καθέδρα)
—V.L. KÁTEDRA > *chaiere* > *chaire*, BRACCHIUM (βραχίων)—
V.L. BRAKJU > *braz* > *bras*, but later borrowings show *f* for
φ in accordance with the change in Greek pronunciation:
ORPHANUS (ὀρφᾰνός)—V.L. ORFANU + -INU > *orfenin, orfelin*;
ζ appears in the earliest borrowings as *s*: MASSA (μάζα) > *masse*,
later as *dj*: ZELUS (ζῆλος) + -ōSUS—V.L. DJELǫSU > *jaloux*, and
still later as *z*: *zèle*; υ appears as Y in C.L. (V.L. as ǫ):
CRYPTA (κρυπτή)—V.L. KRǪPTA > O.F. *croute*, since replaced
by *grotte* (It. grotta), but later borrowings show V.L. *i* and *ę*:
CYMA (κῦμα)—V.L. KIMA > *cime*; PRESBYTERUM (πρεσβύτερος)
—V.L. PRESBĘTERU > O.F. *prouvoire*. Greek accentuation is
maintained in popular borrowings: BÚTYRUM (βούτυρον)
> *beurre*. Learned borrowings are normally accented according
to Latin rules (κάμηλος—CAMÉLUS), but Learned imitation of
Greek is responsible for a number of exceptions (μοναρχία—
MONARCHÍA—*monarchie*)

CELTIC

503. French vocabulary contains a fair number of words
of Celtic origin, the majority dating from the V.L. period.[1]
Some were borrowed early and are common to the Romance
languages (except Roumanian): ALAUDA > *alou*(*ette*), BECCUM

---

[1] They are for the most part known to us only in a Latinized form.

> *bec*, BRACA > *braie*, CABALLUM > *cheval*, CAMBIARE > *changer*, CARRUM > *char*, *CLETA > *claie*, *CUMBA > *combe*, *LANDA > *lande*. Others either remained confined to the Latin of Gaul or were introduced into it at a later date: *AREPENDE(M) (for AREPENNEM) > *arpent*, BODINA > *borne* (O.F. *bodne, bonne, bosne*), CARRUCA > *charrue*, LEUCA > *lieue*, *SOCCUM > *soc*, TUNNA > *tonne*. It should, however, be noted that of this category a certain number later passed from French to other Romance languages, e.g. VASSALLUM > *vassal*, whence It. vassallo, Sp. vasallo. It is possible that a certain number of words have come down from pre-Celtic languages (Ligurian, etc.) through the intermediary of Celtic or directly, e.g. *peautre* (< *PELTRUM Ligurian?). Such words would naturally survive more frequently on the fringes of Gaul, where they were not submerged by the Celtic and Romance strata, notably in the Alpine region (*avalanche, chalet, luge*).

504. Borrowings from the Celtic idiom of the Gauls were completely naturalized in the V.L. period (cf. § 4), and therefore develop in exactly the same way as the original Latin elements. They are to be carefully distinguished from later Celtic borrowings from Breton. These are transposed with little change, the terminations being generally assimilated to the native terminations: *baragouin* < b a r a 'bread' + g w i n 'wine', *bijou* < b i z o u, *bouette* 'bait for cod-fishing' < b o e d. Others, mostly nautical and archaeological terms, retain their original form and have a limited currency (*bernicle, cromlech, dolmen, goéland, menhir*).

GERMANIC

505. Even before the occupation of the various portions of the Empire by Germanic tribes, contact with the latter had resulted in the introduction of certain words into Latin: GANTA (> O.F. *jante*) and SAPO (> *savon*) are found in Pliny, BRUTA in inscriptions of the third century. But with few such exceptions Germanic loan-words remained confined to the spoken language during the V.L. period. J. Brüch (*op.*

cit.) has estimated the total number of Germanic words borrowed before A.D. 400 at roughly 100. The intermediaries were on the one hand the Roman soldiers, officials, and traders, who for longer or shorter periods remained in contact with Germanic tribes, and on the other hand Germanic mercenaries and slaves, who were drafted into the Empire in large numbers. Consequently, many of these early borrowings concern military operations and equipment, the habits and conditions of life of the soldiery: bind-a (binde) > *bande*, bras-a (Scand. brase) > *braise*, būkōn (bauchen) > *buer*, frummjan (frommen) > *fournir*, hardjan (härten) > *hardir*, whence *hardi*, hari-berg- (heer + bergen) > Prov. *auberc, auberga*, whence *auberge*, harp-a (harfe) > *harpe*, helm- (helm) > *heaume*, hraustjan (rösten) > *rôtir*, kausjan (kiesen) > *choisir*, krattōn (kratzen) > *gratter*, likkōn (lecken) > *lécher*, mark-a (mark) > *marche*, skal-ja (schale) > *écaille*, sparanjan (sparen) > *épargner*, spor-on (sporn) > *éperon*, supp-a (suppe) > *soupe*, trapp-a (treppe) > *trappe*, warjan (wehren) > *guérir*, warnōn (warnen) and warnjan > *garnir*; commerce and trades: alisn-a (ahle, North Engl. elsen) > *alêne*, ball-a (ballen) > *balle, ballon*, brakk-on (bracke) > *braque, brachet, braconnier*, marþr- (marter) > *martre*, skūm- (schaum) > *écume*; domestic architecture, husbandry, etc.: balk- (balken) > *bauc* (*balcon* through Italian), bank- (bank) > *banc*, bastjan > *bâtir*, brekan (brechen) > *broyer*, fanj- (dial. fenn, Engl. fen) > *fange*, first (first) > *faîte*, garb-a (garbe) > *gerbe*, older *jarbe*; adjectives of colour (perhaps originally applied only to horses): blank- (blank) > *blanc*, brūn- (braun) > *brun*, falw- (falb) > *fauve*, grīs- (greis) > *gris*; miscellaneous: brūþ- (braut) > *bru* (O.F. *bruz—brut*), hank-a (L.G. hancke) > *hanche*, sinn- (sinn) > *sen* 'direction' preserved in *assener, forcené*, urgōl- (O.E. orgol) > *orgueil*, wīs-a (weise) > *guise*. The words listed above were taken up into Vulgar Latin before the various Romance languages became differentiated, and many of them have been preserved in several of these languages; but French possesses a larger number than any other, owing to the closer contact with the Germanic tribes. The Germanic roots are here given in their West Germanic (hypothetical) form, followed by their phonetic descendants or nearest cognate forms in Modern German, or alternatively in other Germanic idioms. The French equivalents are not in every case the direct descendants of the Germanic forms, but may have been remodelled later under the influence of Franconian.

506. The occupation of Northern Gaul by the Salian Franks and the rapid romanization of the latter resulted in much more extensive and varied borrowing. Whereas the Vulgar Latin borrowings had been of general West Germanic provenance, this second series (*ca.* 400–800) is almost entirely Franconian. The Germanic roots are given in their Old Franconian (hypothetical) form, but it is to be noted that in many cases the form attested in later Franconian is identical with that here given: alin-a (elle) > *aune,* al-ōd (Old Saxon ōd 'landed property'; cf. Mod.G. kleinod) > *alleu,* bakk-on (backe) > *bacon,* bann- (bann) > *ban,* bannjan > *bannir,* ber-a (bahre) > *bière* 'bier', bidil (büttel) > *bedeau,* bis-a (biese) > *bise,* blāw- (blau) > *bleu,* blettjan > *blesser* (O.F. *blecier*), bord (bord) > *bord,* bottan (Engl. to butt) > *bouter* and *bouton,* dansōn (O.H.G. dansōn) > *danser,* fehu- (vieh) > *fief* (O.F. *fieus—fieu*), flad-on (fladen) > *flan* (O.F. *flaon*), gund- 'battle'+fan-on (fahne) > *gonfanon,* whence by dissimilation *gonfalon,* haist- (Gothic haifsts 'strife', O.H.G. heist 'violent') > *hâte* 'haste', harst- (O.H.G. hersten, M.L.G. harsten 'to roast') > *hâte* 'spit', haigir-on (O.H.G. heigir) > *héron,* hag-a (hag) > *haie,* hall-a (halle) > *halle,* happ-ja (cf. O.H.G. happa) > *hache,* hatjan (hassen) > *haïr,* hauniþ-a > *honte,* heriberg-a > *héberge* (O.F. *herberge*), hestr- (M.L.G. hester) > *hêtre,* hring- (ring) > *rang* (O.F. *renc*), huls- (Germ. dial. hulst) > *houx,* kott-a (O.H.G. chozza) > *cotte,* kripp-ja (krippe) > *crèche,* krūk-a (krug) > *cruche,* krupp-a (kropf) > *croupe,* laid- (leid) > *laid,* laub-ja (cf. laube) > *loge,* maising-a (meise) > *mésange,* raub-a (rauben) > *robe,*

rīk- (reich) > *riche,* sin-i 'old' (cf. Gothic sinista 'elder') +
skalk-> *sénéchal,* skankj-on (schenk) > *échanson,* skerp-a
> *écharpe,* skīn-a (schien-bein) > *échine,* sparwār-i (sper-
ber) > *épervier,* spehōn (spähen) > *épier* (through Prov.
espiar?), speut- (spiess) > *épieu* (O.F. *espiet* later *espiel,*
espieu ≠ pieu), treuw-a (treue) > *trêve,* waddj- (wette)
> *gage,* waht-a (wacht) > *guaite,* whence *guaitier* > *guetter,*
whence *guet,* want- (L.G. wanten) > *gant,* werpan (wer-
fen) > *(dé)guerpir.*

507. During the O.F. period borrowings from Germanic
are comparatively rare. The Frankish element of the population has been completely absorbed, and new borrowings filter
in through Picardy from the Low German peoples of the
Netherlands, through Normandy from the Norse invaders
and from Anglo-Saxon. Borrowings from High German are
few (bercvrit> *berfroi, beffroi;* riben > *riber,* whence *ribaud*),
owing to the severing of contact with those parts of Germania
where West Germanic had developed High German peculiarities (the High German sound-shift was completed by the
end of the eighth century). Borrowings from Old Norse and
Anglo-Saxon (ninth to tenth century) are almost confined
to nautical terms, and it is a striking fact that French took
from Anglo-Saxon the terms to denote the points of the
compass. Old Norse: húnn> *hune,* kriki (Engl. creek)
> *crique,* sigla> *cingler* (O.F. *sigler*), skipa> *équiper,* þilja
> *tillac,* vinda> *guinder,* vind-ás> *guindas,* vág-r> *vague*
'wave'. Anglo-Saxon: bát> *bat-eau,* bowline> *bouline,*
éast> *est,* flóta> *flotte,* norþ> *nord,* rád> *rade,* stæg> *étai,*
súþ> *sud,* west> *ouest,* wræc> *varech,* and perhaps wimpel
> *guimple> guimpe.* Low German furnishes a number of
nautical words and terms denoting commodities: aanmaren
> *amarrer,* bak> *bac,* dune> *dune,* havene> O.F. *havene*
> *hâvre,* micke> *miche,* ralijk> *ralingue,* schelling> *escalin,*
stapel> *étaple* and *étape,* vrecht> *fret,* wach-arme!> *va-
carme.*

508. In the Middle French period close commercial relations with the Low Countries are reflected in continued

borrowings from Dutch or Flemish: brosekin > *broissequin* later *brodequin* (15th c.), under the influence of *broder*, buiten > *butiner*, whence *butin*, droge > *drogue*, kerkmisse > *kermesse*, kiel > *quille* 'keel', stockvisch > *stockfisch*, wimpelkin > *wimbelkin* later *vilebrequin*, are attested from the fourteenth century; bolwerc > *boulever* later *boulevard*, dik > *digue*, lamper-kin > *lambrequin*, mande-kin > *mandequin* later *mannequin* 'little basket', mannekin > *mannequin*, plak > *plaque*, from the fifteenth century; bakboord > *bâbord*, boecskin > *bouquin*, stierboord > *estribord* > *tribord*, verlaten > *frelater*, wase > *vase*, from the sixteenth century.

509. German mercenaries are mainly responsible for the introduction of the following High German words: burgmeister > *bourguemaistre* later *bourgmestre*, halber-ent > *halbran*, from the fourteenth century; bettelaere > *belleudre* later *bélître*, elen > *hellent* later *élan* (*du cerf*), halskragen > *hallecrète* later *halecret*, landsknecht > *lansquenet*, ros > *rosse*, from the fifteenth century; bier > *bière* 'beer', Eulenspiegel > *espiègle* (abbreviation of *Ulespiègle*, which suggests the Dutch form *Uilenspiegel* as the intermediary), garaus > *carous* later *carrousse* (17th c.), Eidgenosse > *huguenot*, halt > *halte*, hase > *hase*, hütte > *hutte*, pfife > *fifre*, reiter > *reître*, trinken > *trinquer*, from the sixteenth century.

510. Apart from an increasing number of words adopted by Anglo-Norman writers and passed on by them (*gotelef, wibet, welke* in Marie de France, *lovendrincs* in Beroul, *welcomer, outlaghe* and its derivatives), which had a limited circulation, borrowings from English are rare. *Estellin* (or *esterlin*) is attested in the twelfth century but is perhaps not derived directly from English sterling. The Hundred Years' War resulted in but few importations, dating mostly from the fifteenth century, when the common soldiery of English speech took a more prominent part: by God > *bigot*, fellow > *falot* (cf. Rabelais, *il est goud fallot*), God dam > *goddam, godon*, whence *godenot* (17th c.). From the same period date: dog > *dogue*, hobby > *hobin* (15th c.) later *aubin* (17th c.), milord > *milord, millour*. In the sixteenth century English furnishes but little.

511. From the seventeenth century onwards borrowings from English show a rapid increase, while those from Dutch and German show a corresponding decline. Dutch: afhalen > *affaler*, bylander > *bélandre*, dok > *dogue* > *dock* under the influence of English dock (17th c.); brandewin > *brandevin*, kombuis > *cambuse* (18th c.). German: biwache > *bivouac*, blenden > *blinder*, haubitze > *obus*, habersack > *havresac*, sabel > *sabre*, rheingraf > *rhingrave* 'breeches' (XVII, 39), schibe > *cible*, nudeln > *nouille*, *zigzag*, *zinc* (17th c.); blagen > *blague* 'tobacco-pouch', *blende*, *cobalt*, *feldspath*, kirsch-wasser > *kirsch-wasser* later (*eau de*) *kirsch*, was ist das? > *vasistas*, *vampire*, *vermout* (18th c.); *bock*, *dolman*, *képi*, *landau*, frühstück > *frichti*, sūrkrūt (dial.) > *choucroute*, walzer > *valse* (19th c.).

512. Seventeenth-century borrowings from English begin to reflect the growing interest in English affairs. Beside nautical and commercial terms (*ballast*, *brig* or *brick*, *drague*, *flanelle*, *guinée*, *paquebot*, *rhum*), such words as *boulingrin* (bowling-green), *contredanse* (country-dance), *comité*, *pamphlet*, *pique-nique* appear in the course of the seventeenth century. The admiration which English letters and institutions engendered in the eighteenth century, and the 'anglomanie' which for a time prevailed, led to the adoption of such varied words as *club*, *importation*, *jockey*, *partenaire*, *redingote* (riding-coat), *sentimental*, *spleen*. Such borrowings continue in the nineteenth century (*bifteck*, *châle*, *dandy*, *festival*, *keepsake*, *rail*, *rosbif*, *sinécure*, *tramway*, *wagon*), but they are outnumbered by the countless terms taken from the technical language of trade, industry, and above all of sport: *actuaire*, *chèque*, *stock*; *celluloïd*, *gutta-percha*, *ticket*; *bicycle*, *cricket*, *dead-heat*, *football*, *hockey*, *sport*, *sportsman*, etc., etc.

513. The result of this wholesale borrowing has often been that words originally taken over by English from French have been borrowed back. Sometimes the original French word has in the meantime disappeared, or become archaic (*budget*, *square*, *mess*, *verdict*), but frequently the result is an etymological doublet: *cabane—cabine*, *connétable—constable*, *entrevue—interview, étiquette—ticket, étoffe—stuff, exprès—express, façon—fashion, gentilhomme—gentleman, rapporteur—reporter, reille —rail, compote—compost, humeur—humour.*

ARABIC

514. The Arab invasions and the occupation of Spain, the superior culture of the Arabs, the translation of many of their scientific works into Latin, and finally the Crusades, resulted in the introduction of many Arabic words into the vocabulary of the Western nations. French received the bulk of this vocabulary at second hand, through Low Latin (13th c. *alchimie, barbacane, nuque*; 14th c. *zénith*; 15th c. *amalgame*; 16th c. *alcool*), Spanish (12th c. *algalife, papegai*; 16th c. *abricot, pateque* later *pastèque*; 17th c. *lilac—lilas*), Portuguese (14th c. *épinard*), Italian (13th c. *arsenal, chiffre, girafe*; 14th c. *cramoisi, magasin, tare*; 17th c. *carafe, mesquin, tarif*). Some words passed through several languages before reaching French. Particularly interesting are the peregrinations of *albatros, divan—douane, mohair—moire*. Arabic al qa dūs 'bucket' was the name applied to the pelican from its supposed water-carrying habit; adopted by Spanish and Portuguese (al-catraz 'pelican'), it passed thence into English in the form algatross (17th c.), albatross (18th c.), the latter being borrowed by French in the eighteenth century. Arabic di wān 'custom-house' was apparently borrowed directly into French in the form *douwaine* (15th c.), which gave way in the sixteenth century to *dogane, douane* (< Italian do(g)ana <diwān); the same word having passed through Persian and Turkish was re-borrowed in the sixteenth century in the form *divan*. Arabic mukhayyar 'choice, select' gave English mohair, whence French *mouaire, moire* (17th c.); *mohair* was re-borrowed with a slightly changed meaning in the nineteenth century, English returning the compliment by borrowing *moire*. Direct borrowings from Arabic include: 12th c. *azur, coton, jupe*; 13th c. *alambic, ambre, élixir, gazelle*; 14th c. *nadir*; 17th c. *harem*; and in more recent times, thanks

to the occupation of Algeria, 19th c. *burnous, cheik, zouave*, and many more of limited currency.

ITALIAN

515. Apart from Italianisms to be found in the works of Italians writing French (Brunetto Latini, Rusticiano of Pisa), borrowings from Italian were few in the O.F. period. They consist for the most part of words which Italian passed on from other languages (*arsenal, chiffre, girafe*); *catacombe, citrouille, francolin, porcelaine* date from the end of the thirteenth century. In the fourteenth century, intercourse with Italy becomes more and more frequent and borrowings increase (*alarme, brigade, brigand, brigue, calibre, canon, cassette, citadin, ducat, falot, florin, voguer*). The cultural superiority of the Italians does not assert itself until the fifteenth and sixteenth centuries, when military expeditions, commercial relations, literary influences, and ultimately dynastic alliances, result in a wholesale introduction of Italian words. The extent of Italian influence is due not merely to cultural superiority but to the fact that Italy anticipated in such striking fashion the general movement of ideas at this time. In a word, the French language, suddenly called upon to meet all the needs created by the Renaissance, had recourse to the language which provided ready-made the bulk of the vocabulary required. If for a time Italianisms tended to swamp the language and to reduce it in the hands of certain writers to an Italianized jargon, it is undeniable that Italian contributed in a very large measure to the creation of the refined medium for the classical literature of the seventeenth century. Leaving out of account borrowings which have not survived, we find that the fifteenth century already presents a most varied list: *arborer, banquet, bastion, calmer, câpre, cavalcade, citadelle, dôme, émeri, escadre, escadron, esplanade, fracas, golfe, médaille, moustache, pilote, révolter, tribune*. The Italian monopoly of the banking system is reflected in the large number of banking terms adopted (*banque, banqueroute, bilan,* *crédit, escompte, faillite, risque, trafic*). These were current in the fifteenth century, but did not pass into the literary language until the following century. Sixteenth-century borrowings have been carefully listed, examined, and classified by B. H. Wind. The divers categories, arts and sciences (*arcade, architrave, balcon, corniche, façade, grotesque, pilastre, volute*), literature (*cantilène, madrigal, sonnet*), music (*ballet, fougue, sourdine, trombone, violon*), war (*bataillon, camp, caporal, soldat, vedette*, and with meaning later generalized: *alerte, contraste, corridor, escapade, escorte, solde*), marine (*accoster, boussole, escale, frégate, gondole, remorquer*), industry (*artisan, brocard, carton, damasquin, faïence, majolique*), public and private life (*antichambre, appartement, bosquet, bulletin, cabinet, cadre, camisole, campagne, capuchon, capucin, carrosse, charlatan, contrebande, courrier, courtisan, escroc, festin, gazette, majordome, mascarade, masque, nonce, pantalon, plage, populace, postillon, raquette, récolte, renégat, saltimbanque, soutane, travestir*), show how deep and lasting was the influence of Italy in this age. It was inevitable that the Italian word should often find itself in competition with a native term. The latter was sometimes kept with a restricted meaning or utilized to distinguish shades of meaning (*camp—champ, cargue—charge, escapade—échappée, escale—échelle, récolte—cueillette*), sometimes eliminated as being old-fashioned or crude (*espie, soudart* give way to *espion, soldat*). In many cases the native word was re-modelled under the influence of the Italian cognate word (*embuschier* + imboscare > *embusquer*), or its meaning was affected without change of form (§§ 576, 582). Sometimes the Italian word had itself been borrowed from Old French (O.F. *bauçenc*—It. balzano —*balzan*). Borrowings decline in the seventeenth century but are still varied (*bagne, bandit, céleri, costume, esquisse, filigrane, gigantesque, gradin, imbroglio, lésine, manège, opéra, polichinelle, salon, svelte*); later importations are generally of a technical character, musical terms being particularly numerous (18th c. *aquarelle, camée, dilettante, pittoresque, villégiature*; *adagio, arpège, crescendo, solfège, sonate, ténor*; 19th c. *fantoche*; *brio, fioriture, trémolo*).

SPANISH AND PORTUGUESE

516. The earliest borrowings from Spanish date from the twelfth and thirteenth centuries. They are generally words which Spanish had itself borrowed from Arabic (*auqueton*, later *hoqueton*), and many have not outlived the O.F. period (*algalife, almaçor, amirafle*). Of the 1100 Spanish words listed by Ruppert, less than one hundred date from the Middle Ages (*tournesol, genet* are attested from the fourteenth century, *laquais, infant* from the fifteenth century). Much more extensive borrowing results from the closer contact between the two nations in the sixteenth and seventeenth centuries. In the sixteenth century Spain's military and naval ascendancy and the wars with France led to the adoption of *alezan, casque, escouade, parade, camper, camarade, caparaçon, caracole, morion; caboteur, cabotier, cabotière, canoe* (f.) later *canot*. Her far-flung colonial possessions made her the intermediary for many new commodities together with their names: *patate, mélasse, mermelade, maïs, abricot*; also *cannibale, nègre, savane*. Her influence in political and social matters is reflected in such borrowings as *alguazil, matassin*. In the following century the borrowing of military and nautical terms is rare, but words denoting colonial products and exotic terms are represented by *vanille, marmelade, alpaca, cacao, chocolat; mulâtre, moustique, lilac*. Literary influences, which are marked towards the middle of the sixteenth and again about the middle of the seventeenth century, are responsible for the introduction of many terms such as *parangon, guitare, cédille* (16th c.) and *sarabande, romance, quadrille* (17th c.). Spanish influence declines in the eighteenth century; characteristic borrowings are *adjudant, cigare, embarcadère, embarcation, flottille, mérinos, récif, sieste, tomate*. After 1800 borrowings are comparatively few (*saynète*), some two-score in all. Many of the words listed above and others have come through Spanish from other languages: Arabic (*alcôve, matassin, abricot, alguazil, récif*, etc.), American native idioms (*ananas, cacao, chocolat, maïs*, from Brazil, Chile, Mexico, Haiti respectively).

Here, as in the case of Italian, the borrowing often results in the creation of an etymological doublet: *adjudant—aidant*, *duègne—dame*, *hombre—homme*, *infant—enfant*, *menin—mignon*, *nègre—noir*. The common development of pejorative meaning in borrowed words is illustrated by *duègne*, *hâbler*.

Very few native Portuguese words have been borrowed: *pintade* (17th c.), *autodafé* (18th c.), *caste* (18th c.). Portugal shares with Spain the rôle of intermediary for many terms denoting colonial products and institutions (*acajou* from Brazil), particularly from Africa and the Far East: *bambou*, *banane*, *marabout*, *mandarin*, *palanquin* from the sixteenth and seventeenth centuries; *fétiche* from the eighteenth century.

OTHER ROMANCE IDIOMS

517. Borrowings from the Romance idioms and dialects descended from the common Gallo-Roman stock are often difficult to localize owing to the wide distribution of certain phonetic developments (e.g. hard *c* before *a*, common to Norman, Picard, and Provençal). Further, among the many words introduced from Provençal, it is not always easy to segregate those which Provençal has merely transmitted from Italian (*salade*) or from Spanish (*bourrique*). Unmistakably Provençal are the earliest borrowings resulting from the influence of the Troubadour poetry and the refined culture it represents (12th c. and 13th c. *amour*, *aubade*, *ballade*, *donzelle*), or the superiority of Southern craftsmen in certain trades (*elme*, *osberc*, *velours*). Later borrowings are of the most varied kind, many denoting products of the Midi: 14th c. *abeille*, *bastide*, *bastille*, *cabrer*, *cap*, *emparer*, *escargole* later *escargot*, *gabelle*, *soubresaut*; 15th c. *banquette*, *câble*, *cadeau*, *cape* 'sail', *cigale*; 16th c. *accolade*, *badaud*, *badin*, *barrique*, *cadastre*, *cadenas*, *carnassier*, *caserne*, *escalier*, *fadaise*, *fat*, *gavotte*, *milan*, *mistral*, *troubadour*, *yeuse*; 17th c. *soubrette*; 18th c. *amadou*, *farandole*, *nougat*; 19th c. *béret*, *bouillabaisse*. Franco-Provençal and Swiss dialects have furnished *avalanche*, *chalet*, *crétin*, *glacier*, *luge*, *mélèze*, *moraine*.

Borrowings from Northern dialects are comparatively rare;
from Norman or Picard: *achopper, barbouquet, bercail, bocage,
cabaret, caboche, caillou, étiquette, étriquer, gavion, grincheux, quai,
stopper* 'to repair'; from West or South-West dialects: *aiguayer,
caniche, varaigne.* Many so-called borrowings are more correctly described as dialectal pronunciations which have prevailed over Central French. It sometimes happens that a
word which has disappeared from the standard language is
re-introduced from a dialect: Picard *fabliau* (16th c.) for
O.F. *fablel*, Picard *affiquet* for O.F. *affichet*, Norman *benêt* for
O.F. *ben(e)oit* (cf. § 369). Genuine borrowings take place
when new needs arise which the dialects are in a position
to meet and satisfy. Thus the dialects on the Northern and
Western sea-board provide many nautical and fishing terms
(*aplet, crevette, esturgeon, requin, salicoque, vergue*). Local industries,
when they become of national importance, bring with them
a new vocabulary (from the North-East come *escarbille, houille,
tôle, torque*).

Borrowing from the technical vocabularies of trades and
professions goes on constantly. Here special mention may
be made of borrowings from thieves' slang: 15th c. *dupe,
fourbe, gueux*; 16th c. *matois, matou, narquois*; 17th c. *argot,
polisson, trucher*; 19th c. *cambrioleur, flouer, larbin, mioche, roublard,
voyou.*

PHONETIC TREATMENT AND ASSIMILATION OF BOR-
ROWED WORDS (OTHER THAN LATIN AND GREEK)

518. The treatment of borrowed words often throws an
interesting light on the phonetic constitution of a language
at the time of the borrowing, but generally upon that of the
creditor rather than the debtor language. The subject is one
of peculiar difficulty, for one must take into account the
pronunciation of both languages (and their dialects) at the
time of the borrowing, the manner of transmission (oral or
literary), and the peregrinations of the word (through dialects,
special languages, etc.). A broad distinction may be drawn
between oral and written borrowings. The former take place

mostly when there is prolonged contact between two races and to some extent interpenetration (e.g. the Frankish conquest). Early Germanic borrowings (before 800) are oral. The same may be said of borrowings from Low Latin in the earliest period of the language, to a lesser degree of Italian borrowings of the fifteenth and sixteenth centuries; but, in general, borrowings since the Middle Ages have taken place through the written language. Yet the distinction is often difficult to maintain. Normally the borrowed word, if it is naturalized and no longer felt to be foreign, will share phonetic developments that supervene after its introduction. We have seen how the evolution of a word borrowed from Latin may be retarded by the continued existence of the Latin word by the side of it. The same applies to words borrowed orally from foreign languages, if they are still felt to be foreign words: they keep close to the original form and are held in check by it. The influence of spelling is here particularly potent (*club*, borrowed from English in the eighteenth century and pronounced *klǫb* or *klöb*, has in the nineteenth century come to be pronounced *klüb* under the influence of the spelling).

Broadly speaking, words borrowed orally are transposed as accurately as possible: sounds which are foreign to French are rendered by their nearest equivalent. Only once in the history of the French language have foreign sounds been introduced, viz. as a result of the Frankish conquest and the fusion of the Frankish invaders with the native population: *'h*, which has since become mute (h a u n j a n > *'honnir* > (*h*)*onnir*; cf. § 115), and *w* (> *gu* > *g*: w a r d ō n > *guarder* > *garder*; cf. § 103).

The treatment of Latin and Greek borrowings is discussed in §§ 499–502. Celtic (Gaulish) borrowings are known to us only in their Latinized forms, which develop regularly. In the case of the earlier borrowings from Germanic, those sounds which existed in Vulgar Latin or Gallo-Roman persist, the remainder are rendered by their nearest equivalents. Thus *u* appears as *o* (f u r b j a n—V.L. FORBIRE > *fourbir*) *eu* appears as *ę-o* (streup—V.L. ESTRĘOPU > O.F. *estrieu*; cf. § 44 *a*), *ai* appears as *a* (waidanjan—V.L. GUADANJARE > *gaaignier* > *gagner*); for details see Schwan-Behrens, § 30. In later borrowings from German, *h* continues to be rendered by *ʻh* (*halbran*), *ie* (= i) is rendered by *je* (*bière*), *oe* (= ö) by *oe* in written borrowings (*Goethe*, now pronounced *göt*, formerly rimed with *poète*). Borrowings from English are rendered variously according to the method of transmission and the influence of the written word: *u* is rendered by *ö* or *o* in earlier (oral) borrowings (*club*; see above), but by *ü* in later (written) borrowings (*jury*); *ʻ-er* appears as *-re* in early *cotre* (cutter), as *-ęr* in late *ulster*; *ow* appears as *ou* (= u) in both early and late borrowings (*bouline, boulingrin*; *out!* at lawn-tennis). Italian *c* (= tš) appears as *s*, suggesting Piedmontese provenance, in *céleri, fantassin*, but as *š* in *chiffre, chiourme, polichinelle*; *š* for Italian *ch* (= k) in *niche* (nicchia) indicates a literary borrowing, the *k* of *Michel Ange* is due to Learned influence; *u* appears as *ou* (= u) in *bravoure, coupole*, but as *ü* in *buste, costume*. Spanish *ch* (= tš) appears as *š* (*chocolat*). *j* (= χ) is variously rendered, partly in accord with the evolution of this consonant in Spanish, partly under the influence of spelling: by *ž* or *š* in 16th–17th c. *jonquille, Quichotte*; by *k* in 18th c *kérès* (Jerez), sometimes by uvular ʀ in later borrowings, *Rota* (Jota) (according to Dauzat, p. 183); *z* (= t)—*s* (cigarro—*cigare*), *b* (= ḅ)—*b* (zarabanda—*sarabande*), *d* (= ḍ)—*d* (parada—*parade*), *an*—*ã* (romance—*romance*), final *a*—*ə* (patata—*patate*).

Combinations of sounds which are foreign to French are generally simplified (*bifteck, rosbif, paquebot* for packet-boat, *fifre* for Germ. pfife), or a difficult group is broken up by the intercalation of a glide-vowel: Anglo-Saxon wræc > *varech*, Franconian hnapp > *hanap*, Germ. halskragen > *hallecrète*, landsknecht > *lansquenet*. The accentuation of literary borrowings is generally modified in accordance with French linguistic habits: *revolver, ulster, pamphlet*; *adagio, macaroni, incognito, opéra*; *alpaca*; *blocus* (blochuus). But this applies also to many oral borrowings, even very early borrowings:

they are given a French intonation. The following show the normal treatment of oral borrowings: *cotre* (cutter), *page* (paggio), *parapet* (parapetto), *frichti* (frühstück), *reître* (reiter), *obus* (haubitze). Sometimes the written form later reacts on the spoken: *quacre* (quaker) replaced by *quaker*, 14th c. *gondre* (góndola) replaced by 16th c. *gondole*.

519. Among the disturbing factors which produce hesitation, and sometimes a new pronunciation, the chief is the knowledge of the foreign tongue (not always perfect) possessed by a section of the population. This more cultured section will often endeavour to keep as near as possible to the foreign pronunciation. The rest of the population, familiar only with the word as a written word, will pronounce more or less *à la française*. This applies particularly to modern borrowings from English: *meeting* first pronounced mẹtẽg, but in an attempt to reproduce the English pronunciation, mitĩg or mitin; *square* pronounced skwa:r and skwẹ:r; *Shakespeare* pronounced *-e-ar* in the eighteenth century, *-i:r* in the nineteenth century. Further examples of hesitation are furnished by *club*, *humour*, *rail* (raj or rẹl), *wagon*, *ulster*, *jury*, *high-life* (commonly pronounced *iglif*), *dead-heat* (which we have heard pronounced dẹadẹat). The adoption of large numbers of English words, fully adopted but keeping the English spelling, has led to the suggestion (made by Remy de Gourmont) to spell in French fashion: *boucmacaire*, *speche*, *fivocloque*; but this suggestion is hardly to be taken literally (cf. however *rosbif*, *bifteck*, and the like).

520. The adaptation of borrowed words to native habits of speech takes the form, not only of rendering foreign sounds by the nearest equivalents, but of various kinds of assimilation. The commonest is the assimilation of the ending: *redingote* (riding-coat), *boulevard* (bolwerc), *macaron* (maccherone), *huguenots* (Eidgenossen), *blocus* (blochuus), *tarentelle* (tarantella); this is sometimes merely orthographic: *dogue* (dog), *flanelle* (flannel).

Often the form of the word is modified owing to association with a native word of similar form or meaning. (*a*) Substitu-

tion of one element: blackball + *boule* > *blackbouler*, puli-
tezza + *poli* > *politesse*, terzetto + *tiers* > *tiercet*, burgmeister
+ *maistre* > *bourguemaistre* later *bourgmestre*. (*b*) Crossing of a
foreign word with a native (cf. § 19): Germ. hōh + ALTUM
> V.L. HALTU > *haut*, wesp-a + VESPA > V.L. GUESPA > *guêpe*,
wad- + VADUM > V.L. GUADU > *gué*, wōst- + VASTARE > V.L.
GUASTARE > *guaster* > *gâter*, wulf + *VULPĪCULUM > *goupil*,
widarlōn + DONUM > *guerredon*, wiper-a + VIPERA > *guivre*;
Gr.-Lat. *CATA-UNUM + QUISQUE UNUM > V.L. CASCUNU > *chascun*; Celtic *crit- + TREMERE > *criembre*, *craindre*, ordiga
+ ARTICULUM > *orteil*, marchese + O.F. *marchis* > *marquis* (cf.
§ 515). (*c*) Folk-etymology, the association in the popular
mind of a little-known word (usually foreign) with a better-
known word, with which it is fancied to have some
etymological connection: *beaucuit* (buckwheat), *contredanse*
(country-dance), *choucroute* (sūrkrūt), *hallecrète* (halskragen), *jeu de l' âne salé* (game of Aunt Sally); cf. Nyrop,
I, §§ 528–30.

C. *WORD-FORMATION*[1]

DERIVATION BY SUFFIX

521. Derivation by the addition of suffixes has always
been the chief source of new words. Suffixes may be defined
as particles which have lost what independent existence they
had, but can be detached from words in which they occur
and joined to other words or stems of words. So long as
suffixes are capable of being thus extended by analogy they
are said to be productive. In the course of time a suffix may
cease to be productive either because it ceases to be recognized as a suffix, e.g. -ŬLUM (CINGULA > *sangle*) which continued to form new derivatives only in Italy; or because other
forms of derivation are preferred. Suffixes are added to
substantives, adjectives or verbs in order to modify their
meaning by adding a new (secondary) meaning. The latter

[1] Cf. Nyrop, III, and Darmesteter, *Cours*, III. Most of the examples in
the following pages (306–19) are taken from these two works.

does not always remain constant. A suffix which has become unproductive may also cease to convey any such secondary meaning, particularly if the simple word has dropped out of use, e.g. *-as* in *frimas* (< Germ. *hrīm- + -ACEUM); or in *plâtras* beside *plâtre*.

522. Most of the suffixes employed in French have been inherited (Popular) or borrowed (Learned) from Latin. A few have been borrowed from other languages. A further series of suffixes has been developed in French by a modification in the form of inherited or borrowed suffixes. Such secondary formations often result from a wrong analysis, the final consonant or vowel or syllable of the stem being interpreted as part of the suffix; e.g. on the basis of *chevalerie*, etc., interpreted as *cheval-erie*, *-erie* has been added to other words (*diablerie*). A secondary suffix may result from the combination of two primary suffixes: *-onner*, *-iller*, *-icisme*, *-erot*.

523. Contamination and substitution of one suffix for another are extremely common: *-ation* for *-aison*, *-ier* for *-er*, *-ade* for *-ée*, *-ail* for *-al* (see below). Phonetic change has often caused two or more suffixes to fall together, in which case purely orthographic change is common: *cadenas* for *cadenat*, *hautain* for *hautin*, *brelan* for *brelanc*, *filet* for *filé*. The final syllable of a word may be wrongly interpreted as a suffix and its form modified accordingly: *allemand*, O.F. *alemant* for older *aleman*. The final syllable of borrowed words is particularly subject to this form of assimilation: *abricot* (Sp. albaricoque), *falot* (It. falò) 'lantern'; cf. § 520.

524. Suffixes may be classified under the headings Verbal and Nominal, according as they serve to form verbs or nouns (substantives and adjectives). Of the Nominal suffixes some are both substantival and adjectival, others have in the course of time changed from substantival to adjectival or vice versa.

VERBAL SUFFIXES

New verbs are formed in French by the addition of the verbal suffixes *-er* and *-ir*. The former, which continues to be productive, often appears in enlarged forms presenting either (*a*) the addition of a consonant (*-der, -ter*: *bazarder, numéroter*), or (*b*) that of a nominal suffix (*-asser, -eter, -onner, -oter*: *écrivasser, marqueter, mâchonner, tapoter*), or (*c*) the continuation of a Latin enlarged form: *-ailler* (< -ACŬLARE): *tirailler*; *-oyer, -ayer, -eyer* (< Gr.-Lat. -IZARE, also < -ECARE, -EGARE, -ĬCARE, -ĬGARE): *guerroyer, plaidoyer, nettoyer, charroyer, bégayer, grasseyer*; *-eler* (< -ĬLLARE): *denteler*; *-iller* (< -ICŬLARE): *sautiller*; *-iner* (< -INARE): *trottiner*; *-ouiller* (< -UCŬLARE): *bredouiller*; Learned *-(i)fier* (-(I)FICARE): *personnifier*; Learned *-iser* (Gr.-Lat. -IZARE): *américaniser*.

The suffix *-ir* was fairly productive in the medieval period and gradually displaced *-er* for the formation of verbs from adjectives (cf. § 290), but it is now practically unproductive.

NOMINAL SUFFIXES

525. The following list comprises suffixes which have remained productive throughout. For convenience the secondary suffixes of French formation are added, without any attempt at fixing the date of their appearance.

-able (< -ABILEM, itself an enlarged form of -BILEM and generalized at the expense of -IBILEM in the pre-literary period: *croyable*, O.F. *creable* for CREDIBILEM) is one of the most productive suffixes in French. In the modern period it can have only a passive meaning (*supportable*), but a number of older formations with active meaning have survived (*redevable*).

-age (< -ATICUM), extremely productive in the earlier periods (*sauvage, voyage*), is now less productive and added only to verbal stems (*blanchissage, chauffage*) to denote the action or the result. Secondary: *-tage* (*agiotage*).

-aille (< -ALIA n.pl. of -ALIS), generally collective (*broussaille, épousailles*), but readily assumes pejorative meaning, which predominates in modern formations (*ferraille*); but cf. *trouvaille*.

-ais (< -ENSEM), used to form adjectives from place-names (*bordelais, irlandais*). A collateral form is *-ois* (cf. §§ 72–3).

-asse (< -ACEA), formerly *-ace*; originally augmentative (*milliasse*), but now generally pejorative (*paperasse*).

-e (< -A), frequently added to proper names to indicate objects connected with a place or person (*berline, guillotine, mansarde*).

-é (< -ATUM) was used as a substantival suffix to denote a dignity or office (*duché, archevêché*), but is much more productive as an adjectival suffix (*cuivré*).

-ée (< -ATA) has been used to form a wide range of derivatives, generally collective and used to denote quantity, duration and the like (*bouchée, année, journée*).

-eau (O.F. *-el*), *-elle* (< -ELLUM, -ELLA, extended in V.L. at the expense of -ULUM, -ILLUM, etc.). It has as a rule lost its original diminutive meaning (*chevreau*) and is not recognized as a suffix in many words (*taureau, prunelle*). Secondary: *-ereau* (*hobereau* from *hobe* 'hobby-hawk'; *sauterelle*).

-el (< -ALEM), formerly much used, but has gradually given ground before its Learned doublet *-al*, with which it formerly alternated in many words (*temporel, -al*, etc.), whence, with differentiation of meaning, *journel—journal, originel—original, partiel—partial*. Secondary: *-iel* (*torrentiel*).

-ement (< -AMENTUM, an enlarged form, with A from -ARE stems, which was extended in pre-literary times at the expense of -IMENTUM), extremely productive in Mod.F. of substantives indicating the action or the object of the action denoted by the verb from which they are derived (*avènement, battement*). Many older forms have fallen into disuse (*acordement, naissement*).

-et, -ette (< -ĬTTUM, -ĬTTA) has become the most favoured diminutive suffix, although in some derivatives the diminutive force has in time been effaced (*feuillet, mulet, alouette, serviette*). Secondary: *-elet* (*gantelet*), *-iquet* (*tourniquet*); also *-eton, -etel, -eteau*.

-(e)eur (< -(AT)OREM) has remained very productive of substantives denoting the agent of the action (*vainqueur*) and is in Mod.F. also added to nouns (*chroniqueur*). Secondary: *-teur* (*agioteur*).

-eux, -euse (< -OSUM, -OSA), particularly productive in the sixteenth century (*estoilleux, perleux*, etc.) and continues to

form adjectives denoting quality and abundance (*courageux, boueux*). The feminine form is common in Mod.F. names of machines (*moissonneuse*). Secondary: *-teux* (*caillouteux*), *-ueux* (*majestueux*).

526. *-ien* (< -ANUM preceded by a palatal: PAGANUM > *paiien* > *païen*) is productive of many new forms (*paroissien, parisien*).

-ier, *-ière* (< -ARIUM, -ARIA), one of the most productive suffixes. Substantives in *-ier* denote the person connected in some way (maker, seller, etc.) with the object denoted by the root-word (*bijoutier, fermier, gantier, hôtelier, rentier*) and the tree producing the fruit or flower denoted by the root-word (*pommier, rosier*). Another meaning, which also dates from Latin, is that of a receptacle and the like (*grenier, théière, pépinière*). Adjectives in *-ier* denote the quality associated with or denoted by the root-word (*coutumier, dépensier, princier*). In many words *-ier* has been substituted for earlier *-er* (*bachelier, sanglier, soulier*), but has itself been reduced to *-er* after *š, ž, l', n'* (*porcher, étranger*). Secondary: *-dier* (*boyaudier*), *-tier* (*bijoutier*); *-yer* is an alternative spelling employed after vowels (*écuyer* < SCUTARIUM); §§ 75, 319.

-ille (< -ĪCULA). The original diminutive force has often been obliterated: *cheville* (< CLAVICULA), *charmille, béquille*.

-in (< -ĪNUM), originally diminutive and sparingly used, but has come to be used extensively and with a variety of meanings (adjectives denoting origin, matter; substantives denoting persons and objects): *limousin, argentin, galopin, moulin*. *-ine* serves as the feminine of *-in* (*limousine*) and as an independent suffix (*routine*). Secondary: *-tin* (*tableautin*), *-elin* (*gosselin*).

-oir, *-oire* (< -ORIUM, -ORIA) denotes receptacle, place, instrument (*tiroir, trottoir, assommoir, balançoire*).

-ois (< -ENSEM), used to form adjectives of nationality and the like; these may of course be used substantivally (*suédois, villageois, courtois, bourgeois*); cf. *-ais*.

-u (< -ŪTUM), commonly used to form adjectives of the type *pointu*.

-(e)ure (< -(AT)URA), used to form collective and abstract substantives (*chevelure, droiture*), and often denotes the result of the action (*blessure*).

527. The following nominal suffixes have in Mod.F. come to be used sparingly or not at all. In some cases the secondary form has continued to be productive at the expense of the primary.

-aie (< -ĒTA) forms substantives denoting plantations (*chênaie*). Secondary: *-eraie* (*pineraie*). Cf. §§ 72-3.

-ail (< -ACULUM or -ALIUM): *attirail, soupirail.*

-ain, -aine (< -ANUM, -ANA), formerly very productive (*vilain, lointain, châtelain*) and used to form collective numerals (*huitain, douzaine, centaine*). Cf. § 222.

-aison (< -ATIONEM), gradually crowded out by its Learned doublet *-ation* (*comparaison, liaison*; but *dérivation* for older *derivaison*).

-ance (< -ANTIA), generalized in the pre-literary period at the expense of -ENTIA; formerly very productive (*naissance*), but now practically evicted by the Learned *-ence*.

-er (< -AREM) has been replaced by *-ier* (O.F. *bacheler, sangler, souler*).

-esse (< L.L. -ISSA < Gr. -ισσα): *abbesse*; or (< -ĬTIA): *finesse.*

-ie (< L.L. -ÍA for '-IA under the influence of Gr. -ία), formerly very productive (*jalousie, compagnie, Normandie*), but now displaced by the secondary forms *-erie* (*diablerie, orfèvrerie*) or *-terie* (*bijouterie*).

-is, O.F. *iz* (< -ĪCIUM): *châssis.*

-ise (< -ĪTIA?): *fainéantise.*

-ison (< -ĪTIONEM): *garnison.*

-oison (< -OTIONEM): *pâmoison.*

-on (< -ONEM) has produced many substantives and adjectives, often with a diminutive meaning (*dindon, vallon*). Secondary: *-eron* (*bûcheron*), *-ichon* (*cornichon*), *-illon* (*cotillon*).

-ot (< -OTTUM), still productive but much less so than formerly (*cachot, manchot*). The original diminutive meaning has sometimes given place to a depreciatory meaning (*vieillot*) or has been effaced (*fagot*). As a suffix of endear-

ment it has often been added to proper names (*Pierrot, Margot*). *-otte* serves as the feminine of *-ot* and also as an independent suffix (*calotte*). Secondary: *-elot* (*angelot*), *-illot* (*maigrillot*).

-té (< -ITATEM): *bonté, fierté*; generally replaced by *-ete* (*fermeté* for O.F. *ferté*; *sûreté*) or the Learned *-ité* (*vérité* for O.F. *verté*). Secondary: *-auté* (*privauté*).

528. Other less productive suffixes are: *-agne* (< -ANEA n.pl. of -ANEUS): *champagne*; *-ange* for older *-enge* (< -EMIA): *vendange, louange, vidange*; *-as*, O.F. *-az* (< -ACEUM): *frimas, plâtras*; *-âtre* (< -ASTRUM), used to form adjectives of the type *grisâtre* and substantives with a pejorative meaning (*marâtre*); *-euil* (< -OCULUM or -OLIUM): *bouvreuil*; *-eul* (< -IOLUM): *filleul*; *-if* (< -ĪVUM): *sportif*; *-il* (< -ĪLE): *fournil* or (< -ĪCULUM): *grésil*. With the exception of *-âtre, -if, -il*, this group of suffixes are now unproductive.

529. The most commonly used Learned suffixes are: *-ique* (Gr.-Lat. -ĪCUM): *vocalique*; *-isme* (Gr.-Lat. -ISMUM): *romantisme, bolchévisme*; *-iste* (Gr.-Lat. -ISTA): *humaniste, bolchéviste*; *-ité* (-ITATEM): *banalité*. The following are less prolific: *-aire* (-ARIUM): *annuaire, humanitaire*; *-al* (-ALEM): *banal, gouvernemental*; *-at* (-ATUM): *électorat, externat, assassinat*; *-ateur* (-ATOREM): *accélérateur*; *-ation* (-ATIONEM): *centralisation*; *-ite* (-ῖτις): *bronchite, méningite*; *-ose* (-ωσις): *gastrose, névrose*; the two last-mentioned being extensively used for the creation of technical terms.

FOREIGN SUFFIXES

530. *-ade* is found in many words borrowed from Provençal, Italian, and Spanish (§§ 515–18). From the sixteenth century onwards it has become productive of a large number of substantives (*fusillade*), sometimes with a pejorative meaning (*gasconnade*).

-ais (*-ois*) (< Germ. -isk + Gr.-Lat. -ISCUM): frankisk + FRANCISCUM > *franceis* > *François* and *français*; FRANCISCA > O.F. *francesche*, early supplanted by the analogical fem. *franceise* > *Françoise* and *française*. Cf. §§ 72–3.

-art (< Germ. -h a r t), fem. *-arde*, whence by analogy the spelling *-ard* for *-art* (*Renart, campagnard, canard*) ; has gradually developed a pejorative meaning (*richard*).

-aut, O.F. *-alt* (< Germ. -h a l t), fem. *aude*, O.F. *-alde*, whence the spelling *-aud* (*Arnaud, Michaut, héraut, crapaud*) ; is generally pejorative (*ribaud, nigaud*).

-enc (-i n g) found in Germanic loan-words (*chambrelenc, Flamenc, Loherenc*) and used to form a few O.F. words (*gardenc* 'guardian'), but early confused with the more common *-an*(*t*), *-ain*, *-ien* (*chambellan, flamand, lorrain, gardien*).

531. The addition of a suffix generally leaves the form of the stem unaffected (*fruit—fruitier*), but, once constituted, the derivative may evolve in such a way as to bring about a deviation from the simple word (*lièvre—levrette, oisif—oisiveté, frein—effréné*). Analogical influences are here particularly potent, and the regular phonetic evolution of the derivative may be retarded or checked under the influence of the simple word (*chevalier* < CABALLARIUM has been influenced by *cheval*) or it may be re-modelled (*fierté* for O.F. *ferté* ≠ *fier*). On the other hand, apophony regularly subsisting between such forms as *lièvre—levrette, arc—arceau* may be introduced into new derivatives (*levraud, jonc—joncer*) formed after the sound-law which produced the apophony has ceased to operate. It is therefore very hazardous to attempt the dating of derivatives on purely phonetic grounds.

Other adaptations consist in the elimination of the final consonant (*faubourg—faubourien*), vowel (*Canada—canadien*) or syllable (*Thomas—thomiste, violet—violâtre*), in the intercalation or substitution of a consonant (*rein—éreinter; tabac—tabatière*) ; cf. also the adaptation in such words as *inamovibilité* from *inamovible*. Sometimes the change is purely graphic (*république—républicain, long—longueur*). Forms derived from verbs are based on the stem of the present (*blanchir—blanchissage, recevoir—receveur*).

FORMATION BY PREFIX

532. Prefixes are employed indifferently for the formation of verbs and nouns, with the exception of a few (*avant-*, *plus-*, *sans-*, *vi-*) which are used only for nouns. The formation of new verbs by the addition of a prefix was already extremely common in Latin[1] and has continued. The creation of new nouns was accelerated by the breakdown of the flexional system. All prefixes were originally adverbs or prepositions. Many, such as RE-, had ceased to be used as independent particles in Latin; others have since ceased to function as such (BIS, EX, PRAE, etc.), while a certain number still fulfil both functions (*avant*, *plus*, *sans*, etc.). It is consequently difficult to maintain a rigid distinction between derivation by prefix and composition. The same prefix may be used syntactically with prepositional force (*contre-sens*, i.e. against common sense) or merely juxtaposed with adverbial force (*contre-coup*, i.e. a blow against).

533. The prefixes employed by French are nearly all of Latin origin. Many of the C.L. prefixes fell into disuse, and, as the need for new prefixes arose, adverbs and prepositions were pressed into service: *avant* (*avant-coureur*, *avant-dernier*), *mé(s)* < MINUS (*mésaventure*, *méconnaître*), *non* (*non-sens*, *nonchalant*), *for(s)* < FORIS (*forclore*, *formariage*);[2] *en* (< INDE) was very extensively used in O.F. with verbs of movement to indicate the point of departure; but this notion is in many cases practically obliterated, and *en* tends to become a mere particle: *s'enfuir*, *s'ensuivre* (used only in the 3rd pers.), *s'envoler* show complete fusion in Mod.F.; orthography and grammar maintain *s'en aller* (*Il s'en est allé*), but in popular speech the tendency is to treat *en aller* as a single word (*Il s'est en allé*); cf. *Quand s'est-il en allé?* (Musset) and other

---

[1] Cf. §§ 22 (*d*), 285.

[2] *for(s)* has absorbed the German prefix *fur-* (Mod. Germ. *ver-*), which may be postulated for such forms as *forfaire* (*forfait*, *forfaiture*), *forboire* (*forbu*, *fourbu*), *forvêtu*; cf. Germ. *vertun*, *vertrinken*, *verkleidet*. On the other hand, *for* = Germ. *vor* in O.F. *forborc*, later *forsbourg* and by popular etymology *fau(x)bourg*. For *més-*, cf. Bloch, *Dict*

examples cited by Nyrop, III, 474. Alternatively, Learned prefixes were borrowed (§ 536).

534. Learned reaction and the influence of Learned words has frequently resulted in the re-modelling of Popular prefixes or their replacement by the collateral Learned form (see below). In some cases the re-modelling affected in the first place spelling and was subsequently carried into pronunciation (*adjuger* for O.F. *ajugier*, *absoudre* for O.F. *asoudre*). Other substitutions are less common than in the case of suffixes: *accorder* (CONCORDARE), *allumer* (ILLUMINARE), *arracher* for O.F. *esrachier*. The prefix is sometimes added to a form which is already compound: *accueillir* (AD + COLLIGERE), *rasseoir*, *parachever*.

POPULAR PREFIXES

535. *a-* (< AD-). Under Learned influence *d* has often been restored or the following consonant doubled (*acompte*, but *adjuger*, *apporter*).

bé(s)- (< BIS-) has not remained productive and has been replaced by Learned *bis-* in *bisaïeul*, *biscuit* (cf. *becuis*, XI, 36); found in *bévue*.

dé- (*dés-* before vowel) (< DIS-): *détourner*, *désordre*; sometimes replaced in Mod.F. by Learned *dis-* (*discordance*).

é-, O.F. *es-* (< EX-): *échanger*; sometimes replaced by Learned *ex-*: *exploiter* (for O.F. *esploitier*), *extraire* (for O.F. *estraire*), which gives many modern formations, as in English (*ex-roi*).

en- (*em-* before labial) (< IN-, IM-): *entrain*, *embattre*. For *en-* (< INDE), see above.

entre- (< INTER-) with a variety of meanings: *s'entr'aider*, *entrelacer*, *entrevoir*; often replaced by Learned *inter-* (*intervenir*).

mal-, *mau-* (< MALE-): *malaise*; *l* has generally been restored before consonants: *maltraiter*, *maldisant*; but cf. *maudire*.

outre- (< ULTRA-), rarely used (*outrecuidant*, *outremer*), whereas the Learned *ultra-* has of late become excessively common (*ultra-royaliste*, *ultra-violet*).

par- (< PER-): *parfaire, pardessus*; as an intensive particle it was separable in O.F. (*Moult par est fols*).

pour- (< PRO-): *pourparler, poursuivre*. Learned reaction pro duced hesitation in the sixteenth and seventeenth centuries between *pour-* and the Learned *pro-* (or *prou-*): *prouvoir*, etc.; the latter has triumphed in *promener, profil, profit* (cf. XII, 14).

re- (< RE-). In O.F. *re-* was still separable and was often prefixed to the auxiliary verb in compound tenses or to modal verbs: *nem revueil encombrer* (Alexis, 188); *Et les dames se resont mises* (G. de Dole, 287); *Or vous reveut paier* (Rutebeuf, *Théophile*, 315). Before a vowel *re-* is regularly elided (*rappeler, rhabiller, rouvrir*), but in new formations the Learned form *ré-* is often employed (*réagir, réélire, réactif*) and has sometimes displaced older *r* (*réarmer* for O.F. *rarmer*). If the root-word begins with *s*, the unvoiced sound is preserved and denoted in spelling by *ss* (*ressentir, ressembler*). *re-* conveys a variety of meanings, such as repetition (*redire*), whence the idea of thoroughness, completeness (*rechercher, ressentir*), return or restoration (*revenir, retourner, regagner, rétablir*). In O.F. it often serves to stress the contrast or comparison of two persons performing the same action or different actions: *Or me reconseilliez dou mien* 'now do you in your turn counsel me [as I have counselled you]'; cf. VI, 7.

sans- (< SINE): *sans-gêne*.

sou(s)- (< SUBTUS): *soulever, sous-officier*. The Learned prefix *sub-* has replaced *sous-* in *subdiviser*.

sur- (< SUPER-): *surcharger, surabondant*. The Learned form of this prefix is common in commercial jargon (*super-fin*).

tre(s)- (< TRANS-): *trépasser, tressaillir*. Learned form *trans-*: *transatlantique*.

vi-, O.F. *vis-* (< VICE-): *vicomte, vidame*. Learned form *vice-*: *vice-président*.

LEARNED PREFIXES

536. In addition to those already mentioned, the following Learned prefixes have been the most productive of new formations (quite apart from their prevalence in borrowed words):

anté- (*anténuptial*, *antéchambre* replaced by *antichambre*); *anti-* (*anti-républicain*); *archi-*, much favoured in familiar language (*archi-bon*); *com-*, *con-*, *co-* (*complaire*, *convenir*, *coreligionnaire*); *extra-* (*extra-légal*), common in commercial language (*extra-fin*); *in-* with assimilation before consonant (*inautorisé*, *illisible*, *imperméable*, *irréprochable*; *infiltrer*, *incruster*); *post-* (*postdater*); *pré-* (*prédisposer*); *quasi-* (*quasi-mort*).

PARASYNTHETIC FORMATIONS

537. Many new formations, called parasynthetic, result from the addition of a prefix and at the same time of a suffix. They are for the most part verbs: *a-bord-er*, *contre-rôle-er* > *contrôler* (formerly *contrerôler*), *for-sen*(Germ. **sinn**)-*er*, O.F. *forsener* whence *forcené*, *détacher*, *enivrer*; *encolure*, *souterrain*.

BACK-FORMATIONS

538. Back-formations consist in the elimination of a prefix or suffix, or of a syllable which is regarded as such (*diplomate* from *diplomatie* and *diplomatique*). The commonest type is that which consists in the dropping of the verbal ending (post-verbal formation). Such verbal substantives usually denote the action (*combat*) or its result (*pli*, *amas*), less frequently the agent (*garde*) or the instrument (*presse*).

The older formations are as a rule masculine and show the accented form of the stem (*appui*, *maintien*, *relief*, *espoir*, *pleur*). Modern formations are nearly always derived from -*er* verbs, end in -*e*, and are feminine (*recherche*, *demande*). Many verbal substantives have gone out of use, being replaced by other derivatives: *consulte* by *consultation*, *proteste* by *protestation*, *trompe* by *tromperie*.

COMPOSITION

The formation of a new word by the linking of two full words (not merely stems) was rare in Latin but was freely developed in the Romance languages. Except in the earliest formations, the component words remain phonetically intact, only the meaning and accentuation indicating that they are compounds.

539. The two elements may be co-ordinate and are found in the following combinations:

Subst. + subst., one (usually the second) qualifying the other; rare in Latin (ARCU BALLISTA > *arbalète*), more common in French (*commis-voyageur, chou-fleur; maître-autel, chef-lieu*).

Subst. + adj. The place of the adjective varies and sometimes reflects changing usage; not very common in Latin (RESPUBLICA), but developed in Romance (*DIA DOMINICA > *dimanche*, ALBA SPINA > *aubépine*, PRIMA VERA > O.F. *primevoire*, AVIS TARDA > *outarde*) and relatively common in French (*basse-cour, gentilhomme, malaise, printemps, bonjour, moyen âge; amour-propre, vinaigre, fait divers*).

Poss. pron. + subst.: *monsieur, messire, monseigneur, madame, mademoiselle, Notre-Dame.*

Adj. + adj.: *clair-obscur, gris-pommelé, ivre-mort.*

540. One element may be subordinate to the other in the following combinations:

Subst. + subst. In Latin the qualifying substantive stood in the genitive (AURI FABER > *orfèvre*, LUNAE DIEM > *lundi*, etc., cf. § 173). With the reduction of the cases to two, the rôle of the genitive was taken over by the oblique case, whence such O.F. formations as *chiendent, hôtel-Dieu*. After the breakdown of the two-case system such compounds become rare, and they are to be considered as imitations (*timbre-poste*, cf. § 209).

Subst. + prep. + subst. or inf. This type is extremely common in French (*gendarme, chef-d'œuvre, boîte aux lettres, char-à-bancs, salle à manger, arc-en-ciel, bachelier ès lettres, tabac à priser*).

Verb + subst. Compounds of the type AGRICOLA, in which the stem of the substantive and the stem of the verb are juxtaposed, became rare in later Latin and gave place to formations consisting of the imperative of the verb + subst. (or infinitive used substantivally): *cache-nez, garde-manger*. Such compounds were much favoured by sixteenth-century writers, but the majority of their creations have perished (*casse-loix*, *dompte-ennui*, *porte-laine*). Other parts of the verb are rarely used (*lieutenant*).

Other compounds consist of phrases, such as (*un homme*), *comme il faut*, (*des*) *on dit*, (*le*) *qu'en dira-t-on*, (*un*) *sauve qui peut*, (*un*) *je ne sais quoi*.

DERIVATION BY CHANGE OF FUNCTION

One may distinguish two types:

541. (*a*) The change of function results from ellipsis. This is generally the case when adjectives come to be used as substantives: FONTANA (AQUA) >*fontaine*, HIBERNUM (TEMPUS) > *hiver*, SINGULARIS (PORCUS) > *sanglier*, FICATUM (JECUR) 'liver of a goose fattened with figs' >*foie*, ALBA (VESTIS) > *aube* 'alb', ALBA (DIES) > *aube* 'dawn', none of which survive as adjectives in French. Similarly (*ville*) *capitale*, (*vêtement*) *complet*, *première* (*représentation*), (*train*) *rapide*, *un* (*homme*) *pauvre*, *riche*, *saint*, *malade*, etc.

542. (*b*) One part of speech used for another. This is extremely common, and we have already observed the readiness with which the particles (adverbs, prepositions, conjunctions) pass from one category to another. The substantival use of the various parts of speech, to which the article is simply prefixed, presents many varieties. Leaving aside the purely occasional changes of function (*le moi*, *le pourquoi*), the following chief types may be distinguished:

Subst. used as adj. (*une robe marron*, *un homme colère*), rarely as pron. (*on* < HOMO), as adv. (*se lever matin*), as interj. (*peste!*). Note also the use of proper names as common nouns: *dinde* < (*coq*) *d'Inde*, O.F. *ladre* < *Lazarus*.

Adj. used as subst. (*le droit*), as adv. (*sentir bon*; cf. § 212).

Adv. as adj. (*prêt* < PRAESTO, *un homme debout*), as subst. (*le bien*, *les biens*, *le mal*, *les maux*).

For change of function between particles, see §§ 442–82.

Verb. For the substantival use of the infinitive, see § 295. All participles can be used as adjectives (§§ 305, 372) and like ordinary adjectives, are often used substantivally (*un fiancé—une fiancée, un écrit, une saillie*; *un amant—une amante, le croissant, la variante*; cf. also *savant* beside *sachant*, *puissant* beside *pouvant*, §§ 302–3). The imperative is often used as an interjection (*voici, voilà, tiens*). Other parts of the verb are rarely used with change of function: *soit* as an interjection or conjunction; *le doit* 'debit' (cf. also the Learned forms *débit, crédit, déficit*); O.F. *espoir* (1st sing. pres. ind. of *esperer*) was used as an adverb with the meaning 'perhaps'.

D. *CHANGE OF MEANING*[1]

543. We have defined a word as a sound or group of sounds recognized as a unit in virtue of the meaning it conveys. A word does not describe an object or an idea. It is a symbol which evokes the notion of the object or idea, and it is generally charged with the function of evoking a series of notions. The hearer is guided in the interpretation of the symbol by the context and by various auxiliary devices. In speech-activity the point of departure is the notion. To render the notion of a new object or a new idea, or new varieties or aspects of them, a language has recourse to two devices: (*a*) it may create or borrow a new word (§§ 494–542), or (*b*) it may charge an existing word with the function of conveying the new meaning. In the same way a language may abandon the traditional symbol of an object or idea in favour of another which is felt to be more expressive, more precise, more fashionable, more acceptable for a variety of reasons (considerations of taste, feeling, etc.).

544. Considering the question from the formal point of view of the symbol (word) employed, we therefore find that the number of notions the word conveys may be increased (extension of meaning) or decreased (restriction of meaning), or increased in one direction and decreased in another (shifting of meaning). The number of notions it conveys may

[1] In addition to the works mentioned in the Bibliography, cf. Nyrop, IV, and Dauzat, *Histoire*, pp. 244–77.

vary, not only in time, but as between different sections of the community (specialization of meaning). The extension of meaning may be carried to such a point that the word is overburdened, and it becomes necessary to transfer some of its meanings; otherwise, being overworked, it dies. The restriction of meaning may reduce it to the rôle of a mere particle or it may be lost entirely. The specialization as between different classes of the community may remain constant, or there may be in special languages (technical and regional) survival of words or meanings which have been abandoned by the standard language, or again, the specialized meaning may find its way into standard usage.

545. Changes in meaning may result from changes in the object itself, in the mental and moral attitude of those who speak the language (the setting up of finer distinctions, etc.) and the conditions in which they live (political and social factors), or from various associative influences (influence of form on meaning, etc.). We must distinguish between such factors, which make a change of meaning desirable or necessary, and the logical processes involved in the attribution of a new meaning to a word or the elimination of an old one. The latter represent a modification in the normal connection between the notion (the thing denoted) and the symbol (word), e.g. a word may be utilized to evoke, not merely the primary or traditional notion, but other notions which stand in some sort of logical connection or present some analogy with the primary notion. Thus the notion of a concrete object is associated with the notion of the abstract idea, and the word denoting the latter may be used to denote the former (*potence*; cf. § 549). The word may continue to evoke the primary notion as well as the secondary, or it may cease to evoke the primary; e.g. *chef* (CAPUT) no longer evokes the primary notion 'head'. These processes have been classified by grammarians under the following headings: Synecdoche, extension or restriction of acceptation whereby the name of the part stands for the whole, or that of the whole for the part; Metonymy, change of acceptation whereby a notion is denoted by a word which normally denotes another notion, the two standing in some constant relation with each other (cause and effect, etc.); Metaphor, change of acceptation whereby a notion is denoted by a word which normally denotes another notion, the two having some trait in common which allows of their being associated or compared.

SYNECDOCHE AND METONYMY

546. Genus for species: *bâtiment*, in the sense of 'ship'; *jument* (originally a beast of burden), in the sense of 'mare'; *viande* (< VIVENDA), originally and still in the seventeenth century denoted 'food in general'; *flotte* down to the sixteenth century denoted 'an assemblage of persons or objects', whence 'army', 'armament', cf. § 576; *mousse*, borrowed in the fifteenth century from Sp. mozo or It. mozzo, but early restricted to 'cabin-boy'; *courage* (< *COR-ATICUM) continued to be used as late as the seventeenth century in the original sense of 'mood', 'disposition'; *ouvrer* (< OPERARE), now restricted to the meaning 'to fashion', 'to make up' (*ouvrer du bois, du linge*); *traire* and *labourer*, used throughout the Middle Ages in the general sense 'to draw', 'to work' respectively; *converser*, still commonly used in the eighteenth century in the medieval sense of 'to sojourn', 'to associate with'.

Species for genus: *homme* for 'Man', *chrétien* for 'man'; *gagner*, O.F. *gaaignier* (Germ. waidanjan), originally 'to go hunting', 'to go in search of sustenance', shows at the same time metonymy of cause and effect.

Proper name for common noun: *un tartufe, un suisse, un bohémien, un assassin* (originally the name of the followers of the Old Man of the Mountain, famous in medieval lore); *renard* (Germ. Reginhart), as the proper name of the fox in the famous *Roman de Renart*, came to replace the common noun *goupil* (cf. § 520).

Common noun becomes proper name: *Champagne* (= *campagne*), *La Ferté* (O.F. *ferté* 'stronghold'), *Lefèvre* or *Le Fèvre* (< FABER), *Molière, Racine, Corneille, La Fontaine*, etc.

547. Whole for the part: *tableau* for the painting on it; *hermine* for the fur of that animal.

Part for the whole: *une mauvaise langue, un rouge-gorge, drapeau* (dim. of *drap*) for the whole standard.

Container for contents: *boire un verre; la ville se souleva; la Chambre a été élue; la cour* (< COHORTEM), originally 'enclosed space', whence 'rural property', then 'royal domain', 'residence', 'court', and by extension, 'the persons composing the court'.

Contents for container: *collège* (COLLEGIUM), extended to denote the building which houses it; *dépôt* (< DEPOSITUM) 'the thing deposited', extended to 'the place where it is deposited'.

Material for the manufactured article: *verre*, extended to mean 'drinking-glass', 'watch-crystal', 'lens', etc.; *bonnet* originally denoted a kind of material, but as early as the thirteenth century it seems to have been used to denote the article.

Place of origin or producer for the product: *du bordeaux, du camembert, un terre-neuve.*

548. Cause or agent for effect or result: *timbre* (TYMPANUM) 'bell', whence 'sound produced by bell'; *secourir* (SUCCUR-RERE) 'to run towards', then 'to hasten to one's aid', finally 'to aid'. The reverse is less common: *parfum*, extended to denote the preparation; *araignée* originally denoted the web of the spider (O.F. *araigne*), but began to denote the spider as early as the fifteenth century; the meaning 'web' is still found in La Fontaine; *les pâles maladies* 'illnesses causing paleness'; *goddam* (or *goddem, godon*), name applied to the English soldiery at the time of the Hundred Years' War after their favourite oath.

The action for (*a*) the person performing it or the object to which it is attributed: *garde, manœuvre, entourage, suite, témoin* (< TESTIMONIUM), of which the original meaning 'testimony' survives in *en témoin de quoi*; (*b*) the object or result of the action: *amas, bâtiment* 'building', *connaissance, mélange, peinture, recueil*; (*c*) the place or circumstances of the action: *demeure, entrée, étude, marché, passage, sortie*; (*d*) a variety of notions: *batterie* has come to denote both the subject 'battery of artillery' and the object 'kitchen utensils of beaten metal', 'wall of a tennis-court', 'percussion instruments of an orchestra'; *chasse* has come to denote, on the one hand, the agent 'huntsmen' and the object which chases or urges something forward, 'powder', 'charge' and the like, and, on the other, 'game', 'preserve'; *gouvernement* 'the governing body', 'government house', 'territory governed'; *prison* (< PREHEN-SIONEM), continued to be used as an abstract noun as late as the sixteenth century, but O.F. also used *la prison* in the sense of 'prison', *le prison* in the sense of 'prisoner'.

549. Quality for the person or object possessing it, and the like: *un génie, une jeunesse* (in familiar use), *des amitiés, des honneurs, potence* (POTENTIA) 'strength', whence 'support' (abstract and concrete), 'bracket', also specialized in the sense of 'crutch', later 'gibbet'; *faveur* has derived its meaning 'ribbon' from the use of ribbons, sashes and the like as signs of a lady's favour; *jalousie*, applied to the lattice-screen, and then to a Venetian blind, as being a precautionary contrivance of the jealous husband; *discipline*, applied to the 'scourge' as the instrument of ascetic discipline.

Object for the quality associated with it: the heart being regarded as the seat of the affections and passions, *cœur* comes to be used in a variety of meanings: 'inmost thoughts', 'secret disposition', 'courage', etc.; *humeur, bile, colère* are similarly used in accordance with the ancient belief that there were in man four humours (literally fluids) upon which his character depended: blood, phlegm, yellow bile (productive of anger), black bile (productive of melancholy; cf. the subtitle of Molière's *Misanthrope*, 'L'atrabilaire amoureux'); *humeur* continued to be used in the sense of 'fluid', 'humidity' as late as the fifteenth century, but in the sixteenth it is already used in the abstract sense, and in the seventeenth it is much employed to denote 'moral character' or 'temporary disposition'; *bile* (and its synonym *colère* < CHOLERA) came to denote 'anger', 'evil temper'.

550. Object for action associated with it: *la Grève* as a proper name denoted a place on the bank of the Seine where unemployed workmen in search of work foregathered, whence *être en grève* involuntarily 'to be out of work' and thence voluntarily 'to be on strike', *la grève* coming ultimately to mean 'strike'; *toilette* 'small piece of linen placed on the dressing-table', thence by extension 'toilet-table' and ultimately 'the act of washing, dressing, etc.'; from the latter is derived the modern concrete sense of 'fine attire'; *livraison* denotes not only the act of 'delivery', but by extension the 'thing delivered' or 'an instalment'.

551. The following may serve to illustrate further how a word sometimes goes through a succession of semantic developments of the above types: *bureau* is a derivative of *bure* 'rough serge' and was specialized in the sense of 'cloth used to cover a table', thence the table itself, thence the room in which it is situated and finally all those at work in the room (cf. in English such terms as The Office of Works); *grisette* is a derivative of *gris*, and from 'a greyish colour' came to denote a 'cheap grey cloth', then a garment made of such material, and finally a girl clad in clothes of such material, etc.

METAPHOR

552. The metaphorical use of words is one of the commonest semantic developments. A metaphor is in effect a comparison, condensed and implicit. The two terms of the comparison may be concrete objects (*l'arête d'un toit, un fauteuil manchot, moucher une chandelle*), or one may be concrete, the other abstract, the commonest metaphor consisting in the investing of a concrete term with an abstract meaning: *penser* (PENSARE), originally 'to weigh'; *navrer*, originally 'to wound'; *divertir*, originally 'to turn aside'; *étiquette*, originally 'stick', then by metonymy 'a stick bearing a label', 'a label or ticket', and finally the metaphorical use as an abstract noun; *comprendre*, originally concrete 'to grasp'; *flatter*, 'to stroke with the flat of the hand', 'to caress'. The term so employed may continue to convey both notions (*étiquette*) or the primary (concrete) meaning may entirely disappear (*navrer*). In the former case the metaphor is alive, in the latter it is dead; but its demise is a gradual process, and the concrete meaning may be dimly felt even after it has ceased to be definitely expressed. One may say that it is not safe to mix metaphors until they are dead or moribund, but writers of the sixteenth and seventeenth centuries were less particular in this matter than those of the present day: *La gloire n'est due qu'à un cœur qui sait fouler aux pieds les plaisirs* (Fénelon); Molière has not failed to exploit the mixed metaphor for comic effect, but it is sometimes difficult to draw the line between his conscious and his unconscious mixing of metaphors. The following clearly belong to the first category: *Votre œil en tapinois me dérobe mon cœur. Au voleur! (Préc. Rid.* IX); *Vous avez plus de peur que de mal, et votre cœur crie avant qu'on l'écorche.—Comment diable! il est écorche depuis la tête jusqu'aux pieds (Préc. Rid.* IX).[1] The same metaphor may be alive to some and dead to others; the philologist is in such cases generally to be numbered with the former: for him the language has or should have a fuller flavour than for others.

553. The sources of metaphors are of the most divers kind and almost any concrete term may be used metaphorically, but for the metaphor to be generalized it is essential that the implicit comparison should be easily apprehended and felt to be apt. The closer the community of interests, the more daring can the metaphor be; and the smaller the general vocabulary possessed by a speech-community, the greater will be the number of metaphorical meanings attributed to current words. Hence, on the one hand, the development of many metaphorical uses in the restricted polite society of the seventeenth century, and on the other, the fondness for metaphor which characterizes the special languages of the various trades and callings, and popular speech in general (cf. the countless slang expressions for 'head', beginning with *tête* itself: *boule, citron, poire, pomme,* etc., etc.).

[1] Cf. Livet, *Lexique de Molière*, s.v. *cœur.*

554. It is hardly necessary to stress the importance of metaphor as a literary device, but literary metaphors derive their force and picturesqueness from the very fact that they are not current, have not become hackneyed and, as images, moribund. The generalization of such metaphors in current speech is the exception, while that of popular and technical metaphors is dependent only upon the familiarization of the general public with the objects and conditions which gave birth to the metaphor.

FACTORS WHICH DETERMINE CHANGES IN MEANING

555. The factors which determine semantic developments are commonly classified under the headings Historical, Psychological, and Formal; but such a division is justified only by its convenience. A full account of the factors which have been responsible for the semantic evolution of French vocabulary would mean nothing less than retracing the mental, moral, and material evolution of the French people. Not only has the meaning of words altered as the direct result of social and political changes, but the psychological and formal factors have not remained constant. For example, the demand for the setting up of finer distinctions, the penchant for euphemistic expression[1] are not peculiar to French or to any one period, and they have not operated with uniform force throughout its history, nor in the same way as in other languages. We may say that the genius of the French race has found expression in the precision of its vocabulary, the rationalistic abstract bias, the setting up of fine distinctions, etc., but it is precisely upon such features that we base our conception of the 'genius of the race'.[2] It is true that in the adaptation of the vocabulary inherited

[1] Cf. the interesting chapter on French euphemisms in Nyrop, IV, pp. 257–321.

[2] For a short but excellent appreciation of French vocabulary as compared with English, see the Introduction (pp. 1–59) in R. L. Græme Ritchie and J. M. Moore, *Translation from French*, Cambridge, 1919.

from Vulgar Latin a number of general tendencies have been persistent, but they too have not been constant or uniform. The difficult and delicate problems raised by such considerations cannot in the present state of our knowledge be answered with any precision. We shall content ourselves with presenting a number of typical examples, loosely grouped under the headings indicated above, and drawing such general inferences as appear to be warranted.

556. I. Changes in meaning determined by a change in the object denoted. We include here changes in meaning that result directly from changes in political and social institutions and conditions. Striking examples are furnished by such common notions as 'house', 'road', 'town', 'horse'.[1]

'House.' The barbarian invasions resulted in the destruction of the patrician DOMUS, leaving the humble countryman's hut together with its name CASA (O.F. *chiese*, Sp.-It.-Prov.-Cat. c a s a), superseded in more prosperous times by MANSIONEM (> *maison*), originally a country-house, and by HOSPITALEM (> *ostel* > *hôtel*), originally 'a hostel', then specialized in the sense of (*a*) 'hospital' (cf. *hôtel-Dieu*), later replaced by the Learned *hôpital*, (*b*) 'town-house', sc. capable of receiving guests, in Modern French restricted to the meaning 'mansion', (*c*) the modern 'hotel'. For the humbler dwelling, in default of CASA, O.F. employed the derivatives *maisnil, maisnel, maisil*; *maisonnette* has survived from the twelfth century to develop a specialized meaning in our day; *ferme* has become the generic term for a farmhouse. *Masure* (< * MANSURA), originally 'a dwelling' (twelfth century), has fallen upon evil days and competes upon unequal terms with such borrowings as *hutte* (Germ. h ü t t e, sixteenth century), *cabane* (Prov. c a b a n a, fourteenth century), *bicoque* (It. b i c o c c a, sixteenth century), *cassine* (It. c a s s i n a, sixteenth century). It is a sign of modern fashion that *cottage* (Engl.), *villa* (It.), *chalet* (Swiss) have found their way into French vocabulary.

557. 'Road.' The Latin generic VIA survived in the form

---

[1] The following notes (§§ 556–60) are partly based upon Dauzat, *Histoire*, pp. 272–4.

veie, voie, but its place appears from the beginning to have been largely usurped by the Celtic *CAMMINO (> *chemin*), which has remained the generic term. The VIA STRATA LAPIDE persists as O.F. *estrée* (It. s t r a d a, Sp. e s t r a d a), which disappeared in Gaul with the destruction of the Roman roads, and was followed by the Merovingian (VIA) *CALCIATA (> *chaussée*; Sp. c a l z a d a is borrowed from Prov.), and later by the (VIA) RUPTA (> *route*), originally a road driven through wooded country. O.F. *eire, oire* (< ITER) shared with *veie, voie* the more abstract meaning 'way', which *voie* has kept. RUGA, 'wrinkle', 'crease', came to be used metaphorically in V.L. in the sense of 'road', but was early restricted to 'street'. The derivative *charrière* formerly denoted a cart-track.

558. 'Town.' With the disappearance of the Roman CIVITAS as a political entity, the name came to be used in the sense of URBS and was so used throughout the O.F. period, surviving in *l'île de la Cité, la Cité de Carcassonne,* etc., to designate the older portion of the town as opposed to the modern (*ville*). VILLA originally denoted a country domain, which in the Gallo-Roman period frequently became the centre of agglomerations and eventually of a town (*ville*). The village was denoted by the derivative *VILLATICUM (> *village*). The Germanic invaders were responsible for the introduction of the fortified BURGUS (b u r g), the name of which was extended to include the dependent village (*bourg*), and for the hamlet (*hameau*).

No less interesting is the development of the derivatives *vilain, bourgeois, citoyen. Vilain* means in O.F. 'countryman', 'peasant', consequently 'commoner', and as such 'unversed in the rules of courtly etiquette'; *vilain* thus became the antithesis of *courtois* (later of *gentilhomme*) and developed naturally the modern meanings 'common', 'ugly'. *Bourgeois* has suffered in another way. Originally applied to the inhabitant of a *bourg*, it was extended to denote 'a citizen of the middle class', an enviable status for the greater part of the Middle Ages. However, exposed to the envy of the have-nots and looked down upon with scorn by the nobles, whom he was inclined to ape, he became the butt of satire and mockery, and *bourgeois* became in the seventeenth century the antithesis of *galant*. Since then the term has become a taunt employed by artists, novelists, and communists, but can still upon occasion be used without pejorative meaning. *Citoyen* (O.F. *citeain*, *citeyen*) denoted in the Middle Ages, more specifically than *bourgeois*, a 'town-dweller'; but it appears to have developed at an early date the wider meaning 'citizen of the state', probably under Latin influence (cf. *Hist. Anc.* 49: *la bataille citoienne* 'civil war'), and as such became the sole title recognized by the Revolution. Its place has been partly taken by the Italian cittadino > *citadin* (fourteenth century) and the Learned *urbain*; the latter is found as early as the fourteenth century, but its extensive use is a recent development (cf. the parallel extension of Engl. urban).

559 'Horse.' The Latin equus was in V.L. supplanted by the popular caballus (probably Celtic and originally 'nag'), which survived as the generic term in all the Romance languages (Fr. *cheval*, It. cavallo, Sp. caballo). The feminine equa gave O.F. *ive*, Sp. yegua, Prov. ega. Jumentum denoted in C.L. a beast of burden (horse, mule, ass, etc.) and survived with this meaning in Italian (giumento) and originally in French; but in the extreme north of France it early came to be restricted to the 'mare', the chief beast of burden in those parts, just as in Spanish it was restricted to the 'ass' (jumento). From the North the use of *jument* in the restricted sense 'mare' spread to Paris and displaced *ive* throughout Northern France. *Cavale* (< cavalla) was borrowed from Italian towards the end of the Middle Ages and has largely displaced *ega* in the South. The stallion, not being employed in the fields, was called the stall-horse, L.L. stallonem (Germ. stall) > *étalon*. Admissarius and cantherius went out of general use in the Western Empire. The gelding re-appears in the sixteenth century, first of all in Hungary, whence came the name *hongre*. *Poulain* (< pullamen), originally the young of any animal (cf. C.L. pullus equinus, pullus asininus, etc.), is used as early as the twelfth century in the restricted sense 'colt'.[1] To denote the different varieties of horse, French, like Latin, has recourse to adjectives (*postier, mallier, limonier*) or their equivalents (*de selle, de course, pur sang*) or to borrowed words: *genet* (fourteenth century), the small Sp.-Arab. jinete; *barbe* (sixteenth century), the It.-Arab. barbero (Berber); *bidet*, the humble It. bidetto; *haquenée* (< ? Engl. hackney); *cob*; *pony*; sometimes with secondary pejorative meaning: *rosse* (fifteenth-century Germ. ross). Old French distinguished between the *palefrei* (< PARAVEREDUM = παρά + VEREDUM 'an extra post-horse, a remount') 'a saddle horse for general utility purposes', the *destrier* (< DEXTRARIUM) 'charger', so called because it was led into battle on the right of the squire until required by the knight for actual combat, the *coursier* (der. of *cours*) 'the fleet horse', and the *roncin* (L.L. RUNCINUM) 'the pack horse', which has become *roussin* (≠ *roux*). Cognate Sp. rocín furnished Cervantes' Rocinante, whence French *rossinante*.

560. The introduction of Christianity brought about many changes of meaning, which are, however, not the work of the people; they had already taken place in written Latin, and to some extent in Greek: PRESBYTER (πρεσβύτερος) 'elder', 'elder or presbyter in the Christian Church' (*prêtre*); EPISCOPUS (ἐπίσκοπος) 'overseer', 'bishop' (*évêque*); PARABOLA (παραβολή) 'comparison', 'parable', 'word of God', 'word' (*parole*); the meaning 'parable' is taken over by the borrowed form *parabole* and 'the word of God' by VERBUM (*le Verbe*); MIRACULA, VIRTUTES, SIGNA similarly took the meaning 'miracles of the faith' (O.F. *merveille, vertu, signe*); CENARE is appropriated by the Church, and its place is taken by *DIS-JEJUNARE (*déjeuner* and *dîner*); the Devil is the enemy, hence ADVERSARIUS > *li aversiers* 'the Devil'; *TROPARE 'to invent tropes' shows a popular generalization of meaning to *trouver* 'to invent', 'to find'. As paganism proved most tenacious in the country districts, PAGANUS (der. of PAGUS) 'country-

---

[1] *Poulain* is used in the modern jargon of sport to denote a young aspiring athlete, probably in imitation of the English use of 'colt'.

dweller', 'peasant', became ultimately in Church Latin the equivalent of 'heathen' (*païen*).

561. Changes in political organization and social relations are reflected in such words as the following:

SENIOREM 'the senior', 'the elder' becomes *seigneur* 'the person in authority', 'the lord', preserved as a title of honour and long employed in addressing persons of noble birth (cf. its use in classical tragedy); also *le Seigneur* 'the Lord', and *monseigneur* restricted to bishops since the eighteenth century. The nominative *sendre* (<SENIOR) early disappeared (cf. I, 12). The contracted form *sire* (< *SEIOR), originally a more familiar form of address, came to be used in addressing royalty and was also the title of certain feudal lords (Jehan, sire de Joinville). Later it came to be associated with certain offices and to be used ironically or pejoratively; *messire = mes* (nom. of *mon*) + *sire*, shows a similar degradation. *Sieur* (< *SEIOREM) shows an even more rapid depreciation, but in combination with *mon-* became a title of respect. *Monsieur* was applied in the first instance to persons of high rank, but was gradually extended until it became a polite formula, used when speaking to or about a person and prefixed to *votre père*, *votre frère*, etc., which would sound familiar if used by themselves. Under the ancien régime it was still something more than a mere polite formula and stood but a degree below *monseigneur* (this is its force in XIV, 55).

562. DOMINUS has not survived except in the ecclesiastical *dom*, formerly also employed to render the Sp. *don*. In O.F. it is found in the form *dam(e)* (cf. *vidame*), nom. *danz*, used before proper names or titles; also in *Damnedeu*, *Damedieu*, *Damledeu*.

DOMINA > *dame*, whence *madame*, formerly both titles of honour (*Dame Marie*, *Notre-Dame*, *les dames de France* 'daughters of the King') applied to married and unmarried ladies alike; they were gradually extended to ladies of the middle class, and since the ancien régime *madame* has been reserved for married ladies in general, while *dame* has ceased to be used as a form of address.

*DOMINICELLUM > *damoiseau*, in O.F. 'squire' and loosely 'young nobleman', but in the seventeenth century had developed the modern pejorative meaning 'lady-killer'.

*DOMINICELLA > *demoiselle*, which (like *mademoiselle*) was originally applied to a lady (married or unmarried) of noble birth, but began to be used of the middle class in the seventeenth century. The restriction to single ladies takes place at the end of the ancien régime.

The evolution of *monsieur, madame*, etc., as polite forms of address continues, and one might almost say that each generation in this way brings with it modifications in the finer shades of characteristic French politeness, the complete mastery of which is for the foreigner no mean achievement.

563. COMES, COMITEM 'companion' became in Roman times 'companion of the prince' and thus a title of honour (O.F. *cuens, conte*), which later carried with it a feudal domain (*comté*, Engl. county); its original meaning was taken over by *CUMPANIO -ONEM (> *compagnon*), modelled on a Germanic word (cf. Gothic gahlaiba = ga- 'with' + hlaiba 'bread', i.e. 'one who breaks bread with'). The compound COMES STABULI gave by corruption *connétable*, originally 'the officer in charge of the royal stable', extended to denote a 'cavalry commander', 'governor of a fortified place', and ultimately 'commander in chief of the royal army'. *Maréchal* (Germ. marah 'horse' + skalk 'servant') shows a similar development.

O.F. *marchis* (Germ. mark-a + -ENSIS) 'lord of the marches' was re-modelled under the influence of It. marchese, and in the form *marquis* became a title conferring precedence over a *comte* but ranking below a *duc*.

564. *Chétif* (CAPTIVUM), originally 'prisoner', and still used in this sense in the sixteenth century; but the modern meaning 'weak', 'wretched' had developed in the pre-literary period and is eloquent of the treatment accorded to prisoners.

Gêne and *gêner* continue O.F. *gehine* 'an extorted confession', a derivative of *jehir* (Germ. jehan) 'to confess', 'to force a confession', and developed the meaning 'torture', 'instrument of torture' owing to the means employed to extort a confession. Both *gêne* and *gêner* preserved much of this force as late as the seventeenth century: *Ah! que vous me gênez!* (*Andromaque*); *Allons, vite...des juges, des gênes, des potences!* (*L'Avare*). Since then they have been still further weakened until they imply nothing more than discomfort, constraint.

565. *Sergent* (< SERVIENTEM) 'the serving man' developed in O.F. the special meaning 'soldier', 'squire'; in Mod.F., while retaining the notion of service, it has come to denote an officer, public or military (non-commissioned): *sergent de ville, sergent, sergent-major.*

Artillerie, a derivative of *artiller* (der. of *art*), in conformity with its etymology denoted in O.F. the contrivances, instruments, missiles of warfare in general (cf. Engl. use in I Samuel xx, 40: "And Jonathan gave his artillery (i.e. missiles) unto his lad, and said unto him, Go, carry them to the city"). The modern restricted meaning had not been completely accepted in the seventeenth century.

566. *Manant* (pres. part. of *manoir* < MANĒRE), originally 'one who has a fixed dwelling, who is settled upon the land', 'a peasant', has shared the depreciation of *vilain*.

O.F. *recreant* (pres. part. of *recroire* 'to renounce') 'one who renounces God, his leader or his cause', hence 'one who declares himself beaten', 'recreant'.

567. *Parlement*, originally abstract, denoting 'the act of speaking', 'interview', and by metonymy 'assembly', became specialized under the ancien régime 'a sovereign court of justice' and specifically the *Parlement de Paris*. The *Parlement* perished in the Revolution, but the name has, in imitation of the English Parliament, come to be applied to the representative chambers (*Chambre des Députés + Sénat*). Many other words, such as *intendant, procureur, conseiller, ministre*, reflect in a similar way changes in government and administration, i.e. changes in the object denoted.

Libertin (borrowed in sixteenth century from LIBERTINUS; cf. Bloch, *Dict.*), originally merely a free-thinker, but as the seventeenth-century free-thinkers were in many cases in revolt, not only against authority in matters of religion, but against austerity in conduct, their condemnation by the Church began to invest the word even at that time with the taint of loose morals.

Boulevard (Dutch bolwerc) 'a rampart', 'defensive fortification' (cf. Hugo, *Préface de Cromwell: sans en faire un boulevard à son ouvrage*). With the razing of the old ramparts of Paris and their transformation into avenues lined with trees, the word has developed its modern meaning and is applied to avenues in other towns as well.

Artisan (It. artigiano, sixteenth century) kept the meaning 'artist', 'craftsman' throughout the seventeenth century, since when a sharper distinction has become necessary (*artiste—artisan*).

Librairie, originally 'library', came to be restricted after the seventeenth century to a 'book-seller's shop' with its library-like arrangement, *bibliothèque* (dating from the fifteenth century) taking its place.

568. *Roman* (older *romant*) is the analogical accusative of O.F. *romanz* (< * ROMANICE,[1] which was originally applied to the Romance language as spoken throughout the Roman Empire, but was eventually applied to works composed in the Romance vernacular of France, Spain, etc., as opposed to Latin). In Old French, *romanz—roman* came to denote specifically narrative poems of an entertaining nature, but it could also be applied to legends and chronicles in the vernacular. The modern meaning, which represents both a restriction and an extension (applied to a novel in any language), dates from the later Middle Ages when the verse romances passed into prose.

Espiègle, patelin, and the like, reflect the former popularity of literary works and figures (*Till Eulenspiegel, La Farce de Maître Pierre Patelin*). Similarly *gavroche* 'street-urchin' goes back to the character Gavroche in Hugo's *Les Misérables*.

569. The semantic development of terms denoting articles of attire, furniture, and commodities of various kinds furnishes

---

[1] = 'in Roman (Romance) fashion' (ROMANICE LOQUI).

matter for many a chapter in social history (e.g. *chapeau, armoire, lampe*).

Guêtre, originally the rough footwear of the peasant, is transformed in the nineteenth century into the 'gaiter'. The old meaning survives in the expression *Il est venu en guêtres à Paris* (i.e. penniless).

Fauteuil represents O.F. *faldestuel* (< Germ. *faldistōl- = faldan 'to fold' + stōl- 'stool', 'chair'), which denoted a folding chair reserved for distinguished persons.

CAPPA 'cloak' (first found in Isidore of Seville) shows an interesting development. It gives in the first place French *chape* 'cloak', early restricted to 'cope', 'priestly vestment', and developed a variety of metaphorical meanings (*sous chape*). The diminutives CAPPELLA 'small cloak or cope' and CAPPELLUS 'head-gear', 'chaplet' developed early; CAPPELLA was by metonymy applied to the resting-place 'chapel' in which was kept and venerated the cloak of St Martin of Tours, whence the general meaning of *chapelle*.

CAPPELLUM > *chapel*, Mod.F. *chapeau*; derivative: *chapelet*, which has preserved the old meaning 'chaplet', formerly also 'small hat'.[1]

570. The Revolution has left its mark in many semantic evolutions, which the following may serve to illustrate:

Jacobin, derived from the name of the street *Saint Jacques* (JACOBUS) in which was situated the chief convent of the Dominican order in Paris. Hence the meaning 'a monk of the Dominican order'; but the same convent having served as the meeting-place of a revolutionary club, the name *jacobin* was applied to members of the club and by extension to those who held similar views.

Sans-culotte, reputed to have been first applied by the abbé Maury in the Constituante to the representatives of the people because they wore, not the fashionable *culotte*, but the common *pantalon*. Adopted by the revolutionaries themselves

---

[1] CAPPA is further represented by a vast number of derivatives (*chaperon, chapier, chapelier*), including many borrowings from Italian (*capot, capucin*).

as an honourable epithet, *sans-culotte* became the equivalent of 'radical revolutionary'.

Libéral, radical, socialiste, and other political labels present a semantic development which reflects the whole political history of recent times.

571. II. It is more difficult to assess the importance of historical facts in those semantic developments which reflect a change in mental and moral outlook, except in so far as the latter reveals definite pre-occupations.

For the pre-literary period we have abundant evidence of those metaphorical uses and extensions or restrictions of meaning which we associate with a popular language. The pre-occupation with things of the soil is reflected in such developments as the following: PONERE > *pondre*, CUBARE > *couver*; ARISTA, BRANCA, TIBIA, metaphorically used, receive the meaning of *arête, branche, tige*; SATIONEM 'the sowing season' is for the countryman *the* season and becomes *la saison*; MINARE 'to urge on (cattle) by means of cries' comes to mean 'to lead' (*mener*). Trade and barter furnish: CAMBIARE 'to change money' > 'to change' (*changer*); EXAGIUM, TALENTUM, *ARRIPARE 'to land' are similarly extended (*essai, talent, arriver*). Soldiers' language furnishes the metaphor PAPILIONEM, applied to a tent (*pavillon*) because of its flaps recalling the wings of a butterfly; INGENIUM by metonymy denotes the product *engin* 'a war machine', also 'contrivance', 'trick', 'trap', beside abstract 'deceit', 'trickery'. Other abstract terms are pressed into service to denote concrete objects: VECTURA > *voiture*, VENATIONEM > *venaison*; simple abstract notions are often denoted by concrete terms used metaphorically: ANGUSTIA > *angoisse*. Popular metaphors of the slang variety are: TESTA 'pot', 'potsherd' for 'head' (*tête*); GABATA 'bowl' for 'cheek' (> *GAUTA > joue*), beside the doublet *jatte* 'dish'; MANDUCARE (> *manger*), after a character in comedy (MANDUCUS) pictured with wide-open mouth. The lack of precision in general (as opposed to technical) vocabulary, which is characteristic of popular speech, may be regarded as partly responsible for such shifting of meaning

as we have in COXA 'hip' > 'hip-bone' > 'thigh' (*cuisse*);
BUCCA 'puffed-out cheek' > 'oral cavity' > 'mouth' (*bouche*);
GAMBA 'hoof' > 'hoof-joint' > 'leg' (*jambe*); SPONSUM 'betrothed' > 'spouse' (*époux*); NEPOTEM 'descendant' > 'grand-
son' > 'nephew' (*neveu*).

572. In the following period (O.F. and Mid.F.) the same
factors operate, in so far as the language remains popular
and pre-occupations the same. A noticeable feature is the
number of metaphors furnished by the chase, the favourite
relaxation of the upper classes: *acharner* (der. of *charn*, later
chair) 'to excite dogs or hawks with the taste of flesh', 'to
inspire with animosity or to intense effort'; *ameuter*; *amorce*;
appât; *chasser*; *dépister*; *hagard* (der. of Germ. h a g - a > *haie*) 'a
hawk caught in the hedges', hence 'wild', 'haggard';
hobereau 'hobby-hawk', derisively applied to a poor country
squire; *leurre* 'decoy'; *niais* 'young falcon captured in his
nest', 'simpleton'; locutions: *être aux abois*, *être à l'affût*, *marcher
sur les brisées de quelqu'un* (from the broken branches marking
an animal's course), *revenir bredouille* 'to return empty-handed,
at a loss'.

573. But there is a growing tendency to abstraction and
the metaphorical use of concrete terms for abstract notions.
This is closely bound up with the utilization of the language
for literary purposes. In this connection K. Vossler[1] has
brought out very clearly how Old French poets concentrate
upon the moral aspects of a situation or action rather than
the pictorial, and how the vocabulary, without becoming
definitely abstract, is given a decided twist in this direction (e.g. *adrecié* 'made straight' > 'instructed', 'versed',
'equipped') and words already abstract are given a more
subjective meaning (*achever* 'to bring to an end' > 'to succeed'). One may add that this is no purely literary movement, for it is hardly too much to say that to the medieval
mind life itself was a metaphor. Consequently, in default
of analysis, the medieval poet is led to a species of continuous
metaphor, allegory. The result is not only the investing of

[1] *Op. cit.* pp. 87–95.

concrete terms with abstract meaning but that personification of abstract notions which is characteristic of later medieval literature (*male bouche* 'evil tongue', having come to denote 'scandal', is personified and appears as a character in the *Roman de la Rose*). In Middle French there is on balance a marked general tendency towards abstraction. This finds expression in the breaking down of a barrier, in the intermingling of the concrete and the abstract, rather than in the metaphorical use of concrete terms (which declines); for the rapid influx of abstract Learned words easily met requirements in this direction. By their adoption the concrete terms were set free for the rendering of those pictorial values which begin to find recognition and expression towards the end of the Middle Ages.

574. As a result of these developments the sixteenth century presents an extraordinary uncertainty and confusion in semantic values, complicated by the attribution of classical or foreign meanings to native forms, sometimes accompanied by a formal re-modelling: *soudart* (together with *soudoyer*), the old medieval man-at-arms, gives way to *soldat*, the new (Italian) conception of what a soldier should be; the re-modelling of O.F. *afaitier* 'to prepare carefully' to *affecter* took place before the sixteenth century and facilitated the attribution of the Latin meaning 'to strive'. But often there is no external sign. The lateness of such attributions is often borne out by the absence of the new meaning in words borrowed into English from French at an earlier date.

575. In the following list the meanings borrowed in the sixteenth century from Latin follow the plus sign: *arête* 'fishbone' + 'beard of corn'; *conférer* 'to transfer' + 'to compare'; *déduire* 'to amuse', 'to deduce' + 'to deduct'; *défiance* 'defiance' + 'mistrust' (associated with Lat. DIFFIDENTIA); *desservir* 'to deserve' + 'to serve diligently'; *dispenser* 'to dispensate' + 'to distribute'; *édifier* 'to erect' + L.L. 'to edify'; *estrade* (It. strada) 'road' + 'platform'; *exaucer* 'to raise' + 'to gratify a wish'; *grâce* 'favour', 'mercy' + 'graciousness', 'gracefulness'; *ingrat* 'thankless' + 'unpleasing'; *office* 'office', 'post'+'duty'. Much more numerous are the borrowed meanings which are found in individual writers only, or have not survived, although common in the sixteenth century: *aliéné*, meaning 'strange'; *étude* 'inclination'; *libertin* 'freedman'.

576. Attribution of Italian meanings: *air* 'tune' (aria); *attaquer*, military meaning 'to attack' (attaccare); *créature* —*être la créature de qqn.* 'to owe him everything one is'; *dévotion* 'devotion to persons or causes other than God' (divozione); *estampe* 'stamping instrument'+'engraving' (stampa); *estoc* 'tree-stump'+'rapier' (stocco); *loge* 'bower', 'lodge'+'loggia'; *pause* (O.F. also *pose*) 'interruption'+'musical rest'; *serviteur* and *service* receive their gallant meaning from Italian. In many cases it is impossible to decide whether the borrowed meaning is due to Italian or to Latin influence. *Flotte* 'army', 'armament' owes its meaning 'fleet' to the influence of Sp. flota.

577. We have already alluded to the important changes which French vocabulary underwent in the seventeenth century (§ 10). For a full account of the semantic developments in this period the reader should consult Brunot, III, i, pp. 226–61 (*Travail sémantique*). Two main tendencies are to be distinguished, one making for greater precision, the other for abstraction. Both are to a considerable extent manifestations of the growing rationalism of the age and the general desire for order and regularity, but depend largely upon the preponderant rôle played by the salon and the fact that in essentials there was a close agreement between grammarians, Précieuses, and writers. The grammarians, beginning with Malherbe, are intent upon introducing regularity into the chaotic vocabulary of the sixteenth century, upon the elimination of synonyms or what were sometimes treated as synonyms in the preceding age: *aspect—spectacle, débile—faible, dormir—sommeiller, continu—assidu, contraire—différent, simple—unique, chaire—chaise, consommer—consumer, fatal—funeste, fureur—furie, reliques—restes, soupçonneux—suspect, effroyable—redoutable—terrible—horrible*, etc. The abstract and the concrete terms are

no longer to overlap, the simple word is to be distinguished from its derivative: *jardin—jardinage, luire—reluire, lever—élever*. The same precision is aimed at throughout the vocabulary, obsolete and obsolescent acceptations being pruned away and connotations eliminated as far as possible, the abstract meaning being thus preferred to the pictorial and poetic values. The pre-occupation with questions of the mind and heart, which is characteristic of seventeenth-century society and literature, demanded such precision and the elaboration of an extensive abstract vocabulary for the rendering of the finest shades of thought and feeling. These needs were met by a rational and discerning utilization of the abundant raw material handed on by the sixteenth century; also by the liberal use of concrete terms in an abstract sense: *amorce, appas* (XVII, 21), *assiette, démordre de qqch., dessein, enflamme* (XVII, 58), *entrailles, essuyer, feu, guindé, ressort, trait*.

578. The Précieuses contributed powerfully to this process of purifying, standardization, and abstraction. We are not here concerned with their more laboured, ingenious, and highly artificial attempts to avoid the 'terme propre' (*l'ameublement de la bouche* for *les dents*, and the like), their hyperbolic figures of speech and exaggerations (*furieusement* for 'very', *dernier* for 'utmost'), nor with such antithetic expressions as *tristement doux, sombrement éclairci*, and the use of *chose* and *affaire* as passe-partout words in place of the word one cannot call to mind at the moment or affects to forget. Such aberrations are the products of a society intent upon avoiding the trite and banal no less than the vulgar, and some of them might be paralleled from other periods. Their influence is to be seen in the forced and mixed metaphors which abound in writers of the time, even in Molière, though he himself ridiculed this foible (cf. § 552). By their avoidance of the 'terme propre' and in their happier metaphors (*billet doux, un tour d'esprit, travestir sa pensée, châtier son œuvre*) the Précieuses helped to form the language of the classical writers and have left their mark permanently upon the French language (*beau* (XVII, 35), *esprit, bel esprit, précieux, cœur, vœux* (XVII, 20),

soupirant (XVII, 28), *blondin, damoiseau, commerce*). The abundance of metaphorical uses which developed in this period is due to the fact that writers and Précieuses formed part of a compact society with common interests, and therefore quick to seize upon the comparison implied in the metaphor. It was in the salon that the ideal of the *honnête homme* was evolved, and a whole volume by Faret (1630)[1] did not suffice to bring out all the shades of meaning with which the word *honnête* was endowed; some of these shades are still apparent, e.g. if we compare *un honnête homme* with *un homme honnête*. Cf. also Brunot's interesting study of the word *galant* (*op. cit.* pp. 237–40). The Précieuses are also responsible for the large number of euphemisms which developed in the seventeenth century, but it is well to bear in mind that their sensitiveness is of a different kind from that of the Puritan and did not prevent their calling a spade a spade with a freedom which sometimes comes as a shock.

579. The spell which the Classical writers of Rome threw over the writers of this period is reflected in a number of borrowed meanings: *admirer* 'to admire' + 'to wonder at'; *dénier* 'to deny' + 'to refuse to give'; *fatal* 'inevitable' + 'ordained', sometimes in a favourable sense; *fureur* 'fury' + 'madness'. The following have not survived: *célèbre*, often used in the sense of 'solemn', 'stately'; *conseil*, in Fénelon and Bossuet, 'prudence'. Meanings borrowed from Italian: *accuser* 'to confirm' (*Je vous accuse réception de votre lettre*); *négoce* 'affair' + 'business'.

580. The semantic developments which have taken place since the seventeenth century are numerous, as a glance at such a compilation as Cayrou's[2] will show. But the fundamental character of the vocabulary as then constituted has not altered, in spite of the Revolution, the Romantic reaction (which affects primarily the literary language), the growing popular influence, the gradual infiltration into the standard language of meanings and metaphors taken from the technical

---

[1] *L'Honneste homme, ou l'art de plaire à la Cour.*
[2] Cited in the Bibliography.

languages. If we compare the vocabulary of standard Modern French with that of English we find that it is distinguished by those qualities which the seventeenth century developed and perfected, and it may be claimed that this is so because in that age the French genius found its truest expression. However that may be, it remains true that from the seventeenth century onwards usage has been more thoroughly standardized and the conserving factors have been more powerful in French than in any other language. Thus we may still say of Modern French that its vocabulary is less vague, less charged with connotations, more abstract, more suitable as a language of psychological analysis, richer in metaphors which reflect the life of the salon than, say, English. The tendency to abstraction, which French educational methods perhaps foster, is further reflected in the common use of many abstract terms which would sound slightly pedantic or 'learned' in English.

581. Among the more striking semantic changes since the seventeenth century one may instance the development of many technical meanings connected with the arts (colour and design). This is closely bound up with the development of artistic criticism since Diderot, and with the vindication and exploitation by the Romantics and later literary movements of pictorial and evocative values in vocabulary. The range of adjectives denoting colours and shades was already very large in Old French, which offers a striking contrast with Latin in this respect. Old French had resorted to various devices to satisfy a desire for greater precision and finer distinctions: derivatives (*rosé, roset, rosin, rosenet, rosal, roselent, rosenc, rosaz*), composition (*enrosé*), new formations (*flori, cendreux, vain*), borrowings, chiefly from Germanic (*blanc, gris, blau, bloi, bleu, brun, blond, saur, fauve*, and derivations from these). The seventeenth century made few additions, and many of the O.F. terms were dropped or had gone out of use. In Modern French, with the development of artistic criticism and of word-painting ('transposition d'art'), particularly from Hugo and Gautier onwards, there has been

a striking increase, a favourite device being the use of substantives as adjectives to denote or suggest the colour of the object or material specified (*acajou, ardoise, groseille, marron, or, puce, saumon*). Terms denoting design, line, etc. have been similarly multiplied in recent times by semantic changes.

582. Borrowed meanings from Latin have been few since the seventeenth century; eighteenth-century: *indulgent* 'indulgent towards' + 'yielding to'; *perdition* 'perdition' + 'process of destruction or loss'; *compétence* 'competence' + 'competition', since lost; *détriment* 'disadvantage' + 'detritus', since lost; nineteenth-century: *mode* (m.) + 'manner'; *fréquent* + 'numerous'; *candeur* + 'whiteness'; *labeur* + 'travail', since lost. From Italian; eighteenth-century: *rivière* 'plain adjoining bank or shore' + 'Riviera'; *natif* 'native, born in' + 'inborn'; *paillasse* + 'clown' (pagliaccio); nineteenth-century: *horaire* 'hourly' + 'time-table' (orario).

583. A growing number of meanings have been borrowed from English cognate words; eighteenth-century: *commodité* 'convenience' + 'commodity' (com.); *pétition* 'postulation' + 'petition' (pol.); *adresse* + 'political address or petition'; *juré* + 'juryman'; *motion* + 'resolution'; *planteur* + 'planter' (col.); *session*; *voter*; nineteenth-century: *ballade* 'medieval genre' + 'ballad', a poem dealing with a popular legend; *attraction, confort, exhibition, importer, majorité, minorité, plateforme, surprise*; and *entraîner, record* used as sporting terms under the influence of English 'train', 'record'. Occasionally *accomplissements, gentilhomme, humeur, lecture* are used with meanings taken from their English cognates. A few meanings have been borrowed from German in modern times: *culture* (kultur), *motif* (leitmotif), *lecteur* (lektor) 'assistant lecturer (foreign) at a university'; *subjectif* and *objectif* probably came to be used as terms of literary criticism under German influence.[1]

584. The following words have since the seventeenth century lost the meanings indicated: *admirer* 'to wonder at',

[1] For further examples, see H. Hatzfeld, *op. cit.*

affecter qqn. 'to like', *amusement* 'waste of time', 'delay', *appui* 'action of supporting, upholding', *assemblée* 'social gathering', *audience* 'hearing', 'attention', *austère* 'sour', *badin* 'foolish', *se barbouiller* 'to compromise oneself', *bâtiment* 'act of building', *brave* 'elegant', *capable* 'capacious', *captiver* 'capture', 'hold prisoner', *célèbre* 'solemn', *change = changement*, *conversation* 'intercourse', *courage* 'heart as the seat of affection', *curieux* 'careful', *d'abord* 'from the beginning', *d'ailleurs* 'from elsewhere', *devis* 'talk', *dévot* 'bigot', 'hypocrite', *domestique* 'person attached to a noble household', *douter* 'to distrust', *entendre à* 'to pay attention to', *époux* 'betrothed', *estime* 'valuation', 'opinion (good or bad)', *estomac* 'chest', *étage* 'social rank', *étrange* 'extraordinary', 'striking' (much stronger in the seventeenth century and used of great catastrophes), *étonner* 'to agitate suddenly' (often concrete), *événement* 'issue', *fâcher* 'to disgust', *fier* 'fierce', *flatter* 'to caress', *gêne* 'torture', 'instrument of torture', *gêner* 'to torture', 'to torment', *gloire* 'good name', *grimace* 'hypocrisy', 'pretence', *impertinent* 'out of place', 'inappropriate', *libertin* (cf. § 567), *ménage, ménagerie* 'domestic administration', *négoce* 'affair' (other than commercial), *nouvelliste* 'a gossip', *partir* 'to divide', 'to share', *plaisant* 'pleasing', *plancher* 'ceiling', *quereller qqn.* 'to accuse' (cf. XVII, 9) or *qqch. à qqn.* 'to blame', *ressentiment* 'pleasant recollection', *réussir* 'to result', *stupide* 'struck with stupor', *succéder* 'to find access', 'to happen'.

585. In the following words the pejorative meaning has developed or been given prominence since the seventeenth century: *amas* (cf. XVII, 38), *artifice, débiter, débonnaire, dispute, embonpoint, faquin* 'porter', *goutte* (as neg. part.), *injure* (still commonly in the seventeenth century 'injury', 'injustice', 'harm', and similarly *injurier, injurieux*), *licence, obséder qqn.* 'to monopolize' (XVII, 13), *pédant, stupide.*

586. The distinction between the following pairs of words is modern, or if made in the seventeenth century, was not strictly and universally observed: *consommer—consumer* (the modern distinction is not etymological, *consommer* meaning not only 'to consummate', but 'to consume profitably' as opposed to *consumer* 'to consume destructively'), *aïeux—aïeuls*, *lever—élever*, *fureur—furie*, *jour—journée*, *amant* 'accepted lover' —*amoureux* 'person in love' (XVII, 3; but cf. Corneille, *Le Cid*), *original—originel*, *procès—procédé*, *recouvrer—recouvrir*, *fatal—funèbre—funeste*; *étrange*, *regards* are no longer used for *étranger* and *égards* respectively, as they were in the seventeenth century.

587. We have seen how the meaning of many words has changed under the influence of foreign words of similar form. To such cases might be added those in which formal association with a native word (not a derivative) has induced semantic change; they are difficult to prove, but the following may be advanced with tolerable certainty: *affirmer* + 'to consolidate' ≠ *affermir*; *bizarre* 'brave' + 'queer' ≠ *bigarré*; *classique* + (*édition*) *classique* 'school (edition)' ≠ *classe*; *décréditer* 'to discredit' + 'to decry' ≠ *décri*; *étourneau* 'starling' + 'giddy person' ≠ *étourdi*; *forain* 'foreign', 'wandering' + 'wandering showman' ≠ *foire*; *fronder* 'to sling' + 'to find fault', 'to revolt' ≠ *Fronde* 'sling', metaphorically applied to the revolutionary movement in the seventeenth century; *génie* + 'engineering corps' ≠ *ingénieur*; (*h*)*abiller* 'to equip' + 'to clothe' ≠ *habit*, whence also *h*; *hébéter* 'to dull' + 'to stupefy' ≠ *bête*; *honorer* + 'to pay' ≠ *honoraire*; *orient* + 'lustre' ≠ *oriental* in *perles orientales*, etc.; *parade* + 'display' ≠ *parer*; *peuplier* + 'the tree of the people, revolutionary symbol' ≠ *peuple*; *plantureux* 'plentiful' + 'fertile', 'luxuriant' ≠ *plante*; *ridicule* + 'bag' ≠ *réticule*; *souffreteux* 'needy' + 'ailing' ≠ *souffrir*; *voltiger* 'to vault' + 'to flutter' ≠ *voleter*.

E. *LOSS OF WORDS*

588. In the preceding pages we have had occasion to observe that words or certain meanings of words gradually gain or lose currency. The currency of a word is like that of any token and (more than most) it is constantly changing. Not only is the value of the token subject to fluctuation, but its circulation may be restricted or extended. Although no longer generally current, it may continue to be accepted as

'legal' tender within a narrower sphere. When it ceases completely to circulate and to serve as a medium of exchange, it becomes a part of history and important as such, but it can no longer be used except for ornamental purposes. If it is used, it is in the manner of the guinea which lives on convention, just as the poet continues under licence to use words which have ceased to circulate. We may carry the analogy further and say that, just as the currency of a token is menaced by excessive deflation or inflation, so the overloading of a word with meanings or the progressive restriction of meaning may drive it out of circulation. Another token is preferred, one which has an unmistakable and definite value. But it is obvious that our analogy ceases to serve once we examine in detail the causes and processes by which words suffer loss of currency or go out of circulation.

589. The simplest case is that of loss through the disappearance of the object for which the word is the token. Revolutions, whether political, administrative, religious or social, result in the disappearance of objects, institutions, and conceptions; these generally carry with them the terms by which they are denoted, unless the term is preserved and applied to analogous objects. The break-up of the Roman Empire and the introduction of Christianity resulted in the abandonment of the vocabulary of paganism and of many words identified with Roman conditions of life. Similarly, the decay of the feudal system, the revolution in methods of warfare, in arms and equipment, and in conditions of life generally at the end of the Middle Ages, result in the loss of many words. The disappearance of the social and political institutions of the ancien régime marks another series of losses at the end of the eighteenth century, but in this case many words were adapted to new uses (see above). Less striking, but still fairly numerous, are the losses resulting from social and industrial changes since the Revolution.

590. More complicated is the case of an object which remains, but for which another term is preferred. The factors which determine this preference are of various kinds, and

two or more may combine to drive a word out of circulation.

(1) Change in the nature of the object. Striking examples are furnished by the vocabulary of dress and costume or of vehicles (French has abandoned *char-à-bancs* and quite inexplicably prefers *car* for the modern sight-seeing conveyance).

(2) Change in the mentality of those who speak the language, in their state of culture, their pre-occupations, etc. We have here to do with psychological factors that are partly constant, partly variable and dependent upon social conditions (see above).

(*a*) The demand for precision is far from constant. A decline in culture involves the abandonment of fine distinctions, so far as the general vocabulary is concerned. This is clearly revealed in the abandonment in Vulgar Latin of many words which are more or less synonymous. Brunot (1, 109) cites the interesting example of the many Classical Latin equivalents of 'to shine', reduced in Vulgar Latin to a mere half-dozen. The subtle shades of meaning and connotation which distinguish apparently synonymous words, and which characterize a literary language, are lost or ignored; and absolute synonymity is a luxury no language can afford. The French writers of the sixteenth century allowed themselves to indulge in this luxury, with a consequent sacrifice of precision. It was left to the seventeenth century to bestow upon the French language that precision which has remained its chief virtue. This was accomplished by setting up clear distinctions between so-called synonyms (§ 577) or by dropping one of the synonymous words. In this way, quite apart from other pruning methods, the actual number of words was greatly reduced, but precision was achieved.

(*b*) The demand for greater expressiveness and vividness is more constant. A new and apt metaphor tends to replace a faded one, a word which conjures up the object or action more vividly is generally preferred (§ 552 ff.)

591. (*c*) The demand for clearness is more closely associated with the formal aspect of the language. Clearness

requires that the symbol shall be unmistakable and un-equivocal, that the word shall have body, and that it shall not be liable to confusion with another word of identical or similar form. These requirements are closely connected, for the shorter the word (i.e. the fewer the constituent sounds), the more likely is the same combination of sounds to recur in the language (pẽ = *pain, peins, peint, pin*). The phonetic evolution of French has been, as a whole, so rapid and the process of erosion so extensive that a large number of homonyms has been created. A distinction in spelling is often retained and sometimes introduced. So long as such auxiliary devices and the context suffice to distinguish homonyms, no sacrifice of clearness is entailed (*louer* 'to praise' is unlikely to be confused with *louer* 'to let'), but if the homonyms belong to the same order of ideas, there is obviously a danger of confusion; the result is a struggle for existence which often means the elimination of the weaker, i.e. of the word most easily dispensed with (e.g. O.F. *e(s)mer* collided with *aimer* and was eliminated, the Learned *estimer* being at hand to take its place). The conflict is therefore more than a pure 'collision homonymique', and a variety of factors may intervene to decide the issue. Thus it is difficult to believe that BELLUM 'war' would have been eliminated by BELLUM 'beautiful' had war itself not come to be largely a Germanic affair and to be denoted by the Germanic werra (> *guerre*). Homonymity is best described as a disability which renders a word less able to compete with its semantic rivals. Vulgar Latin already presented many words suffering from this disability (VIR collided with VERUM, VERO, VER; HABENA with AVENA; FIDIS with FIDES), and their number was greatly increased in French, particularly towards the end of the Middle Ages, when final consonants and final ǝ were eliminated. We have already seen that hesitation in pro-nunciation and the restoration of final consonants particularly affect short words and were freely utilized as therapeutic devices (§ 125 ff.). The tendency to prefer the long to the short word can be abundantly illustrated from Vulgar Latin

(FORTIA, BUCCA, CAMPANIA preferred to VIS, OS, RUS) and
partly accounts for the prevalence of derivatives (*SPERANTIA,
HIBERNUM, *GENUCULUM, AURICULA, AVICELLA, AGNELLUS, for
SPES, HIEMS, GENU, AURIS, AVIS, AGNUS). Similarly in French:
mul replaced by *mulet*, *tor* by *taureau*, *ef* (< APEM) by *abeille*.

592. (3) Loss of currency may also result from a variety
of associative influences. A word which is one of a series of
cognate or derivative forms derives support from that association, whereas a word which stands alone and is seldom used ·
is at a disadvantage (*binocle* and *missive* have been unable to
stand against *lorgnon* and *lettre*). A word may lose caste
owing to its unpleasant associations (*garce* ousted by *fille*,
replaced in its turn by *jeune fille*), or may fall a victim to the
fickleness of fashion (*précieux*, *fable*, *intellectuel*). One may
regret the preference so commonly shown in modern times for
the Learned word as against the Popular (*perturber* preferred
to *troubler*, *émotionner* to *émouvoir*).[1]

593. There remain a large number of words which have
simply dropped out of use for no apparent reason, words
which lose currency, come to be considered old-fashioned or
archaic, and as such are completely disowned. Countless
Old French words were abandoned in this way, as a glance
at Godefroy's *Lexique* will show: *ouïr* (because it is too short?),
isnel (because it is isolated?), *bouter*, *roiste*, etc.; *déconfit*, *guerdon*
have been abandoned in more recent times. *Accort* 'adroit',
amiable, *appas*, *appointeur*, *arroi*, *baisemain*, *braverie*, *chopper*,
congruent, *conjouir*, *consolatif*, and many other words now
obsolete or obsolescent, were still current in the seventeenth
century. The following have lost currency since the beginning
of the nineteenth century: *boulingrin*, *déconstruire*, *déité*, *délect-
able*, *fredon*, *guéret*, *peinturer*, *ris*, *sauvagine*;[2] and the process
continues. Many new words coined at the time of the Revolu-
tion (names of the months in the Revolutionary calendar and
the like) had but a short existence.

---

[1] Cf. Dauzat, *Histoire*, p. 228.
[2] Examples taken from *Petit de Julleville* (Brunot), VIII, p. 868; cf. also
VII, pp. 842–4.

594. As has been indicated above, loss of currency can take place by degrees, and words are labelled by lexicographers as archaic, obsolete, obsolescent, poetic, popular, according to the degree and range of their currency. While it is possible to say of many words that they are now no longer current in such and such a sphere or with such and such a meaning, it is quite another undertaking to establish the currency of particular words in earlier periods of the language. From the sixteenth century onwards we have more precise data to go upon; we know, for example, that many of the words used by sixteenth-century writers had no currency in the spoken language and represent conscious archaism or an attempt at resuscitation.[1] The gradual elimination of words from general currency can be observed in our own day, and in special cases almost from year to year.

595. Words which have lost currency in the standard language may continue to be used or artificially revived for literary purposes. The literary language of the seventeenth century afforded little shelter for such words, but in the sixteenth, and again in the nineteenth, archaisms were freely employed (sixteenth century: *gab, grevance, laidanger, merir*; nineteenth century: *admonester, feurre, pantois, remembrance*; cf. *Petit de Julleville* (Brunot), VIII, pp. 738–42). Many words find a last refuge in popular speech or patois (*avaricieux, bailler, choir, cotte*). Others are preserved in fixed locutions (*à huis clos, faire bonne chère, au fur et à mesure, par monts et par vaux, sain et sauf*), become petrified (*règne animal*), or, devoid of meaning, continue to serve a functional purpose (*rien*).

[1] Cf. Brunot, II, pp. 182–8.

Appendix A

SELECTIONS

The following extracts are partly intended to illustrate the development of the French language as a literary medium, from the terse and pithy lines of the unknown author of the *Sequence of Eulalia* to the classical Alexandrines of Molière, from the direct, naïve, and simple narrative of Villehardouin to the exuberant, racy prose of Rabelais and the artistic nonchalance of Montaigne's *Essais*. It is impossible to find space for the illustration of every type, and in any case we have thought it preferable to enable the reader to observe the progress made in one or two genres: the writing of history from Villehardouin to Froissart, the treatment of the same theme by Marie de France and by La Fontaine. It is not our aim to present what we consider the best passages of the best writers, but rather characteristic specimens.

At the same time these extracts are intended to serve as linguistic documents, and we were therefore bound to begin with the earliest extant piece of French prose, the *Strasburg Oaths*. We have endeavoured to ensure that, so far as possible, each extract shall serve as an authentic document. For Extracts I–V, VIII, X, we have reproduced without corrections, except those indicated in the text[1] or in the footnotes, the manuscript named. Abbreviations have been expanded, diacritic signs and punctuation added, *i* and *j*, *u* and *v* distinguished, but no attempt has been made to correct or standardize spelling. The remarks on orthography made in Chapter IV may thus find their partial illustration here. To obviate any difficulty in interpretation created by this close adherence to spellings and dialectal forms, we have added a few brief notes and have translated a number of extracts.

Similarly, we have considered it to be of some interest to

[1] Letters or words placed in square brackets are not in the manuscript and are to be supplied; letters or words to be suppressed are placed in parentheses.

reproduce without change (except s for ʃ) contemporary editions of Molière and La Fontaine. For Extract XIII we have reproduced F. Heuckenkamp's exact reprint of the first edition of the *Quinze Joyes de Mariage*, perhaps one of the first books to be printed with movable type.

Bibliographical indications will be found in P Studer and E. G. R. Waters, *Historical French Reader*, Oxford, 1924; and in the separate editions of the works from which our extracts are taken. The following works dealing with French versification may here be mentioned: L. E. Kastner, *A History of French Versification*, Oxford, 1903; M. Grammont, *Le Vers français*, Paris, 2nd ed. 1913; A. Tobler, *Vom französischen Versbau*, Leipzig, 5th ed. 1910, and French translation by K. Breul and L. Sudre, *Le Vers français ancien et moderne*, Paris, 1885. For the development of Modern French prose, see G. Lanson, *L'Art de la Prose*, Paris, 13th ed. 1909.

I. *STRASBURG OATHS*

Date of Composition: 842.   Date of Manuscript:[1] about 1000

[*The oaths taken by Louis the German and by the followers of Charles the Bald at Strasburg in 842, the occasion being the forming of an alliance against Lothair. We have omitted the corresponding German oaths taken by Charles the Bald and by the followers of Louis the German.*]

Lodhuvicus, quoniam major natu erat, prior haec deinde se servaturum testatus est:

'Pro Deo amur et pro christian poblo et nostro commun salvament, d'ist di in avant, in quant Deus savir et podir me dunat, si salvarai eo cist meon fradre Karlo et in ajudha et in   5
cadhuna cosa, si cum om per dreit son fradra salvar dift, in o quid il mi altresi fazet, et ab Ludher nul plaid nunquam prindrai qui, meon vol, cist meon fradre Karle in damno sit.'

TRANSLATION. For the love of God and the salvation of the Christian people and our common salvation, from this day forward, in so far as God grants me knowledge and power, I will succour this my brother Charles in aid and in every thing, as one ought by right to succour one's brother, provided that he does likewise by me, and I will never undertake any engagement with Lothair which, by my consent, may be of harm to this my brother Charles.

[1] Paris, Bibliothèque Nationale, lat. 9768, fol. 13.

Sacramentum autem quod utrorumque populus quique propria lingua testatus est, romana lingua sic se habet:

'Si Lodhuvigs sagrament, que son fradre Karlo jurat, conservat, et Karlus meos sendra de suo part lo fraint, si io returnar non l'int pois, ne io ne neuls cui eo returnar int pois, in nulla ajudha contra Lodhuwig nun li iv er.'

NOTES. 12 *lo fraint*] MS. *n̄ lostanit*, which has been variously interpreted. 14 *iv* (<IBI) = Mod.F. *y*; cf. *int* (<INDE) = Mod.F. *en*. For notes on the orthography, see § 152.

If Louis keeps the oath which he swore to his brother Charles and Charles my master, for his part, breaks it, if I cannot deter him therefrom, neither I nor anyone else whom I can deter from it will be of any assistance to him against Louis.

II. *SEQUENCE OF SAINT EULALIA*

Date of Composition: about 880.   Date of Manuscript:[1] before 900.

[*The poet has imitated very closely the form of a Latin Sequentia. Eulalia was a Spanish saint of Merida, who died a martyr's death under Maximian.*]

> Buona pulcella fut Eulalia,
> Bel auret corps, bellezour anima.
> Voldrent la veintre li Deo inimi,
> Voldrent la faire diaule servir.
> Elle no'nt eskoltet les mals conselliers,
> Qu'elle Deo raneiet, chi maent sus en ciel,
> Ne por or ned argent ne paramenz,
> Por manatce regiel ne preiement;
> Niule cose non la pouret omque pleier
> La polle sempre non amast lo Deo menestier.   10

NOTES. The poem was composed in the Picard-Walloon area (probably at St Amand-les-Eaux) and shows the following characteristic dialectal forms: 4 *diaule*; 6 *raneiet* (<RENEGET); 13 *lei* (< *ILLAEI); 13 *chielt* (§ 153); 20 *coist* (<COXIT); 23 *kose* (<CAUSA); 24 *seule* (<SAECULUM); 27 *auuisset* (<HABUISSET); 19 *lo* perhaps for Picard *le* (<ILLAM). Cf. §§ 153, 496.

10 Paratactic structure, the subjunctive (*amast*) alone indicating that the clause is virtually dependent upon *pleier*. Cf. §§ 395, 482.

TRANSLATION. A virtuous maiden was Eulalia, fair was her body and fairer yet her soul. The enemies of God would fain have vanquished her, would make her serve the Evil One. But she heeds not the wicked counsellors, counselling her to renounce God who dwells on high, nay not for gold or silver or fine apparel nor a king's threats or pleading. Nothing could ever bend her from steadfast love for the service of her

E por o fut presentede Maximiien,
Chi rex eret a cels dis soure pagiens.
Il li enortet, dont lei nonque chielt,
Qued elle fuiet lo nom christiien.
    Ell' ent adunet lo suon element;   15
Melz sostendreiet les empedementz
Qu'elle perdesse sa virginitét;
Por os furet morte a grand honestét.
    Enz enl fou lo getterent com arde tost;
Elle colpes non auret, por o nos coist.   20
    A czo nos voldret concreidre li rex pagiens;
Ad une spede li roveret tolir lo chieef.
    La domnizelle celle kose non contredist:
Volt lo seule lazsier, si ruovet Krist;
    In figure de colomb volat a ciel.   25
Tuit oram que por nos degnet preier
    Qued auuisset de nos Christus mercit
Post la mort et a lui nos laist venir
    Par souue clementia.

13 *chielt* (< CALET) 'it matters', 'it concerns'.   15 An obscure line usually interpreted 'she gathers together her strength (or resolution)'; for a new interpretation, cf. John Orr, "Sur un vers de l'"Eulalie"", in *Archivum Romanicum*, XIV, 3.   17 *Qu'elle* = *Que qu'elle*.   18 *os* = *o* (HOC) + *se*; cf. similar cases of enclisis: 19 *enl* = *en* + *le*, 20 and 21 *nos* = *non* + *se*.

The use of the pluperfect indicative as a preterite is noteworthy: *auret* (HABUERAT) 2, 20; *voldret* (VOLUERAT) 21; *pouret* 9; *furet* 18; *roveret* 22. Cf. § 436.

Lord. For this she was brought before Maximian, who in those days ruled over the pagans. He exhorts her (but little does it reck her) to flee the name of Christian. It does but make her summon up her strength: rather would she bear with persecution than that she should lose her virgin innocence. For this she died with great honour. They cast her into the flames, there to consume quickly. There was no sin in her, therefore she went unscathed. To this the pagan king would not submit; with a sword he ordered her head to be cut off. The maiden did not resist this thing; she wished to leave the world, and so she calls upon Christ. In the semblance of a dove she flew toward Heaven. Let us all pray that she may deign to pray for us to Christ, that He may have mercy upon us when we die, and that He may by His Grace let us come to Him.

III. *LIFE OF SAINT ALEXIS*[1]

Date of Composition: 11th century.   Date of Manuscript: about 1150.

[*The poet followed a tenth-century Latin version of the very popular legend of Sain Alexis. He employed the common ten-syllable lines of the 'chansons de geste', here linked by assonance to form five-line stanzas.*]

> Bons fut li secles al tens ancïenur,
> Quer feit i ert e justise et amur,
> S'i ert creance, dunt or(e) n'i at nul prut;
> Tut est müez, perdut ad sa colur,
> Ja mais n'iert tel cum fut as anceisurs.   5

NOTES. The poem was composed in the Île de France or in that part of Normandy adjoining it. We have reproduced the text of the earliest MS. (Hildesheim = L), which was executed in England and shows the peculiarities to be expected of an Anglo-Norman scribe of the twelfth century. The majority of the mistakes in declension are certainly not to be ascribed to the poet: *tel* 5, *vailant* 8, *ampairét* 10, *un* 13; *bien* (10) and *Eufemïen* (16) might reasonably be attributed to the poet. *Tut* (4, 9), although used adverbially, is normally inflected in O.F. *Filz* (15, etc.) is used as an accusative from an early date and may have been so used by the poet. The scribe's nationality is further revealed by the following features: *e* for *ie* (*secles* 1, 8, 38; *Velz* 9; *ampairét* 10; *melz* 20); *a* for *ə* (*Nostra* 12; *tuta, cuntretha* 20; *batesma* 29; *cambra* 31, 46; *cesta* 40; *ela* 46; *dama* 53; *estra* 55; *guardarai* 57); *ai* for *ei* (*ampairét* 10); *o* for *ue* (*voil* 15; *dol* 50; *vols* 56); *il* for *l'* (*muiler* 27); *in* for *n'* (*plainums* 59; *seinur* 60); *pois* for *puis* 42; *frai* for *ferai* 60. *c* for *ch* is not specifically Anglo-Norman (*rices* 14; *cambre* 31, 44, 46).

The spelling *u* for tonic free *ǫ*, while not peculiar to Anglo-Norman, is particularly favoured by Anglo-Norman scribes. The spelling *an, am* for countertonic *en, em* is also to be attributed to the scribe (*ansemble* 21, 55, 59; *amfant* 22, 25; *an* 31, 47, 54). The scribe hesitates between *th* and *d* as a spelling for the intervocal dental, which had by the date of this poem been reduced to a spirant and was tending to disappear (*parede* 46; *depredethe* 48; etc.); similarly, final *d* beside the more common *t* (*fud* 14; *fut* 13; etc.). Cf. § 101.

TRANSLATION. Good was the world in the time of them of old, for there was faith, justice, and love; trust there was too, which now is of small profit. It (the world) is quite changed, bereft of its colour; never will it be as in the time of our forefathers. In the time of Noah, in the

[1] Editions: G. Paris, *La Vie de Saint Alexis, texte critique* (Classiques fr. du moyen âge), Paris, 1911. M. Rösler, *Sankt Alexius* (Rom. Übungstexte xv), Halle, 1928. J.-M. Meunier, *La Vie de Saint Alexis*, Paris, 1933.

Al tens Nöé et al tens Abraham
Et al David, qui Deus par amat tant,
Bons fut li secles, ja mais n'ert si vailant;
Velz est e frailes, tut s'en vat declinant:
Si'st ampairét, tut bien vait remanant.   10

Puis icel tens que Deus nus vint salver,
Nostra anceisur ourent cristïentét,
Si fut un sire de Rome la citét:
Rices hom fud, de grant nobilitét;
Pur hoc vus di, d'un son filz voil parler.   15

Eufemïen—si out a(n) num li pedre—
Cons fut de Rome, des melz ki dunc i ere[n]t;
Sur tuz ses pers l'amat li emperere.
Dunc prist muiler vailante et honurede,
Des melz gentils de tuta la cuntretha.   20

Puis converserent ansemble longament,
N'ourent amfant; peiset lur en forment;
E Deu apelent andui parfitement:
'E! Reis celeste, par ton cumandement
Amfant nus done ki seit a tun talent.'   25

Tant li prïerent par grant humilitét
Que la muiler dunat fecunditét:

9 For *vat declinant* the scribe, influenced by the following line, wrote *vat remanant*. 22 For *N'ourent amfant* the other MSS. have *Qued amfant n'ourent*, which is to be interpreted as a consecutive clause: 'They lived together for a long time without having any children; this grieves them sorely.' Other scribal errors are noted in the text.

time of Abraham and in that of David, whom God loved so, the world was good; never again will it be so worthy. It is old and frail, quite declining, it has grown worse: all good deeds go undone. From that time when God came to save us, our forefathers held the Christian faith. And there was a noble man of Rome the city; a mighty man was he and of high degree. I tell you this for the reason that I would speak of a son of his. Eufemian—thus was the father named—was a count of Rome, of the best that then were there; above all his peers the emperor loved him. Then he took a wife, worthy and honoured, of the most noble in all the land. Then they lived for a long time together, but had no children; this grieves them sorely, and they both fervently call upon God: 'O heavenly king, by thy command give us a child that shall be according to thy desire.' So much they prayed with great humility that he granted the woman fertility; a son he gives them, and they were

Un filz lur dunet, si l'en sourent bon(t) gret;
De sain[t] batesma l'unt fait regenerer,
Bel num li metent sur la cristïentét.   30

(1–30)

Quant an la cambra furent tut sul remés,
Danz Alexis la prist ad apeler:
La mortel vithe li prist mult a blasmer,
De la celeste li mostret veritét;
Mais lui est tart quet il s'en seit turnét.   35

'Oz mei, pulcele! Celui tien ad espus
Ki nus raens[t] de sun sanc precïus!
An ices[t] secle nen at parfit amor,
La vithe est fraisle, n'i ad durable honur;
Cesta lethece revert a grant tristur.'   40

Quant sa raisun li ad tute mustrethe,
Pois li cumandet les renges de s'espethe
Et un anel, a Deu l(i) ad comandethe.
Dunc en eissit de la cambre sum pedre;
Ensur[e] nuit s'en fuit de la contrethe.   45

(61–75)

'Cambra,' dist ela, 'ja mais n'estras parede,
Ne ja ledece n'ert an tei demenede.'
Si l'at destruite cum(dis) l'ait host depredethe;
Sas i fait pendre, curtines deramedes;
Sa grant honur a grant dol ad (a)turnede.   50

Del duel s'asist la medre jus(que) a terre;
Si fist la spuse danz Alexis a certes.

---

grateful to him for this. With holy baptism they made him to be regenerate; a fair name they lay upon him according to the Christian law....When they were left all alone in the chamber, sir Alexis began to upbraid her, greatly did he begin to condemn this earthly life, and shows her the truth of the heavenly; but he is impatient to be gone. 'Hear me, maiden! Take him to spouse who redeemed us with his precious blood. In this world there is no perfect love: life is frail, there is no lasting honour, this joy turns to great sorrow.' When he has told her his whole mind, then he commits to her the baldric of his sword and a ring; he commends her to God. Then he went forth from the chamber of his father. During the night he flees from the country....'Chamber!' said she, 'nevermore wilt thou be adorned, nor shall joy be displayed in thee!' And so she destroyed it as though an army had pillaged it; sacks and torn curtains she has hung in it; she has turned its great splendour to great mourning. With grief the mother sat down upon the ground, and so in truth did the wife of sir Alexis. 'Lady,' said she, 'I have suffered such a great loss.

'Dama,' dist ele, 'jo i ai si grant perte,
Ore vivrai an guise de turtrele:
Quant n'ai tun filz, ansembl' ot tei voil estra.'   55

Ço di[st] la medre: 'S(e) a mei te vols tenir,
Sit guardarai pur amur Alexis,
Ja n'avras mal dunt te puisse guarir.
Plainums ansemble le doel de nostre ami,
Tu (de) tun seinur, jol f[e]rai pur mun filz.'   60

(141–155)

Henceforth I shall live in the manner of a turtle-dove: since I have not thy son, I would remain together with thee.' Thus spake the mother: 'If thou wouldst remain with me, I will keep thee for love of Alexis. Thou shalt never have ill from which I can protect thee. Let us mourn together the loss of our dear one, thou thy lord, and I shall do likewise for my son.'

IV. *LA CHANSON DE ROLAND*[1]

Date of Composition: about 1100.   Date of Manuscript: about 1140.

Li empereres se fait e balz e liez:
Cordres ad prise et les murs peceiez,
Od ses cadables les turs en abatiéd;
Mult grant eschech en unt si chevaler
D'or e d'argent e de guarnemenz chers   5
En la citét nen ad remés paien
Ne seit ocis u devient chrestïen.
Li empereres est en un grant verger,
Ensembl' od lui Rollant e Oliver,
Sansun li dux e Anseïs li fiers,   10
Gefreid d'Anjou, le rei gunfanuner,
E si i furent e Gerin e Gerers;
La u cist furent, des altres i out bien,
De dulce France i ad quinze milliers.
Sur palies blancs siedent cil cevaler,   15
As tables juent pur els esbaneier,
E as eschecs li plus saive e li veill,
E escremissent cil bacheler leger.
Desuz un pin, delez un eglenter,
Un faldestoed i unt fait tut d'or mer;   20
La siét li reis ki dulce France tient.

[1] Editions: T. A. Jenkins, *La Chanson de Roland*, New York, 1924. J. Bédier, *La Chanson de Roland*, Paris; i (Text and Translation), 1922; ii (Commentary and Glossary), 1927.

Blanche ad la barbe e tut flurit le chef,
Gent ad le cors e le cuntenant fier;
S'est kil demandet, ne l'estoet enseigner.
E li message descendirent a pied,   25
Sil saluerent par amur e par bien.

(96–121)

Li empereres en tint sun chef enclin,
De sa parole ne fut mie hastifs,
Sa custume est qu'il parole(t) a leisir.
Quant se redrecet, mult par out fier lu vis.   30
Dist as messages: 'Vus avez mult ben dit;
Li reis Marsilies est mult mis enemis:
De cez paroles que vos avez ci dit,
En quel mesure en purrai estre fiz?'
'Voet par hostages,' ço dist li Sarrazins,   35
'Dunt vos avrez u dis u quinze u vint.
Pa[r] nun d(e) ocire i metrai un mien filz,
E si'n avrez, ço quid, de plus gentilz.
Quant vus serez el palais seignurill,
A la grant feste seint Michel del Peril,   40
Mis avoëz la vos sivrat, ço dit;
Enz en voz bainz, que Deus pur vos i fist,
La vuldrat il chrestïens devenir.'
Charles respunt: 'Uncor(e) purrat guarir.' Aoi.

(139–156)

Notes. The poem was probably composed in that part of Normandy which adjoins the Île de France. The manuscript (Oxford, Bodleian, Digby 23) is the work of an Anglo-Norman scribe, as can be seen from various dialectal features (cf. No. III, Notes): *e* for *ie* (*chevaler* 4, 15, 47; *chers* 5; *chef* 22, 27, 89; *ben* 31; *Oliver* 60; *melz* 66; *culcét* 88; etc.); *murra* for *murrai* 61; *oi* for *üi* (*oi* 56; *pois* 58; *noit* 87, 90); *u* for *o* (cf. No. III and § 155). Of the numerous mistakes in declension the majority are to be attributed to the scribe (*chrestïen* 7 (cf. l. 43), *gunfanuner* 11, *repairét* 63, *paiens* 69, *chevaler* 71, *Francs* 78, *culcét* 88, *nasfrét* 96, *dunét* 100, *baruns* 101); others might possibly be ascribed to the poet, although when he wrote the two-case system was still well maintained on the Continent (proper names: *Sansun* 10, *Gerin* 12, *Oliver* 9, *Rollant* 9, etc.; the Learned forms *arcevesque* 70, *monie* 75; and after *cum*: 47, 64). Analogical *s* (*empereres* 1, etc.; *cumpainz* 62), *descendirent* for *descendierent* 25 (cf. § 343), may also be due to the poet. *c* for *ch* is not specifically Anglo-Norman (*cadables* 3; *cevaler* 15 (cf. *chevaler* 4); *Carlon* 53; *culcét* 88; *cascun* 94; *Carles* 97).

23 *e le c.*] MS. *e la cuntenance.*   24 *kil = ki + le*; similarly *sil = si* (sic) *+ le*   26; *nes = ne + les* 77, 103, *= ne + se* 90; *nel = ne + le* (cf. § 139).   37 *Par nun* (=*nom*) *de* 'by the name of', whence 'in token of', 'postulating', 'at the risk of'.   38 *si'n = si* (sic) *+ en*; *quid < COGITO*.

24-2

Rollant reguardet es munz e es lariz;   45
De cels de France i veit tanz morz gesir,
E il les pluret cum chevaler gentill:
'Seignors barons, de vos ait Deus mercit,
Tutes voz anmes otreit il pareïs,
En seintes flurs il les facet gesir!   50
Meillors vassals de vos unkes ne vi.
Si lungement tuz tens m'avez servit,
A oés Carlon si granz païs cunquis;
Li empereres tant mare vos nurrit!
Tere de France, mult estes dulz païs,   55
Oi desertét a tant ruboste exill!
Barons franceis, pur mei vos vei murir,
Jo ne vos pois tenser ne guarantir;
Aït vos Deus ki unkes ne mentit!
Oliver frere, vos ne dei jo faillir,   60
De doel murra[i], s(e) altre ne m'i ocit.
Sire cumpainz, alumi referir.'

Li quens Rollant el champ est repairét,
Tient Durendal, cume vassal i fiert,
Faldrun de Pui i ad par mi trenchét,   65
E .xxiiii. de tuz les melz preisez;
Ja mais n'iert home, plus se voeillet venger.
Si cum li cerfs s'en vait devant les chiens,
Devant Rollant si s'en fuient paiens.
Dist l'arcevesque: 'Asez le faites ben: 70
Itel valor deit aveir chevaler
Ki armes portet e en bon cheval set;
En bataille deit estre forz e fiers,
U altrement ne valt .iiii. deners,
Einz deit monie estre en un de cez mustiers,   75
Si prierat tuz jurz por noz peccez.'
Respunt Rollant: 'Ferez, nes espar(i)gnez!'
A icest mot l'unt Francs recumencét:
Mult grant damage i out de chrestïens.
                                        (1851–1885)
Li emperere ad prise sa herberge;   80
Franceis descendent en la tere deserte,
A lur chevals unt toleites les seles,

---

53 *oés* (<OPUS) 'need', 'use'.   54 *mare* (<MALA HORA) 'in an evil hour', 'ill-fated', 'in vain'.   56 MS. *rubostl.*   73 An imperfect line from the metrical point of view; read: *E en bataille* (?), which would give a correct cæsura.   83 *e* may be a scribal lapse for *ē* (=*en*).

Les freins a or, e metent jus les testes;
Livrent lur prez, asez i ad fresche herbe;
D'altre cunreid ne lur poeent plus faire.   85
Ki mult est las, il se dort cuntre tere;
Icele noit n'unt unkes escalguaite.

Li emperere s'est culcét en un pret,
Sun grant espiét met a sun chef li ber,
Icele noit ne s(e) volt il desarmer,   90
Si ad vestut sun blanc osberc saffrét
Laciét sun elme ki est a or gemmét,
Ceinte Joiuse, unches ne fut sa per,
Ki cascun jur muet .xxx. clartez.

Asez savum de la lance parler   95
Dunt nostre Sire fut en la cruiz nasfrét:
Carles en ad la mure, mercit Deu;
En l'orét punt l'ad faite manuvrer.
Pur ceste honur e pur ceste bontét
Li nums Joiuse l'espee fut dunét.   100

Baruns franceis nel deivent ublïer;
Enseigne en unt de Munjoie crïer;
Pur ço nes poet nule gent cuntrester.

(2488–2511)

V. *LE MYSTÈRE D'ADAM*[1]

Date of Composition: about 1150.   Date of Manuscript: 12th–13th century.

[DIABOLUS]. Eva, ça sui venuz a toi.
E[VA]. Di moi, sathan, e tu pur quoi?
D[IABOLUS]. Jo vois querant tun pru, t(un) honor.
E. Ço dunge Deu!
D.   N'aiez poür!
Mult a grant tens que j(o) ai apris   5
Toz les conseils de paraïs!

NOTES. The play was probably composed in England, as one would
conclude from the rime *ǫ : ü* (*criator : dur* 27, 28) which is an Anglo-
Norman trait. The single manuscript (belonging to the Municipal
Library of Tours) presents a large number of Anglo-Normanisms, but

TRANSLATION.
   Here have I come, fair Eve, to speak with thee.
   — And tell me, Satan, pray, why hast thou come?
   — I do but seek thy profit and thy honour.
   — God grant that it be so! — Pray, have no fear!
   Long since have I learnt Eden's secrets all!

[1] Edition: P. Studer, *Le Mystère d'Adam*, Manchester, 1918.

Une partie t'en dirrai.

E. Or(e) le comence, e jo l'orrai.

D. Orras me tu?

E.   Si f[e]rai bien,
Ne te cur[e]cerai de rien.   10

D. Celeras m'en?

E.   Oïl, par foi.

D. Iert descovert!

E.   Nenil par moi.

D. Or me mettrai en ta creance,
Ne voil de toi altre fiance.

E. Bien te pois creire, a ta parole!   15

D Tu as esté en bone escole;
Jo vi Adam, mais trop est fols.

E. Un poi est durs.

D.   Il serra mols!
Il est plus dors que n'est emfers.

E. Il est mult francs.   20

D.   Ainz est mult sers.
Cure n'en voelt prendre de soi;
Car la prenge sevals de toi.
Tu es fieblette e tendre chose,

owing to the presence of a number of Provençal forms it is assumed to
have been copied by a Provençal scribe from an Anglo-Norman manuscript. In our extract the following Anglo-Normanisms are to be noted:
Confusion of *ǫ* and *ü* (*dors* 19; cf. *dur* 28); of *oi* and *ui* (*pois* 15); *frai* 9,
curcerai 10; the writing of double consonants for single (*dirrai* 7, 35;

—————————

A part thereof I'd now divulge to thee.
— Go to, thy tale begin, and I will hear.
— Wilt thou hear me? — That will I, verily,
Nor will I anger thee in any wise.
— My secret wilt thou keep? — I will, forsooth.
— 'Twill be revealed! — Nay, Satan, not by me.
— Then will I place myself in thy safe-keeping;
No other surety do I ask of thee.
— And I, well may I believe thee, on thy word.
— Now dost thou show how well thou hast been schooled;
I saw Adam, but he's, alas, a fool.
— He's somewhat harsh. — Fear not, he'll soon be soft!
But now he's harsher even than Hell itself.
— Yet is he noble. — Nay, rather is he servile.
For not a thought will he take for himself;
Let him at least take thought for thee, his mate.
For thou art a frail and tender thing, sweet Eve,

E es plus fresche que n'est rose;
Tu es plus blanche que cristal,   25
Que neif que chiet sor glace en val,
Mal cuple em fist li criator:
Tu es trop tendre e il trop dur;
Mais neporquant tu es plus sage,
En grant sens as mis tun corrage.   30
Por ço fait bon traire a toi;
Parler te voil.

E.   Ore i ait fai!
D. N'en sache nuls!
E.   Ki l(e) deit saver?
D. Neïs Adam.
E.   Nenil, par veir.
D. Or te dirrai, et tu m'ascute!   35
N'a que nus dous en ceste rote,
E Adam la, qu'il ne nus ot.
E. Parlez en halt, n'en savrat mo(l)t.
D. Jo vus acoint d'un grant engin,

serra 18; *corrage* 30) and single for double (*seüsez* 53); mistakes in declension (*Deu* 4; *dur* 28; *que* for *qui* 26, 40; *tuit* for *tut* 54); confusion of 2nd sing. and 2nd pl. (51–54); fondness for subjunctive forms in -*ge* (*dunge* 4; *prenge* 22). Most of these features were doubtless shared by scribe and poet, but it is noteworthy that the poem presents no rimes of *ei* with *oi, ai*, or *e*, although the scribe freely writes *oi, ai, e* for *ei* (*toi* 1, *quoi* 2, etc.; *fai* 32; *saver* 33, 47).

The following MS. readings have been rejected: 20 *serf* for *sers*; 27 *culpe* for *cuple*; 34 *par moi* for *par veir*.

Thou art fresher far than any new-blown rose,
Whiter than crystal, yes, and than the snow
That falls upon the ice a-down the vale.
An ill-assorted couple God made here:
Thou art too tender, Adam is too harsh,
And ne'ertheless thou art the wiser far,
Thy mind thou hast set upon things sensible.
Therefore 'tis pleasant to draw nigh to thee;
With thee I'd speak. — 'Tis well, let there be trust!
— Let none know of it! — And who shall know, I pray?
— Not Adam even. — Nay, nay, forsooth, not he!
— And now will I tell thee, do thou hear me!
Alone we are, we twain, to keep this tryst,
And Adam there, who hears not what we say.
— Speak out, Satan, no word he'll hear, I wot.
— 'Tis of a vile deceit I would acquaint you,

Que vus est fait en cest gardin: 40
Le fruit que Deus vus ad doné,
Nen a en soi gaires bonté;
Cil qu'il vus ad tant defendu,
Il ad en soi [mult] grant vertu;
En celui est grace de vie, 45
De poësté, (e) de seignorie,
De tut saver, [e] bien e mal.

E.   Quel savor a?
D.   Celestïal.

A ton bel(s) cors, a ta figure,
Bien covendreit tel aventure, 50
Que tu fusses dame del mond,
Del soverain e del parfont,
E seüsez quanque a estre,
Que de[l] tuit fuissez bone maistre.

(205–258)

Wherewith you have been servèd in this garden:
The fruit which God has given unto you
Has in it wondrous little virtue, yet
The fruit which he has told you is forbidden,
That has in it all the grace of life,
Of worldly power, and of over-lordship,
The knowledge of all things, both good and evil.
— Pray, tell me of its savour. — 'Tis divine!
Well would this destiny become thy form,
Thy body fair, that thou shouldst ever be
The queen of all the world, both high and low,
Shouldst know all that which is, and be, in fine,
The true mistress.

VI. CHRÉTIEN DE TROYES: *EREC ET ENIDE*

Date of Composition: 1160–1170.   Edition: W. Foerster (1909)

[*Erec, driven forth by the reproaches of his wife Enide, emerges sorely wounded from the last of his knightly adventures.*]

Erec tote voie ne fine
De chevauchier a grant esploit
La ou Enide l'atandoit,
Qui mout an avoit grant duel fet,
Et cuidoit bien tot antreset, 5
Qu'il l'eüst guerpie del tot.
Et cil restoit an grant redot,

Qu'aucuns ne l'an eüst menee,
Qui la l'eüst sole trovee;
Si se hastoit mout del retor.   10
Mes la chalors qu'il ot le jor,
Et les armes tant li greverent,
Que les plaies li escreverent
Et totes les bandes tranchierent.
Onques ses plaies n'estanchierent   15
Tant que il vint au leu tot droit
La ou Enide l'atandoit.
Cele le vit, grant joie an ot;
Mes ele n'aparçut ne sot
La dolor, dont il se pleignoit;   20
Que toz ses cors an sanc beignoit
Et li cuers faillant li aloit.
A un tertre qu'il avaloit,
Cheï tot a un fes a val
Jusque sor le col del cheval.   25
Si come il relever cuida,
La sele et les estriers vuida,
Et chiet pasmez con s'il fust morz.
Lors comança li diaus si forz,
Quant Enide cheoir le vit.   30
Mout li poise, quant ele vit,
Et cort vers lui si come cele
Qui sa dolor mie ne cele.

NOTES. Chrétien was a native of East Champagne, and his language shows a number of dialectal traits.[1] In *Erec et Enide* these are more numerous than in his later works, the language of which approximates more and more to Central French. The language of the scribe (Guiot) corresponds very closely with that of Chrétien. The following features are to be noted: $\tilde{a}$ ($<\bar{e}$) is denoted phonetically by *an*, *am* (*atandoit* 3; *an* 4, etc.; *andemantiers* 70; *fame* 84; *an* (=*en* for *on*) 109). Tonic *ai* (=ϱ) appears as *e* before a final consonant (*fet* 4, etc.; *fes* 24; *et* 58; *sohet* 65; *tret* 66; also *trest* 111), but as *ei* in *atreire* 110; *feire* 109, 131. Pre-tonic *ai* (=ϱ) appears as *ei* (*eidier* 59; *soheidier* 60; *reison* 63; cf. also *pleignoit* 20, *beignoit* 21). ϱl and *uel* followed by a consonant appear as *iau* (*biaus* 39; *biautez* 97; *viaut* 59; *diaus* 29; cf. *duel* 86). Note also *aus*=*eus* (ILLOS) 138 and *leu*=*lieu* (LOCUM) 16. *aï* and *eï* rime (l. 61); when tonic, both are written *ai* (*plains* 69; *painne* 124; *daingne* 55; *çainte* 62); when pre-tonic, *ei* (*pleignoit* 20). For *porroiz* 93, see § 323; for *vost* 76, see § 356; for *chalors* 11, see § 178.

5 *antreset* (<IN TRANSACTUM) 'assuredly'. 24 *a un fes* 'all of a heap'.

[1] A full account of Chrétien's language will be found in Foerster-Breuer, *Kristian v. Troyes: Wörterbuch*, 1st ed., pp. 210–23.

An haut s'escrie et tort ses poinz;
De robe n'i remest uns poinz   35
Devant son piz a descirer.
Ses crins comance a detirer,
Et sa tandre face descire.
'Ha! Deus!' fet ele, 'biaus douz sire,
Por quoi me leisses tu tant vivre?   40
Morz! car m'oci, si t'an delivre!'
A cest mot sor le cors se pasme.
Quant ele revint, si se blasme:
'Ha!' fet ele, 'dolante Enide,
De mon seignor sui omecide,   45
Par ma parole l'ai ocis.
Ancor fust or mes sire vis,
Se je come outrageuse et fole
N'eüsse dite la parole,
Por quoi mes sire ça s'esmut.'   50

                              (4580–4629)

'Deus! que ferai? Por quoi vif tant?
Morz que demore et que atant,
Que ne me prant sanz nul respit?
Trop m'a la morz an grant despit!
Quant ele ocirre ne me daingne,   55
Moi meïsme estuet que je praingne
La vanjance de mon forfet.
Einsi morrai, mal gre an et
La morz qui ne me viaut eidier.
Ne puis morir por soheidier,   60
Ne rien ne m'i vaudroit conplainte
L'espee, que mes sire a çainte,
Doit par reison sa mort vangier.
Ja n'an serai mes an dangier
N'an proiiere ne an sohet.'   65
L'espee fors del fuerre tret,
Si la comance a regarder.
Deus la fist un po retarder,
Qui plains est de misericorde.
Andemantiers qu'ele recorde   70
Son duel et sa mesavanture,
A tant ez vos grant aleüre
Un conte a grant chevalerie,

---

60 *soheidier* = Mod.F. *souhaiter*.   66 *fuerre* 'scabbard'.   70 *Andemantiers que* 'while'; cf. § 471.

Qui de mout loing avoit oïe
La dame a haute voiz crïer. 75
Deus ne la vost mie oblïer:
Que maintenant se fust ocise,
Se cil ne l'eüssent sozprise,
Qui tolue li ont l'espee
Et arriere el fuerre botee. 80
Puis desçandi li cuens a terre,
Si li comança a anquerre
Del chevalier, qu'ele li die,
S'ele estoit sa fame ou s'amie.
'L'un et l'autre,' fet ele, 'sire! 85
Tel duel ai, ne vos puis plus dire.
Moi poise que je ne sui morte.'
Et li cuens mout la reconforte:
'Dame!' fet il, 'por Deu vos pri,
De vos meïsme aiiez merci! 90
Bien est reisons que duel aiiez,
Mes por neant vos esmaiiez;
Qu'ancor porroiz assez valoir.
Ne vos metez an nonchaloir,
Confortez vos! ce sera sans, 95
Deus vos fera liee par tans.
Vostre biautez, qui tant est fine,
Buene avanture vos destine;
Que je vos recevrai a fame,
De vos ferai contesse et dame. 100
Ce vos doit mout reconforter;
Et j'an ferai le cors porter,
S'iert mis an terre a grant enor.
Leissiez ester ceste dolor,
Que folemant vos deduiiez.' 105
Cele respont: 'Sire! fuiiez!
Por Deu merci, leissiez m'ester!
Ne poez ci rien conquester.
Riens qu'an porroit dire ne feire,
Ne me porroit a joie atreire.' 110
A tant se trest li cuens arriere,
Et dist: 'Feisons tost une biere,
Sor quoi cest cors an porterons,
Et avuec la dame an manrons
Tot droit au chastel de Limors; 115

96 *liee* (<LAETA); cf. 121 *liez* (<LAETUS). 105 *vos deduiiez*, 2nd pl.
pres. ind. of *se déduire* 'to behave', usually 'to amuse oneself'.

La iert an terre mis li cors.
Puis voudrai la dame esposer,
Mes que bien li doie peser;
Qu'onques mes tant bele ne vi
Ne nule tant n'an ancovi.   120
Mout sui liez, quant trovee l'ai.
Or faisons tost et sanz delai
Une biere chevaleresce;
Ne vos soit painne ne peresce!'
Li auquant traient les espees,   125
Tost orent deus perches copees
Et bastons liiez a travers.
Erec ont sus couchié anvers,
S'i ont deus chevaus atelez.
Enide chevauche delez,   130
Qui de son duel feire ne fine,
Sovant se pasme et chiet sovine;
Mes li chevalier pres la tienent,
Qui antre lor braz la soztienent,
Si la relievent et confortent.   135
Jusqu'a Limors le cors an portent
Et vienent el palés le conte.
Toz li pueples aprés aus monte,
Dames, chevalier et borjois.
Anmi la sale sor un dois   140
Ont le cors mis tot estandu,
Lez lui sa lance et son escu.

(4655–4746)

118 *Mes que* 'although', 'however much'.   120 *ancovi*, 1st sing. pret.
of *ancovir* (<*INCUPIRE) 'to desire'.   140 *dois* (<DISCUM) 'dais', 'table',
'high table'.

VII. MARIE DE FRANCE: *FABLES*

Date of Composition: last quarter of 12th century.

Edition: Warnke (*Bibl. Norm.* VI)

(*a*) *De Lupo et Agno* (II)

Ci dit del lou e de l'aignel,
Ki beveient a un duitel.
Li lous en la surse beveit,
E li aignels a val esteit.
Ireement parla li lous,

Ki mult esteit cuntrarious,
Par maltalent parla a lui.
'Tu me fes,' dist il, 'grant ennui.'
Li aignelez a respundu:
'Sire, de quei?'—'Dunc ne veiz tu?   10
Tu m'as ceste ewe trublee,
N'en puis beivre ma saülee.
Altresi m'en irai, ceo crei,
Cum jeo vinc ça, murant de sei.'
Li aignelez dunc li respunt: 15
'Sire, ja bevez vus a munt!
De vus me vint ceo qu'ai beü.'
'Quei!' fet li lous, 'maldiz me tu?'
Cil li a dit: 'N'en ai voleir.'
Li lous respunt: 'J'en sai le veir.   20
Cest meïsmes me fist tis pere
A ceste surse, u od lui ere,
Ore a sis meis, si cum jeo crei.'
'Que retez ceo,' fet il, 'a mei?
Ne fui pas nez, si cum jeo quit.'   25
'E quei pur ceo?' li lous a dit,
'Ja me fez tu ore cuntraire
E chose que tu ne deis faire.'
Dunc prist li lous l'aignel petit,
As denz l'estrangle, si l'ocit.   30

    Ço funt li riche robeür,
Li vescunte e li jugeür
De cels qu'il unt en lur justise.
False achaisun par coveitise
Truevent asez pur els confundre;   35
Suvent les funt a plait somundre:
La char lur tolent e la pel,
Si cum li lous fist a l'aignel.

NOTES. Marie de France was a native of France, but wrote in England, where the best[1] of the twenty-three manuscripts of her *Fables* and two of the manuscripts of her *Lais* were executed. She tells us that her Fables are translated from an English version (in its turn translated from the Latin) by a certain Alfred, whom she identifies with Alfred the Great.

(*a*) 2 *duitel* 'brook'. 12 *ma saülee* 'my fill'. 24 'Why do you blame that on me?' 25 *quit* < COGITO. 27 *cuntraire* 'offence'. 34 *achaisun* 'accusation'. 37 *tolent*, 3rd pl. pres. ind. of *tolir* 'to take away'.

(b) *De formica et cicada* (XXXIX)

D'un criket cunte la maniere,
Ki desqu'a une furmiëre
El tens d'yver esteit alez.
Par aventure est enz entrez.
Viande demanda e quist;   5
Kar n'en aveit niënt, ceo dist,
En sa maisun n'en sun recét.
Dist li furmis: 'Qu'as tu dunc fet,
Quant tu deüsses guaaignier
E en aüst tei purchacier?'   10
'Jeo chantai,' fet il, 'e deduis
A altres bestes, mes ne truis
Ki me vueille guereduner:
Pur ceo m'estuet issi aler.'
Dist li furmis: 'Chante ore a mei!   15
Par cele fei que jeo te dei,
Mielz fust que tu te purchaçasses
El meis d'aüst e guaaignasses,
Que tu fusses de freit muranz
A mun us viande queranz!   20
Pur quei te durreie a mangier,
Quant tu a mei ne puez aidier?'

Pur ceo defent que nuls ne vive
En nunchaleir ne en oisdive.
Sulunc ceo que chescuns deit faire   25
Se deit pener de bien atraire;
Plus en est chiers s'il a que prendre,
Que s'a altrui se deit atendre.

(b) 7 *recét* 'dwelling'. 10 *tei purchacier* 'to make provision for your-self'. 11 *deduis*, 1st sing. pret. (cf. § 354) of *deduire* 'to play'. 12 *truis* 1st sing. pres. ind. of *trover*; cf. § 326. 14 *estuet* 'it is necessary' cf. § 392. 20 *us* (=*huis*) 'door'. 24 *oisdive* 'idleness'.

VIII. *CHANSON DE TOILE*

Date of Composition : 12th century.   Date of Manuscript:[1] 1250–1300.

Quant vient en mai, que l'on dit as lons jors,
Que Franc de France repairent de roi cort,
Reynauz repaire devant el premier front;
Si s'en passa lez lo meis Arembor,
Ainz n'en dengna le chief drecier amont.   5
  E ! Raynaut amis !

Bele Erembors a la fenestre au jor
Sor ses genolz tient paile de color;
Voit Frans de France qui repairent de cort,
E voit Raynaut devant, el premier front;   10
En haut parole, si a dit sa raison.
  E ! Raynaut amis !

'Amis Raynaut, j'ai ja veü cel jor,
Se passisoiz selon mon pere tor,
Dolanz fussiez, se ne parlasse a vos.'   15
'Jal mesfaïstes, fille d'empereor,
Autrui amastes, si oblïastes nos.'
  E ! Raynaut amis !

16 *Jel*, the MS. reading, has been corrected to *jal* (=*ja*+*le*).

TRANSLATION.

When comes the month of May and days grow long,
The men of France return from court of king,
Raynaut returns, the first, well in the van;
He passes by the house of Erembor,
And never does he deign to raise his eyes.
  Ah ! Raynaut dear !

Fair Erembor sits by the window bright,
A coloured silk is spread upon her knee;
She sees the men of France return from court,
Raynaut she spies, the first, well in the van;
Aloud she speaks, and this is what she says:
  Ah ! Raynaut dear !

'Dear Raynaut, well do I recall the day
When, passing by my father's tower, thou
Didst sigh with grief if I spake not with thee.'
''Tis thou hast wronged me, daughter of a king:
Another didst thou love, forgetting me.'
  Ah ! Raynaut dear !

  [1] Paris, Bibliothèque Nationale, fr. 20050, fol. 69.

'Sire Raynaut, je m'en escondirai:
A cent puceles sor sainz vos jurerai,   20
A trente dames que avuec moi menrai,
C'onques nul home fors vostre cors n'amai
Prennez l'emmende et je vos baiserai.'
　　　E! Raynaut amis!

Li cuens Raynaut en monta lo degré,   25
Gros par espaules, greles par lo baudré,
Blonde ot lo poil, menu recercelé:
En nule terre n'ot si biau bacheler.
Voit l'Erembors, si comence a plorer.
　　　E! Raynaut amis!   30

Li cuens Raynaut est montez en la tor,
Si s'est assis en un lit point a flors,
Dejoste lui se siet bele Erembors.
Lors recomence[nt] lor premieres amors.
　　　E! Raynaut amis!   35

―――――――――

'Sir Raynaut, do but let me plead my cause:
Before an hundred maidens will I swear,
And thirty dames whom I shall bring with me,
By all the saints, that none I loved save thee;
Accept this reparation and my kiss.'
　　　Ah! Raynaut dear!

Then quickly doth count Raynaut mount the stair;
So broad of shoulder, slim of waist is he,
So fair his hair, waving with many a curl:
No fairer knight was there in all the world;
At sight of him she may not stay her tears.
　　　Ah! Raynaut dear!

Count Raynaut speedily ascends the tower,
Upon a couch broidered with flowers he sits,
Beside him sits the lovely Erembor.
All is forgiven, their love begins anew.
　　　Ah! Raynaut dear!

IX. GUILLAUME DE FERRIÈRES, VIDAME DE CHARTRES: *CHANSON*

Date of Composition: end of 12th century.   Edition: Brakelmann.[1]

Combien que j'aie demoré
Hors de ma dolce contree
Et maint grant traval enduré
En terre maleüree,
Por ce n'ai je pas oblïé   5
Le dolz mal qui tant m'agree,
Dont ja ne quier avoir santé,
S'en France ne m'est trovee.

Si me doinst Deus joie et santé!
La plus belle qui soit nee   10
Molt me conforte en sa bialté
Qui si m'est el cuer entree.
Et se je muir en cest pensé,
Bien cuit m'ame avoir salvee;
Car m'eüst or son liu presté,   15
Deus! cil qui l'a esposee!

TRANSLATION.

Though I have tarried long,
Far from my native strand,
And great travail endured
In an ill-favoured land,
Yet have I not forgot
The sweet-soothing malady
For which I crave no leech,
Unless in France it be.

God grant me joy and health!
The fairest of the fair,
Her beauty comforts me
Which in my heart I bear.
If with this thought I die,
Methinks my soul is saved;
Ah! would that he were I,
Who holds her wed, enslaved!

[1] Jules Brakelmann, *Les plus anciens chansonniers français*, Marburg, 1896 (p. 26).
A critical edition of Guillaume de Ferrières' poems is being prepared by
J. A. Noonan.

Hé Deus! trop sui maleürez
Se cele n'ot ma proiere,
A qui je me sui toz donez,
Si ne m'en puis traire arriere.   20
Molt longement me sui celez
Por cele gent malparliere,
Qui ja lor cuers n'auront lassez
De dire mal en derriere!

Ha! dolce riens, ne m'ocïez!   25
Ne soiez cruels ne fiere
Vers moi qui plus vos aim qu'assez
D'amor leal et entiere.
Et se vos por tant m'ocïez,
Las! trop l'achaterai chiere   30
L'amor, dont trop serai grevez;
Mais or m'est dolce et legiere!

Ill-fated then am I
If she hear not my prayer,
To whom I'm given o'er
Nor can forget this care.
Long have I hid my love
For fear of slanderers vile,
Who ne'er desist from spite
To spill their secret bile.

Ah! sweet one, slay me not,
Nor be thou cruel and cold
Toward me who love thee true,
With faithfulness untold.
If 'tis thy will I die,
Too dearly must I pay
The love which grieves me so,
And yet 'tis blithe and gay.

X. VILLEHARDOUIN: *CONQUEST OF CONSTANTINOPLE*[1]

Date of Composition: about 1210.   Date of Manuscript: 14th century.

Lors se partirent del port d'Avie tuit ensemble. Si peussiez
veoir flori le Braz-Sain-Jorge contremont de nes et de galies et
de uissiers; a mult grant mervoille ere la bialtez a regarder.

[1] Edition: N. de Wailly, *Geoffroi de Ville-Hardouin: Conquête de Constantinople*
Paris, 1874 (§§ 127–40).

Et ensi corrurent contremont le Braz-Sain-Jorge, tant que il
vindrent a Saint-Estiene a une abbaïe qui ere a trois lieues de 5
Costantinople, et lors virent tout a plain Costantinople. Cil des
nes et des galies et des uissiers pristrent port et aancrerent lor
vaissiaus. Or poez savoir que mult esgarderent Costantinople cil
qui onques mais ne l'avoient veue, que il ne pooient mie cuider
que si riche ville peust estre en tot le monde. Cum il virent ces 10
halz murs et ces riches tours dont ele [ere] close tot entor a la
reonde, et ces riches palais et ces haltez yglises, dont il i avoit
tant que nuls nel poist croire, se il ne le veist a l'oil, et le lonc
et le lé de la ville qui de totes les autres ere soveraine. Et sachiez
que il n'i ot si hardi cui la car ne fremist; et ce ne fu mie mervoille, 15
que onques si grant affaires ne fu empris de tant de gent puis
que li monz fu estorez.

Lors descendirent a terre li conte et li baron et li dux de
Venise; et fu li parlemenz ou mostier Saint-Estiene. La ot maint
conseil pris et doné. Totes les paroles qui la furent dites ne vos 20
conterai mie li livres. Met la summe del conseil si fu tiels que
li dux de Venise se dreça en estant et lor dist: Seignor, je sai
plus del convine de cest païs que vos ne faites, car altre foiz i ai
esté. Vos avez le plus grant afarie et le plus perillous entrepris
que onques genz entrepreissent; por ce si convendroit que on 25
durast sagement. Sachiez, se nos alons a la terre ferme, la terre
est granz et large, et nostre gent sont povre et diseteus de la viande.
Si s'espandront par la terre por querre la viande; et ill i a mult
grant plenté de la gent el païs; si ne porriens tot garder que nos

Notes We reproduce without change the text of the excellent Bodleian
manuscript (Laud Misc. 587, fol. 13 a, line 11 ff.), which has never received the attention it deserves. It dates from the fourteenth century
and is probably the work of a Venetian scribe, who took few liberties
with his text. There is no reason to suppose that the forms and spellings
differ markedly from those of Villehardouin, whose language, while
approximating to the standard literary language, reflects his Champenois
origin (cf. the Notes to No. vi). Our extract presents the following
deviations from standard forms: *iau* (*ial*) for *eau* (*eal*) (*vaissiaus* 8, *biax* 56,
chastials 41, *bialtez* 3); *als* for *els* 77, 87 (cf. *els* 93); *o* for *eu* or *ue* (*empereor* 53,
planteurose 64, *oil* 13, *oel* 56); *poist* for *puist* 13; *leus* for *lieus* 54; *liue* for
lieue 98 (but cf. 5, 69); *aust* for *eust* 49, 51; *camps* for *champs* 65; *cevaus* 98
(but cf. 61); *iki* for *ici* 33; *haltez* for *haltes* 12; *aront* for *avront* 43 (but
cf. 36); *conterai* for *contera* 21 (cf. No. xi, Notes).

2 *nes*, obl. pl. of *nef* (<NAVEM). 3 *uissiers* (der. from *huis*) 'transport ship'.
9, 16, 30 *que* causal (cf. § 469). 9 *cuider* 'to think', 'to conceive'. 14 *lé*
'breadth'. 17 *estorez* 'created'. 22 *se dreça en estant* 'stood up'. 23 *convine*
'condition'. 26 *durast* 'that one should bide'. 29 *el*] MS. *il*; 'and so

n'en perdissiens. Et nos n'avons mestier de perdre, que mult avons 30
poi de gent a ce que nos volons faire. Ill a isles ci pres, que vos
poez veoir de ci, qui sont habitees de genz et laborees de blez et
de viandes et d'autres biens. Alons iki prendre port, et recuillons
les blés et les viandes del païs; et quant nos avrons mis les viandes
recuillies, alomes devant la ville, et ferons ce que Nostre Sires 35
nos avra porveu. Quar plus seurement guerroie cil qui a la viande
que cil qui n'en a point.' A cel conseil s'acorderent li conte e li
baron, et s'en ralerent tuit a lor nes chascuns et a ses vaissiaus.
Ensi repouserent cele nuit. Et al maitin (fu le jor de la feste
mon seignor sain Johan-Baptiste, en juing) furent dreciés les 40
banieres et li confanon es chastials des nes et les bosches des
escuz, et portenduz les bors des nes. Chascuns regardoit ses armes
tels con a lui convint, que de fi seussent que par tens en aront
mestier.

Li marinier traistrent les ancres et laissent les voilles al vent 45
aler; et Diex lor done bon vent tel con a els convint. Si s'en
passent tres par devant Costantinople, si pres des murs et des
tours que a maintes de lor nes traist on. Si i avoit tant de gent
sor les murs et sor les tours que il sembloit que il n'aust se la non.
Ensi lor bestorna Diex Nostre Sires le conseil qui fu pris le soir 50
de torner es ysles, ausi con se chascuns n'en aust onques oï parler.
Et maintenant traient a la ferme terre plus droit que onques
il puent, et pristrent port devant un palais l'empereor Alexis,
dont li leus estoit appellez Calchidoines; et fu endroit Costantinople, d'autre part del Braz, devers la Turchie. Cil palais fu uns 55
des plus biax et des plus deletables que onques oel peussent
esgarder, de(s) toz les (liz) deliz que il convint a cors d'ome, que
en maison de prince doit avoir.

Et li conte et li baron descendirent a la terre et se herbergierent
el palais et en la ville entor, et li plusor tendirent lor paveillons. 60
Lors furent li cheval trait fors des uissiers, et li chevaler et li
serjant descen[diren]t a la terre a totes lor armes, si que il ne
remest es vaissiaus que li marinier. La contree fu bele et riche
et planteurose de toz bien, et les moies des blez, qui estoient
messoné par mi les camps, tant que chascun en volt prendre, si 65
en prist cum cil qui grant mestier en avoient. Ensi sejornerent
en cel palais l'endemain. Et al tierz jor lor dona Diex bon vent;
et marinier resachent lor ancres et drecent lor voilles al vent ensi
qu'il s'en vont contreval le Braz, bien une lieue desor Costanti-

we could not help losing some'. 30 *mestier* 'need' (cf. 44, 66, 80).
41 *confanon* 'standards'; *bosches* 'bosses'. 43 *de fi* 'assuredly'. 49 'that
it seemed as though there were nothing else (save people)'. 50 *bestorna*
'caused to go awry'. 53 *puent*; cf. § 321 (*pouvoir*). 64 *moies* 'stacks'.

nople, a un palais qui ere l'empereor Alexis, qui ere appellex 70
'Escutaire. Enki se ancreerent les nes et les uissiers et totes les
galies.

Et la chevalerie qui era erbergié el palais de Calcedonie ala
costoiant Costantinople par terre. Ensi s'erbergierent sor le Braz-
Sain-Jorge a l'Escutaire et contremont l'ost des François. Et quant 75
ce vit l'emperere Alexis, si fist la soe ost issir de Costantinople;
si se herberja sor l'autre rive, d'autre part, endroit als; si fist
tendre ses paveillons por ce que cil ne peussent prendre terre par
force sor lui. Ensi sejorna l'ost des François par nuef jorz, et
porcaça de viande cil que mestier en ot; et ce furent tuit cil de 80
l'ost.

Dedenz cel jor issi une compaigne de mult bone gent por
garder l'ost que on ne li feist mal; et les foriers (et) cerchierent
la contree. En cele chompaigne fu Odes li Champenois de
Camlite et Guillelmes ses freres et Ogiers de Sain-Cheron et 85
Manassiers de l'Isle et li cuens Cras, uns cuens de Lombardie,
qui ert del marchis de Monferrat; et orent bien avec als quatre-
vins chevaliers de mult bone gent. Et choisierent el pié de la
montaigne paveillons bien a trois lieues de l'ost; et ce estoit li
megedux l'empereor de Costantinople, qui bien avoit cinc cenz 90
chevaliers de Grius. Quant nostre gent les vit, si ordenerent lor
gent en quatre batailles, et fu lor consels tiels que iroient combatre
a els. Et quant li Grieu les virent, si ordenerent lor genz et lor
batailles et rengierent par devant les paveillons et les attendirent;
et nostre gent les alerent ferir vigueroisement a l'aïe de Dieu 95
Nostre Seignor. Petiz dura cil estors, et li Grieu lor tornent les
dos; si furent desconfis a la premiere assemblee, et li nostre les
enchaucent bien une liue grant. La gaaignerent assez cevaus et
roncins et palefrois, et muls et mules, et tentes et paveillons, et
tel gaing con a tel besoigne aferoit. Ensi se revindrent en l'ost, 100
ou il furent mult volentiers veus; et departirent lor gaing si con
il durent.

73 *era* for *ere* (3, 5, etc.); cf. § 333.   83 *foriers* 'foragers'.   84 *chompaigne*
for *compaigne* (82).   88 *choisierent* 'perceived'.   90 *megedux* 'grand-duke'.
92 *consels* = *conseus* (cf. § 185).   98 *enchaucent* 'pursue'.   100 *aferoit* 'was
fitting'.

XI. JOINVILLE: *HISTOIRE DE SAINT LOUIS*

Date of Composition: 1304–1309.   Edition: Natalis de Wailly (1906).

187. Il nous couvient premierement parler dou flum qui vient
par Egypte et de Paradis terestre; et ces choses vous ramentoif-je
pour vous faire entendant aucunes choses qui affierent a ma
matiere. Cis fleuves est divers de toutes autres rivieres; car quant
plus viennent les autres rivieres aval, et plus y chiéent de petites 5
rivieres et de petiz ruissiaus; et en ce flum n'en chiet nulles:
ainçois avient ainsi que il vient touz en un chanel jusques en
Egypte, et lors giete de li sept branches, qui s'espandent parmi
Egypte.

188. Et quant ce vient aprés la saint-Remy, les sept rivieres 10
s'espandent par le païs et cuevrent les terres pleinnes; et quand
elles se retraient, li gaaingnour vont chascuns labourer en sa terre
a une charrue sanz rouelles, de quoy il tornent dedans la terre
les fourmens, les orges, les comminz, le ris; et viennent si bien
que nulz n'i savroit qu'amander. Ne ne sait l'on dont celle creue 15
vient, mais que de la volontei Dieu; et se ce n'estoit, nul bien
ne venroient ou païs, pour la grant chalour dou soleil qui arderoit
tout, pour ce que il ne pluet nulle foiz ou pays. Li fluns est
touzjours troubles; dont cil dou païs, qui boire en vuelent, vers
le soir le prennent, et esquachent quatre amendes ou quatre 20
feves; et l'endemain est si bone a boire que riens n'i faut.

189. Avant que li fluns entre en Egypte, les gens qui ont
acoustumei a ce faire, gietent lour roys desliées par mi le flum au
soir; et quant ce vient au matin, si treuvent en lour royz cel
avoir de poiz que l'on aporte en ceste terre, c'est a savoir gingimbre, 25
rubarbe, lignaloey et canele. Et dit l'on que ces choses viennent

NOTES. Joinville's native dialect (E. Champagne) is revealed in such
features as: *ei* for *e* (*volontei* 16, *acoustumei* 23, *trouvei* 42, *citei* 60, *teix* 59);
ou for *eu* (*chalour* 17, *aioul* 64, *lour* 69). Other features of still wider
currency in E. and N.E. dialects are: *iau* for *eau* (*ruissiaus* 6, *yaue* 30);
-aige for *-age* (*passaige* 53, *pelerinaige* 86); omission of glide *d* (*venroient* 17,
85, *tenroient* 85); intercalation of *e* (*arderoit* 17, *averoit* 86); *penre* for *prendre*
66; *tailliés* for *tailliées* 40; *aus* for *eus* 55; *consoil* for *conseil* 58. Other
dialectal forms are: *Signour* for *Seigneur* 79; *bisson* for *buisson* 90. For
soufferroit 57 and *mousterrai* 77, see § 336.

1 *flum* (< FLUMEN), nom. *fluns* 22, 'river'. 2 *ramentoif*, 1st pres. ind.
of *(ra)mentevoir* (< MENTE HABERE) 'to recall'. 3 *affierent* 'pertain'. 5 For
chiéent (also *chiet* 6 and *cheoit* 41), see § 321. 12 *gaaingnour* 'husbandmen'.
14 *comminz* 'caraway'. 20 *esquachent* 'squash'. 23 *roys* (RETIS) 'nets'.
26 *lignaloey* 'aloe wood'.

de Paradis terrestre; que li venz abat des arbres qui sont en
Paradis, aussi comme li venz abat en la forest en cest païs le
bois sec; et ce qui chiet dou bois sec ou flum, nous vendent li
marcheant en ce païz. L'yaue dou flum est de tel nature, que 30
quant nous la pendiens (en poz de terre blans que l'en fait ou
païs) aus cordes de nos paveillons, l'yaue devenoit ou chaut dou
jour aussi froide comme de fonteinne.

190. Il disoient ou païs que li soudans de Babiloine avoit
mainte foiz essaié dont li fluns venoit; et y envoioit gens qui 35
portoient une maniere de pains que l'on appelle becuis, pour ce
que il sont cuit par dous foiz; et de ce pain vivoient tant que il
revenoient arieres au soudanc. Et raportoient que il avoient
cherchié le flum, et que il estoient venu a un grant tertre de
roches taillies, la ou nulz n'avoit pooir de monter. De ce tertre 40
cheoit li fluns; et lour sembloit que il y eust grant foison d'arbres
en la montaigne en haut; et disoient que il avoient trouvei
merveilles de diverses bestes sauvaiges et de diverses façons, lyons,
serpens, oliphans, qui les venoient regarder dessus la riviere de
l'yaue, aussi comme il aloient en amont. 45

191. Or revenons a nostre premiere matiere, et disons ainsi
que quant li fluns vient en Egypte, il giete ses branches aussi
comme je ai ja dit devant. L'une de ses branches va en Damiete,
l'autre en Alixandre, la tierce a Tenis, la quarte a Raxi. Et a
celle branche qui va a Rexi, vint li roys de France atout son ost, 50
et si se logea entre le flum de Damiette et celui de Rexi; et toute
la puissance dou soudanc se logierent sur le flum de Rexi, d'autre
part, devant nostre ost pour nous deffendre le passaige: laquex
chose lour estoit legiere a faire; car nulz ne pooit passer ladite
yaue par devers aus, se nous ne la passiens a nou. 55

---

554. Tandis que li roys estoit a Jaffe, l'on li dist que li soudans
de Damas li soufferroit bien a aler en Jerusalem, et par bon
asseurement. Li roys en ot grant consoil; et la fins dou consoil
fu teix, que nulz ne loa le roy que il y alast, puis que il couvenist
que il lessast la citei en la main des Sarrazins. 60

555. L'on en moustra au roy un exemple qui fu teix, que
quant li grans roys Phelippes se parti de devant Acre pour aler
en France, il lessa toute sa gent demourer en l'ost avec le duc
Hugon de Bourgoingne, l'aioul cesti duc qui est mors nouvellement. Tandis que li dus sejournoit a Acre, et li roys Richars 65
d'Angleterre aussi, nouvelles lour vindrent que il pooient penre
l'endemain Jerusalem se il vouloient, pour ce que toute la force
de la chevalerie le soudanc de Damas s'en estoit alee vers li, pour

36 becuis 'biscuit'. 50 atout 'with', cf. § 464. 55 a nou = à la nage.

une guerre que il avoit a un autre soudanc. Il atirierent lour
gent, et fist li roys d'Angleterre la premiere bataille, et li dus de 70
Bourgoingne l'autre aprés, atout les gens le roy de France.

556. Tandis que il estoient a esme de prendre la ville, on li
manda de l'ost le duc que il n'alast avant; car li dus de Bourgoingne s'en retournoit ariere, pour ce, sanz plus, que l'on ne
deist que li Anglois eussent pris Jerusalem. Tandis que il estoient 75
en ces paroles, uns siens chevaliers li escria: 'Sire, sire, venez
jusques ci, et je vous mousterrai Jerusalem.' Et quant il oy ce,
il geta sa cote a armer devant ses yex tout en plorant, et dist a
Nostre Signour: 'Biaus sire Diex, je te pri que tu ne seuffres que
je voie ta sainte citei, puis que je ne la puis delivrer des mains 80
de tes ennemis.'

557. Ceste exemple moustra l'on au roy, pour ce que se il, qui
estoit li plus grans roys des Crestiens, fesoit son pelerinage sanz
delivrer la citei des ennemis Dieu, tuit li autre roy et li autre
pelerin qui aprés li venroient, se tenroient tuit apaié de faire lour 85
pelerinaige aussi comme li roys de France averoit fait, ne ne
feroient force de la delivrance de Jerusalem.

558. Li roys Richars fist tant d'armes outre mer a celle foys
que il y fu, que quant li cheval aus Sarrazins avoient poour
d'aucun bisson, lour maistre lour disoient: 'Cuides-tu, fesoient-il 90
a lour chevaus, que ce soit li roys Richars d'Angleterre?' Et
quant li enfant aus Sarrazinnes breoient, elles lour disoient: 'Tay-
toi, tay-toi, ou je irai querre le roy Richart, qui te tuera.'

72 *a esme* 'of a mind'.   85 *apaié* 'satisfied', 'quit'.

XII. FROISSART: *CHRONICLES*

Date of Composition: 1386–8.   Edition: Luce-Raynaud (1869–1931),
                                                    Vol. x, pp. 117–21.

[Anno 1381.] Che propre jour au matin, s'estoient asamblé et
quelliét tous les mauvais, desquels Wautre Tieullier, Jake Strau
et Jehan Balle estoient cappitainne, et venu parlementer en une
grande place que on dist Semitefille, ou li marchiés des chevaulx
est le vendredi, et la estoient plus de vint mille, tout de une 5
aliance; et encores en i avoit biaucop en la ville, qui se des-
junoient et buvoient par les tavernes a le grenace, a le malevissie
chiés les Lombars, et riens ne paioient: encores tout ewireus qui
leur pooit faire bonne chiere. Et avoient ces gens, qui la estoient
asamblés, les banieres dou roi que on leur avoit bailliét le jour 10
devant, et estoient sus un propos cil glouton que de courir Londres

et reuber et pillier ce meïsmes jour, et dissoient les cappitainnes:
'Nous n'avons riens fait: ces franchisses que li rois nous a donnét
nous portent trop petit de pourfit, mais soions tout d'un acord.
Courons ceste grosse ville et riche et poissans de Londres, avant 15
que cil d'Exsexs et de Sousexsexs, de Cambruge, de Beteforde
et les autres contrees estrangnes d'Arondiel, de Waruich, de
Redinghes, de Barkesiere, d'Asquesufort, de Gillevorde, de Con-
ventré, de Line, de Staffort, de Gernemue, de Lincolle, de Iorc
et de Durames viegnent; car tout venront, et sai bien que Bakier 20
et Listier les amenront, et, se nous sommes au dessus Londres,
de l'or et de l'argent et des ricoisses que nous i trouverons et qui
i sont, nous arons pris premier, ne ja nous ne nous en repentirons,
car, se nous les laissons, cil qui vienent, che vous di, le nous
torront.'   25

NOTES. Our extract is taken from Froissart's graphic account of Wat
Tyler's rebellion (Livre II, ch. XIII). The language of the *Chronicles* shows
abundant traces of Froissart's native dialect (Picard-Hainault), in spite
of the fact that the scribes eliminated them in varying degrees. The
following are the most striking Picardisms: *ch* (=š) for Central French
c (=s) (*che* 1, 24, 30, etc., *chelle* 27, *chi* 36, *ochiiés* 37, 97, 99, *chils* 71,
commencha 72, *garchons* 75, *perchurent* 96, *anchois* 110, *fachons* 114); also *fach*
(<FACIO) 36, 86, from which *ch* was extended in Picard to the 1st pers.
of other verbs); *c* (=k) for *ch* (=š) (*ricoisses* 22, *cose* 31, 111, *cascun* 100,
camps 113, *lasque* 90); preservation of final unsupported *t* (*quelliét* 2,
bailliét 10, *donnét* 13); omission of glide *d* (*venront* 20, and with assimilation
of *l* to *r*, *torront* 25, *vorrons* 39); -(*e*)*ule* for -*ble* (-BILEM) (*paisieule* 63,
paisiule 109); *men* for *mon* (54, 58); *au* for *ou* (<*ǫl*) (*vaudrai* 55); *le* for *la*
def. art. (7?, 7?, 55, 57, 84, 99), for *la* pron. (70, 72, 95); *se* for *sa*
(64); *en* for *an* (*mengerai* 78); *ie* for *e* (<*ę* blocked) (*Engletiere* 39, *priés* 50,
61, *deviers* 62); early loss of *e* in hiatus with the following tonic vowel
(*crant* 46); *ewireus* for *eureus* (8); *estiemes* for *estiiens*, *estions* (75). Other
dialectal traits of wider currency are: *iau* for *eau* (<*ęl*) (*biaucop* 6); *li* for
la (nom. of def. art.) (*li espee* 74); *o* for *eu* (*jones* 38), for *ou* (*biaucop* 6,
cops 79); tendency of pre-tonic *e* to become *a* (*dalés* 33) and elimination
of *v* before *r* in the future of *avoir* (23, 64, 78, 115) and *savoir* (31) are
particularly common in Picard; *signeur* for *seigneur* (32, etc.), *consilliét* for
conseillé (112); *maries* for *mairies* (64); *sieue* for *siue*, 3rd pres. subjv. of
sivre 'to follow' (103); *vela* for *voila* (35). Orthographic confusion of
single and double consonants (§ 158), notably *ss* for *s*, is particularly
common in Picard (*cappitainne* 3, *valloit* 113; *aliance* 6; *dissoient* 12, *apaisse*
45, *maissons* 117, *ossés* 82, *franchisses* 13, etc.; *asamblé* 1); also *ll* or *l* for
l' (*quelliét* 2, *voel* 35, etc.).

2 *quelliét*, p.p. of *cueillier*; cf. § 294.   7 *grenace* (normally masc.) 'wine
from S.W. France'; *malevissie* (Mod.F. *malvoisie*) m. or f. 'Greek wine'.
11 *sus un propos* 'of a single mind'.   12 *reuber* 'to rob'.

A ce conseil estoient il tout d'accord, quant evous le roi qui
vient en chelle place, acompaigniés de soissante chevaulx, et ne
pensoit point a eulx, et quidoit passer oultre et aler son chemin
et laissier Londres. Enssi que il estoit devant l'abbeïe de Saint
Betremieu qui la est, il regarde et voit che peuple. Li rois s'arreste 30
et dist que il n'iroit plus avant, si saroit de ce peuple quel cose il
leur falloit, et, se il estoient tourblé, il les rapaisseroit. Li signeur
qui dalés li estoient s'arresterent; che fu raisons, quant il s'arresta.

Quant Wautre Thieullier veï le roi qui estoit arestés, il dist a
ses gens: 'Vela le roi, je voel ale[r] parler a lui. Ne vous mouvés 35
de chi, se je ne vous acene, et, se je vous fach che signe ([si] leur
fist un signe), si venés avant, et ochiiés tout horsmis le roi. Mais
au roi ne faites nul mal: il est jones, nous en ferons nostre volenté,
et le menrons partout ou nous vorrons en Engletiere, et serons
signeur de tout le royaulme, il n'est nulle doubte.' 40

La avoit un juponnier de Londres, que on appeloit Jehan Ticle,
qui avoit aporté et fait aporter bien soissante jupons, dont aucun
de ces gloutons estoient revesti, et Thieullier en avoit un vesti.
[Si] li demandoit Jehans: 'Hé sire! qui me paiera de mes jupons?
Il me faut bien trente mars.' — 'Apaisse toi, respondi Tieulliers, 45
tu seras bien paiiés encores anuit. Tient t'ent a moi: tu as crant
assés.'

A ces mos, il esperonne un cheval sur quoi il estoit montés,
et se part de ses compaignons, et s'en vient droitement au roi
et si priés de li que la queue de son cheval estoit sus la teste dou 50
cheval dou roi. Et la premiere parolle qu'il dist, il parla au roi
et dist enssi: 'Rois, vois tu toutes ces gens qui sont la?' — 'Oïl,
dist li rois, pourquoi le dis tu?' — 'Je le di pour ce que il sont
tout a men commandement, et m'ont tout juré foi et loiauté a
faire che que je vaudrai.' — 'A le bonne heure, dist li rois, je voel 55
bien qu'il soit enssi.' Adont dist Tieulliers, qui ne demandoit que
le rihotte: 'Et quides tu, di, rois, que cils peuples qui la est, et
otant a Londres, et tous en men commandement, se doie partir
de toi enssi sans porter ent vos lettres? Nenil; nous les emporterons
toutes devant nous.' Dist li rois: 'Il en est ordonné, et il le faut 60
faire et delivrer l'un apriés l'autre. Compains, retraiiés vous tout
bellement deviers vos gens et les faites retraire a Londres, et soiés
paisieule, et pensés de vous, car c'est nostre entente que cascuns
de vous par villages et maries ara se lettre, enssi comme dit est.'
A ces mos, Wautre Tieullier jette ses ieus sus un escuier dou roi 65
qui estoit deriere le roi et portoit l'espee dou roi, et haoit cils

26 *evous* for *es* (ECCE) *vous* 'behold'; cf. VI, 72.   36 *acene* 'beckon'.
46 *anuit* 'this night'; *crant* 'security'.   56 *adont* 'then'.   57 *rihotte* 'riot'.
66 *haoit*, 3rd sing. impf. of *haïr*; cf. § 291.

Tieulliers grandement cel escuier, car autrefois il s'estoient pris
de parolles, et l'avoit li escuiers vilonné: 'Voires, dist Tieulliers,
es tu la? Baille moi ta daghe.' — 'Non ferai, dist li escuiers,
pour quoi le te bailleroie je?' Li rois regarde sus son vallet, et 70
li dist: 'Bailles li.' Chils li bailla moult envis. Quant Tieulliers
le tint, il en commencha a juer et a tourner en sa main, et reprist
la parolle a l'escuier et li dist: 'Baille moi celle espee.' — 'Non
ferai, dist li escuiers, c'est li espee dou roi; tu ne vaulx mies que
tu l'aies, car tu n'iés que uns garchons, et, se moi et toi estiemes 75
tout seul en celle place, tu ne diroies ces parolles ne eusses dit
pour ossi grant d'or que cils moustiers de Saint Pol est grans.' —
'Par ma foi, dist Tieulliers, je ne mengerai jamais, si arai ta
teste.' A ces cops estoit venus li maires de Londres, li dousimes
montés as chevauls et tous armés desous leurs cottes, et rompi 80
la presse, et veï comment cils Tieulliers se demenoit; si dist en
son langage: 'Gars, comment es tu si ossés de dire tels parolles
en la presence dou roi? C'est trop pour toi.' Adont li rois se
felenia et dist au maieur: 'Maires, mettés le main a li.' Entrues
que li rois parloit, cils Tieulliers avoit parlé au maieur et dit: 85
'Et, de ce que je di et fach, a toi qu'en monte?' — 'Voire, dist
li maires, qui ja estoit avoés dou roi, gars puans, parle[s] tu enssi
en la presence de mon naturel signeur? Je ne voel jamais vivre,
se tu ne le comperes.' A ces mos il traïst un grant baselaire que
il portoit, et lasque et fiert che Tieullier un tel horion parmi la 90
teste que il l'abat as piés de son cheval. Sitos comme il fu cheus
entre piés, on l'environna de toutes pars, par quoi il ne fust veus
des assamblés qui la estoient et qui se dissoient ses gens. Adont
descendi uns escuiers dou roi, que on appelloit Jehan Standuich,
et traïst une belle espee que il portoit et le bouta ce Tieullier 95
ou ventre, et la fu mors. Adont se perchurent ces folles gens la
asamblés que leur cappitains estoit ochis. Si commenchierent
a murmurer ensamble et a dire: 'Il ont mort nostre cappitaine!
alons! alons! ochions tout!' A ces mos, il se rengierent sus le
place par maniere de une bataille, cascun son arc devant li, qui 100
l'avoit. La fist li rois un grant outrage, mais il fu convertis en
bien, car, tantos comme Tieulliers fu aterés, il se parti de ses
gens tous seuls, et dist: 'Demorés chi. Nuls ne me sieue.' Lors
vint il au devant de ces folles gens, qui s'ordonnoient pour venger
leur cappitainne, et leur dist: 'Signeur, que vous fault? Vous 105

68 *vilonné* 'insulted'. 71 *envis* 'unwillingly'. 79 *li dousimes* 'he being
the twelfth', i.e. 'with eleven others'. 84 *se felenia* 'became angry';
entrues que 'while'. 86 *a toi qu'en monte* 'what does that matter to
you?' 89 'if you do not pay for it'; *baselaire* 'cutlass'. 95 *bouta*
'thrust'.

n'avés autre cappitainne que moi: je sui vostre rois; tenés vous
en pais.' Dont il avint que li plus de ces gens, sitos comme il
veïrent le roi et oïrent parler, il furent tout vaincu et se commenchierent a de.uir, et che estoient li paisiule; mais li mauvais
ne se departoient mies, anchois se ordonnoient et monstroient 110
que il feroient quel [que] cose. Adont retourna li rois a ses gens
et demanda que il estoit bon à faire. Il fu consilliét que il se
trairoient sus les camps, car fuirs ne eslongiers ne leur valloit
riens, et dist li maires: 'Il est bon que nous fachons enssi, car
je suppose que nous arons tantos grant confort de ceuls de Londres, 115
des bonnes gens de nostre lés, qui sont pourveus et armés, eux
et leurs amis, en leurs maissons.'

111 *quel*; cf. § 276. 116 *lés* 'side'.

XIII. *LES QUINZE JOYES DE MARIAGE*

First edition: 15th century (as reprinted by F. Heuckenkamp, 1901).[1]

La quarte joye de mariage sy est quant celui qui a esté marié
et a esté en son mesnage, et demeure sept ou huyt ans, et a six
ou sept petis enfans, et a passé tous les maulx jours et males
nuits et toutes les malleuretés dessusdictes, et dont il a eu maint
maulvaiz bont, et est sa jeunesse fort refroydee, tant qu'il fust 5
temps de soi repentir, s'il peust: car il est aussi mat du mesnage
et si tres-las que il ne lui en chault plus de femme, ne qu'elle
die, ne qu'elle face. Car il est aussy aduré comme asne a l'aguillon.
Le pouvre homme a ugne fille ou deux a marier, et leur tarde
l'eure, et sont es jeux. Et a l'advanture le bon homme n'a pas 10
grant chevance; car il fault aux filles ou autres enfans chausses,
pourpoins et autres vitailles, et plusieurs autres choses. Et mesmement les filles il faut tenir joliement pour trois choses: l'une
pource qu'elles en seront plus tost demandees de plusieurs galans;
l'autre si est que se le preuxdomme n'en vouloit rien faire, il 15
n'en seroit rien pour lui, car la dame, qui a passé par ycelle
voye comme elles font, ne le souffriroit pas; l'autre si est pource
que les filles ont le cuer bon et gay de leur coustume, et jamais
ne seront aultrement qu'elles ne soyent jolies; et a l'advanture,
qui ne les tiendroit, ilz trouveroient maniere d'avoir leure joly- 20
vetés, de quoy je me taiz. Et ainsi le bon homme est esbahy
de tous les costés, et porte les grans charges, qui sera, a l'advanture,
mal habillé. Et ne lui en chault mais qu'il vive; et aussi lui

[1] Cf. p. 352. We have introduced diacritic signs, punctuation, and the distinction between *i* and *j*, *u* and *v*. We adopt the editor's *suspec* for *suepec* (65).

souffit bien, comme au poisson qui est en la nasse, qui auroit bon
temps s'on le laissast vivre en languissant, mais on lui abrege [25]
ses jours: si fait on au povre homme qui est mis en la nasse de
mesnage pour les tourmens que j'ay dis, et autres innumerables.
Et pource, lui voiant les charges et les choses que il a [a] faire,
comme j'ay dit, il ne lui chault mes qu'il vive; et met tout a non
chaloir, comme un cheval recreu ne fait compte des esperons [30]
ne de chose qui oncques lui fut faicte. Ce non obstant, il fault
qu'il trote et aille dehors pour gouverner sa terre selon l'estat
dont il est. Il a a l'adventure deux povres chevaux, ou ung, ou
nul. Maintenant s'en va trente ou quarante lieues a ugne assise
ou en parlement pour une vielle cause qui a duré long temps. [35]
Il a unes botes qui ont trois ou quatre ans; et ont esté apareillees
par bas tant que ce qui souloit estre aux genoulx est au millieu
de la jambe. Il a uns esperons du temps au roy Cloutaire, dont
l'un n'a point de molete, et une robe de parement qui a bien
dix ans; mais il n'a acoustumé de la porter, si non aux bonnes [40]
festes et quant il alloit dehors; et est de vielle façon, pource que
depuis qu'elle est faicte, il est venu d'autres nouvelletés de robes.
Et quelques jeux ou instrumens qu'il voie, il lui souvient tousjours
de son mesnage. Il vit povrement sur les chemins, et les chevaux
[de] mesmes, s'il en a; et ung varlet tout desgaroté, qui a au [45]
costé une vielle espee toute enroullie que son maistre gaigna en
la bataille de Flandres. Il porte unes vielles bouges ou le povre
homme porte son harnoys de jambes a la bataille. Briefvement,
le bon homme fait le mieulx qu'il peut, et a petis despens,
car il a assés a la maison qui lui despent. Et aussi est il plus [50]
empesché d'advocas, de sergens et de greffiers. Et s'en vient
le plus tost qu'il peut en sa maison; et a l'adventure que l'eure
est aussi pres du matin comme du soir, et ne trouve que souper,
car la dame et tout son mesnage sont couchés; et le bon homme
prent tout en pascience, car il l'a bien acoustumé. Et s'il advient [55]
que le bon homme arrive de bonne heure, fort las et travaillé,
et a le cuer pencif et chargé et angoisseux de ses besongnes, et
cuide bien estre arrivé—combien que il a maintes fois eu aussi
bien qu'il pense d'avoir—la dame tance et tempeste par la
maison. Et sachez que, quelque chose que le bon homme com- [60]
mande ou die, les serviteurs n'en feront compte, car ilz seront
tous de la dame, et les aura tous endoctrinés. Et pource il pert
sa peine de riens commander, s'il ne plait a la dame. Se le povre
varlet qui a esté avecques luy demande chose pour lui ou pour
ses chevaux, il sera suspec et rebouté, et n'ousera rien dire. Et [65]
aussy le bon homme, qui est sage et ne veult point fayre de noise,
prent tout en pascience et dit: 'Dame, vraiement vous faictes

bien des vostres!' Et la dame respont: 'Vous avés plus perdu
que vous ne gaingnerés de deux ans. Je vous avoie piesça bien
dit de par tous les dyables que vous feissiés fermer nostre polallier: 70
la martre m'a mengié trois de mes vielles gelines, dont vous vous
apercepvrés bien du dommage. Par Dieu, se vous vivés vostre
aage, vous serés le plus povre homme de vostre lignage.' 'Belle
dame,' ce fait il, 'ne me dictes point telles paroles. Dieu mercy,
j'ay assés, et auray, se Dieu plait; et y a de bonnes gens en mon 75
lygnaige.' 'Ha, voy!' fait elle, 'en vostre lignage! Par saincte
Marie, je ne sçay ou il sont, mais au moins je n'en voy gueres!'
'Par ma foy,' fait il, 'dame, il en y a de bons et qui vous valent
bien.' 'Eulx,' fait elle, 'qu'ilz me valent!' 'Oy,' fait le preudomme.
'Par Dieu,' fait elle, 'vostre fait fust bien petit se ne fussent mes 80
amis.' 'Et pour Dieu, belle dame, laissés ester ces paroles.'
'Certes,' fait elle, 'ilz vous respondroient bien, se vous leur parliés
de cestes paroles!' Lors le bon homme se taist, car a l'advanture
il a doubte qu'elle le die a ses parens.

Et adoncques se prent a plourer l'un des petis enfans; et la 85
dame le prent et bat tres-bien de bonnes verges, par despit du
bon homme plus que pour autre chose. Lors dit le preudomme:
'Belle dame, ne le batés plus,' et se cuide courroucer. Et la dame
commence a tencer et dit: 'Ha! de par tous les diables, vous
n'avés pas la peine de les gouverner, ne ilz ne vous coustent 90
gueres; et je suis tout les jours aprés: que malle mort s'y puist
mectre.' 'Haa! belle dame,' fait il, 'c'est tres-mal dit.' 'Havoi!
mon seigneur,' ce fait la nourrisse, 'vous ne sçavez pas la peine
qui y est et qu'il nous fault endurer a les nourrir.' 'Par ma foy,'
dit la chamberiere, 'c'est grant honte a vous: quant vous venés 95
de dehors, la maison deust estre resjouye de vostre venue et vous
ne faictes que noise et debat.' Et ainsy le bonhomme, soy voiant
aculé de toutes pars, et voit qu'il n'y peut riens gaigner, s'en va
coucher sans souper, et par avanture tout moullié et morfondu;
et s'il soupe, Dieu scet comment il est aise et quelle plaisance 100
il a. Puis s'en va coucher, et oit toute la nuit les enfans crier;
et la dame et la nourrisse les laissent crier tout en esciant, pour
despit du puvre homme. Et ainsi passe la nuyt en soussy et en
tourment, et tient tout a joye, veu qu'il ne vouldroit pas autrement. Pource y est et demourra tousjours et finira miserablement 105
ses jours.

XIV. RABELAIS: *GARGANTUA*

Edition: Abel Lefranc (Champion, 1913).

Comment Gargantua laissa la ville de Paris pour secourir son païs,
et comment Gymnaste rencontra les ennemys

Chapitre xxxiv

En ceste mesmes heure, Gargantua, qui estoyt yssu de Paris
soubdain les lettres de son pere leues, sus sa grand jument venant,
avoit jà passé le pont de la Nonnain, luy, Ponocrates, Gymnaste
et Eudemon, lesquelz pour le suivre avoient prins chevaulx de
poste. Le reste de son train venoit à justes journées, amenent tous 5
ses livres et instrument philosophique.

Luy arrivé à Parillé, fut adverty par le mestayer de Gouguet
comment Picrochole s'estoit remparé à La Roche Clermaud et
avoit envoyé le capitaine Tripet avec grosse armée assaillir le
boys de Vede et Vaugaudry, et qu'ilz avoient couru la poulle 10
jusques au Pressouer Billard, et que c'estoit chose estrange et
difficile à croyre des excès qu'ilz faisoient par le pays. Tant qu'il
luy feist paour, et ne sçavoit bien que dire ny que faire. Mais
Ponocrates luy conseilla qu'ilz se transportassent vers le seigneur
de La Vauguyon, qui de tous temps avoit esté leur amy et con- 15
federé, et par luy seroient mieulx advisez de tous affaires, ce
qu'ilz feirent incontinent, et le trouverent en bonne deliberation
de leur secourir, et feut de opinion que il envoyroit quelq'un
de ses gens pour descouvrir le pays et sçavoir en quel estat
estoient les ennemys, affin de y proceder par conseil prins scelon 20
la forme de l'heure presente. Gymnaste se offrit d'y aller; mais
il feut conclud que pour le meilleur il menast avecques soy
quelq'un qui congneust les voyes et destorses et les rivieres de
l'entour.

Adoncques partirent luy et Prelinguand, escuyer de Vauguyon, 25
et sans effroy espierent de tous coustez. Ce pendent Gargantua
se refraischit et repeut quelque peu avecques ses gens, et feist
donner à sa jument un picotin d'avoyne: c'estoient soisante et
quatorze muys troys boisseaux. Gymnaste et son compaignon
tant chevaucherent qu'ilz rencontrerent les ennemys tous espars 30
et mal en ordre, pillans et desrobans tout ce qu'ilz povoient;
et, de tant loing qu'ilz l'aperceurent, accoururent sus luy à la foulle
pour le destrouser. Adonc il leurs cria:

'Messieurs, je suys pauvre diable; je vous requiers qu'ayez de
moy mercy. J'ay encores quelque escu: nous le boyrons, car c'est 35

aurum potabile, et ce cheval icy sera vendu pour payer ma bien
venue; cela faict, retenez moy des vostres, car jamais homme ne
sceut mieulx prendre, larder, roustir et aprester, voyre, par Dieu!
demembrer et gourmander poulle que moy qui suys icy, et pour
mon *proficiat* je boy à tous bons compaignons.'   40

Lors descouvrit sa ferriere et, sans mettre le nez dedans, beuvoyt
assez honnestement. Les maroufles le regardoient, ouvrans la
gueule d'un grand pied et tirans les langues comme levriers, en
attente de boyre apres; mais Tripet, le capitaine, sus ce poinct
accourut veoir que c'estoit. A luy Gymnaste offrit sa bouteille, 45
disant:

'Tenez, capitaine, beuvez en hardiment, j'en ay faict l'essay,
c'est vin de La Faye Monjau.

— Quoy, dist Tripet, ce gautier icy se guabele de nous! Qui
es tu?   50

— Je suis (dist Gymnaste) pauvre diable.

— Ha! (dist Tripet) puisque tu es pauvre diable, c'est raison
que passes oultre, car tout pauvre diable passe partout sans peage
ny gabelle; mais ce n'est de coustume que pauvres diables soient
si bien monstez. Pour tant, Monsieur le diable, descendez que 55
je aye le roussin, et, si bien il ne me porte, vous, Maistre diable,
me porterez, car j'ayme fort q'un diable tel m'emporte.'

Comment Gymnaste soupplement tua le capitaine Tripet et aultres gens de Picrochole

Chapitre xxxv

Ces motz entenduz, aulcuns d'entre eulx commencerent avoir
frayeur et se seignoient de toutes mains, pensans que ce feust
un diable desguisé. Et quelq'un d'eulx, nommé Bon Joan, 60
capitaine des Franc Topins, tyra ses heures de sa braguette et
cria assez hault: '*Agios ho Theos*. Si tu es de Dieu, sy parle! Sy tu
es de l'Aultre, sy t'en va!' Et pas ne s'en alloit; ce que entendirent
plusieurs de la bande, et departoient de la compaignie, le tout
notant et considerant Gymnaste.   65

Pour tant feist semblant descendre de cheval, et, quand feut
pendent du cousté du montouer, feist soupplement le tour de
l'estriviere, son espée bastarde au cousté, et, par dessoubz passé,
se lança en l'air et se tint des deux piedz sus la scelle, le cul tourné
vers la teste du cheval. Puis dist: 'Mon cas va au rebours.'   70

Adoncq, en tel poinct qu'il estoit, feist la guambade sus un pied
et, tournant à senestre, ne faillit oncq de rencontrer sa propre
assiete sans en rien varier. Dont dist Tripet:

'Ha! ne feray pas cestuy là pour ceste heure, et pour cause.

— Bren! (dist Gymnaste) j'ay failly; je voys defaire cestuy 75 sault.'

Lors par grande force et agilité feist en tournant à dextre la gambade comme davant. Ce faict, mist le poulce de la dextre sus l'arçon de la scelle et leva tout le corps en l'air, se soustenant tout le corps sus le muscle et nerf dudict poulce, et ainsi se tourna 80 troys foys. A la quatriesme, se renversant tout le corps sans à rien toucher, se guinda entre les deux aureilles du cheval, soudant tout le corps en l'air sus le poulce de la senestre, et en cest estat feist le tour du moulinet; puis, frappant du plat de la main dextre sus le meillieu de la selle, se donna tel branle qu'il se assist sus 85 la crope, comme font les damoiselles.

Ce faict, tout à l'aise passe la jambe droicte par sus la selle, et se mist en estat de chevaucheur sus la croppe.

'Mais (dist il) mieulx vault que je me mette entre les arsons.'

Adoncq, se appoyant sus les poulces des deux mains à la crope 90 davant soy, se renversa cul sus teste en l'air et se trouva entre les arsons en bon maintien; puis d'un soubresault leva tout le corps en l'air, et ainsi se tint piedz joinctz entre les arsons, et là tournoya plus de cent tours, les bras estenduz en croix, et crioit ce faisant à haulte voix: 'J'enrage, diables, j'enrage, j'enrage! 95 Tenez moy, diables, tenez moy, tenez!'

Tandis qu'ainsi voltigeoit, les marroufles en grand esbahissement disoient l'ung à l'aultre: 'Par la mer Dé! c'est un lutin ou un diable ainsi deguisé. *Ab hoste maligno, libera nos, Domine.*' Et fuyoient à la route, regardans darriere soy comme un chien qui 100 emporte un plumail.

Lors Gymnaste, voyant son advantaige, descend de cheval, desguaigne son espée et à grands coups chargea sus les plus huppés, et les ruoit à grands monceaulx, blessez, navrez et meurtriz, sans que nul luy resistast, pensans que ce feust un diable 105 affamé, tant par les merveilleux voltigemens qu'il avoit faict que par les propos que luy avoit tenu Tripet en l'appellant *pauvre diable*; sinon que Tripet en trahison luy voulut fendre la cervelle de son espée lansquenette; mais il estoit bien armé et de cestuy coup ne sentit que le chargement, et, soubdain se tournant, 110 lancea un estoc volant audict Tripet, et, ce pendent que icelluy se couvroit en hault, luy tailla d'un coup l'estomac, le colon et la moytié du foye, dont tomba par terre, et, tombant, rendit plus de quatre potées de souppes, et l'ame meslée parmy les souppes.

Ce faict, Gymnaste se retyre, considerant que les cas de hazart 115 jamais ne fault poursuyvre jusques à leur periode et qu'il convient à tous chevaliers reverentement traicter leur bonne fortune, sans la molester ny gehainer, et, montant sus son cheval, luy donne

des esperons, tyrant droict son chemin vers La Vauguyon, et
Prelinguand avecques luy. 120

XV. PIERRE DE RONSARD

Edition: P. Laumonier (Société des Textes Français Modernes, 1914–1928).

(a) *A la fontaine Bellerie*[1]

(Livre II, Ode ix)

O Déesse Bellerie,
Belle Déesse cherie
De nos Nimphes, dont la vois
Sonne ta gloire hautaine
Acordante au son des bois, 5
Voire au bruit de ta fontaine,
Et de mes vers que tu ois.

Tu es la Nimphe eternelle
De ma terre paternelle,
Pource en ce pré verdelet 10
Voi ton Poëte qui t'orne
D'un petit chevreau de laict,
A qui l'une & l'autre corne
Sortent du front nouvelet.

Sus ton bord je me repose, 15
Et là oisif je compose
Caché sous tes saules vers
Je ne sçai quoi, qui ta gloire
Envoira par l'univers,
Commandant à la memoire 20
Que tu vives par mes vers.

L'ardeur de la Canicule
Toi, ne tes rives ne brule,
Tellement qu'en toutes pars
Ton ombre est epaisse & drue 25
Aus pasteurs venans des parcs,
Aus beufs las de la charue,
Et au bestial epars.

[1] Ed. Laumonier, I, p. 203, reproducing the text of the first edition (1550).

Tu seras faite sans cesse
Des fontaines la princesse, 30
Moi çelebrant le conduit
Du rocher persé, qui darde
Avec un enroué bruit,
L'eau de ta source jazarde
Qui trepillante se suit. 35

(b) *Ode à Cassandre*[1]

Mignonne, allon voir si la rose
Qui ce matin avoit declose
Sa robe de pourpre au soleil,
A point perdu, cette vesprée,
Les plis de sa robe pourprée, 5
Et son teint au vostre pareil.
Las, voiés comme en peu d'espace,
Mignonne, elle a dessus la place
Las, las, ses beautés laissé cheoir !
O vraiment maratre Nature, 10
Puis qu'une telle fleur ne dure
Que du matin jusques au soir.
Donc, si vous me croiés, mignonne :
Tandis que vôtre âge fleuronne
En sa plus verte nouveauté, 15
Cueillés, cueillés vôtre jeunesse :
Comme à cette fleur, la vieillesse
Fera ternir vôtre beauté.

XVI. MONTAIGNE: *LES ESSAIS*

Edition: F. Strowski (Bordeaux, 1906).[2]

Livre I, Chapitre xx

Que Philosopher c'est apprendre à mourir

Cicero dit que Philosopher ce n'est autre chose que s'aprester
à la mort. C'est d'autant que l'estude & la contemplation retirent

---

[1] Ed. Laumonier, v, p. 196, reproducing the text of the first edition (*Les Amours*, 1553).

[2] The text is that of the so-called 'exemplaire de Bordeaux', a copy of the 1588 edition with corrections and additions in Montaigne's own hand. The latter are here printed in italics and Montaigne's spellings have been strictly preserved (as in F. Strowski's edition), but the punctuation (including the use of the apostrophe) has been regularized.

aucunement nostre ame hors de nous, & l'embesongnent à part
du corps, qui est quelque aprentissage & ressemblance de la
mort; ou bien, c'est que toute la sagesse & discours du monde 5
se resout en fin à ce point, de nous apprendre à ne craindre *point*
à mourir. De vray, ou la raison se mocque, ou elle ne doit viser
qu'à nostre contentement, & tout son trauail tendre en somme
à nous faire bien viure, & à nostre aise, comme dict la Saincte
escriture. Toutes les opinions du monde en sont là, *que le plaisir* 10
est nostre but, quoy qu'elles en prennent diuers moyens; autrement
on les chasseroit d'arriuée: car qui escouteroit celuy qui pour sa
fin establiroit nostre *peine et mesaise?*

    Les dissantions des sectes philosophiques, en ce cas, sont uerbales.
"Transcurramus solertissimas nugas." Il y a plus d'opiniatreté et de 15
picoterie qu'il n'apartient a une si seincte profession. Mais quelque
personage que l'home entrepraigne, il ioue tousiours le sien parmy. Quoi
qu'ils dient, en la uertu mesme le dernier but de nostre uisee c'est la
uolupté. Il me plait de battre leurs oreilles de ce mot qui leur est si fort
a contreceur. Et s'il signifie quelque supreme plaisir et excessif contente- 20
mant, il est mieus deu a l'assistance de la uertu qu'a null'autre assistance.
Cette uolupte, pour estre plus gaillarde, nerueuse, robuste, uirile, n'en est
que plus serieusement uoluptueuse. Et luy deuions doner le nom du plaisir,
plus fauorable, plus dous et naturel: non celuy de la uigur, duquel nous
l'auons denomee. Cett'autre uolupté plus basse, si elle meritoit ce beau 25
nom, ce deuoit estre en concurrance, non par priuilege. Ie la treuue moins
pure d'incommoditez & de trauerses que n'est la uertu. Outre que son
goust est plus momentanee, fluide & caduque, ell'a ses ueillees, ses iunes,
& ses trauaus, & la sueur, et le sang; & en outre particulierement ses
passions tranchantes de tant de sortes, & a son coste une satieté si lourde 30
qu'elle equipolle a pœnitāce. Nous auons grand tort d'estimer que ces
incommoditez luy seruent d'eguillon et de condimant a sa douceur, come
en nature le contrere se uiuifie par son contrere, et de dire, quand nous
uenons a la uertu, que pareilles suites & difficultez l'accablent, la rendēt
austere & inaccessible, la ou, beaucoup plus propremant qu'a la uolupte, 35
elles annoblissent, esguisent, et rehaussent le plaisir diuin et parfaict
qu'elle nous moiene. Celuy la est certes bien indigne de son acointance,
qui contrepoise son coust a son fruit, et n'en conoit ny les graces ny l'usage.
Ceus qui nous uont instruisant que sa queste est scabreuse et laborieuse, sa
iouissance agreable, que nous disent ils par la, si non qu'elle est tousiours 40
desagreable. Car quel moien humain arriua iamais a sa iouissance? Les
plus parfaicts se sont bien contantez d'y aspirer et de l'aprocher sans la
posseder. Mais ils se trompent: ueu que de tous les plaisirs que nous
conessons, la poursuite mesme en est plaisante. L'entreprinse se sent de la
qualite de la chose qu'elle regarde, car c'est une bone portion de l'effaict 45
et consubstantielle. L'heur et la beatitude qui reluit en la uertu, ramplit

toutes ses apartenances & auenues iusques a la premiere entree et extreme
barriere. Or des principaus bienfaicts de la uertu est le mespris de la
mort, moien qui fournit nostre uie d'une molle tranquillité, nous en done
le goust pur et amiable, sans qui tout'autre uolupté est esteinte.   50

Voyla pourquoy toutes les *regles* se rencontrent & conuiennent
à *cet* article. Et bien qu'elles nous conduisent aussi toutes d'vn
commun accord à mespriser la douleur, la pauureté, & autres
accidens à quoy la vie humaine est subiecte, ce n'est pas d'vn
pareil soing, tant par ce que ces accidens ne sont pas de telle 55
necessité (la pluspart des hommes passent leur vie sans gouster
de la pauureté, & tels encore sans sentiment de douleur & de
maladie, comme Xenophilus le Musicien, qui vescut cent & six
ans d'vne entiere santé) qu'aussi d'autant qu'au pis aller la mort
peut mettre fin, quand il nous plaira, & coupper broche à tous 60
autres inconuenients. Mais quant à la mort, elle est ineuitable,

> Omnes eodem cogimur, omnium
> Versatur vrna, serius ocius
> Sors exitura & nos in æter-
> Num exitium impositura cymbæ.   65

Et par consequent, si elle nous faict peur, c'est vn subiect con-
tinuel de tourment, & qui ne se peut aucunement soulager.
Il n'est lieu d'ou elle ne nous uieigne; nous pouuons tourner sans cesse la
teste ça & la come en païs suspect: "*quæ quasi saxum Tantalo semper*
impendet". Nos parlemens renuoyent souuent executer les criminels 70
au lieu où le crime est commis: durant le chemin, promenez les
par *des* belles maisons, faictes leur tant de bonne chere qu'il
vous plaira,

> non Siculæ dapes
> Dulcem elaborabunt saporem,   75
> Non auium cytharæque cantus
> Somnum reducent,

pensez vous qu'ils s'en puissent resiouir, & que la finale intention
de leur voyage, leur estant ordinairement deuant les yeux, ne
leur ait alteré & affadi le goust à toutes ces commoditez?   80

> Audit iter, numerátque dies, spacióque viarum
> Metitur vitam, torquetur peste futura.

Le but de nostre carriere c'est la mort, c'est l'obiect necessaire
de nostre visée: si elle nous effraye, comme est il possible d'aller
vn pas auant, sans fiebure? Le remede du vulgaire c'est de n'y 85
penser pas. Mais de quelle brutale stupidité luy peut venir vn si
grossier aueuglement? Il luy faut faire brider l'asne par la queuë,

> Qui capite ipse suo instituit vestigia retro.

Ce n'est pas de merueille s'il est si souuent pris au piege. On faict peur à nos gens, seulement de nommer la mort, & la plus- 90 part s'en seignent, comme du nom du diable. Et par-ce qu'il s'en faict mention aux testamens, ne vous attendez pas qu'ils y mettent la main, que le medecin ne leur ait donné l'extreme sentence; & Dieu sçait lors, entre la douleur & la frayeur, de quel bon iugement ils vous le patissent. 95

Parce que cette syllabe frappoit trop rudement leurs oreilles, & que cette voix leur sembloit malencontreuse, les Romains auoyent apris de l'amollir ou de l'estendre en perifrazes. Au lieu de dire: il est mort; il a cessé de viure, disent-ils, il a vescu. Pourueu que ce soit vie, soit elle passée, ils *se consolent*. Nous en 100 auons emprunté nostre feu Maistre-Iehan.

XVII. MOLIÈRE: *LE MISANTHROPE*

Edition: Paris, 1674 (Denys Thierry et Claude Barbin).[1]

Act II, Scene i

ALCESTE

Madame, voulez-vous que je vous parle net?
De vos façons d'agir je suis mal satisfait:
Contr'elles, dans mon Cœur, trop de Bile s'assemble,
Et je sens qu'il faudra que nous rompions ensemble.
Oüy, je vous tromperois de parler autrement, 5
Tost ou tard nous romprons, indubitablement;
Et je vous promettrois mille fois le contraire,
Que je ne serois pas en pouvoir de le faire.

CELIMENE

C'est pour me quereller donc à ce que je voy,
Que vous avez voulu me ramener chez moy? 10

[1] The only changes we have made consist in the expansion of $\bar{a}$ to *an* (13, 37, 63), $\bar{e}$ to *en* (21), $\bar{o}$ to *on* (13, 17, 32, 35, 37), $\bar{o}$ to *om* (43, 52); cf. § 167.

The 1667 edition (Paris, Jean Ribou) is less carefully printed (misprints: 18 and 80 *les*] *le*; 23 *Arme*; 54 *voyez*; and perhaps 82 *Amant*] *Amour*). It shows a much more sparing use of *j* and *v* and of the hyphen. The use of capitals is identical, but the comma is employed much more freely. The bar ($\bar{a}$, $\bar{o}$, etc.) and the accent (acute or circumflex) are sometimes used merely to economize space. The following are the chief orthographical variants: 5 and 76 *Ouv*; 12 *accez*; 17 *fond*; 25 *presentez*; 27 *estenduë*; 31 *Merite*; 38 *a-t'il*; 40 *gaigné*; 45 *Procez*; 47 *Proces*; 50 *reçeu*; 51 *r'asseoir*; 60 *souffire*; 61 *assûrera*; 64 *la*; 66 *dedis*; 67 *méme*; 69 *r'atrape*; 70 *beniray*; 73 *éforts*; 84 *Demeslez*.

ALCESTE

Je ne querelle point; mais vostre humeur, Madame,
Ouvre au premier venu trop d'accés dans vôtre Ame;
Vous avez trop d'Amans, qu'on voit vous obseder,
Et mon cœur de cela ne peut s'accommoder.

CELIMENE

Des Amans que je fais, me rendez-vous coupable?   15
Puis-je empescher les Gens, de me trouver aimable?
Et lors que pour me voir, ils font de doux efforts,
Dois-je prendre un Baston, pour les mettre dehors?

ALCESTE

Non, ce n'est pas, Madame, un Baston qu'il faut prendre,
Mais un Cœur à leurs vœux moins facile & moins tendre. 20
Je sçai que vos Appas vous suivent en tous Lieux,
Mais vostre accüeil retient ceux qu'attirent vos yeux;
Et sa douceur offerte à qui vous rend les Armes,
Acheve sur les Cœurs l'Ouvrage de vos Charmes.
Le trop riant Espoir que vous leur présentez,   25
Attache autour de vous leurs assiduitez;
Et vostre Complaisance, un peu moins étenduë,
De tant de Soûpirans chasseroit la Cohuë.
Mais, au moins, dites-moy, Madame, par quel Sort,
Vostre Clitandre a l'heur de vous plaire si fort?   30
Sur quel fonds de Mérite, & de Vertu sublime,
Appuyez-vous, en lui, l'honneur de vostre Estime?
Est-ce par l'Ongle long, qu'il porte au petit Doigt,
Qu'il s'est acquis, chez vous, l'Estime où l'on le voit?
Vous estes-vous renduë, avec tout le beau Monde,   35
Au mérite éclatant de sa Perruque blonde?
Sont-ce ses grands Canons, qui vous le font aimer?
L'amas de ses Rubans a-t-il sçeu vous charmer?
Est-ce par les appas de sa vaste Reingrave,
Qu'il a gagné vostre Ame, en faisant vôtre Esclave?   40
Ou sa façon de rire, & son ton de Faucet,
Ont-ils de vous toucher sçeu trouver le secret?

CELIMENE

Qu'injustement, de lui, vous prenez de l'ombrage!
Ne sçavez-vous pas bien, pourquoi je le ménage?
Et que dans mon Procés, ainsi qu'il m'a promis,   45
Il peut interesser tout ce qu'il a d'Amis.

ALCESTE

Perdez vostre Procés, Madame, avec constance,
Et ne ménagez point un Rival qui m'offence.

CELIMENE

Mais de tout l'Univers, vous devenez jaloux.

ALCESTE

C'est que tout l'Univers est bien receu de vous.   50

CELIMENE

C'est ce qui doit rasseoir vostre Ame effarouchée,
Puis que ma Complaisance est sur tous épanchée:
Et vous auriez plus lieu de vous en offencer,
Si vous me la voyiez sur un seul ramasser.

ALCESTE

Mais, moy, que vous blâmez de trop de jalousie?   55
Qu'ay-je de plus qu'eux tous, Madame, je vous prie?

CELIMENE

Le bon-heur de sçavoir que vous estes aimé.

ALCESTE

Et quel lieu de le croire, à mon Cœur enflamé?

CELIMENE

Je pense qu'ayant pris le soin de vous le dire,
Un aveu de la sorte a dequoy vous suffire.   60

ALCESTE

Mais qui m'assurera que, dans le mesme instant,
Vous n'en disiez, peut-estre, aux autres tout autant?

CELIMENE

Certes, pour un Amant la Fleurette est mignonne,
Et vous me traitez là de gentille Personne.
Hé bien, pour vous oster d'un semblable soucy,   65
De tout ce que j'ay dit, je me dédis icy:
Et rien ne sçauroit plus vous tromper, que vous-mesme;
Soyez content.

ALCESTE

                    Morbleu, faut-il que je vous aime?
Ah! que si de vos Mains je r'attrape mon Cœur,
Je béniray le Ciel de ce rare Bon-heur!   70

Je ne le cele pas, je fais tout mon possible
A rompre de ce Cœur l'attachement terrible;
Mais mes plus grands efforts n'ont rien fait jusqu'icy,
Et c'est pour mes Pechez que je vous aime ainsi.

CELIMENE

Il est vray, vostre ardeur est pour moy sans seconde.   75

ALCESTE

Oüy, je puis là-dessus défier tout le Monde,
Mon amour ne se peut concevoir, & jamais
Personne n'a, Madame, aimé comme je fais.

CELIMENE

En effet, la Méthode en est toute nouvelle,
Car vous aimez les Gens, pour leur faire querelle;   80
Ce n'est qu'en Mots fâcheux, qu'éclate vostre ardeur,
Et l'on n'a veu jamais, un Amant si grondeur.

ALCESTE

Mais il ne tient qu'à vous, que son chagrin ne passe;
A tous nos Démeslez, coupons chemin, de grace,
Parlons à Cœur ouvert, & voyons d'arrester..   85

XVIII. LA FONTAINE: *FABLES*

Edition: Paris, 1678 (Denys Thierry et Claude Barbin).

(a) *La cigale & la Fourmy* (I, 1)

La Cigale ayant chanté
    Tout l'Esté,
Se trouva fort dépourvuë
Quand la bise fut venuë.
Pas un seul petit morceau   5
De mouche ou de vermisseau.
Elle alla crier famine
Chez la Fourmy sa voisine;
La priant de luy prester
Quelque grain pour subsister   10
Jusqu'à la saison nouvelle.
Je vous payray, luy dit-elle,
Avant l'Oust, foy d'animal,
Interest & principal.
La Fourmy n'est pas presteuse;   15
C'est là son moindre défaut.

Que faisiez-vous au temps chaud?
Dit elle à cette emprunteuse.
Nuit & jour à tout venant
Je chantois, ne vous déplaise.   20
Vous chantiez? j'en suis fort aise.
Et bien, dansez maintenant.

(b) *Le Loup & l'Agneau* (i, 10)

La raison du plus fort est toûjours la meilleure.
    Nous l'allons montrer tout à l'heure
    Un Agneau se desalteroit
    Dans le courant d'une onde pure.
Un Loup survient à jeun qui cherchoit avanture,   5
    Et que la faim en ces lieux attiroit.
Qui te rend si hardi de troubler mon breuvage?
    Dit cet animal plein de rage:
Tu seras châtié de ta temerité.
Sire, répond l'Agneau, que vostre Majesté   10
    Ne se mette pas en colere;
    Mais plutost qu'elle considere
    Que je me vas desalterant
        Dans le courant,
    Plus de vingt pas au dessous d'elle;   15
Et que par consequent en aucune façon
    Je ne puis troubler sa boisson.
Tu la troubles, reprit cette beste cruelle,
Et je sçai que de moy tu médis l'an passé.
Comment l'aurois-je fait si je n'estois pas né?   20
    Reprit l'Agneau, je tete encore ma mere.
    Si ce n'est toy, c'est donc ton frere:
    Je n'en ay point. C'est donc quelqu'un des tiens:
    Car vous ne m'épargnez guéres,
    Vous, vos bergers, & vos chiens.   25
On me l'a dit: il faut que je me vange.
    Là-dessus au fond des forests
    Le Loup l'emporte, & puis le mange,
    Sans autre forme de procés.

Appendix B

SELECT BIBLIOGRAPHY[1]

GENERAL[2]

A. Darmesteter. *Cours de grammaire historique de la langue française.* Paris. Published posthumously by E. Muret (vol. I, 1891) and L. Sudre (vols. II–IV, 1894–7); later editions by L. Sudre, whose name we use as a short reference for examples taken from vol. IV.

Kr. Nyrop. *Grammaire historique de la langue française.* 6 vols. Copenhagen, 1899–1930.

F. Brunot. *Histoire de la langue française des origines à 1900.* Paris, 1905 ff. Twelve volumes (tomes I–V, VII and part of VI, IX) have so far appeared.

—— 'La langue française', in L. Petit de Julleville's *Histoire de la langue et de la littérature française.* 8 vols. Paris, 1895–1900.

—— *Précis de grammaire historique de la langue française.* Paris, 1887. New edition (in collaboration with Ch. Bruneau) 1933.

W. Meyer-Lübke. *Historische Grammatik der französischen Sprache.* Heidelberg. Vol. I. *Laut- und Flexionslehre,* 1908; 3rd ed. 1913. Vol. II. *Wortbildungslehre,* 1921.

K. Vossler. *Frankreichs Kultur im Spiegel seiner Sprachentwicklung. Geschichte der französischen Schriftsprache von den Anfängen bis zur klassischen Neuzeit.* Heidelberg, 1913; 2nd ed. 1929.

L. Clédat. *Manuel de Phonétique et de Morphologie historique du français.* Paris, 1917.

A. Dauzat. *La langue française, sa vie, son évolution.* Paris, 1926.

—— *Histoire de la langue française.* Paris, 1930.

A. Hatzfeld, A. Darmesteter et A. Thomas. *Dictionnaire Général de la langue française* (preceded by *Traité de la formation de la langue*). Paris, 1892–1900.

W. Meyer-Lübke. *Romanisches etymologisches Wörterbuch.* Heidelberg, 1911; 3rd ed. in course of publication (A–T).

L. Clédat. *Dictionnaire étymologique de la langue française.* Paris, 1912; 12th ed. 1929.

W. von Wartburg. *Französisches etymologisches Wörterbuch.* Bonn-Leipzig, 1922 ff. Twenty-three fascicules (A–F) have appeared.

---

[1] Further bibliographical indications on points of detail and special aspects are given in the foot-notes. For other recent publications the reader should consult *The Year's Work in Modern Language Studies,* edited by W. J. Entwistle. London. Vols. I–III, 1931–3. Also the periodicals listed below.

[2] The bibliographical indications for separate chapters should be completed by references to the relevant sections of the larger works here quoted.

E. Gamillscheg. *Etymologisches Wörterbuch der französischen Sprache*. Heidelberg, 1926–9.

O. Bloch et W. von Wartburg. *Dictionnaire étymologique de la langue française*. Paris, 1932.

F. Godefroy. *Dictionnaire de l'ancienne langue française et de tous ses dialectes du IXe au XVe siècle*. 10 vols. Paris, 1880–1902.

—— *Lexique de l'ancien français*, p.p. J. Bonnard et Am. Salmon. Paris, 1901.

A. Tobler–E. Lommatzsch. *Altfranzösisches Wörterbuch*. Berlin, 1915 ff. Fifteen fascicules (A–De) have appeared.

J. Gilliéron et E. Edmont. *Atlas linguistique de la France*. Paris, 1900–12; *Supplément*, 1920.

J. Gilliéron et M. Roques. *Études de géographie linguistique*. Paris, 1912.

K. Jaberg. *Sprachgeographie*. Aarau, 1908.

A. Dauzat. *La géographie linguistique*. Paris, 1922.

—— *Essais de géographie linguistique*. Paris, vol. i, 1921; vol. ii, 1928.

A.-L. Terracher. *L'histoire des langues et la géographie linguistique*. Oxford, 1929.

J. Orr. Reviews in *Modern Language Review*, xxiv (1929), pp. 364–70; xxv (1930), pp. 365–70; *Times Literary Supplement*, March 21, 1929.

PERIODICALS

Archiv für das Studium der neueren Sprachen (Herrigs Archiv). 1846 ff.

Romania. Paris, 1872 ff.

Revue des Langues romanes. Montpellier, 1870 ff.

Zeitschrift für romanische Philologie. Halle, 1877 ff.

Zeitschrift für französische Sprache und Literatur. Berlin, 1878 ff.

Literaturblatt für germanische und romanische Philologie. Leipzig, 1880 ff.

Romanische Forschungen. Erlangen, 1885 ff.

Modern Language Notes. Baltimore, 1886 ff.

Revue de Philologie française et provençale. Paris, 1887 ff.

Modern Philology. Chicago, 1903 ff.

Modern Language Review. Cambridge, 1906 ff.

Romanic Review. New York, 1910 ff.

Archivum Romanicum. Geneva, 1917 ff.

Revue de Linguistique romane. Paris, 1925 ff.

Medium Ævum. Oxford, 1932 ff.

CHAPTER I

G. Gröber. *Grundriss der romanischen Philologie*. Strasburg, vol. i, 2nd ed. 1906.

W. M. Lindsay. *The Latin Language*. Oxford, 1894.

—— *A Short Historical Latin Grammar*. Oxford, 1895; 2nd ed. 1915.

SELECT BIBLIOGRAPHY 401

A. Meillet. *Esquisse d'une histoire de la langue latine.* Paris, 1928; 2nd ed. 1931.

W. Meyer-Lübke. *Grammatik der romanischen Sprachen.* 4 vols. Leipzig, 1890–1902. French translation: *Grammaire des langues romanes.* Paris, 1890–1906.

—— *Einführung in das Studium der romanischen Sprachwissenschaft.* Heidelberg, 1901; 3rd ed. 1920.

C. H. Grandgent. *An Introduction to Vulgar Latin.* Boston, 1907.

E. Bourciez. *Éléments de linguistique romane.* Paris, 1910; 3rd ed. 1930.

Schwan-Behrens. *Grammatik des Altfranzösischen.* Leipzig, 12th ed. 1925. French translation by O. Bloch: *Grammaire de l'ancien français.* Leipzig, 4th ed. 1932.

J. Anglade. *Grammaire élémentaire de l'ancien français.* Paris, 1918.

K. von Ettmayer. *Vorträge zur Charakteristik des Altfranzösischen.* Fribourg, 1910.

D. A. Paton. *Manuel d'ancien français.* London, 1933.

A. Darmesteter et A. Hatzfeld. *Le seizième siècle en France. Tableau de la littérature et de la langue, suivi de morceaux choisis.* Paris, 1878; 13th ed. 1920.

Ch.-L. Livet. *La grammaire française et les grammairiens au XVIe siècle.* Paris, 1859.

E. Lerch. 'Die französische Sprache im 19. und 20. Jahrhundert', in *Neuphilologische Monatsschrift,* i, pp. 99–111, 145–58. Also separately.

E. Richter. 'Der Entwicklungsweg des neuesten Französischen', in *Herrigs Archiv,* clviii, pp. 60–83, 222–42.

G. Rohlfs. *Volkssprachliche Einflüsse im modernen Französisch.* 1928.

D. Mornet. *Histoire de la clarté française.* Paris, 1929.

H. Suchier. 'Die französische und provenzalische Sprache und ihre Mundarten', in Gröber's *Grundriss,* i, pp. 712–840. French translation by P. Monet (Paris, 1891).

H. Morf. *Zur sprachlichen Gliederung Frankreichs.* Berlin, 1911.

A. Dauzat. *Les Patois.* Paris, 1927. (Contains a useful bibliography.)

L. Sainéan. *L'argot ancien* (1455–1850). Paris, 1907.

—— *Les sources de l'argot ancien.* 2 vols. Paris, 1912.

A. Dauzat. *Les Argots.* Paris, 1929. (Contains a useful bibliography.)

—— *L'argot de la guerre.* Paris, 1918; 2nd ed. 1919.

J. Lacassagne. *L'argot du 'milieu'.* Paris, 1929.

G. Gougenheim. *La langue populaire dans le premier quart du XIXe siècle.* Paris, 1929.

L. Sainéan. *Le langage parisien au XIXe siècle.* Paris, 1920.

H. Bauche. *Le langage populaire. Grammaire, syntaxe et dictionnaire du français tel qu'on le parle dans le peuple de Paris.* Paris, 1920. New ed. 1927.

L. E. Kastner and J. Marks. *A Glossary of Colloquial and Popular French.* London, 1929.

Bulletin du parler français au Canada. Quebec, 1902 ff.

Glossaire du parler français au Canada, préparé par la Société du parler français au Canada. Quebec, 1930.

A. RIVARD et S. A. LORTIE. *L'origine et le parler des Canadiens français.* Quebec-Paris, 1903.

A. RIVARD. *Les dialectes dans le parler franco-canadien.* Quebec, 1907.

J. GEDDES et A. RIVARD. *Bibliographie du parler français au Canada.* Quebec-Paris, 1906.

N.-E. DIONNE. *Le parler populaire des Canadiens français.* Quebec, 1909.

———

J. VISING. *Étude sur le dialecte anglo-normand du XIIe siècle.* Upsala, 1882.

—— *Anglo-Norman Language and Literature.* Oxford, 1923. (Contains an excellent bibliography.)

L. E. MENGER. *The Anglo-Norman Dialect.* New York, 1904.

F. J. TANQUEREY. *L'Évolution du verbe en anglo-français.* Paris, 1915.

M. K. POPE. *Étude sur la langue de Frère Angier.* Paris, 1903.

CHAPTER II

H. PAUL. *Prinzipien der Sprachgeschichte.* Halle, 5th ed. 1920.

F. DE SAUSSURE. *Cours de linguistique générale.* Paris, 2nd ed. 1922.

A. MEILLET. *Linguistique historique et linguistique générale.* Paris, 2nd ed. 1926.

J. VENDRYES. *Le langage.* Paris, 1921.

O. JESPERSEN. *Language, its Nature, Development and Origin.* London, 1922.

A. H. GARDINER. *The Theory of Speech and Language.* Oxford, 1932.

A. DAUZAT. *La Vie du langage.* Paris, 3rd ed. 1922.

—— *La Philosophie du langage.* Paris, 6th ed. 1929.

F. BRUNOT. *La pensée et la langue.* Paris, 2nd ed. 1927.

H. DELACROIX. *Le langage et la pensée.* Paris, 1924.

CH. BALLY. *Le langage et la vie.* Paris, 1926.

—— *Linguistique générale et linguistique française.* Paris, 1932.

M. BARTOLI. *Introduzione alla neolinguistica.* Geneva, 1925.

G. BERTONI–M. BARTOLI. *Breviario di neolinguistica.* Modena, 1925.

CHAPTER III

A. C. JURET. *Manuel de phonétique latine.* Paris, 1921.

—— *La phonétique latine* (abridged). Strasburg, 1929.

M. NIEDERMANN. *Historische Lautlehre des Lateinischen.* Heidelberg, 2nd ed. 1931. French translation: *Précis de phonétique historique du latin.* Paris, 2nd ed. 1931.

H. SUCHIER. *Les voyelles toniques du vieux français.* Paris, 1906. (Translated from the German by C. GUERLIN DE GUER.)

H. E. BERTHON et V. G. STARKEY. *Tables synoptiques de Phonologie de l'ancien français.* Oxford, 1908.

E. Bourciez. *Précis historique de phonétique française.* Paris, 7th ed. 1930.

Ch. Thurot. *De la prononciation française depuis le commencement du XVIe siècle, d'après les témoignages des grammairiens.* 2 vols. Paris, 1881–3.

Th. Rosset. *Les Origines de la prononciation moderne étudiées au XVIIe siècle.* Paris, 1911.

E. Herzog. *Historische Sprachlehre des Neufranzösischen.* I. Teil: *Einleitung. Lautlehre.* Heidelberg, 1913.

G. Rydberg. *Zur Geschichte des französischen ?.* Upsala, 1896–1907.

Kr. Nyrop. *Manuel phonétique du français parlé.* Paris, 4th ed. (translated by E. Philipot) 1924.

M. Grammont. *Traité pratique de prononciation française.* Paris, 6th ed. 1928.

H. Langlard. *La liaison dans le français.* Paris, 1928.

H. Klinghardt and M. de Fourmestraux. *French Intonation Exercises.* Cambridge, 1923. (Translated from the German and adapted by M. L. Barker.)

H. Michaelis et P. Passy. *Dictionnaire phonétique de la langue française.* Hanover, 2nd ed. 1924.

A. Barbeau et E. Rodhe. *Dictionnaire phonétique de la langue française.* Stockholm, 1930.

CHAPTER IV

Ch. Beaulieux. *Histoire de l'orthographe française.* Vol. i, *Formation de l'orthographe.* Vol. ii, *Les accents et autres signes auxiliaires.* Paris, 1927.

F. Brunot. *La réforme de l'orthographe.* Paris, 1905.

H. Sensine. *La ponctuation en français.* Paris, 1930.

CHAPTER V

A. Ernout. *Morphologie historique du latin.* Paris, 2nd ed. 1927.

P. Fouché. *Le Verbe français. Étude morphologique.* Strasburg, 1931.

J. Gilliéron. *La faillite de l'étymologie phonétique (Étude sur la défectivité des verbes).* Neuveville, 1919. Cf. L. Clédat in *Revue de Philologie française,* xxxiv (1922), pp. 1–21.

A. C. Juret. *Système de la syntaxe latine.* Strasburg, 1926.

F. Stolz und J. H. Schmalz. *Lateinische Grammatik.* Munich, 5th ed. 1928.

P. Horluc et G. Marinet. *Bibliographie de la syntaxe française.* Lyons-Paris, 1908.

L. Foulet. *Petite syntaxe de l'ancien français.* Paris, 3rd ed. 1930.

E. Huguet. *Étude sur la syntaxe de Rabelais.* Paris, 1894.

A. Haase. *Französische Syntax des XVII. Jahrhunderts.* Oppeln-Leipzig, 1888. French translation by Mlle Obert: *Syntaxe française du XVII siècle.* Paris, 1898.

K. SNEYDERS DE VOGEL. *Syntaxe historique du français*. Groningen, 2nd ed. 1926.

C. DE BOER. *Essais de syntaxe française moderne*. Groningen-Paris, 1923.

J. DAMOURETTE et E. PICHON. *Des mots à la pensée. Essai de grammaire de la langue française*. 3 vols. Paris, 1930–2.

K. ETTMAYER. *Zur Theorie der analytischen Syntax des Französischen*. Vienna, 1929.

—— *Analytische Syntax der französischen Sprache, mit besonderer Berücksichtigung des Altfranzösischen*. Halle, 1930 ff. (To be complete in about ten parts; eight parts have appeared to date.)

E. LERCH. *Historische französische Syntax*. Leipzig, 1925 ff. (To be complete in four volumes; the first two have appeared.)

A. TOBLER. *Vermischte Beiträge zur französischen Grammatik*. Leipzig, Reihe I–III, 2nd ed. 1902–8; Reihe IV, 1908; Reihe V, 1912 (pp. 1–29).

E. RICHTER. *Zur Entwicklung der romanischen Wortstellung aus der lateinischen*. Vienna, 1903.

—— 'Grundlinien der Wortstellungslehre', in *Zeitschrift für rom. Phil.* XL, pp. 9–61, XLII, pp. 703–21.

A. BLINKENBERG. *L'ordre des mots en français moderne*. I. Copenhagen, 1928.

H. FREI. *La grammaire des fautes*. Paris, 1929.

CHAPTER VI

H. BERGER. *Die Lehnwörter in der französischen Sprache ältester Zeit*. Leipzig, 1899.

G. PARIS. 'Les plus anciens mots d'emprunt', in *Journal des Savants*, 1900, pp. 294–307, 356–75; reprinted in *Gaston Paris: Mélanges Linguistiques*, p.p. MARIO ROQUES, pp. 315–52. Paris, 1909.

W. HAUPRICH. *Der Einfluss des Christentums auf den französischen Wortschatz*. Bonn, 1930.

TH. CLAUSSEN. 'Die griechischen Wörter im Französischen', in *Romanische Forschungen*, XV (1904), pp. 774–883.

G. DOTTIN. *La langue gauloise*. Paris, 1920.

R. THURNEYSEN. *Keltoromanisches*. Halle, 1884.

E. MACKEL. *Die germanischen Elemente in der französischen und provenzalischen Sprache*. Heilbronn, 1887.

E. GAMILLSCHEG. 'Germanisches im Französischen', in *Festschrift der Nationalbibliothek in Wien* (1926), pp. 235–49.

D. BEHRENS. *Über deutsches Sprachgut im Französischen* (Giessener Beiträge, Zusatzheft I). Giessen, 1924.

—— *Über englisches Sprachgut im Französischen* (Giessener Beiträge, Zusatzheft IV). Giessen, 1927.

E. BONAFFÉ. *Dictionnaire étymologique et historique des anglicismes*. Paris, 1920

P. BARBIER. *English Influence on the French Vocabulary*. Oxford, 1921. Also in *Modern Language Review*, XVI (1921), pp. 138–49, 252–64; and in *Modern Languages*, IV (1923), pp. 139–46, 175 ff.

M. Kuttner. 'Anglomanie im heutigen Französischen', in *Zeitschrift für frz. Spr. und Lit.* XLVIII, pp. 446–65.

M. Scherer. *Englisches Sprachgut in der französischen Tagespresse der Gegenwart* (Giessener Beiträge, XI). Giessen, 1923.

M. Valkhoff. *Étude sur les mots français d'origine néerlandaise.* Amersfoort, 1931.

B. H. Wind. *Les mots italiens introduits en français au XVIe siècle.* Deventer, 1928.

G. Kohlmann. *Die italienischen Lehnworte in der neufranzösischen Schriftsprache seit dem 16. Jahrhundert.* Kiel, 1901.

W. F. Schmidt. 'Die spanischen Elemente im französischen Wortschatz' (*Zeitschrift für rom. Phil.* Beiheft LIV). 1914.

R. Ruppert. *Die spanischen Lehn- und Fremdwörter in der französischen Schriftsprache.* Munich, 1915.

————————

A. Darmesteter. *De la création actuelle de mots nouveaux dans la langue française.* Paris, 1877.

—— *Traité de la formation des mots composés.* Paris, 1874; 2nd ed. 1894.

—— *La vie des mots.* Paris, 1886.

M. Bréal. *Essai de sémantique.* Paris, 1897; new ed. 1908.

G. Esnault. *L'imagination populaire.* Paris, 1925.

F. Boillot. 'Les métaphores fournies à la langue française par l'art littéraire', in *French Quarterly*, IX (1927), pp. 245–59.

—— *Répertoire des métaphores et mots français tirés des noms de villes et de pays étrangers.* Paris, 1930.

L. Sainéan. 'La création métaphorique en français et en roman' (*Zeitschrift für rom. Phil.* Beihefte I and X). Halle, 1905–7.

—— *Les sources indigènes de l'étymologie française.* 3 vols. Paris, 1925–30.

H. Hatzfeld. *Leitfaden der vergleichenden Bedeutungslehre.* Munich, 1924.

—— *Über Bedeutungsverschiebung durch Formähnlichkeit.* Munich, 1924.

—— *Über die Objektivierung subjektiver Begriffe im Mittelfranzösischen.* Munich, 1915.

F. Brunot. *Les mots témoins de l'histoire.* Paris, 1928.

Ch. Bally. *Traité de stylistique française.* 2 vols. Heidelberg, 2nd ed. 1919–21.

J. Gilliéron. *Pathologie et thérapeutique verbales*, I–III. Paris, 1915–21.

—— *Généalogie des mots qui désignent l'abeille.* Paris, 1918.

—— *Les étymologies des étymologistes et celles du peuple.* Paris, 1922.

—— *Thaumaturgie linguistique.* Paris, 1923. Cf. Mario Roques, *Bibliographie des travaux de Jules Gilliéron.* Paris, 1930.

————————

W. Foerster und H. Breuer. *Kristian von Troyes. Wörterbuch zu seinen sämtlichen Werken.* Halle, 1914; 2nd ed. 1933.

G. Tilander. *Lexique du Roman de Renart.* Göteborg, 1924.

—— *Glanures lexicographiques.* Lund, 1932.

A. G. Ott. *Étude sur les couleurs en vieux français.* Paris, 1899.

E. Huguet. *Dictionnaire du XVIe siècle.* Paris, 1925 ff. (A–De).

L. Sainéan. *La Langue de Rabelais.* 2 vols. Paris, 1922–3.

L. Mellerio. *Lexique de Ronsard.* Paris, 1895.

E. Voizard. *Étude sur la langue de Montaigne.* Paris, 1885.

J. Coppin. *Étude sur la grammaire et le vocabulaire de Montaigne.* Lille 1927.

G. Cayrou. *Le français classique. Lexique de la langue du XVIIe siècle.* Paris, 1923.

E. Huguet. *Petit glossaire des classiques français du XVIIe siècle.* Paris, 3rd ed. 1919.

F. Godefroy. *Lexique comparé de la langue de Corneille et de la langue du XVIIe siècle en général.* 2 vols. Paris, 1862.

Ch.-L. Livet. *Lexique de la langue de Molière comparée à celle des écrivains de son temps.* 3 vols. Paris, 1895–7.

P. Adam. *La langue du duc de Saint-Simon.* Paris, 1920.

F. Gohin. *Les Transformations de la langue française pendant la deuxième moitié du XVIIIe siècle (1740–1789).* Paris, 1903.

M. Frey. *Les transformations du vocabulaire français à l'époque de la Révolution (1789–1800).* Paris, 1925.

M. Fuchs. *Lexique du 'Journal des Goncourt'.* Paris, 1912.

K. Glaser. *Neologismus und Sprachgefühl im heutigen Französischen.* Giessen 1930.

———

A. Longnon. *Les noms de lieu de la France.* Paris, 1920–9.

A. Dauzat. *Les noms de lieux.* Paris, 2nd ed. 1928.

—— *Les noms de personnes.* Paris, 3rd ed. 1928.

Corrections and Additions to the

SELECT BIBLIOGRAPHY

GENERAL

Nyrop. Vol. i, 5th ed. (revised by P. Laurent), 1967. Vol. ii, 4th ed., 1965. Vol. iii, 2nd ed. (revised by K. Sandfeld), 1936.

Brunot. *Histoire*: Tomes i–x, and (by Ch. Bruneau) xii and part of xiii. 1905–53.

Brunot. *Précis*. 4th ed. (by Ch. Bruneau), 1956.

Meyer-Lübke. Vol. i, 5th ed., 1934. Vol. ii (revised by J. M. Piel), 1966.

Add:

W. von Wartburg. *Évolution et Structure de la langue française*. Berne, 8th ed., 1967.

M. K. Pope. *From Latin to Modern French with especial consideration of Anglo-Norman*. Manchester, 1934; reprint 1952.

Ch. Bruneau. *Petite Histoire de la langue française*. 2 vols. Paris, 1955–8. Vol. i, 3rd ed., 1962. Vol. ii, 2nd ed., 1961.

M. Cohen. *Histoire d'une langue: le français*. Paris, 1947. 3rd ed., 1967.

A. François. *Histoire de la langue française cultivée, des origines à nos jours*. 2 vols. Paris, 1959.

J. Fox and R. Wood. *A Concise History of the French Language*. Oxford, 1968.

M. Regula. *Historische Grammatik des Französischen*. 3 vols. Heidelberg, 1956–66.

J. Dubois. *Grammaire structurale du français*. Paris. Vol. i (*Nom et pronom*), 1964. Vol. ii (*Le Verbe*), 1967.

K. Togeby. *Structure immanente de la langue française*. Paris, 1951. 2nd ed., 1964.

L. Kukenheim. *Grammaire historique de la langue française*. Vol. i, Leiden, 1967.

R.-L. Wagner. *Introduction à la linguistique française*. Paris, 1947. *Supplément bibliographique*. Paris, 1955. 2nd ed. (2 vols.), Geneva, 1965.

Meyer-Lübke. 3rd ed., 1935.

W. von Wartburg. Fascicules comprising the letters A–L, part of M, and N–Z, and supplements dealing with foreign elements, have appeared.

The Year's Work in Modern Language Studies. Vol. xxix (edited by N. Glendinning), 1968.

E. Gamillscheg. 2nd ed., 1966 ff.

Bloch et Wartburg. 4th ed., 1964.

Tobler-Lommatzsch. Fascicule 68 (*premier–pro*) appeared in 1968.

Add:

R. Grandsaignes d'Hauterive. *Dictionnaire d'ancien français.* Paris, 1947.

K. Urwin. *A Short Old French Dictionary for Students.* Oxford, 1946.

Dictionnaire de l'Academie française. Paris, 1694. 8th ed. 2 vols., 1931–5.

E. Littré. *Dictionnaire de la langue française.* 4 vols. (1863–73) and *Supplément* (1877). Reprint (incorporating *Supplément*), Paris, 1956.

A. Dauzat. *Dictionnaire étymologique de la langue française.* Paris, 1938. 10th ed., 1954.

A. Dauzat, J. Dubois et H. Mitterand. *Nouveau Dictionnaire étymologique et historique.* Paris, 1964.

P. Robert. *Dictionnaire alphabétique et analogique de la langue française.* 6 vols. 1950–64.

Dauzat. *Géographie.* 3rd ed., 1948.

Add:

A. Dauzat. 'Où en sont les atlas linguistiques de la France', in *Le Français Moderne*, XXII (1954), pp. 81–3.

K. Jaberg. *Aspects géographiques du langage.* Paris, 1936.

PERIODICALS

Add:

Revue Belge de Philologie et d'Histoire. Bruxelles, 1922 ff.

Le Français Moderne. Paris, 1933 ff.

French Studies, Oxford, 1947 ff.

Romance Philology. Berkeley, 1947 ff.

Archivum Linguisticum. Glasgow, 1949 ff.

Forum for Modern Language Studies. St Andrews, 1965 ff.

Revue romane. Copenhagen, 1966 ff.

CHAPTER I

Bourciez. 4th ed. (by J. Bourciez), 1946.

Add:

I. Iordan and J. Orr. *An Introduction to Romance Linguistics.* London, 1937.

L. R. Palmer. *The Latin Language.* London, 1955.

W. D. Elcock. *The Romance Languages.* London, 1960.

V. Väänänen, *Introduction au latin vulgaire.* Paris, 2nd ed., 1967.

Anglade. 5th ed., 1934.

Add:

H. Rheinfelder. *Altfranzösische Grammatik.* Vol. I (*Lautlehre*), 2nd ed., Munich, 1953. Vol. II (*Formenlehre*). Munich, 1967.

G. Raynaud de Lage. *Manuel pratique de l'ancien français.* Paris, 1964.

P. Guiraud. *L'ancien français.* Paris, 1963.

P. Guiraud. *Le moyen français.* Paris, 1963.

G. GOUGENHEIM. *Grammaire de la langue française du XVIe siècle*. Lyon-Paris, 1951.

P. RICKARD. *La Langue française au XVIe siécle. Étude suivie de textes*. Cambridge, 1967.

L. C. HARMER. *The French Language Today*. London, 1954.

M. GREVISSE. *Le Bon Usage. Cours de grammaire française et de langage français*. 8th ed., Gembloux, 1964.

J.-C. CHEVALIER, C. BLANCHE-BENVENISTE, M. ARRIVÉ ET J. PEYTARD. *Grammaire Larousse du français contemporain*. Paris, 1964.

DAUZAT, *Les Argots*. 2nd ed., 1946.

Add:

P. GUIRAUD. *Patois et dialectes français*. Paris, 1968.

Add:

G. DULONG. *Bibliographie linguistique du Canada français*. Québec and Paris, 1966.

CHAPTER II

F. DE SAUSSURE. 4th ed., 1949. Critical ed. by R. ENGLER, Wiesbaden, 1967.

VENDRYES. 2nd ed., 1939.

GARDINER. 2nd ed., 1951.

DAUZAT. *Philosophie*. 7th ed., 1948.

BRUNOT. 3rd ed., 1936.

DELACROIX. 2nd ed., 1930.

BALLY. *Langage*. 3rd ed., 1952.

BALLY. *Linguistique*. 3rd ed., 1950. 4th ed., 1965.

Add:

L. BLOOMFIELD. *Language*. New York, 1933.

W. VON WARTBURG. *Problèmes et Méthodes de la linguistique*, Paris, 1946. 2nd ed. (with the collaboration of S. ULLMANN), 1963.

W. J. ENTWISTLE. *Aspects of Language*. London, 1953.

J. WHATMOUGH. *Language. A Modern Synthesis*. London, 1956.

A. MARTINET. *Phonology as functional phonetics*. London, 1949.

A. MARTINET. *Éléments de linguistique générale*, Paris, 1960. 2nd ed., 1968. English translation by ELISABETH PALMER. London, 1964.

A. MARTINET. *A Functional View of Language*. Oxford, 1962.

S. POTTER. *Modern Linguistics*. London, 1957. 2nd ed., 1967.

T. B. W. REID. *Historical Philology and Linguistic Science*. Oxford, 1960.

L. KUKENHEIM. *Esquisse historique de la linguistique française et de ses rapports avec la linguistique générale*. Leiden, 1961. 2nd ed., 1966.

R. H. ROBINS. *General Linguistics*. London, 1964.

R. A. HALL, jr. *Introductory Linguistics*. Philadelphia, 1964.

CHAPTER III

BOURCIEZ. 10th ed., 1967.

GRAMMONT. 10th ed., 1941.

KLINGHARDT. 2nd ed., 1933.

Add:

A. MARTINET. 'Phonology as Functional Phonetics' and 'Les traits généraux de la phonologie du français', in *Publications of the Philological Society*. London, 1949.

A. MARTINET. *Économie des changements phonétiques*. Berne, 1955. 2nd ed., 1964.

P. FOUCHÉ. *Phonétique historique du français*. Vol. I, *Introduction*. Vol. II, *Les Voyelles*. Vol. III, *Les Consonnes et index général*. Paris, 1952–61.

P. FOUCHÉ. *Traité de Prononciation française*. Paris, 1956. New ed., 1959.

L. E. ARMSTRONG. *The Phonetics of French*. London, 1932. Latest ed., 1949.

H. N. COUSTENOBLE AND L. E. ARMSTRONG. *Studies in French Intonation*. Cambridge, 1937.

W. ZWANENBURG. *Recherches sur la prosodie de la phrase française*. Leiden, 1965.

M. GRAMMONT. *Le Vers francais, ses moyens d'expression, son harmonie*. 5th ed., Paris, 1964.

G. LOTE. *Histoire du vers français*. 3 vols. Paris, 1949–55.

W. T. ELWERT. *Traité de versification française des origines à nos jours*. Paris, 1965.

CHAPTER V

ERNOUT. 3rd ed., 1935.

FOUCHÉ. New ed., 1967.

HAASE-OBERT. 5th ed., 1965.

DAMOURETTE-PICHON. 7 vols. 1930–50. Glossary and Tables. 1949–56.

LERCH. 3 vols. 1925–34.

BLINKENBERG. Vol. II. 1933.

Add:

G. ET R. LE BIDOIS. *Syntaxe du français moderne. Ses fondements historiques et psychologiques*. 2 vols. Paris, 1936–8. New ed., 1967.

E. GAMILLSCHEG. *Historische französische Syntax*. 1957.

L. TESNIÈRE. *Éléments de syntaxe structurale*. Paris, 1959. 2nd ed., 1965.

CHAPTER VI

Add:

J. BRÜCH. *Der Einfluss der germanischen Sprachen auf das Vulgärlatein*. Heidelberg, 1913.

F. MACKENZIE. *Les relations de l'Angleterre et de la France d'après le vocabulaire*. 2 vols. Paris, 1939.

P. GUIRAUD. *Les mots étrangers*. Paris, 1964.

DARMESTETER. *Vie*. 19th ed., 1937.

BRÉAL. 6th ed., 1924.

BALLY. 3rd ed., 1951.

Add:

S. ULLMANN. *The Principles of Semantics.* Glasgow, 1951. 2nd ed., 1957.
S. ULLMANN. *Précis de sémantique française.* Berne, 1952. 3rd ed., 1965.
J. ORR. *Words and Sounds in English and French.* Oxford, 1953.
E. GAMILLSCHEG. *Französische Bedeutungslehre.* Tübingen, 1951.
M. SCHÖNE. *Vie et mort des mots.* Paris, 1947.
J. MAROUZEAU. *Précis de stylistique française.* 5th ed., 1964.
H. A. HATZFELD. *A Critical Bibliography of the New Stylistics applied to the Romance Literatures,* 1953–65. Chapel Hill, 1966.
G. MATORÉ. *La Méthode en lexicologie.* Paris, 1953.

E. HUGUET. *Dictionnaire du XVIe siècle.* 7 vols. Paris, 1925–68.
CAYROU. 2nd ed., 1948.

Add:

J. DUBOIS ET R. LAGANE. *Dictionnaire de la langue française classique.* Paris, 1960.

Add:

A. DAUZAT. *Dictionnaire étymologique des noms de famille et prénoms de France.* Paris, 1931. 3rd ed. (revised by M.-T. MORLET), 1961.
A. DAUZAT ET CH. ROSTAING. *Dictionnaire des noms de lieux.* Paris, 1963.
E. NÈGRE. *Les noms de lieux en France.* Paris, 1963.

Index Verborum

escarbille, 517
escargot, 517
escient, 77
escompte, 515
escorte, 515
escouade, 516
escroc, 515
†esmer, 102, 591
espace, 201
†espardre: *past def.* 352
espérer: *indic. pres.* 310
espiègle, 509, 568
espion, 515
esplanade, 515
espoir, 538, †542
esprit, 500, 578
esquisse, 515
essai, 493, 571
essuyer, 577
est, 507
estampe, 120, 576
†ester: *indic. pres.* 321; *past def.* 342,
  345, 350, 352
esterlin, 510
estime, 584
estimer, 591
estoc, 576
estomac, 584
†estouvoir, 392; *past def.* 352
estrade, 575
†estre (*prep.*), 458
†estrée, 557
†estrieu, 44, 518
esturgeon, 517
et, 221, 466
étage, 584
étai, 507
étalon, 559
étape, 507
étaple, 507
été, 200
éteindre: *past def.* 352, 354
étincelle, 20
étiquette, 513, 517, 552
étoffe, 513
étoile, 120
étonner, 584
étourneau, 587
étrange, 91, 584, 586
étranger, 526, 586
être, 100, 217, 293, 295, 392; *indic. pres.*
  307, 321; *impf.* 49, 333; *past def.* 37,
  351; *fut.* 279, 337; *subjv. pres.* 127,
  323, 326; *impv.* 329; *past part.* 368

étrécir, 290
étreindre: *past def.* 354
étrenne, 80
étrier. *Cf.* estrieu
étriquer, 517
étude, 548, 575
eucharistie, 68
eunuque, 68
eux, 238
évanouir (s'), 384
événement, 584
évêque, 501, 502, 560
examen, 122, 501
exaucer, 575
excellent, 122
excepté, 372, 464
excessif, 497
exclure, 122; *past def.* 354; *past part.* 368
excursion, 118
exemple, 122
exempter, 121
exercer, 122
exercice, 199
exhibition, 583
exploiter, 535
exprès, 513
ex-roi, 535
externat, 529
extra, 118
extra-fin, 536
extraire, 118, 535
extra-légal, 536
extrême, 122

fable, 592
fabliau, 517
façade, 515
face, 174, 465
fâcher, 392, 584
façon, 513
fadaise, 517
fagot, 527
faible, 72, 577
faïence, 515
faillir, 291, 338; *indic. pres.* 315–17;
  fut. 338; *subjv. pres.* 325. *Cf.* falloir
faillite, 515
fainéante, 203
fainéantise, 527
faire, 211, 217; *indic. pres.* 285, 315;
  318; *past def.* 37, 349, 352, 353, 358,
  fut. 337; *subjv. pres.* 55, 323, 325;
  impf. 358, 360; *impv.* 102, 327, 328;
  past part. 45, 92, 102, 126

hébraïque, 206
hébreu, 206
hélas, 127
héraut, 530
hériter, 496
hermine, 157, 547
hermite, 157
héron, 506
héros, 115
herse, 56
hêtre, 506
heur, 23, 44, 68, 198
heure, 68
heureusement, 447
heurt, 127
hiatus, 126, 134
hier, 115, 442
hiéroglyphe, 498
high-life, 519
hiver, 128, 541, 591
†hobe, 525
hobereau, 525, 572
hockey, 512
hollandais, 72
hombre, 516
homme, 179, 182, 183, 516, 546
hongre, 559
honnête, 578
honnêteté, 61
honneur, 198, 549
honnir, 518
honorer, 587
honte, 506
hôpital, 67, 556
hoqueton, 516
horaire, 582
horrible, 577
hors, 464-5
hôtel, 67, 556
hôtel-Dieu, 209, 540
hôtelier, 526
hôtesse, 205
houille, 517
houx, 506
huguenot, 509, 520
†hui (< HODIE), 36, 46, 442
huile, 134
huis, 156, 595
huit, 115
huitain, 527
huitaine, 222
humaniste, 529
humanitaire, 529
humble, 28

humeur, 198, 513, 549, 583
humour, 201, 513, 519
hune, 507
hutte, 509, 556
hygiène, 502
hypothèse, 498

ici, 445
if, 125, 127
ignition, 122
il, 129, 238, 258, 392-3
île, 102
illisible, 536
image, 28, 201
imbroglio, 515
impératrice, 206
imperméable, 536
impertinent, 584
importation, 512
importer, 583
inamovibilité, 531
inamovible, 531
inautorisé, 536
inclus, 368
incognito, 122, 518
incontinent que, 471
incruster, 536
indemnité, 80
indu, 367
indulgent, 582
inexpugnable, 122
infant, 516
infiltrer, 536
ingrat, 575
injure, 585
injurieux, 585
instituer, 289
instruire, 500
instrument, 500
intellectuel, 592
intendant, 567
interdire: indic. pres. 318
interminable, 497
intervenir, 535
interview, 513
irlandais, 525
irréprochable, 536
issue, 363
†ive, 559
ivre-mort, 539

†ja, 93, 156, 442, 474
jacobin, 570
†jaçoit que, 474

servir, 102, 382; *pres. part.* 301; *indic.*
pres. 314, 316; *fut.* 338; *subjv. pres.*
325; *impv.* 327, 328
serviteur, 206, 576
session, 583
seul, 43, 218
si (< SI), 134, 421–6, 466
si (< SIC), 134, 442, 467, 471, 476
siècle, 122
sien, 250
sieste, 516
sieur, 183, 561
signe, 122, 560
signet, 122
signifier: *indic. pres.* 311
silence, 194
sinécure, 512
singe, 91, 102
sinon, 450, 468
sire, 183, 561
sobre, 66
soc, 503
socialiste, 570
sœur, 179, 183, 206
soi, 238, 248
†soif 'hedge', 23
soigner, 83
soin, 83
soit (*conj.*), 468
soit (*interj.*), 127, 542
soldat, 515, 574
solde, 515
soleil, 66
solennel, 80
solfège, 515
somme, 202
son, 63, 134, 250
sonate, 515
sonner, 38
sonnet, 515
sortie, 548
sortir, 295; *fut.* 338; *subjv. pres.* 325
sot, 126, 130, 191
soubresaut, 517
soubrette, 517
soudain, 96, 471
souder, 47
soudoyer, 574
soudre, 102; *past def.* 352; *fut.* 337; *past
part.* 362, 370
souffreteux, 587
souffrir, 284, 290; *indic. pres.* 307, 310;
fut. 338; *impv.* 327
souhait, 58

soulever, 311, 535
soulier, 526, 527
souloir, 43
soupe, 505
soupirail, 527
soupirant, 578
source, 362
sourcil, 129
sourd, 102
sourdine, 515
sourdre, 100; *fut.* 337; *past part.* 362
souris, 193
sous, 464
sous-œuvre, 195
sous-officier, 535
soutane, 515
souterrain, 537
souvenir, 392
spirituel, 120
spleen, 512
splendeur, 120
sport, 512
sportif, 528
square, 513, 519
squelette, 201
stagnant, 122, 171
station, 120
steamer, 128
stock, 512
stockfisch, 508
stopper 'repair', 517
stopper 'stop', 289
stratagème, 502
structure, 498
stuff, 513
stupide, 17, 584, 585
subdiviser, 535
subjectif, 583
subjection, 122
substituer, 118
subterfuge, 121
subtil, 102, 500
succéder, 584
succès, 58
sud, 131, 507
suédois, 72, 526
suer, 17
suffire, 500; *past part.* 368
suisse, 546
suite, 371, 548
suivre, 294; *indic. pres.* 321
sujet, 58, 191
super-fin, 535
supportable, 525

sur, 458, 459, 460
sûr, 60, 68, 102, 168
surabondant, 535
surcharger, 535
sûreté, 527
sur-le-champ, 445
surprise, 583
survivre, 382
sus, 84, 127, 442, 459
svelte, 515
sympathie, 502
symptomatique, 498
symptôme, 121, 498, 502

tabac, 531
tabac à priser, 540
tabatière, 531
tableau, 547
tableautin, 526
tablier, 75
taire (se), 290, 293, 352, 384; *indic. pres.*
   315; *past def.* 350, 352, 355; *fut.* 337
talent, 571
†tandis, 443
tandis que, 123, 471
tant, 442
taon, 102
tapis, 502
tapoter, 524
tard, 101, 102, 442
tarder, 102
tare, 514
tarentelle, 520
tarif, 514
tartufe, 546
taureau, 525, 591
teindre: *past def.* 352, 354
tel, 102, 129, 189, 274
télégramme, 502
téléphone, 502
tellement que, 476
témoigner, 83
témoin, 83, 108, 548
tempête, 19
temporel, 525
temps, 102, 121, 174, 180
tendre: *indic. pres.* 307; *past def.* 345;
   past part. 363
tendre (<TENERUM), 100, 187
tenir, 211, 290; *pres. part.* 303; *indic.*
   pres. 310; *past def.* 37, 342, 345, 349,
   352, 353; *fut.* 335, 337; *subjv. pres.*
   324, 325, 326; *impf.* 360; *impv.* 328,
   542; *past part.* 363, 366

ténor, 60, 515
tente, 362
†terdre, 283; *past def.* 352; *past prat.*
   371
terre, 99
terre-neuve, 200, 547
terrible, 577
tertre, 56
†testimonie, 496
tête, 45, 553, 571
tête-à-tête, 445
théière, 526
thomiste, 531
ticket, 512, 513
tien, 250
tierce, 222
tiercet, 520
tiers, 222
tige, 102, 108, 201, 571
tillac, 507
timbre, 548
timbre-poste, 209, 540
tirailler, 524
tiroir, 526
tison, 47
tisser, 289, 364
titre, 106
toi. 237
toile, 17, 102
toilette, 550
toise, 371
toit, 45
tôle, 517
†tollir: *past part.* 371
tomate, 516
ton, 63, 134, 250
tondre, 283, 292; *past part.* 363
tonne, 503
tonnerre, 22, 72
tonte, 371
topaze, 496
†tor, 591
tordre, 283, 292; *past def.* 352, 354;
   past part. 362, 366, 371
torque, 517
torrentiel, 525
tort, 371
tôt, 67
tour, 202
tourment, 34, 66
tournesol, 516
tourniquet, 525
tousser, 287, 289, 364
tout, 127, 212, 274, 464